the BUSH DOCTOR'S WIFE

NAOMI GAEDE-PENNER

Prescription for Adventure

The Bush Doctor's Wife
Published by Prescription for Adventure
Denver, CO

Copyright © 2021. All rights reserved.

No part of this book may be reproduced in any form or by any mechanical means, including information storage and retrieval systems without permission in writing from the publisher/author, except by a reviewer who may quote passages in a review.

All images, logos, quotes, and trademarks included in this book are subject to use according to trademark and copyright laws of the United States of America.

978-0-9637030-1-9
BIOGRAPHY / Doctors

Bible verses are taken from:
King James Version. Public Domain.
THE HOLY BIBLE, NEW INTERNATIONAL VERSION®, NIV®
Copyright © 1973, 1978, 1984, 2011 by Biblica, Inc.® Used by permission.
All rights reserved worldwide.

Cover photo from the Elmer E. Gaede collection: Pictured from left: Ruth, Naomi, Ruby, and Mark Gaede making homemade ice cream along the Yukon River in front of Tanana, Alaska.
Alaska map by Barbara Spohn-Lillo
Tanana village map by Anna Bortel Church
House sketch by Ruby L. Gaede
Photos within book are from the collections of Elmer E. Gaede and Naomi Gaede Penner

Cover and Interior design by Victoria Wolf, wolfdesignandmarketing.com

All rights reserved by Naomi Gaede-Penner and Prescription for Adventure
Printed in the United States of America.

To the women before me and the women after:
To my mother, Ruby, and my daughter, Nicole

CONTENTS

Introduction 1

Author's Notes 3

Chapter 1: The Bush Doctor's Wife 11

Chapter 2: So This Is Home 25

Chapter 3: Teachers, Toys, and Trikes 35

Chapter 4: Just a Farm Girl and Boy 51

Chapter 5: Going to the Chapel 65

Chapter 6: Childhood, Chicken Coops, and Cows 73

Chapter 7: Getting Acquainted 81

Chapter 8: Swept Off Her Feet 95

Chapter 9: The Wilderness Wife 111

Chapter 10: Picnics 121

Chapter 11: Reaching Across the Miles 131

Chapter 12: Autumn Gives Up 143

Chapter 13: Halloween and Other Entertainment 155

Chapter 14: Christmas Chills and Thrills 167

Chapter 15: The New Year Starts with a Bang 181

Chapter 16: High Society in the Arctic 191

Chapter 17: Census Taking 199

Chapter 18: Valentine's Day and a Little Sweetheart 207

Chapter 19: Igloos and Polar Bears 225

Chapter 20: Caring for One Another 241

Chapter 21: Rumbles of Change 261

Chapter 22: The Happy Days of Summer 275

Chapter 23: The Revolving Door of Hospitality 287

Chapter 24: Loved Ones and More... 299

Chapter 25: Summer's End... 323

Chapter 26: Ruby the Hunter 337

Chapter 27: Everyday Life: Mukluks and Molasses Bread 347

Chapter 28: The Happiest Christmas Ever... 359

Chapter 29: Finding Brightness in the Darkness.................................. 377

Chapter 30: Keeping the Pace, Not Frozen in Place............................. 389

Chapter 31: Up in the Air 401

Chapter 32: Spring Carnival and School Fair 415

Chapter 33: On the Move 425

Chapter 34: Summer Flies By.. 439

Chapter 35: Farewell to Tanana... 453

Chapter 36: Starting Anew 463

Epilogue 467

Resources and Further Reading.. 471

Acknowledgments 477

Reader's Guide 479

Notes 483

Index.. 491

INTRODUCTION

"I WANTED TO BE the best wife and mother possible," my mother, Ruby, told me, as we sat in lawn chairs on the Gaede-80 homestead, and batted at mosquitos. And, she expected to fulfill those roles amidst cornfields and a dairy barn. Instead, in 1957, she found herself patting flour off her hands, dusting them on her apron, and walking from the kitchen to the living room, where instead of farmland, she saw a mile-wide frozen Yukon River with midday dusky sunlight skimming the treetops, as though it was rising and setting all at once.

Her farmer-turned-physician husband changed the course of her future. She exchanged smiling sunflowers for purple-pink fireweed. Kansas humidity for Alaska ice fog. Picnics with watermelon along a muddy creek bed, for campfires and hot dogs on snowy riverbank.

The women before her had imprinted upon her everything she needed to meet this life on the Last Frontier. Although the backdrop of her life was worlds different than she had ever imagined, these women gave her Mennonite cultural traditions and values, faith, and determined, gritty reflexes toward life. These, and a rolling pin, were the ingredients she needed to adapt to a small Athabascan Indian village, where food was ordered for a year and arrived on a river barge. The amenities were three small churches, an elementary school, an expensive general store, and a hospital compound; and temperatures plunged to 50° below zero. In this setting, with four children under the age of eight, she strove to be the best wife and mother possible; in other words, keep her family warm, fed, safe, and even entertained.

AUTHOR'S NOTES

The Bush Doctor's Wife is set in Tanana. Tanana was also the location for some of my father's adventures in *Alaska Bush Pilot Doctor*. Then, I recounted my life, with two years in Tanana, in *From Kansas Wheat Fields to Alaska Tundra: a Mennonite Family Finds Home*. Still, I found more stories, and now my mother, Ruby, is onstage; though her desires were simple, and she did not consider herself to be an adventurer, she faced an extraordinary task.

In one of many letters my mother wrote to her family, I found this request: *"Mom could we asks you to please save our letters, it's not impossible that some day we might try to write a book and we keep no diary and the letters could serve as one. Thanks!"* The letters were saved in shoeboxes.

To write this story, not only did I use my parents' letters, but also my father's many Kodak slides; a cassette-taped interview with my mother about her courtship, childhood, and thoughts and feelings about my father's flying and hunting; communications with missionaries, cousins, and other people who knew my mother; conversations with Anna Bortel, a schoolteacher in Tanana and friend of my mother's, along with the letters Anna had written from Tanana to her parents; letters from my Grandpa

Henry Gaede about his parents; Leppke and Gaede family history books; old documents from Alaska Public Health Services, *The Mukluk Telegraph* newsletters, Tanana *Northern Lights* school newspapers; and other historical documents, books, and websites.

I wanted to keep idioms true to the 1950s era, as well as include common Plautdietsch words and phrases used by my parents in everyday conversation. When quoting my parents' letters, I did not clean up or change vocabulary, spelling, or make them politically correct. It was a different time and place back then.

CHARACTER GUIDE

Ruby's Family
    Isaac Leppke – Ruby's grandfather
    Solomon Leppke – Ruby's father
    Bertha (Litke) Leppke – Ruby's mother
    Lulu Mae – Ruby's older sister
    Margie – Ruby's younger sister
    Wilbur – Ruby's younger brother

Elmer Gaede's Family
    Heinrich and Agata (Knelsen) Gåde - Elmer's great-grandfather and his wife.
    Abraham B. Gaede – Elmer's grandfather
    Henry Gaede – Elmer's father
    Agnes (Ediger) Gaede – Elmer's mother
    Harold – Elmer's older brother
    Lillian – Elmer's younger sister

AUTHOR'S NOTES

MISSIONARIES

Rev. Roy and Margie Gronning – Arctic Missions, Tanana, AK
    Chris and Bethany (children)
Rev. Coleman and Anne Inge – St. James Episcopal Church, Tanana, AK
Russ and Freda Arnold – Ruby (village), AK
    Darris, Sondra, Barry, Lynda (children)
Larry and Maxine Scripter – Kokrines, AK
    Bobby, Shirley, and Nancy (children)
Ken and Vivian Hughes – Lazy Mountain Children's Home, Arctic Missions, Palmer, AK
Mahlon and Hilda Stoltzfus – Mennonite Church, Russian Mission, AK
    Gueen, Ruby, Gareth, and Karl (children)
Mel and Pat Jensen – Arctic Missions, Tanana, AK
    Naoma and Tim (children)

SCHOOLTEACHERS

Harriet Amundson
Anna Bortel
Florence Feldkirchner
Herman Romer

OTHERS

Wally Hanson – Tanana hospital lab technician, shared other side of duplex with the Gaede family.
Paul and Irene Carlson – friends from Anchorage, AK
Dora Tooyak – Mishal's birth mother, from Point Hope, AK
Grandma Elia – older Native woman that everyone referred to as "Grandma"
Leonard Lane – hospital employee, from Point Hope, AK, took Elmer polar bear hunting
Harold and Vera Johnson – CAA/FAA, Birches, AK
    David and Barbara (children)
Sally Woods – Naomi's best friend, Tanana, AK
Jim Orr and family – friends from Anchorage, AK

MAPS AND SKETCHES

AUTHOR'S NOTES

*Soldotna, site of Dr. Gaede's homestead

Map showing Alaskan rivers, territories, towns and cities of "Doc" Gaede's adventures.

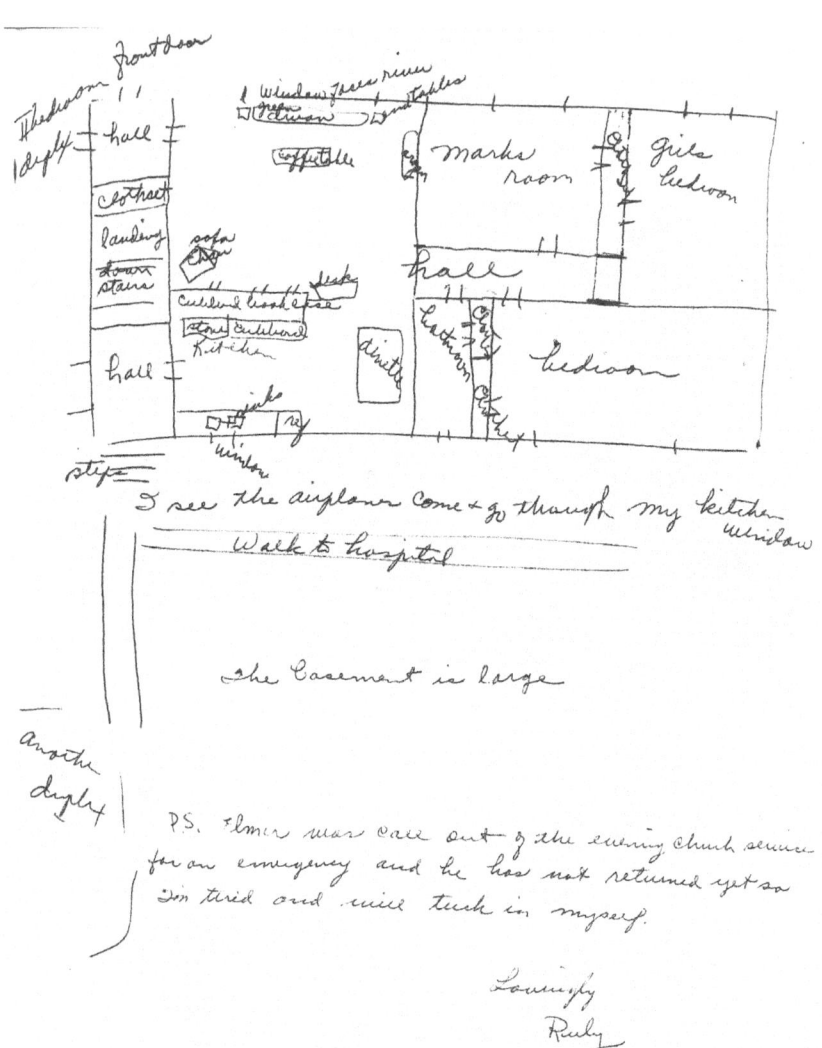

P.S. Elmer was called out of the evening church service for an emergency and he has not returned yet so I'm tired and will tuck in myself.

Lovingly,
Ruby

AUTHOR'S NOTES

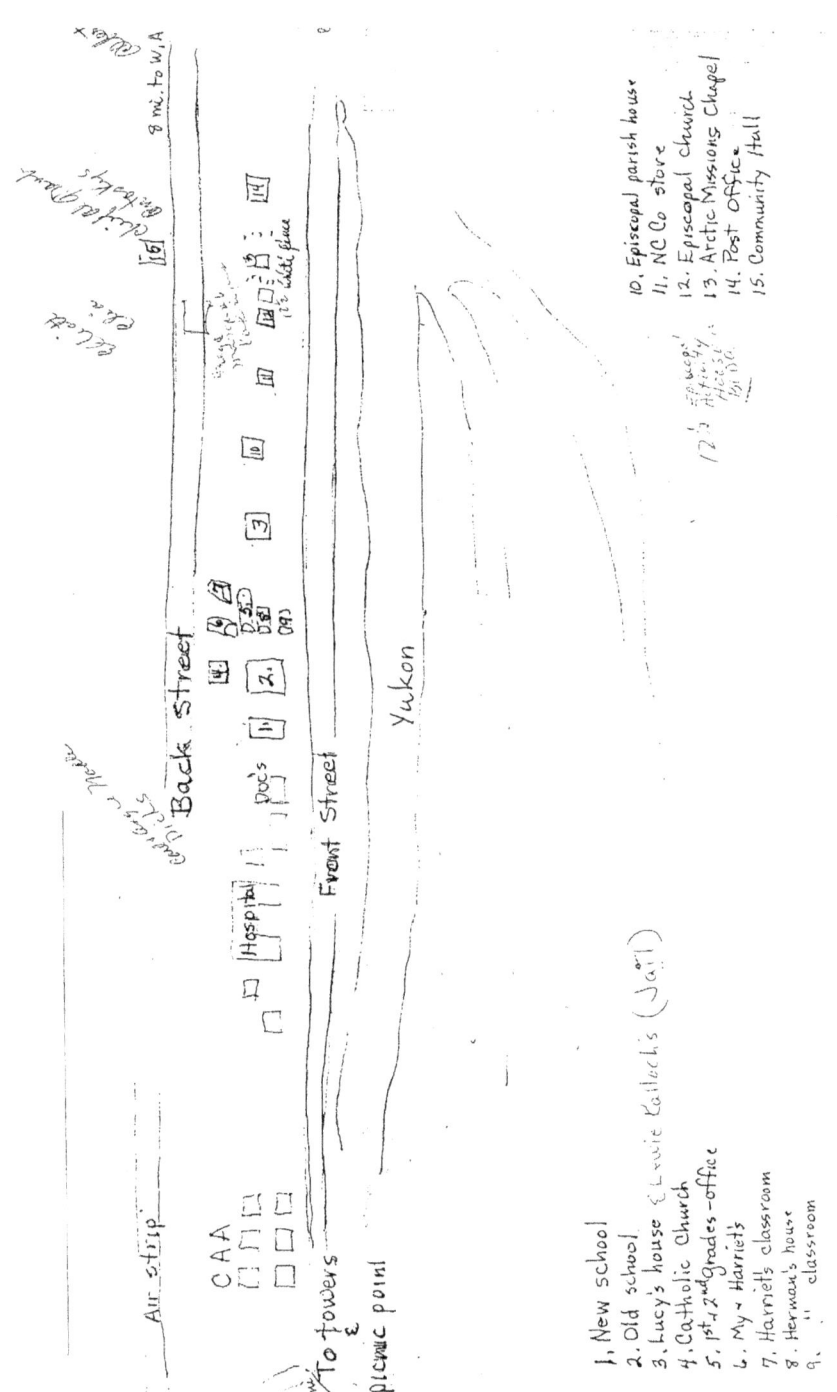

CHAPTER 1

THE BUSH DOCTOR'S WIFE

Tanana, 1957

RUBY HUGGED HER PARKA AROUND herself, pulled the squirrel-fur mittens out of the pockets, opened the back door, and stepped outside. The rush of cold air made her eyes tear. Quickly, she leaned down and reached for the ice cream freezer crank. The handle barely moved. There was no need to top the bucket with ice. At 30° below zero, the mixture of milk, eggs, and sugar could freeze without assistance. Satisfied with the progress, she returned indoors and, despite fogged up glasses, made her way to the closet to hang her coat. The house was unusually quiet.

It was midafternoon, and Ruby was ready for a break from parenting. Mark, nearly age two, was destined to be a plumber, and she'd extracted his busy hands out of the toilet—several times since breakfast. His two sisters, Naomi, age seven, and Ruth, age six, would soon be home from school, and a three-ring circus was possible. Just to know another adult would arrive later in the day would have been encouraging to Ruby. However, her husband, Elmer Gaede (GAY-dee), the only Public Health physician for twenty-two villages up and down the Yukon River in Interior Alaska, would probably not be home for supper—or the entire evening.

The morning alarm had gone off at 7:15 a.m. Elmer had swung his legs over the edge of the bed and headed to the bathroom. Ruby silently got up and wrapped a robe around herself. By the time he had shaved and dressed, Ruby had hot oatmeal and homemade raisin bread toast waiting for him in the kitchen. As a physician, he had learned to eat quickly in case he was called out. Between bites of porridge, as Naomi called it, he and Ruby had exchanged a few words before he pulled on a heavy wool coat and other sub-zero gear to walk the short distance to the Tanana (Ta-nuh-naw) Public Health hospital. Ruby crawled back into bed until it was time to wake the children for school.

After the sun had shyly peeked above the horizon, around 10:30 a.m., Elmer had returned to heat his Piper J-3 airplane's oil on the kitchen stove, which otherwise congealed within the engine, and layer on long johns and wool pants in preparation to fly to a medical emergency downriver.

"I don't know if I'll get back today," he'd said on his way out the door. The "I don't know" depended on being able to stabilize the medical crisis before the sun retreated. The Tanana airstrip didn't have landing lights, and, of course, the frozen river strip, which was often cleared for planes with skis, rather than wheels, didn't either. There was no means to land if he returned after dark. Ruby felt the familiar uneasy tightness in her stomach that transferred to quick annoyance with the children's normal but very busy activity. "Not knowing" seemed to be a standard state of being for the bush[1] doctor's wife.

One thing she did know was that after supper, when she brought in the ice cream freezer, pulled out the dasher in the middle, and placed it on a cookie sheet, her children would shove against each other to spoon up drops of ice cream, and ask, "When is Daddy coming home?" They knew he loved homemade ice cream for a bedtime snack. Once he finished with a bowl or two, they anticipated crowding onto the living room couch where he'd sit and read them bedtime stories. Of course, this would be after their mother reminded them to brush their teeth, and they'd have pulled on their flannel pajamas, warm slippers, and grabbed at least one, if not two, favorite stuffed animals. Each child would have a different book and plead to have his or hers read first. "Not knowing" was all too familiar to the bush doctor's children too.

But at this moment, Ruby stared outside at the fading sunrays on the angular pressure ridges in the frozen mile-wide river. Within moments, the 2:30 p.m. sun slipped down beyond the Yukon River, and all that was left were shadows on the river and the reflection of her face on the frost-edged living room window.

Back home, in the Kansas harvest-time humidity, Ruby's dark brown hair, naturally highlighted with auburn, had responded with full, thick waves. Here, she used a Toni permanent kit to give it fullness. The straight line of her short bangs appeared as though someone had carefully marked a pencil line and then cut with precision. Her hazel eyes looked out from behind glasses that had dark upper frames and sparkles in the corners. Red lipstick brightened her winter-pale face, which, with more potent sunlight than Alaska offered, would have been olive-tanned. Oftentimes, she dabbed some of the lipstick on her cheeks and then blended it with her fingers—as a substitute for rouge. There was no Kansas heat to flush her face.

A worn-soft bib apron shielded her from the cloud of flour she'd just worked into a pile of dough. Bread making was usually a twice-weekly routine, except when company was invited for dinner or missionaries flew into the village and needed a place to stay for a weekend, or a week or two. Then she baked nearly daily, and the yeasty aroma was prolonged within the house.

Never in her wildest dreams could she have imagined herself in this setting: Tanana, Alaska, a village of approximately three hundred people, mostly Athabascan (ath-uh-BASS-kun) Indians, along the renowned Yukon River, and in the heart of the Last Frontier. The location was poles away from her and Elmer's heritage in the Mennonite farming settlement of Central Kansas, where she'd expected to perpetuate a lifestyle like that of her parents and their parents—the Leppkes and Litkes. By no means had she anticipated that the ordinary farm boy, Elmer Gaede, with the mischievous grin, who had aspired to be a dairy farmer, would instead pursue medicine—in Alaska. Would she have married him if she'd known? Who knows? The girl from the Kansas farm was in love.

Ruby's introduction to Alaska had been in Kansas City, at the Covenant Church, where she and Elmer walked each Sunday during his family practice internship at Kansas University medical school. One afternoon at a ladies' meeting, a missionary woman from Nome, Alaska, showed slides. When the Kansas-bred young woman had seen the pictures, her initial and remaining thought was, "Dark and cold. Who on earth would want to go to Alaska?" During this same time, Elmer crossed paths with a nurse from Bethel, Alaska. She urged him to consider Alaska. "The Public Health Service's pay is fantastic!" she said. "Physicians get $7,000 to $9,000 in salary per year!" This was put in perspective with teachers earning $3,440 to $4,700. And, in the early 1950s, houses sold for $14,000, and cars for $2,000. Another incentive for Elmer was that he would be able to fulfill his military obligation, which he had deferred by working on his parent's farm.[2]

Ruby's musings ended with the yowl of a half-grown kitten bursting into the room in front of a yelling chubby-legged preschooler. Mark lost his balance in the pursuit of the kitten and slipped on the floor. The kitten perched with arched back on the couch and watched the boy scream until tears rolled down his cheeks. Before Ruby could respond, a blast of foggy, frozen air entered from the hallway door by the kitchen, signaling that school was out for Naomi and Ruth. The stomping of their feet on the back porch could never be heard with the padded silence of the moose-skin mukluks they wore.

In synchronized motion, the grade-schoolers pushed back fox-fur ruffed red parka hoods and shook loose their tangled brown braids. Naomi's short bangs mirrored her mother's and retained its morning neatness. In contrast, her younger sister's hair was softened by wisped edges that pulled out and curled or stood up in a cowlick wherever it pleased.

"The handle won't turn on the ice cream freezer!" declared Naomi. Surprisingly she had not started the question with a "why." Her first observation about nearly anything was not "what" but "why." In this situation, it *would* have been appropriate to ask *why* ice cream was even being made, rather than hot cocoa dotted with bouncing marshmallows or steaming chicken noodle soup with soggy crackers floating atop.

Wintertime in Interior Alaska was certainly an odd time to be making homemade ice cream; nevertheless, it was Ruby's propensity to make ice cream with glacier ice, river ice, and this time, to curiously experiment with making it without any ice at all. Perhaps this was a means of staying linked to her home place, where cousins, aunts, and uncles regularly took time off on a Sunday afternoon from the hard work of carving a life out of the prairie and gather for the simple enjoyment of sharing chilly bowls of rich dessert, combined from the pure ingredients of farm eggs and milk from their own chickens and cows.

Ruby cherished those memories. Often when she cranked the ice cream freezer, she talked softly to anyone around, about the way it was back then, intermittently giving a quick laugh of amusement or pleasure. Today, she was not cranking or reminiscing, and her experimental ice cream inclination may have been just one more way she found fun in the ordinary or difficult routines of life. She was often the instigator of celebrations and parties, not necessarily in spectacular dramas, but in spontaneous and homey ways that made an observer or participant chuckle, "Who would ever think of that?" Making ice cream on a dark winter afternoon in the Last Frontier was one of those occasions.

"Mark, you leave my cat alone!" Ruth said in an unusually loud voice. More typically, she defended her little brother and believed he could do no wrong. Furthermore, she did not like to draw attention to herself and often remained in the background. Obviously, she felt strongly about cat torment, or at least the well-being of her gray and white kitten, Yukon.

Mark thrashed around on the floor in a temper tantrum, banging his reddish-brown curls on the square linoleum tiles; his blue eyes squeezed shut. Ruby walked down the hall toward the bedrooms to find a tissue to wipe Mark's teary eyes and running nose. By the time she returned to the kitchen, Ruth had disappeared to the basement, where she was most likely rearranging the toy villages and farms around the electric train track.

Chances are, the first-grader was crouched over or sitting on the floor with legs spread beneath her like a *W*, beside the electric train track her father had carefully laid out and tacked to a large piece of quarter-inch plywood. She would be putting precisely the right amount of magical drops in the engine smokestack. There, in her serene after-school retreat, the electric train chugged around the track, past a herd of Guernsey cows and a pen of pink pigs, puffing subtle but enchanting bursts of smoke. Who knows where the cat had fled.

Naomi plopped herself at the table, ready to report on every piece of trivia from the school day. It all seemed so astonishing and important to her, from the ice around the outhouse seat holes to the government-subsidized cheese[3] that so-and-so refused to eat, to her broken silver crayon that she had rationed for only special pictures. "What will I ever do?" She asked anyone in hearing distance, of which there was only her mother.

Ruby listened with only one ear because Mark, who had finally realized that flailing on the floor would not make the kitten cuddle with him, had climbed up inside the built-in Hi-Fi[4] cabinets, where he scratchily started and stopped and restarted his record-player. She had had just about enough of *The Little Engine That Could*, who thought-he-could and thought-he-could. She really wished that that train *could* get itself up the hill and out of her hearing range.

It was 1957. President Eisenhower was in office. Alaska was not a state;[5] however, as a result of Seward's Folly[6] it was a territory of the United States. Purchased for two cents an acre from Russia, it was nearer to Russia than to the United States. During the years of the Cold War,[7] this close proximity caused uneasiness for America and much more so for the people in the Last Frontier. They were easily spooked by rumors of Russia lobbing a missile over the short space between the mainlands of the two continents—separated at one point by a mere fifty-five miles across the Bering Sea.

The distance may have been close to Russia, but it was miles and miles from the contiguous United States from which many of the non-Native folks had come. It was not unusual for newcomers to feel isolated from friends and family. At the same time, some individuals actually liked the distance and separation from their past. Ruby did not. She missed dearly her family and the soothing landscapes and schedules of what she had known. She was over five thousand miles from her home place, which was nestled securely in the *middle* of the United States, not in a territory within striking distance from the Soviet Union. If political decisions, or even misjudgments, resulted in a nuclear catastrophe, there would be no road to hurry down or fast train to catch. They were stuck.

Decades later, in 2008, Alaska's governor, Sarah Palin, referred to by some as "the hottest governor in the coldest state," would be the first woman to be selected for a Republican vice presidential running mate, picked by presidential candidate, John McCain. Newscaster Charles Gibson would ridicule her when she responded to a question in an interview about Alaska's proximity to Russia. Palin would say, "They're our next-door neighbors, and you can actually see Russia from land here in Alaska, from an island in Alaska." Comedian Tina Fey, who impersonated Ms. Palin on *Saturday Night Live*, would change the sentence to, "I can see Russia from my house," thus mocking Palin since Palin's home in Wasilla, Alaska, was outside Anchorage, and not along the coast. Nevertheless, Sarah Palin was correct. On a clear day, inhabitants of the Alaskan island of Little Diomede can see the Russian island of Big Diomede, approximately two and a half miles away, and across the international date line.

In 1955, when Ruby and Elmer moved to Alaska, Alaskans would have understood Palin's meaning, as would the older Alaskans in 2008, who remembered always looking over their shoulders or to the sky during the Cold War.

Nothing was easy in this wilderness—in the 1950s—or even today except, perhaps, catching fish and attracting mosquitoes. Alaska had few roads for transportation; this, however, was not unique to 1957. Over sixty years later, the same would hold true, with the vast majority of villages in the Interior wilderness, including Tanana, connected only by riverboats and barges in the summer, dog sleds or snow machines in the winter, and airplanes when the weather permitted or a landing strip was available.

Getting to a doctor was difficult, even in the areas where less than twelve thousand miles of primitive road existed. Fewer than 30 percent were paved, and many were a lane or two of gravel. All were subject to moody permafrost that resulted in frost heaves that made the roads roll like an ocean wave and the asphalt crack. Or with weather variations, the roads would turn to sheets of ice, and strong winds would push semi-trucks on their sides. These trucks carried bananas, Cheerios, mail, and prescriptions. Empty grocery store shelves and mailboxes were typical, and people matter-of-factly stocked up on canned and boxed goods—when available.

Ruby and Elmer had taken for granted the Kansas roads that had been laid out carefully and conveniently in one-square-mile grids across much of the state. If one were to miss a turn, just a mile farther, a second chance could be available. A summer thunderstorm could make the roads impassable with slick mud, and there had been winter blizzards with wind-whipped drifts, but, sooner or later, the roads recovered and provided the services for which they were designed.

In addition to the ample supply of roads, train tracks cut across Kansas. Trains connected towns and hauled cattle, grain, flour, coal, and freight. The Santa Fe Chief, with its red-splashed locomotive and gold emblem, and the Rock Island made regular runs east and west with passengers. Isolation was pounded away with newly laid tracks that kept ripping through prairie sod.

In Alaska, trains did little to modify isolation, although they offered more convenience for transporting freight. They chugged laboriously over 470 miles, connecting the same towns as did the highway, but at half the speed. Just as trucks and cars on a road, the trains contended with heavy snowfall in their pathways and heaved tracks that jolted passengers and tossed about freight. Trains were *not* a quick ambulance for a patient with an emergency or transportation for a physician striking out on a house call. Nor were they available in the Interior, and certainly not to villages in the Bering Coast region or above the Arctic Circle.

For the handful of physicians posted in these desolate areas, medical jurisdiction was not limited to patients within the hospital. Doctors would be summoned to make house calls, which commonly meant climbing into an airplane, and on some occasions, even a dogsled. The implications of the physician's Hippocratic Oath were steeper. The concern of the physician's wives was deeper. Ruby's previous experiences with a doctor-husband had been late nights of medical school in Lawrence and Kansas City, Kansas; endless hours of residency; and shared on-call responsibilities at the Public Health hospital in Anchorage—all locations within twenty or thirty minutes of home. In Tanana, the boundaries expanded, and the lines blurred.

When a physician was called out to a village, he or she relied heavily on nurses remaining at the hospital to make on-the-spot decisions and tend to crises. When a doctor *was* at the hospital, he or she depended on people in other villages to provide adequate and timely healthcare, often with contact via a two-way radio, operated by the schoolteacher, a missionary, or a roadhouse owner.

In 1957, in Alaska's western half of 250,000 square miles, a total of one private practitioner and seven Public Health physicians attempted to perform surgeries, quarantine tuberculosis patients, deliver babies, and even take on dental care when no dentist was available. As if this wasn't enough, they were on call twenty-four hours a day, seven days a week. Elmer, who was the one Public Health physician employed as Medical Officer in Charge at Tanana, had responsibilities covering an area as large as his home state of Kansas.

Elmer's obligations exceeded those of a bush *doctor*; he was a bush doctor *pilot*. Unlike the other physicians, who chartered pilots to fly them to emergencies and field clinics, he owned and operated an airplane. Besides keeping in mind medical instruments and antibiotics, he was heedful of packing a gas funnel and chamois (to filter impurities from the gas), gas cans, and stale chocolate bars for an emergency. Maintenance of his airplane, judgment of suitable landing areas, and flying expertise all rested on his shoulders. He used words like *practical, adventure,* and *convenience* to defend his bush-doctor flying.

These words did not quell Ruby's gloomy imagination. There was no telephone contact to let her know of his safe arrival or even his whereabouts. Electronic means of communication, such as email messaging, fax machines, or cellular phones, would not be options for another thirty years. If forced down by a blizzard or by an empty fuel tank, there was no GPS to point to his whereabouts. The reality of bad weather, winter darkness, deathly freezing temperatures, and flying mishaps crowded her mind.

Why did he choose to put his life in jeopardy? Farming seemed so benign. The farm girl imagined how it could have been, their family together for all meals, running to the barn or mechanic shed to find her husband, or driving a truck to the field. But here, she faced bleak winter nights alone with the children, typically not knowing where he was.

She had to admit, though, home in this wilderness could be breathtakingly beautiful. At the same time, she understood it could be life-takingly cruel. It demanded the respect and endurance of anyone who lived there. It could bring out the best in men and women, particularly those who went with a steadfast mission to provide aid and comfort to fellow human beings, and surprisingly, it sometimes even brought out robust and appreciated qualities in the individuals who tagged along reluctantly behind the intense and venturesome spirits.

The first description fits Elmer Gaede. Beneath his Tabor College (Hillsboro, Kansas) yearbook picture, the caption clearly declared his bold predisposition, "Looking for worlds to conquer." Even with this clue, Ruby had been caught off guard. If she had attended college, what would a captioned yearbook picture have revealed? Perhaps something like, "Content, yet spunky." She was *not* looking for worlds to conquer. She would have been happy to stay in Kansas and live out a traditional script of country wife and mother. Just the same, she followed her husband when he pushed north.

No, Ruby had *not* bargained for any of this; however, she knew no different than to stand by her man, take on household chores and child-raising often by herself, and accommodate other people. The ability to survive adversity was bred deeply inside her and, as time would tell, even the ability to thrive.

DEPRESSION FRUGALITY

> Motto during the Great Depression:
> "Repair, reuse, make do, and don't throw anything away."

Growing up during the Great Depression served Ruby well in her frontier life. Her wants were few, and her needs were basic. Here's a list of things people did during the Great Depression; some continued with these most of their lives.

- Didn't go out to eat.
- Didn't buy processed food.
- All leftovers were saved, reheated (and they didn't have microwaves), or reused.
- Odds and ends of meat or vegetables ended up in soup.

- Bread, oatmeal, crushed crackers, or rice was added to hamburger to stretch a meat dish.
- Never filled the sugar bowl to the top in case it would topple over and spill, and sugar would be wasted.
- Table scraps were passed along to hogs, chickens, cats, and dogs.
- Stale bread ended up in bread pudding, French toast, and stuffing.
- Plastic bags were washed, hung out to dry, and reused.
- Jars were saved as containers for nails, buttons, leftover gravy, and so on.
- Never bought paste; it was made out of flour and water.
- Kerosene was used to "dry clean" woolen clothes.
- Small pieces of soap were heated in water and pressed together to form a new bar.
- Used wrapping paper was ironed smooth for lining dresser drawers or to wrap another gift.
- When a shoe had a hole in the sole, cardboard was cut and placed inside.
- A sheet worn in the center was split lengthwise, and the outside edges stitched together to form a seam down the middle. The raw edges on the outside were hemmed. A sheet beyond salvaging was material for dresser scarves, diapers, dust cloths, and anything white cotton fabric could be used for.
- Women's full skirts were cut and redesigned into dresses or clothes for children or dolls, mending, or quilts.

- Flour, sugar, and animal feed came in plain cloth sacks. By the 1940s, manufacturers realized women emptied the flour and used the "free" fabric to make clothes for themselves and their children, kitchen dishtowels, diapers, curtains, aprons, and more. The manufacturers responded by using floral and other patterns on the sacks.(In the late 1950s, cloth bags were replaced by cheaper paper and plastic.)

- Backs of letter envelopes were used for grocery and to-do lists.

- Plant clippings were shared, rather than purchasing a new plant.

- Women cut their own hair and that of their husband and children.

- Gifts were often crafted, homemade, or re-gifted.

- The only thing inexpensive was automobile gasoline; hence, taking leisurely Sunday afternoon drives around the countryside was a relatively cheap form of entertainment. Thus came the phrase, "Sunday afternoon driver."

CHAPTER 2

SO THIS IS HOME

Tanana, September 1957

FORTUNATELY, Ruby's initial arrival into Tanana wasn't met with below zero temperatures, a frozen ice cream freezer on the steps of her new home, airplane oil warming on a stove, or a toddler and cat tormenting each other. Rather, it was on a cool, first of September evening with the Alaska sun still high overhead that she and the children had flown into Tanana with a bush pilot from Fairbanks. Elmer had arrived in early summer, in his Piper J-3 airplane on floats, and had begun his Public Health rotation at the thirty-five-bed hospital.

Aspen leaves, touched with gold, announced the ending summer. The Alaska winter would not be a complete shock to the family. From 1955 to 1957, they had experienced two winters in Anchorage, where Elmer had worked for Public Health Services at the Alaska Native Services hospital. However, that had been in a city, not a remote village with few conveniences and services. Also, Tanana was at a higher latitude than Anchorage so winter daylight hours would be shorter.

In March, Elmer had previewed the village. He had brought back pictures and descriptions. Approximately 11.6 square miles comprised their new location, with somewhere around twenty miles of road. No need for a car. They could walk nearly everywhere. Amenities included a post office, Northern Commercial Company (NCC) general store, school—grades one through eight— three churches, a 4,400-foot airstrip, the Civil Aeronautics Administration (CAA),[8] and a community hall. Added to this was the medical compound. Neither was there a fabric store, full-service grocery store, or gas station.

Moreover, in Elmer's enthusiasm, he failed to inform his wife that there was no library, floral shop, malt shop, hotel, or café. Not that she and Elmer ever spent money on eating out, but it would have been nice to know that she could have splurged with the purchase of a root beer float for twenty-three cents—if she'd wanted to. Burger King (1954), Dunkin' Donuts (1950), and McDonald's (1955)[9] had recently germinated in the United States, ushering in the era of fast food; nevertheless, in Tanana, there were no such luxuries then or ever after.

Once reality hit, it would be a toss-up which she would miss most, a fully stocked grocery store or a Five and Dime store with rickrack and zippers for sewing, round paper doilies for fancy entertainment, wax for candle making, birthday cards, anklets for the girls, diaper pins, pleated paper cupcake cups, bubbles to blow, spinning tops, cap guns, hairbrush sets with matching brush, hand mirror, and comb, and Brylcreem or Elmer's hair—with the advertisement of "A little dab will do you!"

Even though Tanana was predominantly an Athabascan Indian village, there were eight to ten CAA couples who were White. One family had blonde girls who stood out among the dark-haired Native children at school. The medical staff and support people were both Native and non-Native. The employees of the White Alice site[10], approximately six miles up a hill behind Tanana, were White, as were many of the seasonal construction men.

Ruby tried to get a sense of the village as the pilot flew over the accumulation of buildings strung along the river. She wondered, "Would she find friends with common interests? Would she feel stuck in the middle of nowhere?" The unknown was about to become known.

No one landed on the sandy gravel airfield or up the riverbanks without word spreading like an outbreak of measles. Elmer had heard the plane landing and drove out to greet his family in a red jeep that had been converted into an ambulance and which served as ordinary transportation when necessary. Now, at the edge of the landing field, he walked toward his family.

Naomi ran ahead and into her father's arms. Mark toddled as fast as his short legs could go on the uneven surface, babbling, "Daddy, Daddy!" Ruth walked beside her mother, who was happy to see her husband and relieved to have her children stop huddling around her. She had spent days as a single parent and was ready for some backup support.

The pilot hefted two suitcases through the split doors in the rear of the makeshift ambulance-taxi. Ruby and the children crawled inside. She started to giggle at the oddity of the situation but then checked her fatigued nervousness and smoothed her full-skirted dress. Ruth snuggled nearer her mother, and Mark bounced around trying to climb toward his daddy.

The short drive took them along the CAA housing perimeter to the hospital compound, which included the hospital, construction of new nurses' quarters, the hospital staff housing, several other buildings, and two new duplexes. The ambulance-taxi stopped in front of the duplex facing the Yukon River.

The two living quarters of the duplex had joint foyers in the front and the back of the building, with common doors outside, as well as a stairway to the basement. The basement was to be shared, although at this time, no one lived in the opposite duplex and the Gaedes literally had full run of the space. The narrow, rectangular basement windows stood barely three feet above ground and let limited light into the basement.

In contrast to the other, older medical-related buildings, the roof was gray, rather than red, rolled asphalt. Plain, concrete exterior stairs, with a narrow landing, brought people into the house. Most frequently, everyone entered through the back door. As is typical in many homes in Alaska, the enclosed foyer served as an arctic entry and captured the frigid air when the exterior door opened, without letting it penetrate the rest of the dwelling, when the door into the main living area was opened.

Tanana Hospital complex. The Gaedes lived along Front Street, facing the Yukon River, in the duplex with the gray roof.

Ruby gazed across the dirt street to the nearby, swiftly flowing gray water. Her eyes moved across the expanse until they rested on land, a half-mile away—and that being an island—rather than the actual opposite banks of the Yukon River. She had grown up with an endless horizon where weather could be seen brewing miles away and where the sun took its time to glide like a slippery ball down from the sky. In Anchorage, she had felt suffocated and encapsulated by the mountains surrounding the city. It had seemed the only openness was the land about to slide into Cook Inlet.

Here, she immediately liked the broad breathing space. To the east, the hillsides gradually climbed high above the riverbanks yet did not cut off the sky. In the same way, mountains grew to the northwest, although not in any hurry, and at such a distance, they left plenty of flatness in all directions of the village. She had the feeling that this exposed terrain would nurture her spirit.

Right now, her spirit was weary from weeks of traveling, which had originated in Kansas where she and the children had been warmed through and through by the hot, sticky sun, as well as being immersed in the family enclaves and Mennonite farming community she knew and understood. Next, they had journeyed to California, where the family had visited Elmer's parents in Reedley.

She sighed when she walked through the doors of what would be her home for the next two years. The sigh was filled with a mix of emotions: relief for finally arriving at this destination, surprise and pleasure about the duplex, and dismay at the realization that their personal belongings would not arrive for another week or two. She wondered what she would do to entertain three children without toys.

Nevertheless, within moments what she saw boosted her outlook. There were three bedrooms. During many years of marriage, she and Elmer had lived in places with only one or maybe two bedrooms, sometimes only one room in total. In most cases, one of the children had shared their bedroom. Here, there was a bathroom with a sink, tub, and commode, just for their family's use! In Anchorage, they had shared a house with another couple, and everyone used the same tiny bathroom.[11] They were fortunate to have indoor plumbing since the schoolchildren, missionaries, and Native people used outhouses. In the middle of nowhere, this new home seemed luxurious. Public Health certainly took care of its people.

"Mommy, come see!" Ruth and Naomi grabbed her arms and towed her into a bedroom with twin beds. Before she could completely survey the room, they pulled her into another room with a crib. "Look. Mark has his own room too." She acknowledged their excitement and continued the tour with repeated exclamations of, "Elmer, look at this!"

The new quarters were ample and smelled of fresh paint. The furniture, which came with the house, was modern. Ruby sat on the couch and found it stiff and scratchy from lack of use. No soft, worn spots from hours of conversations, bedtime story reading, or social hospitality. That would change.

"I need to look at the kitchen," she said, trying to untangle herself from Mark, who had wrapped his arms around her legs. He was at that annoying stage where he would run from her, and then scare himself by being alone, and come running back.

By choice, as well as need, Ruby would spend much of her time in this room. She inspected it eagerly. White cabinets with narrow chrome handles matched the white kitchen appliances, which were standard for that era. The red countertops were not complemented by the curtains above the double kitchen sink, which were an aqua and brown geometric design on a white background. This design would be retro some fifty to sixty years later and used for women's dresses and skirts. (The blue color would be referred to with descriptors such as lake, rain, and other earthy names.) Beneath all this flamboyance, the dark hardwood floor would show every crumb and be chilly on bare feet. This flooring would also become popular decades later. Even so, Ruby's gratitude showed in her wide smile. She and Elmer had come from previous living situations of damp basement concrete floors and walls and a milk house of large stones that drove the Kansas humidity deep into their bones. This was so much more than adequate.

In unusual fashion, Elmer followed her around unhurried, not rushing off to tend to a patient, his airplane, or wild game he needed to dress out.

"*Somewhere*, we need to find a large area rug," Ruby commented.

He responded with something about all kinds of furniture and "stuff" in the unused second-floor rooms of the hospital. Ruby felt good that he was being resourceful and engaged about creating their home, a comfortable one at that.

For a house in the backwoods, this house had up-to-the-minute furnishings. On the wall between the kitchen and living room was an entire arrangement of built-in cupboards with adjustable shelves for a Hi-Fi. Naomi and Ruth saw the potential for cave dwelling and climbed into the cupboards, pulled shut the doors, and pretended they were hiding—until one giggled too loudly and the other shushed her sister equally loudly.

Energetic combinations of color and design continued in the adjacent eating area, as well as the living room. Slashes of black and pink fought on the silver background of the floor-length drapes in both rooms, with timid white sheers peeping behind. Pink walls softened the impact. Blond end tables joined in the melee with the silver-flecked green couch and gray-black armchair in the living room.

The large living room window competed with any twenty-first-century IMAX screen. Perhaps such a film would be titled *The Cold Beauty of the*

Far North or *Mount McKinley: Alaska's Centerpiece.* Every day Ruby could look at North America's tallest mountain, 20,230 feet high, and marvel at the exquisite splendor; the white frosting of snow or clouds would add to the fascination. The film's subject would change frequently. If Elmer were flying, Ruby would watch the weather form in the broad sky—and either worry or be relieved. At other times, she would see a river barge bring supplies—and anticipate arrivals of staples and necessities. Motorboats catching driftwood or bringing visitors from up or downriver would add to the film's fascination—and what would count as entertainment in the village. A keen observer could pan in closer to the pink and purple fireweed that bunched along the bank, much taller than Mark.

"It faces south!" Ruby exclaimed. By early November, she would crave any semblance of light from the sun that would have swung from the southeast to southwest. Every scrap of the sun would be maximized. The window would try its best to provide this aspect of emotional survival gear. From the opposite side of the house, and through the kitchen and dining room windows, she could catch sight of airplanes landing or taking off, depending on the direction of the wind, and only when they were above the tops of the thin, wilted-looking black spruce trees. If they were landing, she'd anticipate mail, a sporadic newspaper, or an interesting guest in the village.

Even with these unexpected and wonderful amenities, there was more; clean sheets, blankets, and towels were stacked in a closet. On this first day, she was pleased and hopeful by what the house offered. Ruby sketched the upstairs floor plan in one of her weekly letters to her parents.

Unlike her husband, who had explored every inch of Tanana within forty-eight hours, including the frozen river, and the large island within it, Ruby's immediate focus would be settling in her family. Then, she would figure out this new environment.

SO THIS IS HOME

Alaska Native Health Services
National Health Week
May 12-18, 1957

Hospitals: Anchorage, Barrow, Bethel, Kanakanak, Kotzebue, St. George Island, St. Paul Island, Tanana, Fairbanks, PHS Alaska Native Hospital Tanana

<u>General:</u> Tanana is rich in the lore of early Alaska and claims more "old-timers" among its residents than any other village on the Yukon. Located in Tanana, it is the oldest frame building on the Yukon River, now occupied by the Northern Commercial Company manager.

<u>Physical Plant:</u> The hospital is approximately one-fourth mile from the village proper on what was Fort Gibbon, a World War I Infantry Post; some of the old army buildings are still standing. … the larger percent of the patients are pediatric. The hospital plant, constructed in 1949, is well-equipped and in good repair; the wards, surgery, laboratory and X-ray unit, and kitchen, staff dining rooms are located on the main floor. The hospital employs approximately 35 persons and living quarters for ancillary personnel are on the second floor with the laundry, storerooms and maintenance in the basement. … The X-ray unit is a Westinghouse Mattern, 150 MA unit, and there is also a portable unit for use in outlying villages. The hospital maintains its own power plant and water system; electricity is 110 volt, 60 cycle, alternating current and suitable for ordinary household appliances.

Quarters: The nursing personnel are housed in completely furnished single rooms in a four-year-old building and share a comfortably furnished living room, snack kitchen, and bath with hot and cold running water. Two new duplexes were completed in December of 1956, each providing one two-bedroom and one three-bedroom apartment, all of which apartments are completely furnished. Three of these apartments have been assigned to the Medical Officer in Charge, Director of Nurses, and Maintenance Supervisor and the other is presently unoccupied.

Transportation and Communication: Plane and mail service is scheduled four times a week to and from Fairbanks; the flight to Fairbanks is only 70 minutes and the fare is quite reasonable. The hospital radio station has schedules twice daily with the Alaska Communication System, operated by the U.S. Army Signal Corps in Fairbanks; in an emergency, radio traffic is relayed through the Civil Aeronautical Authority. The Medical Officer in Charge maintains two-way radio contact with the surrounding villages four times weekly.

CHAPTER 3

TEACHERS, TOYS, AND TRIKES

Tanana, September 1957

A FEW DAYS AFTER RUBY and her children arrived in their new setting, school started. Ruby had her concerns. Ruth did not respond easily to change or new experiences, and, within the past weeks, change was piled upon new experiences. Ruby was more confident that Naomi would adapt. Her curiosity usually drove her to the edge of an unknown circumstance, which she would assess, and then slowly work her way into it.

That first morning, Ruby walked the girls a scant two minutes to the Tanana Day School, which was a white painted building that had weathered many a season and historical era. The sisters wore dresses with matching anklets and leather shoes; by the time they set foot in the schoolyard, their shoes were covered with dust. A flagpole with the United States flag stood in front of the building. Several bicycles leaned against the building. As they waited on the school grounds, Ruth leaned against her mother. Tears slid down her downturned face. "It's okay," said Naomi softly. "I'm here with you." Ruby placed an arm on each girl's back. Mark, who had just caught up to his family, stared up at Ruth and touched her leg.

First building is the Tanana Day School. The Gaede's duplex is beyond the school with the gray roof. Notice how close these buildings were to Front Street and the Yukon River (far left).

The school bell clanged abruptly. Ruby nudged the girls forward and watched as Ruth clutched her sister's hand tightly. Other students, who had been playing nearby, ran pell-mell toward the building and clustered breathlessly between the front and side of the building. Two teachers, a younger and a middle-aged woman, sorted the students into grades one and two, and three through eight, and then instructed them to line up single file.

Anna Bortel, the teacher in her early thirties, motioned for the first and second-graders to enter the side door. She was dressed neatly in heels, stocking hose, and a full-skirted dress. She made a friendly comment to each student who passed by and often added a pat on the shoulder. There was nothing shy about her, and her personality livened up her plain, pale face. Ruth (first grade) and Naomi (second grade) were relieved to find themselves in the same classroom.

The class areas were separated by large double doors, which could be opened when necessary for common activities. At this time, the doors were closed. Naomi and Ruth stood to the side as students jostled into one another and found their way to desks. Miss Bortel guided first-graders to one side of her room and second-graders to the other. The narrow wood-planked floor creaked beneath their feet. Near the top of one wall was a paper runner with alphabet letters in both stiff straight print and rolling cursive format. In the back of the room was a colorful bulletin board with a September calendar and construction paper autumn leaves.

Naomi warmed quickly to her new teacher, whereas Ruth retreated from the teacher's extroversion, as well as from the enthusiasm of the other students. She slunk down in her seat as if to hide.

At recess, she attached herself to Naomi, like a shadow. She blinked hard and put her hands on her face. Naomi whispered to her forlorn sister, "Don't cry. Be glad we don't have that other teacher."

Florence Feldkirchner, who had summoned the older students to the front doorway, was twenty years older than her teaching partner. Whereas Anna had been hired by the Alaska territory educational system, Florence taught under the Bureau of Indian Affairs (BIA).[12] Tanana was the only school in Alaska that had a teacher from both entities. All the same, the two teachers did not divide the students by Native and non-Native, but by grades. Perhaps it was her years with the government or her naturally restrained manner that made Florence appear unapproachable. Perhaps it was her hairstyle and the no-strand-left-loose dyed bun at her neck. Whatever the case, she was definitely a "mind your p's and q's" type person. She was also the head teacher.

Northern Lights, a newspaper put out by the students, recorded details and descriptions of the start of the 1957 school year. Charles Wheeler, one of the older students, edited the paper and lined up student reporters to bring back reports for publication. In the first issue of the season, there were articles on "Keeping Schools Better," "Hunting Ptarmigans," an untitled paragraph about the progress on the refurbishing of St. James Episcopal Church, and other items of local interest. Helen Wheeler reported on the first day of school.

SCHOOL NEWS

```
There are 27 children in the bigger room. There
are 4 third graders, 5 fourth graders, 1 seventh
grader, 5 eighth graders. And in the littler room,
there are 14 in the first grade and 10 in the
second grade. There are 51 children who are going
to school in the Tanana Day School.
```

Miss Florence Feldkirchner and Miss Anna Bortel are the new teachers at Tanana. Miss Feldkirchner has been a teacher in Alaska for a number of years. She came from Fort Yukon. Miss Bortel taught for three years in Valdez, Alaska before coming to Tanana.[13] They both like the school here very much.

We all miss the students who are attending school at Wrangell.[14] We hope they are enjoying school there.

In subsequent documentation of school life, Mr. William Thomas (BIA), a carpenter from Fairbanks, would be noted for his maintenance tasks. The building, previously a Knights of Columbus meeting place, was aging. New, pastel-colored paint in the classrooms offered aesthetic pleasure but only slightly subdued the musty smell of years of use. The roof was in need of a complete refurbishing, and much of the electric wiring was unsafe. The school paper reported, "Many little things were repaired so that the building is much more comfortable." In reality, the school was one step away from being condemned.

All morning, Ruby thought of the girls. She had forced herself not to run after Ruth and smother away her little girl's anxiety with a hug. Now, between washing breakfast dishes, straightening up beds, and trying to entertain Mark—without his usual toys—she looked often at the black and white round wall clock. Would lunchtime ever come? Would Ruth make it until she and the other students ran home to eat?

In anticipation, Ruby prepared peanut butter and grape jelly sandwiches. Short glasses of powdered milk stood beside the waiting plates. All at once, the back door opened, and the girls burst in. Without a word, Ruth climbed onto her chair.

"How was school?" asked their mother. Ruth looked down at her plate and hunched her shoulders until they nearly touched her ears. Naomi exclaimed, "The windows in the room are too high to see out of … some of the books have torn corners … there are two sets of sisters … Mark! Leave my doll alone!"

The smirking toddler ran when his sister hopped off her chair. Ruby grabbed Mark, his arms and legs thrashing, and put him in the high chair. Quiet prevailed momentarily as both Naomi and Mark focused on their sandwiches. Mark soon had jelly on both cheeks. Ruth reached over and tried to clean his face. He tossed his head to elude her efforts.

"It's time to go," said Ruby gently. Ruth appeared glued to her chair.

"Come on," urged Naomi, not unkindly. She had hopped off her chair and was standing at the door. "You were fine this morning." Ruth wouldn't look at either her mother or sister; she just crossed her arms and joined Naomi. "It's only a few more hours," said Ruby, in a comforting voice. Naomi reached for her sister's hand, and they walked down the steps into the bright midday sunlight.

Ruby remembered her school lunches. She and her siblings attended a country school near Peabody, Kansas. They packed sandwiches of homemade bread that were often spread with rendered lard (a substitute for butter). Sometimes they were filled with liverwurst and mustard. In fall, the sandwiches might be spread with bacon grease, filled with crisply fried bacon, and freshly picked sliced tomatoes. At times, potato salad would be added, stuffed into round French mustard glass jars. All food items were toted in a lunch bucket made from eight-inch-tall Karo syrup cans with lids and wire handles.

Tanana Day School actually wasn't that much different from Ruby's elementary school, which had been a small one-room building with an outhouse behind it. Ruby had done so well in first grade that the teacher moved her on to second grade. She kept up until fourth grade when, for some reason, she would cry and not want to go to school. Her mother and teacher decided she should repeat third grade, after which her attitude toward school improved. Just like Ruth, Ruby had had her ups and downs.

After a few days, Ruth decided she *did* like school; this was a relief to her mother, who had plenty of other things to attend to, and happy children made her tasks easier.

At long last, the barge arrived with the household goods and toys. Everyone had heard and even felt the throb of the barge engine as it made its way

TEACHERS, TOYS, AND TRIKES

down river and a knot of people gathered eagerly at the dirt docking area. The triple-deck barge lay low in the water, and it appeared that water could run over the floor deck at any moment. Tall yellow-gold cranes hoisted off large crates of supplies. Names of the recipients were written in bold marks on the crates and boxes, and whether or not there was a personal shipment, curious and excited speculation and observations wandered through the crowd. "Look what so-and-so got." "Oh, that crate is broken." "I wonder if that's enough coal for the hospital furnace." "Gaede? Oh yes, that is the new doctor." "Oh no. Macaroni everywhere."

Barge docked along the Yukon River riverbank at Tanana.

Elmer borrowed the hospital maintenance man's truck to haul the crated goods to the duplex. Some items were packed in off-white, fifty-five-gallon cardboard packing barrels with steel-ringed tops and bottoms.

It didn't take long for Ruby to unpack. They didn't have much. She pushed away the children's enthusiastic hands as they reached to tear out the packing paper. "Careful! Careful!" she admonished them—to no avail. The children squealed in delight and pulled out stuffed animals and games. Naomi and Ruth lined up their dolls and animals on their beds. Mark wallowed in the paper, tossing it everywhere and laughing happily. Ruby had barely arranged the baking tins when she had bread rising in a large glass bowl. The familiar yeasty smell filled the house, and everyone seemed to relax.

After work, Elmer helped with the large articles, of which there were only two or three. "It made it!" Ruby exclaimed when the tall and ornate vintage pump organ was unbundled and appeared undamaged by the move. She played by ear, not by notes, and this musical instrument gave her pleasure, and more so when she and Elmer sang together. Naomi and Ruth tried to pronounce the scripted words on the smooth white knobs: *Dolce, Forte, Alto*. The volume and timbre changed as these were pulled out and pushed in. Surprisingly, the organ ended up in the basement playroom and not upstairs, where Ruby could have better supervised its use. As active as the children were, the basement would be their mother's saving grace once winter set in.

Along the basement hallway was a recessed area for a clothes washer *and* dryer. Ruby would not have to hang clothes around the house to dry in winter, as she had done in Anchorage, and in summer, she would not have to schedule laundry around sunny days when clothes could dry on the outdoor wire lines. Adjacent to the laundry facility was a spacious closet. Elmer filled it with hunting, fishing, and flying gear. Ruby had her area too. The small room across the hall became a sewing room. Next to it was an oversized pantry with deep shelves from floor to ceiling, which was ready for the year's worth of groceries Ruby had ordered from McDonald's Pike Place Market in Seattle, Washington. At each end of the hall were large undesignated spaces, one for each duplex. The one beneath the Gaede's area evolved into a playroom-guestroom.

Ruby hung a sizeable picture of two white kittens above the pump organ. It was Ruth's favorite picture and resembled her favorite stuffed animal, a white stuffed cat named Puff. Like her mother, Ruth had an ear for music. She sat on the stool, which could be spun higher or lower, and carefully fingered melodies. Her small feet pushed two flat pedals up and down, and the pressure inflated the bellows, which then produced the sound.

In the foreground of the tunes was the racket of Mark racing rowdily, in place, on his jumping horse. "Silver!" he shouted. "Hi-ho," said Naomi in the background. "Away," interjected Ruth. The force of Mark's pursuit lifted the metal tube frame off the concrete floor. It clattered noisily up and down.

Elmer had discovered a large Persian rug on the second floor of the hospital. He and Ruby wrestled it home and spread it on the basement floor. The room was unfinished, so floor joists and utility pipes were visible, and the walls were raw concrete. He hung a swing from the ceiling with ropes. They had brought the plaything from Kansas City, where he had done his residency after completing medical school at Kansas University in Lawrence, Kansas. Metal tubes were welded in a sideways H with the top rung to wrap hands around and the bottom to push with feet. A rope was connected to an eyebolt from the end of the handlebars and the back of the seat. Mark started to pull himself onto the swing. "You're too small. You will fall off," warned Naomi. He climbed on anyway.

The girls set up their toys quickly. With moos, neighs, and oinks, Ruth corralled hard rubber cows, horses, and pigs into clipped together, white plastic fences. The chickens ran loose. Her memories of her grandparent Leppke's Kansas farm were fewer than Naomi's; however, that made no difference in her desire to play farmer.

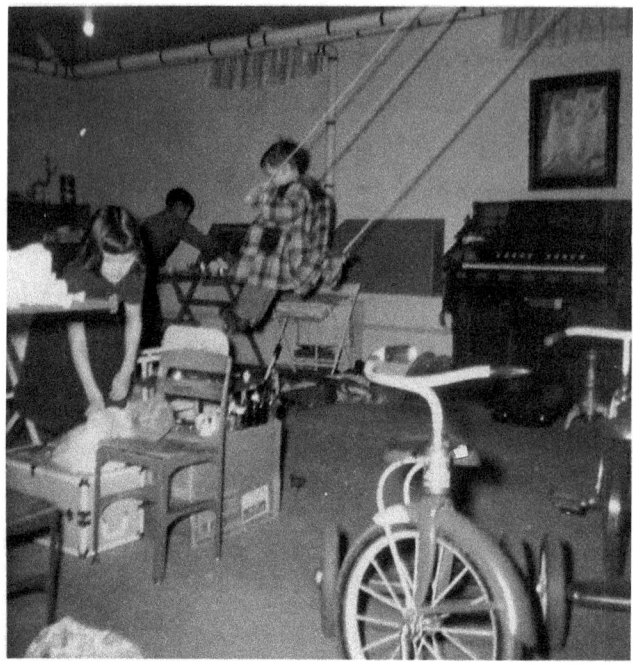

Playroom and guestroom in duplex basement. Mark is on the swing.

Naomi organized her dolls in front of her, sat on a student-size wood-and-metal school chair, and "taught school," complete with handwritten report cards. "Betty is such a good student," she told her mother. "But Pete does not pay attention." This was typical of Naomi—teaching everything that came in front of her, as well as telling her mother, in a somewhat desperate voice, "I have to get organized!"

In addition to the dolls, farm, and swing, there was a clutter of tricycles, roller skates, doll strollers and beds, a train set, and what was intended to be a guest bed. When their parents were not looking, the children jumped up and down on it, thumped one another with the feather-filled pillows, and laughed until nearly frenzied. This beat any bouncy house or trampoline they could have imagined. Fortunately, Ruby had a high tolerance for children's chaos, as long as her offspring were not under her feet, demanding extra attention, or causing harm to each other, themselves, or the plumbing system.

Upon their arrival to Tanana, the playroom was not used as strenuously as later in the season. Even though the early September temperatures dipped to 17° at night, the children were not deterred from playing outdoors in the daytime highs of 40°. Mark could have spent the entire day outside, but without his mother's watchful eye guarding him against river explorations, he was safer indoors.

Resources for the children's outdoor play were limited. There was no grassy front lawn for croquet or badminton. The children had lived without a lawn in both houses in Anchorage, and, except for Naomi's memory of Kansas City, they thought nothing unusual about it.

There were no hedges or flowerbeds to delineate one yard from another. All in all, landscaping and yard work was unheard of. Ruby, the consummate dig-in-the-dirt girl, was determined to "farm" indoor plants. She'd carefully wrapped starts of houseplants from Elmer's parents in California and packed them in her suitcase. As soon as the household goods arrived by barge, and she unpacked the typewriter, she wrote his family:

> *"The philodendron and angle wing begonia that mother Gaede sent along kept nicely and they of course remind me of her as I see them and I do hope that they will shoot roots. They were in a suitcase for a week before they came here to Tanana, the tissue paper was still damp and it had been sufficient for moisture."*

The green foliage of both plants and the pink blossoms on the begonia would give a sense of life through the dead of winter.

Outdoor planting was another story. "There is a garden for hospital employees," Elmer told Ruby. She would have to wait to sink her fingers deep into the sandy Alaska soil and plant a garden that would reward her with the taste of fresh vegetables—an otherwise expensive and difficult to obtain luxury this far north.

The raw ground in front of the duplex blended in with Front Street, a dirt, single-lane driving path that ran the length of the village and along the river. Depending on the season, this was dusty, muddy, icy, or a mix of all. People and vehicles shared this path with no danger to children or adults. There were only a few trucks in the village; those owned by several CAA folks, seasonal construction crew, a handful of Natives, and then the hospital ambulance and coal dump truck. These rumbled along slowly, often without a muffler. One battered pickup lacked glass in its windshield, had both doors ripped off, and the floorboard was a thick litter of Coke bottle caps. Washing one's truck was unheard of. Why bother? There were no garages, carports, or car washes.

The girls rode their bikes on this street, on the dirt around the duplex, and on the bare ground of the hospital circle drive. When it rained, they deliberately pedaled through the mud puddles with as much regard as the *Peanuts'* character, Pigpen. Mark rode his trike or sat in the red American Flyer wagon that Ruth pulled; this was easier on the narrow sidewalk that ran between the two duplexes and the hospital than through mud or snow. His sister, not at all a tomboy or stocky girl, pulled him without complaining, her little girl arms straining with the load of her fat-cheeked, chunky brother. "He's too heavy," said Naomi. "Make him walk." Ruth replied in short gasps, "I ... can do ... it ... myself."

On the same narrow sidewalk, the girls saw other potentials. They colored the surface with muted chalk marks and drew hopscotch outlines. When they became bored with drawing and jumping, the sisters strapped adjustable metal roller skates to the bottoms of their shoes and agilely jumped permafrost cracks. Playing jacks on the south-facing front stoop was another pastime. Ruby had come to expect that the two would figure out what to do. Even though Naomi was bossy, the girls were as inseparable as twins and played well together.

Hospital playground

The hospital playground was across the road from the hospital and enclosed with a forty-eight-inch wire-mesh fence. Ragged grass filled in around the play equipment, with beaten-down spots beneath the swings and the bottom of the slide. Outside this area stood a tall flagpole—without a flag. Below the bank, Elmer tied his airplane on floats.

This was the sole recreational area for children. There were no theaters with Saturday matinees, no amusement parks, no children's museums, no soccer fields. Fair-skinned and dark-skinned children, heads of blonde curls and raven-black braids, romped together. Mark climbed to the top of the slide but was afraid to go down. "I will catch you," Ruth assured him. Naomi became bored with the usual method of sliding and tried to run up the slide, rather than using the ladder, and other times attempted to go down backward.

Ruby allowed Naomi and Ruth to go to the playground alone. In a language understood only by his mother, Mark begged to follow his sisters. Some days, she tried to distract him by letting him stand on a chair alongside the kitchen counter and "help" her bake. Other times, she considered it a welcomed excuse to go outdoors. The fresh air and the feel of the soft sunshine on her face invigorated Ruby's sun-lover heart. Even on a cloudy day, the natural environment refreshed her with the smell of spruce and woodstove smoke, the energy of the Yukon River that raced and tumbled as far as the eye could see, and the display of purple-pink fireweed going to seed with halos of white fluff.

From time to time, women accompanied the children and sat on one of the two wooden benches. The women beaded soft moose skin for slippers or mittens, read a book, or just stared, transfixed by the movement of the churning water. Ruby's hands were always busy, and she carried along her mending. If other women were at the playground, she initiated a conversation. "How do you get water in the winter? Where do you get beads for the moccasins you're making? How do you keep your children from falling into the river?" Their answers were short. They were quiet and reticent. Shy, yet not unfriendly

The playground itself was surprisingly near the riverbank and gave a passerby an alarming impression that if any rambunctious child bumped into the flimsy wire, she or he would topple into the swift current taking along, like netted fish, every other child in the playground. This never happened.

TEACHERS, TOYS, AND TRIKES

DICK, JANE, AND SALLY

In the United States, from the 1930s into the 1960s, the youngsters and main characters in the primary reading books were written by William S. Gray and Zerna Sharp and published by Scott Foresman. Mother, who wore high heels, and Father, in a suit with tie, rounded out the family, while Spot, the energetic black and white spaniel, Puff, the spunky yellow tabby cat, and Tim, the teddy bear, added supplementary surprises and interaction.

Repetition was the emphasis of learning to read. Hence, such phrases:

- See Dick jump. Jump, Dick, jump.
- Jane can run! Run, Jane, run!
- Mother said, Sally, get Puff. No, Mother, no. I do not want Puff. Oh! See Puff jump.
- Where is Spot? There is Spot. See Spot run.

The family setting was a white frame house with a green lawn and a concrete sidewalk. Streets and cars added to the environment that was assumed to be familiar to every child.

Imagine the Native children in a remote Alaska village reading about these people. The Natives lived in one-room, woodstove-heated log cabins with howling husky dogs chained to doghouses; fox, bear, ptarmigan, and moose wandered nearby; no cats chased balloons or jumped into doll buggies. Their parents wore moose-skin mukluks on their feet and fox or wolverine fur-ruffed parkas. Would these children share familiarity with blow-up kiddie swimming pools? Lawn mowers? Honking horns? Television sets? Probably not.

Naomi and Ruth could remember sidewalks and lawns from their early childhood home in Kansas City, Kansas, and kittens from under their Leppke grandparent's farmhouse porch. If any of the Tanana children had had the opportunity to fly to Fairbanks, they would have witnessed one or two busy streets with cars and trucks. Most likely, the percentage of Native children doing so was small, if not zero.

All the same, the Native children were given white-faced, intact families, in a carefully groomed city, to teach them to read. Dick, Jane, and Sally did their best with a red Radio Flyer wagon, and happy and amusing experiences to compel these children to learn "Jump," "Run," "See," and "Look."

CHAPTER 4

JUST A FARM GIRL AND BOY

Kansas 1788–1940s

IT COULD HAVE BEEN SAID that migrating and adjusting to new worlds was in Ruby and Elmer's DNA. Their Mennonite ancestors had originated in Holland and then fled to Poland/Prussia for religious freedom. In 1763, Catherine the Great invited Europeans to settle in various parts of South Russia (Ukraine.) The Mennonites were recognized as good farmers, and in 1788, the first group of Mennonites accepted her offer and left Poland.

In 1878, Heinrich and Agata (Knelsen) Gåde, Elmer's great-grandfather and his wife, along with four children, traveled by ship from the undulating hills of South Russia to the city of New York.[15] The Statue of Liberty welcomed them with the opportunity of prosperity and happiness. They were farmers by birth and proceeded west by train to find dirt to cultivate. During this time period, they and other immigrants, such as Ruby's great-grandparents, the Leppkes and Litkes, stepped off the train at Peabody, Kansas and made their way by wagon and foot twelve miles to Ebenfeld.[16]

They brought with them hopes of finding flourishing farming in the land of freedom. In little time, they discovered the soil was unyielding—nothing like the deep, fertile loam they had turned into Russia's breadbasket.

In this small community, Ruby and Elmer's fathers, Solomon Leppke and Henry Gaede, spent their boyhood together, fishing, exploring creeks, and shooting jackrabbits. As teenagers, they played cornets[17] in the Hillsboro town and Ebenfeld community bands. They both loved fun.

Henry A. Gaede and Sol Leppke as teenagers

Solomon was tall, angular, and quiet, with narrow eyes, an early receding hairline, and prominent nose and ears. He stood erect throughout his entire life; and no matter how hard he toiled on the farm his shoulders never slumped. Henry Gaede's eyes twinkled; he had a quick smile and dark brown wavy hair.

On August 5, 1918, at the age of twenty-four, Henry was drafted for World War I and sent to Fort Riley in North Central Kansas, southwest of Manhattan, Kansas. During this same time, Sol was also drafted, and went to Camp Funston, a part of Fort Riley that served as a detention camp for those men who objected to serving in a war, many of whom were Mennonite, such as Sol. They had no idea what they would encounter.

Solomon was tall, angular, and quiet, with narrow eyes, an early receding hairline, and a prominent nose and ears. He stood erect throughout his entire life, and no matter how hard he toiled on the farm, his shoulders never slumped. Henry Gaede's eyes twinkled; he had a quick smile and dark brown wavy hair.

On August 5, 1918, at the age of twenty-four, Henry was drafted for World War I and sent to Fort Riley in North Central Kansas, southwest of Manhattan, Kansas. During this same time, Sol was also drafted and went to Camp Funston, a part of Fort Riley that served as a detention camp for those men who objected to serving in a war, many of whom were Mennonite, such as Sol. They had no idea what they would encounter.

From their earliest history, the Anabaptist-Mennonites took a stand against war and military service. In the 1550s, Menno Simons, one of the Mennonites' original leaders, said, "The regenerated do not go to war, nor engage in strife. They are the children of peace who have beaten their swords into plowshares and their spears into pruning hooks, and know of no war." For more than two centuries, service in the armed forces was practically unheard of among the Mennonites. Around 1850, it was possible for faith-based objectors to secure exemption from military service by hiring a substitute.

In World War I, the United States government faced the matter of non-combatants, also known as Conscientious Objectors (COs), whose decision was faith-based. They did not know what to do with these men who refused to be part of the military. The Mennonites did not object to serving their new country in peaceful alternatives but in varying ways, refused to be a part of the war machine. For some, this meant not wearing the army uniform or saluting; for most, it meant not carrying a gun.

What complicated matters was most Mennonites in the United States and Canada spoke German dialects during this time.[18] When their new home country was at war with the Germans, and the Mennonites refused to fight, while speaking German in their businesses, homes, and churches, the language immediately put them into a position of being regarded as traitors.

Thus, the Gaede and Leppke families, along with others, sought to integrate hastily, not draw attention to themselves, and blend in. This created the impetus to learn English as quickly as possible. Regardless of Henry's acquisition of the English language, he never really pronounced the *th* sound, which was not a part of the German language, and continued to "Tank the Lord," as well as pronouncing *f* as a *v* and "Praised God the Vater." His *English* gave him away.

At this point, there were no government guidelines for how to manage the non-compliant men. The initial response was to place drafted men into military camps and separate them from the rest of the servicemen. In some cases, the COs were harassed, taunted, and hazed in an attempt to get them to renounce their objection. In a documented case, two men were abused enough to cause their death.

JUST A FARM GIRL AND BOY

Henry A Gaede at Fort Riley, Kansas

In an interview years later, Henry recounted his experience. "They handed you the gun … and when it came to me, I stepped back and wouldn't take the gun. That's when they took me out of the bunch. They wanted to try us out to see if we'd change our minds and go with the regulars." Henry wore a uniform but wouldn't comply with taking a gun. To begin with, he was put in jail with prisoners, after which he and other non-combatants were moved to separate tents and not allowed to talk to one another. "We always tried to do as much as we could," he said. "We'd help clean up the barracks and help clean up outside or make meals, trim trees, and cut grass." Always there were officers with guns guarding them.

Ruby had heard her father talk about his experience. When he was in his eighties, she recorded his story on a cassette. "The officers didn't know what to do with us. We hauled rocks up a hill one day and hauled the same rocks down the next. … We peeled potatoes and helped with meal making," he told her in his gravelly voice. Those were acceptable and fairly benign memories. What made his voice quiver was describing when an officer woke him in the middle of the night, took him outside the main camp, and cocked a gun behind his head. "I expected to be shot to death."

After World War I, the military changed their policies, and future COs were given options of working in the Forestry Service, the National Park Service, the Bureau of Reclamation, and in hospitals.

In 1919, both boys married farm girls within their community. Solomon, at age twenty-three, married Bertha Litke[23]. She was a sturdy and capable girl who would not be easily blown over by the constant Kansas wind; she would be able to shoulder the demands of raising a family, come alongside her husband with fieldwork, and tend the livestock.

At age twenty-six, Henry Gaede married Agnes Ediger, the sister of his good friend, John Ediger. Agnes was a beautiful girl with small features, gentle eyes, and auburn hair. As a teenager, she had assisted neighbors when they were ill or injured, and she desired to be a nurse when she was older. This never happened. However, her son, Elmer, would become a physician, and the next generations would produce healthcare workers as well.

Agnes Ediger Gaede

Henry and Agnes Gaede lived in a sod house, four miles west and three miles south of Hillsboro, Kansas. The early settlers used what was available, and the prairie offered thick sod with a tough root system. The sod was cut into rectangles and stacked into walls. Canvas, plaster, or wallpaper might line the walls. The end product was well insulated but subject to rodents and snakes burrowing through the walls and ceiling and a very muddy floor when there was precipitation. Agnes recalled standing in inches of water after one heavy rainstorm. Harold, their first child, was born on December 23, 1920.

Farming was difficult with dirt clods, dry spells, and bugs. Some Mennonite families headed to Collinsville, Oklahoma, just north of Tulsa, where they had heard there was great prosperity. Solomon and Bertha were among one of the earlier groups to migrate in that direction. In some cases, men jolted in covered wagons on deeply rutted roads with a meager showing of livestock following beside them while the women and children journeyed by train. Ruby's oldest sister, Lulu Mae, was born on April 26, 1920, in Collinsville.

Agnes's parents owned a farm in that area, so on July 30, 1921, she and Henry loaded a freight car with their household goods, furniture, farm implements, and livestock and moved to Oklahoma. Elmer was born in Collinsville on September 8, 1922. His mother described him as "inquisitive."

The obstinate Oklahoma red-dirt prairie did not encourage the settlers, who were destitute to begin with. The two families, now each with a young child, loaded their household and farm goods onto a freight train and returned to Kansas. In four years, the newlywed families had experienced complete upheaval, discouragement, and exhaustion; all the while, the women were doing double duty of farm work, meal-making, tending the livestock, washing clothes by hand—including baby diapers—and dealing with all those things involved with early childcare. They were no sissies.

Ruby was born on April 17, 1924, on the Litke farm. The farm was about three miles from the Ebenfeld Mennonite Brethren Church, where all the Litke relatives attended, and around which many had settled. Solomon and Bertha Leppke had some economic advantages, and shortly after their return to Kansas, Solomon's father, Isaac Leppke, was able to offer land to his sons. No one would have guessed this would be possible since the pioneering immigrant struggled during the drought years to pay on the loans against his own farm. To offset the loss of revenue from oats, which were selling for sixteen cents a bushel, and wheat farming, he'd added hog-raising.[24] Solomon and Bertha were then able to live on this farm, outside of Peabody, Kansas, one mile west of the Rock Island railroad tracks and slowly repay Isaac.

The decision to live at this location was frowned on because it removed the family from the strictly Mennonite community. Solomon and Bertha's children would attend a non-Mennonite school and subsequently make non-Mennonite friends. Both elements would expose them to non-Mennonite ways of thinking, acting, and believing.

Sol and Bertha Leppke moved into the white-sided, red-shuttered two-story house that was already built on the farm. A wood cookstove heated the kitchen, and a heating stove was present during the winter in the main, lower level of the house, which burned either hedge wood or coal. There was no direct heat in the bedrooms upstairs; the smallest bedroom, through which the stove stack ran, was the warmest.

Bathroom facilities initially consisted of an outhouse and a metal bathing tub in the back pantry. With no running water, buckets of water were heated on the stove and poured into the tub. Later, the smaller main level bedroom was turned into a bathroom with indoor plumbing.

Margie was born five years after Ruby, on May 21, 1929. Ruby would forever describe her little sister as "a beautiful little blonde," who contrasted with her older sister, Lulu Mae, who took after their father and was tall, slender, and dark-haired. Margie was the pretty one in the family, and pictures showed her with Shirley Temple curls for special occasions. Finally, on September 4, 1933, a boy blessed the farming family. Ruby cherished her little brother, Wilbur, who was nine years younger than she. Just as Ruby's daughter Ruth would feel about her brother, Mark, Ruby also believed Wilbur could do no wrong. In stature, Wilbur took after his mother's side, the shorter Litkes, although he would have the appearance, strength, and fortitude of his father.

*Ruby, Margie, Solomon, Lulu Mae, Wilbur,
Bertha Leppke on their Peabody, Kansas farm*

These were hard years. Ruby was five when the Great Depression began after the stock market crash of October 1929. Farming communities and rural areas suffered as crop prices fell by approximately 60 percent. To some degree, the family had an advantage over city folks in that they could raise their own food. This advantage was minimized by the Dust Bowl, also known as the Dirty Thirties, which was a period of severe dust storms accompanied by extreme drought that harshly damaged the ecology and agriculture of the United States prairies. Added to this misery were the swarms of grasshoppers and jackrabbits that descended on anything that remained on the parched grasslands. By the end of the decade, the rains returned; these, along with steps instigated by President Franklin D. Roosevelt and soil conservation and agricultural agencies, restored hope and help for the farmlands.

Ruby was born into these hard times. She was a no-frills girl and accepted her lot in life.

JUST A FARM GIRL AND BOY

Elmer's grandfather, Abraham Gaede, could not provide land for his sons, as had Isaac Leppke for Ruby's father and his brothers; consequently, Elmer's father, Henry, struggled to provide for his family. He rented and lived on several farms, but his meager profits went nearly all to the landowner. Then news circulated that Western Kansas offered a promising future. In July of 1926, only three years after returning from Oklahoma, Henry and Agnes packed up and moved to the Ingalls area where other Gaedes lived. Within this time, two of Henry's sisters had married two Penner brothers. Generations later, Elmer and Ruby's oldest daughter, Naomi, would marry one of these Gaede-Penner boys, tying family history together even tighter.

Henry and Agnes again lived in a one-room soddy.[25] They sowed 255 acres of wheat—which the horrendous and terrifying dust storms promptly destroyed. It wasn't as if there were no warnings. The enormous black storms grew on the horizon, billowing, roaring, and towering high in the sky as they approached the small farmhouses and rural towns with thin frame buildings. Livestock suffocated. Men and women wet bandanas and placed them over their mouths and noses, and pulled their crying children toward them to do the same. The dust monster paid no heed to the dampened towels along the windowsills and brazenly slinked inside. Woe to anyone caught in the field or driving on a road when the merciless, shrieking darkness captured and blinded him or her. "Rollers" they were called. These rollers grew into tormenting nightmares for adults and children alike.

Henry and Agnes lost everything. On March 17, eight months after their arrival in what had been a Promised Land, they returned to Hillsboro, Kansas. This time they had no money to transport their belongings by railroad. Horses drew a modified covered wagon and hayrack, with their remaining cattle herded in front. Agnes and the two young boys, Harold and Elmer, rode with a relative in his Model T Ford. Back near their starting point, Lillian was born on September 25, 1927, in Hillsboro, Kansas.

Elmer knew about being poor. He knew no differently. He expected little. Possibly his little-boy wishes and dreams were to have enough to eat and to live in one place. No wonder that during these years, he was malnourished and failed to thrive physically. There was habitually not enough to fill his stomach. As an adult, he revealed to his children, "Harold and I used to fight over crackers and homemade chocolate pudding." His health interfered with his early school learning, and he missed school often. He had to repeat first grade. Surprisingly, as an adult, his eating habits did not compensate for the early deprivation, and, as much as he loved homemade ice cream, he remained wiry and thin his entire life.

When Elmer and Harold weren't milking cows, chopping firewood, or doing other farm work, they earned up to $2.50 from the government for shooting skunks, squirrels, and jackrabbits. These pests ate any green shoot that managed to poke out of the hard clods and survive the wind and pestilence. Adversity made everyone, including the two boys, resourceful. They picked up golf balls from the neighboring golf course, by Sunset Lake, that bounced onto their land or in their creek and, for a few cents, turned these in to a sporting store in Wichita. Other times, they were paid one cent for every row of cockle burrs or sunflower weeds they hacked down. At that time, a pair of shoes cost $2; eventually, the boys had the financial resources to purchase a bicycle—for around $5—and then ordered shoe ice skates from a catalog. (They gave their clamp-on ice skates to neighbor kids.)

Just like Ruby, Elmer's preferred world was outdoors. He and Harold caught catfish by hand in the muddy creeks, sledded over the banks of their creek, and skated on ice-glazed fields. Unlike Ruby, Elmer was foolhardy and tested the limits, trying such daredevil feats as skating on Sunset Lake even when it groaned and split from the edges to the center.

Ruby came from generations of hardy stock. Throughout their migration, they not only survived but found ways to adapt and thrive. Now, did she have the elasticity to stretch into a completely new environment and culture? Could she find contentment alongside the bush doctor? The story was just beginning.

```
          KANSAS                    ALASKA

Nickname: Sunflower State   Last Frontier
Song: "Home on the Range"   "Alaska's Flag"
Flower: Sunflower           Forget-me-not
Tree: Cottonwood            Sitka spruce
Bird: Meadowlark            Willow ptarmigan
Insect: Honey bee           Dragonfly
Mammal: Buffalo             Moose
```

CHAPTER 5

GOING TO THE CHAPEL

Tanana, September 1957

FROM THE FIRST SUNDAY THEY ARRIVED, the Gaedes attended the Arctic Missions Chapel.[26] Ruth was not excited about another new experience. "Can I sit with you, Mommy?" she asked. "Of course," her mother replied. "I mean the whole time," Ruth pleaded. She knew better than to beg to stay home.

For their entire life, the Gaedes had attended church every Sunday, no matter what, and today was no different. And, going to church meant wearing "church clothes." Here in the middle of nowhere, would they give up that tradition? Maybe choose clothes more practical for an unassuming village? No. Part of wearing church clothes was out of honor, respect, and reverence for God; there was something almost sacred about wearing church clothes. Accordingly, they didn't think twice about walking a half-mile on a sandy road to the church service, dressed as though they were in a city—with sidewalks.

Ruby wore a fashionable nipped-in-the-waist dress and even a hat. Elmer took long strides in a gray suit and yellow necktie. Naomi and Ruth were outfitted in matching dresses, designed and sewn by their mother, and white anklets in black patent shoes, shoes that were shiny to begin with, but faded by the time of their arrival.

Their hair had been another matter. Any mother can appreciate what Ruby went through with Naomi's outbursts of "Why isn't my hair pretty like Ruth's?" Naomi's hair didn't quite touch her shoulders, and instead of pulling it into the customary stubby pigtails on Saturday night, Ruby wound the hair in pin curls and covered them with a red nylon stretchy four-inch band. When Naomi did *not* pull out the rigid bobby pins, her hair was full the next day, even if it wasn't in natural ringlets like Ruth's. Her hair had been somewhat curly when she was younger and in the Kansas humidity. "Yes, Naomi, you are pretty too," Ruby tried to assure her oldest, who fought back tears. In most cases, the girls got along well, except for infrequent fits of jealousy. Throughout the coming years, Ruby would say, with exasperation, "The girls were so easy. Then I had Mark."

Family photos illustrated Naomi and Ruth's differences. Their father, who reveled in the attention he got when he showed slides and 8 mm movies of hunting adventures, occasionally took family pictures. Naomi appeared content and at ease, although often in constant motion. She was quick to show off for the camera. Her skin tanned easily, like her mother's. Ruth characteristically hid her face from the sun, which in turn blocked her face from the camera. Slides and snapshots captured a contained child with her face to her chest, hands folded, and slightly bowed legs like her mother's. Movies showed her nervously shifting from one foot to the other, rapidly. Her smile was guarded.

All the same, the girls shared their mother's hazel eyes, and, eventually, their hair would turn as dark as hers. They would, however, surpass her five feet, two-inch frame and grow to five feet four.

Mark, not yet two years old, was a smaller version of his father; that is, in terms of his toddler suit. In a physical sense, at least at this stage of life, the similarities stopped there. Mark had Grandma Agnes Gaede's round nose, blue eyes, and auburn hair; his father's nose was not small and had been hit by a softball, the aftermath leaving a slight bend to one side. Without Ruby's regular haircuts, Elmer's jet-black hair curled in a pile on his head, but it never camouflaged his ears, which stuck out noticeably. Unlike Mark, who had a double chin, Elmer had been a scrawny kid, and even as an adult didn't carry any extra pounds. Someday, Mark would look surprisingly like his father—with the same hair color and trim build. At this point, no one would have guessed that fact.

Ruby and her family must have appeared entirely out of place walking on Tanana's Front Street in their Sunday best. Their route took them along the river and past a few buildings, most of which had corrugated tin roofs with a pitch great enough for snow to slide down easily. The older buildings were weathered gray, while the newer ones were painted brown. Some appeared to be unused sheds. Overhead a few electrical lines ran between the slightly rolling road and the riverbank. A scattering of aspen, cottonwoods, and willows ranged among the buildings, which were filled in with native grass and random patches of stalky remainders of purple, pink, and white wildflowers.

Gaede family walking home from church on Front Street

Elmer pulled Mark in a red wagon. Ruth walked near her brother, stuffing her hands in her pockets when a breeze swept against her. Naomi jumped on crunchy brown leaves that skittered across the road. Everyone puffed to keep up with Elmer's pace.

"See how the fireweed is going to seed? Isn't that something how the flowers turn into cottony strands?" Ruby grabbed a handful of the stringy fibers. She was a careful observer of the natural environment and especially appreciated color and plant life. The wild bush roses were nearly flowerless, and maroon rosehips hid in the remaining leaves. She picked one, bit into it, blinked her eyes, and spit it out. Still sputtering, she hurried to catch up with the small procession.

Elmer studied the sky, evaluating it, as would a pilot.[27] Stringy cirrus clouds. "A bit windy up there," he stated.

Ruby glanced at him without saying a word. It didn't take a mind reader to know she would just as soon he had never learned to fly—even if her general response to anyone who asked was, "I have to trust God." Why couldn't Elmer just be happy on a tractor, she wondered.

On the left side of the road, the Northern Commercial store, with a half-dozen fifty-five-gallon oil drums on the side and a hand-dolly standing near the front door, stood between the new log rectory and St. James Episcopal Church. The rectory showed the handiwork of Reverend Coleman Inge and his wife, Anne, as did the church.[28] Windows had been salvaged from the Old Mission on the edge of town. The installation of these and a new oil furnace would provide a warmer meeting place in winter.

The small village actually had three churches. The Catholic Church sat behind the schoolhouse. The Arctic Missions' chapel, the Gaede's destination, was next door to St. James. The white-sided parsonage and chapel could have used some fresh paint. The same was true for the picket fence, which seemed a bit out of place in the middle of Alaska. The chapel, with a sloped roof, was actually a lean-to attached to the small house. Two chimney pipes for wood-burning stoves—one for the house and one for the meeting room—stuck out of the roof. At least the short boardwalk up to the door helped scuff off dirt or mud stuck to attendees' boots and shoes.

All in all, maintenance of the facility, along with the untrimmed patches of grass in the yard, was probably last on the missionary's to-do list. More important tasks were hauling water, which in winter meant chopping holes in the river ice; in summer, trolling the river with a boat and snagging logs for firewood that had toppled off the riverbanks; keeping a path cleared to the outhouse; and saving souls.

Roy and Margie Gronning were the current Arctic Missions' missionaries. Roy, a strapping blonde Scandinavian of over six feet, towered quietly over his wife, Margie, less than five feet tall. When Elmer had visited Tanana the previous spring, he'd sized up Roy and had told Ruby, "He's an ox of a man, and I bet he can pack out a ton of moose meat." Elmer would find this to be true.

Margie, extraverted and with a sense of humor, made everyone feel as though they were her long-lost friends. She beamed at Ruby, put her arm around her waist, and exclaimed, "I've been waiting to meet you!" Ruby liked this woman instantly. The two started a short conversation before it was time to sit on the cold metal folding chairs that sent a quick chill up one's spine when first seated.

About twenty people filled the chapel with a mix of Native children, an older Native man Margie called "Grandpa Sam," several blond-haired girls with their mother (CAA family), and Naomi and Ruth's schoolteacher, Anna Bortel. When a classmate walked up to Ruth and tried to start a conversation, Ruth leaned into her mother.

Ruby had only met Anna briefly. At that first quick exchange on the school ground, Anna had been smitten with "Markie," and now again, she was captured by his charm. At this instant, Ruby did not see his charm. She was trying to shush him for the church service. His response to such constraints was to grab her glasses and throw them. This was not funny—to Ruby.

Once Mark settled down, Ruby studied Anna. Her light-brown hair was cut tidily into short, wide bangs above her neutral-rimmed glasses. She appeared positive and upbeat about life. Ruby hoped that was true in the long run, and more so in the winter when the darkness sapped the energy out of every living thing.

The service started with Roy leading the singing and Margie playing an autoharp. The hymn was one Ruby knew well, "I Love to Tell the Story." Not only that, she was thrilled to hear harmony parts emerge out of the small group. Elmer sang tenor, Anna found alto parts, Ruby sang soprano, and Roy and Margie picked up anything missing. Children's young voices added to the sound. This made Ruby smile inside and out. The familiarity gave her a sense of continuity, and it was as though she could almost reach back to the little country church on the Kansas prairie that was filled with fond memories of her family. No matter the distance, the same God was here in Alaska. She would need Him for sure.

After the service, Margie beckoned for Ruby to come into their poorly insulated, low-ceiling house. "It's simple, but it's home," she laughed. At least the chapel functioned as an arctic entry; that is, one had to walk through the chapel to access the house. Rather than opening the door into the house directly from the outdoors, the chapel protected it from a direct wintry blast—when that season would come.

Ruby looked around. Off the main room, which included a countertop for a kitchen, a table with chairs, and a few items of living room furniture, there was a bedroom the size of a closet. A wood-burning barrel stove[29] scarcely warmed the air, much less the floor where two-and-half-year-old Chris and seven-month-old Bethany played. And this was only September, not the middle of an arctic winter. There was no indoor plumbing, nor any electricity. "We use lantern light, and there's the outhouse out back," said Margie, reading Ruby's thoughts. Margie didn't murmur or complain, yet Ruby felt guilty about the plushness of the new duplex in which she lived. Not real bush living by any means.

Early on, nearly every letter Ruby sent to loved ones contained a sentence such as: "*A nurse came and got Elmer out of church for an accident.*" Or, "*Elmer was called out of church to check on a woman who had delivered her baby in bed. He pronounced it alive and ran back to church.*" The CAA houses had an inter-house phone system that connected to the airport station, and the airport station could call the hospital. Otherwise, communication was by word-of-walk, rather than word-of-mouth. The bush doctor got his exercise, which was easier in moderate weather than in winter's biting cold. The bush doctor's wife often found herself alone after church, bundling up children and walking home—pulling the wagon, or in the depth of winter, a sled.

But, on that first Sunday, Ruby sensed she had found a kindred spirit in Margie, who would be not only a friend with a buoyant outlook, but a woman of fortitude, and a mother, with whom she could share parenting frustrations. They could totter together when the going got rough. Time would tell about Anna, but if she was captivated by Mark, could entertain the child for a moment or two, *and* have the ability to make Ruth feel comfortable at school, those traits alone would be appreciated and endearing qualities. Adjustment to the small village already felt a bit easier, and more so since Ruth had survived her second new experience in a week.

CHAPTER 6

CHILDHOOD, CHICKEN COOPS, AND COWS

Peabody, Kansas farm 1930s–1940s

WHEN RUBY WAS GROWING UP, and her siblings weren't working, which wasn't often, the children had to come up with their own ideas for play; thus, as a mother, the thought never entered Ruby's head that she should be her children's social activities director, day camp leader, or playmate. She assumed her children would figure out what to do on their own, with one another, or with the natural interaction of children in the neighborhood, the church nursery, or Sunday school. Unlike Kansas City and Anchorage, however, in Tanana, there was no church nursery or Sunday school, and neighbor children lived a distance from the hospital compound. All the same, her children did not lack for indoor or outdoor toys or the imagination to find pleasure in dirt, mud, or snow.

Even though Ruby's childhood free time was rare, she could look back with fondness on several memories. On one hot summer day, she and Lulu Mae were allowed to turn a section of the chicken coop into a pretend restaurant. The chicken coop first had to be cleaned out from years of chicken excrement and feathers, as well as layers of sticky, humid dust that fastened itself to every ladder, board, and screen. Unused chicken feeders and waterers were caked with a mix of poop and mud. The girls used a shovel and broom, both of which kicked up more dust. Ruby and Lulu Mae coughed in unison and solo. Eventually, they hauled a bucket of water from the well and used rags for an even more thorough cleaning.

The girls rummaged behind farm sheds and turned up wooden boxes and scrap boards to construct rudimentary tables. Ruby hunted down a worn-out tablecloth, and Lulu Mae hung some kind of curtains on the windows, perhaps burlap from feed sacks. "We shaped our food out of mud and decorated it with corn and wheat kernels," she told a grown-up Naomi in a life history interview. Ruby laughed with pleasure.

"We made ice cream cones out of the mud. Very attractive foods! Lulu Mae was the cook, of course, and as the budding artist in the family, she made a bird nest and a little bird egg out of mud and put it in the mailbox for the mailman. I don't know if it was appreciated or not, but it was very creative." Their time to play was limited by the constant farmwork and housework, but this bit of creative and imaginative fun was food for Ruby's inner and outer child.

Make no mistake; Ruby was not a perfect child. "One of my fun things that was such a no-no was making mud balls and throwing them against one of the buildings. Ha! And, we weren't supposed to walk in the mud after the rain. The soil was so clay-like that it wouldn't ooze back into a smooth surface. When we kids finally got a toy wagon, we loved to make trails all around the farmyard in the mud. Daddy scolded us. He didn't like driving his car or farm equipment over the hard, dried-in ruts."

On other occasions, probably when the weather was inclement, Ruby played indoors with her life-size baby doll. The doll's fragile plaster head, hands, and feet were attached to a cloth body. When Ruby gently rocked the doll's head side-to-side, its eyes rolled side-to-side too, which made it look eerily alive.

Even though there were these fun times, Ruby's overriding recollections of her earlier years were of work, and, as a result, she didn't want her children to live the life she had; she wanted them to be children and have the playtime she never had.

"As a young child, I carried in bushel baskets of wood for the heating and cooking stoves and corncobs for kindling," Ruby said in her life review. "Mom kept a tin can half-full of kerosene and four corncobs with which she started the fire in the morning."

As Ruby grew older, her responsibilities included feeding the chickens and gathering eggs. There was a routine to the proper care of chickens. In the mornings, their mother, Bertha Leppke, fed the chickens a mash of grain and sour milk. She also set out a large bowl of ashes from the woodstove, in which the chickens rolled and fluffed themselves. This took care of the lice and mites that would bother them. The chickens were likewise given crunched up oyster shells in their food pans, which made the calcium for the eggshells. These were the easy steps. Gathering eggs was not.

The hens, which happily sat in their nests, on top of eggs they carefully mothered, pecked the children's hands. Ruby learned to clutch the neck of the protective hen, hope she wouldn't kick around too much, and grab the fragile eggs. When Ruby grew bigger and bolder, she'd seize the hen by its head and yank the hen out of the nest. As fun and nostalgic as it may sound to gather eggs from a chicken coop, those were scary times for the youngsters.

Around age twelve, Ruby started to help milk the cows. Although both her parents milked, it was mostly her mother's responsibility. In the low ceiling barn that was sticky humid in summers and sharply cold in winter, the milkers sat on short three-legged wooden stools and reached beneath the cows' bellies to squeeze off warm milk that foamed into the bucket between the milkers' knees or setting in front of them. The cows seemed to gain pleasure in flicking their tails into the milkers' mouths or wrapping their tails around their heads. In summer, the cows were sprayed for flies and given some grain or alfalfa to focus their attention elsewhere. When Ruby was fifteen, she won a cow-milking contest. That took strong hands and fingers, as well as technique.

No matter how small the task, farming is physically demanding, and farming families rely heavily on producing sons to help with the work. In the absence of older boys, her father recruited Ruby to help with the fieldwork. He liked having her assistance and called her his "Handy Andy" and "Grease Monkey." Certainly, she knew the smells of grease, oil, gas, and diesel.

As she matured, there were several days each month when she would have preferred getting off her feet and out of the sun. Her mother tried to step in for her but usually had her own hands full with outdoor work too.

Harvest time kept Ruby extra busy. She was short, small, and could slip easily into spots where a grown man would have to squeeze. She could wiggle inside a threshing machine and hold rivets while her father made repairs on the outside. Sometimes, a worker unintentionally dropped his pitchfork on the feeder table, along with a bundle of grain. It was her job to throw in the clutch and stop the machine before it ingested the pitchfork.

July temperatures easily hit 100°, and the labor-intensive workdays extended twelve hours or more. Dust from the dry grain and straw mixed with mugginess. Before the day was half through, Ruby and everyone involved would be coated gray, with streaks of salty sweat running down their backs, bits of straw stuck to any exposed damp skin or even beneath a loose shirt, and hair matted beneath wide-brimmed straw hats.

CHILDHOOD, CHICKEN COOPS, AND COWS

In the blacksmith shop, she turned the forge wheels so the coals would heat and the plowshares would glow red-hot. Her father hammered the huge plowshare until it was sharp and could more easily cut through the prairie sod. If interviewed at that time in her life, she would have burst out bitterly, "I know more about pouring Babbitt,[30] grinding valves, and working on radiators than making an apple pie."

Ruby's arms quickly tanned from daily outdoor exposure, and her arms grew smooth and taut from pulling, climbing, and lifting. The sweltering sun made sweaty dark ringlets around her neck. One spring, she plowed for six days straight on the orange Allis-Chalmers tractor. Her boyfriend didn't understand the lack of attention he received or the unflattering use of her time. "My mother never does that kind of work," he grumbled. The comment smacked on her already sunburnt face. She wiped her perspiring palms on her overalls and turned the tractor around.

Although Ruby resented toiling in the fields, the truth was, she preferred to be outdoors than inside. She took pleasure in feeling the dirt between her fingers and toes, driving a tractor with the rhythmic putt-putt-putt, and hearing and identifying the bird songs in the quiet of a golden wheat field. In Alaska, she would miss the Kansas evenings with the luscious ball of yellow-orange sliding behind hedgerows with rays of light filtering through silhouetted tangled trunks. She could hear in her head the myriad of insects rasping, singing, and whirring. In her mind, she would see the stormy skies with lightning ripping, winds snorting, and clouds swirling.

Reading the clouds in Alaska would be different. She had grown up knowing how crops brought money for clothes, fabric, chicken feed, combine parts, and medicine. A successful harvest depended on storm clouds bringing moisture to newly planted seeds and hot sunshine to ripen wheat kernels and ears of corn. At the same time, storm clouds could bring hail, tornadoes, and destruction. The weather, a nearly personified entity, held in its capricious grasp the ability to grant the favor of desperately needed precipitation during a drought or to change a prosperous day of harvest into a fateful day of hail. She had experienced these hard facts.

Meanwhile, her two sisters worked inside the family house. With no air conditioning, the house was firecracker hot, even sauna-like when chicken was fried and bread baked, or water boiled with ears of corn, but at least there was shade—and some relief from the constant, blowing dust from the fields.

Even if Ruby was an outdoor girl, she longed to feel pretty, womanly, and even a bit fancy—things that happened inside the house. When she would come inside, covered with oil smears on her legs, she would see her sisters embroidering, crimping pastry edges, baking, and canning peaches. They were prepared to be women by doing womanly tasks. Ruby was not.

When girls turned age sixteen, they were expected to find paying jobs outside the home, such as cleaning or cooking for wealthy people in Wichita, helping out women who had just had a baby, and so on.

When Ruby took on such jobs, she faced anxious and embarrassing moments from her lack of culinary skills. Her first pie was a disaster. The crust wouldn't roll out and looked nothing like what she had seen her mother and Lulu Mae make. The meringue pooled instead of whipping into peaks. She was at a loss when the woman of the house gave her a recipe to follow. She had some sense of how to make Mennonite foods, just from watching her mother, but following a recipe for something other than what she recognized was baffling.

As an adult, people would both tease and admire her ability to make or mend anything with baling wire or fishing line. At the same time, guests and family would describe her as an excellent cook, who adeptly, and without a hint of anxiety, served ten to twelve people every Sunday noon after church, and later cooked outdoors or under clear plastic tenting for children's Bible camps in Alaska.[31]

In Tanana, she would need that old-fashioned, roll-up-your-sleeves character she had cultivated on the farm. However, in Alaska, "character" would be better described as roll *down* your sleeves and wrap a wool scarf around your neck to tackle the challenges in front of you. But, she didn't know that growing up. Sometimes life makes more sense long after the fact.

HIDE THE THIMBLE

"Hide the Thimble" was a game Naomi and Ruth learned before going to Alaska, possibly from their Gaede grandparents. With roots emerging from the United States and the United Kingdom in the early 1880s, the game has other names, including "Hot Buttered Beans" and "Hide the Key."

The rules vary. In some versions, everyone (the seekers) leaves the room except the person hiding the thimble (the hider). In other versions, there are multiple hiders and one seeker. The hiders place the thimble behind an object or someplace where it blends in. When the seeker is called in, the hiders give verbal clues of "you're hot" when the seeker moves near to the thimble and "you're cold" when the seeker moves away. Both the hiders and the seekers delight in their opposite successes of hiding or seeking.

CHAPTER 7

GETTING ACQUAINTED

Tanana, 1957

FINALLY, RUBY WAS ABLE to step away from unpacking boxes and organizing rows of canned goods and explore her new surroundings. Truthfully, Anna initiated this. Even with the differences in their personalities, and the short time they'd known each other, there was something that drew Ruby to Anna. Now, given the unknowns of the village, she was content to be the follower of a confident leader.

After a few brief conversations at church, it became evident to Ruby that Anna faced life with personality traits similar to Elmer. If Elmer or Anna were shown some unknown pathway, neither would be satisfied to merely journey to the end of *that* pathway. They would consider it a stepping-stone to something even more adventurous. Both of them had ended up in Tanana due to that restlessness and the reflexive pull to see what was just over another mountain.

In 1955, Elmer left a trail of Kansas dust and drove with his young family to Anchorage, Alaska. Within six months of his work with Public Health in Anchorage, he had impatiently chomped at the bit and desired work in a farther frontier. When he was given options for his second two-year rotation, he chose Tanana, in the Interior. His first flight to the area proved that it *was* more remote, and his work would be more rigorous. He liked that.

Anna's story illustrated the same motivation. In 1954, she had traveled to Alaska from Ohio as a single schoolteacher. She had survived, with equanimity, the waterfront village of Valdez, even though she experienced more than three hundred inches of snow, an unwelcomed ermine house resident, and a stove blowing up in her face—which threatened to burn down her house. After three years, she yearned for *more* demanding experiences in the Last Frontier. Thus, she packed up and drove to Fairbanks for summer school. Her intention was to snag a teaching position in Interior Alaska. She was tickled pink to spot a posted job: Tanana. She arrived shortly before the Gaede family.

In contrast, Ruby was not energized by the unexplored or by testing her physical and mental limits. Elmer and Anna labeled their experiences as adventures, and even though Ruby's life *was* an adventure, she did not frame it as such. Whereas they would entertain guests with captivating stories, Ruby entertained with a pretty table and tasty food, the latter, being an adventure in itself with the limited resources she was able to find.

On the other hand, Ruby was a dependable writer of daily events, which truly read as adventures to the readers. In hindsight, if she had used the telephone to convey this information, the true-life Alaska tales would have evaporated like early season snowflakes hitting a warm surface.

Even though Ruby was cautious and introverted, she responded to Anna's gregariousness with anticipation for a potential friendship. Years later, Ruby would try to explain how it happened. "I was kind of lonely, but there was Anna, whom I'd only recently met. She was friendly and warm, and we started a friendship."

Anna would think back, too, and try to describe how the relationship took shape. "We just hit it off. We had such good times together, especially sharing our spiritual journeys. We were on the same page in our beliefs and could talk for hours." Anna found little things amusing and giggled when she thought back to one occasion. "I remember one time Elmer was gone on a medical field trip, and Ruby had me come and stay with her. We were in bed talking so long that finally, she had us each take a sleeping pill, so we'd shut up!"

Friendships are not a luxury in the northland; they are as essential as any other wilderness survival gear. Whom could Ruby confide in about her worries and fears of living in this rough country? Who could provide that emotional connection and reassurance when she doubted her abilities to mother three lively children. Or when she felt depressed during the holidays, or when four days in a row the sun did not even peak over the horizon because storm clouds shut it out. Who could help when she didn't think she could layer three children with wool socks, two pairs of corduroy pants, parkas, wool neck mufflers, and mittens—for the umpteenth time—and walk to church. Not to mention time and time again when her husband flew to another village for a medical emergency and was late returning. Was he safe at a missionary or schoolteacher's cabin? Or had weather or darkness caused his plane to go down? More often than not, her conclusions were dark.

As small as the village was, making friends did not just happen. It wasn't as if women lived in houses side-by-side, caught sight of one another, and started conversations as a result of weeding their zinnias or marigolds, or hanging just-washed socks and petticoats on a clothesline, or shaking out rugs. They did not meet because one child batted a ball into the neighboring yard.

Likewise, there were no formalized groups for moms. Not that there were any of these resources Outside[32] at this time either. Neither the hospital compound nor the community at large had a clubhouse with activities or a recreation center. None of the three churches sponsored a Ladies' Night Out. If women in Tanana had wanted to plan such a night out, where would they have met? Overall, opportunities for finding similar-minded women were limited to interactions at school activities, participation at one of the churches, or the Native events held at the Community Hall. Ruby, just like Anna, Margie, and the nurses, needed each other to fill the gaps of distant loved ones and previous friends.

When Anna arrived, she lived in the teacherage[33], inside the Tanana Day School; therefore, in a blink of an eye, she could be at the medical compound duplex and could easily share a cup of tea or hot cocoa with Ruby. And, even though Anna was single and had no children, and Ruby was a wife and mother, there was an interest and connection to one another. Anna didn't seem to mind that Ruby's conversations centered on her hectic world of homemaking and child-rearing. In fact, Anna welcomed being included in the Gaede family. She already knew Naomi and Ruth, or "Ruthie," as she affectionately called the youngest daughter, from school. Then there was, of course, Markie. As everyone knows, a mother treasures anyone who makes a fuss over her children. Beyond this, Ruby appreciated Anna's quick chuckle and her positive and humorous renditions of daily teaching incidences. She also valued Anna's backwoods savvy, and, as time went on, the two developed a synergy for social planning.

"She is like my sister," she wrote in her letters to loved ones. Feeling like sisters strengthened their ability to be pioneers, rather than melt into heaps of despair when inconveniences or lack of creature comforts clumped together and for the moment withered their spirits.

GETTING ACQUAINTED

Most certainly, there had been many pioneers in the Tanana area before Elmer, Ruby, and Anna showed up to test *their* grit and courage. The landscape of the 1957 village hid many of the telltale signs of earlier footsteps. The moss, undergrowth, aspen, and spruce trees took back any wilderness that was not continually cleared or maintained. Beneath their jealous guard were evidence of gold-seekers, military, missionaries, mercenaries, and ever-migrating Native people.

Confluence of the Yukon and Tanana Rivers, up from the village of Tanana. The Tanana airstrip runs behind the village

Upriver from the present day Tanana, the Yukon and the Tanana Rivers converged. The Natives identified this as *Nuchalawoyya* (new-cha-la-WOY-uh) — "Place where two rivers meet." For decades, the Koyukon and Tanana Athabascans had met in this area to discuss differences and settle issues.

Outposts came and went downriver. In 1880, Harper Station, thirteen miles below the confluence, served as the only trading post within the area. The following year, the Church of England established a Mission eight miles downriver, but later moved it upriver and on the hill past the present site of Tanana. During its prime, the Mission included a sawmill, school, hospital, cemetery, and several other buildings. Its showpiece was the elegant Mission of Our Savior Church, complete with shake shingles and siding, and a steeple with a belfry. This work of art and awe remained in Tanana in 1957, but in that era was referred to as the *Old* Mission. When Elmer had flown into Tanana to assess it as a viable option for a transfer, he had explored the area and had brought back pictures to show Ruby. She was intrigued by the architecture and eager to see it for herself.

The Old Mission in 1957

Like any archeological site, more layers of history were added. At one time, the area consisted of three sections: the Mission, which was nearest the convergence of the rivers; then slightly downriver of the Mission, the actual site of Tanana that had sprung up when a post office was established in 1889 on Front Street for the benefit of miners, trappers, and traders; and finally, in 1890, the United States Army had constructed Fort Gibbon. The intention was that it would uphold civil order during the raucous era of the Alaska Gold Rush and maintain a telegraph line between Fairbanks and Nome. Ten acres of land were claimed, with some belief that eventually, with its central location in Alaska, it would become the future capital.

Fort Gibbon, along the Yukon River

At Fort Gibbon, trappers and miners in the north country could enjoy the same conveniences of civilization that had spread west, across states and territories of the United States; amenities such as saloons and dances, hotels, boardwalks, and street lights. At Fort Gibbon, there was also a Chinese restaurant, laundry, and slaughterhouse. Photographs show a large hayfield and potato fields. The White folks lived in two-story framed houses that reflected the Victorian era and included picket fences in front and large vegetable gardens in the back. Supposedly, the first vegetable planted was a turnip. The storefront facades on businesses were reminiscent of American frontier towns. Perhaps this style suited the Wild Wild West. Still, the structures were not practical for the Last Frontier, with frigid temperatures dipping easily to minus 50 degrees and reaching effortlessly through thin wood walls and single-paned windows.

The inhabitants of Fort Gibbon and Tanana did not mingle, and history gives evidence of conflicts with mail distribution and telegraph acceptance. Fort Gibbons would not recognize telegrams sent to Tanana, and letters to Fort Gibbons would somehow become lost when sent to Tanana. One old-timer recalled as a child, a fence divided the two sectors, with Native people occupying the upriver end and the others, White folks, the Fort Gibbon's end.

Activity at the post peaked in 1920, with a population of 515 counted within the area defined as Fort Gibbon.[34] Shortly after, when the gold fever subsided, it was abandoned. During World War II, an airbase was established nearby but was closed soon thereafter. Education and healthcare were tied together closely, and in 1926, the Bureau of Education reopened the twenty-bed Fort Hospital. In 1940, the Bureau of Indian Affairs built a new hospital, which was the one Elmer had come to serve. Its significance was enormous, especially during the tuberculosis epidemic; subsequently, Elmer's duties were immense, as it was the only hospital serving Interior Alaska.[35]

Tower House 1957

When Ruby and Elmer arrived in Tanana, one hotel remained, vacated and sagging into a drainage depression on Front Street. A short, narrow wooden bridge crossed the resulting dip in the road, and a pedestrian walking bridge with wood handrails ran alongside. In the summer, wild roses flourished in this draw. Dull gray-black letters, resembling enlarged typewriter font, named this one grand structure the TOWER HOUSE. In previous years, the building had stood remarkably tall with three stories and a cupola, which some historians gave prominence to as the tallest building in Alaska at that time. But when Ruby and Elmer explored Front Street, only two floors remained. Decorative wood corbels, roof cornices, window hoods, transoms, and columns only hinted at its faded glory. Practical? No. These accommodations, as well as the left-over post office structure, were non-functional in the harsh Alaskan climate; yet, image and style tried to persuade the onlooker that, at some point, this had been a place of civilization, development, and substance.

Both buildings had rough log slabs nailed over some of the thin-paned large lower windows. The remaining windows faced south, grabbing any opportunity for tepid winter light to penetrate the insulation-void structure. The two buildings were mysteriously incongruous with the rest of the village. One Sunday after church, Ruby and Elmer had tried to peek curiously inside the TOWER HOUSE to catch glimpses of its history. No hint of stories untold; just littered broken glass, discarded asphalt roofing, a can of nails and screws, and a sleeping bag with its innards spilling out.

And so it was when that one afternoon Anna said to Ruby, "Let's go to Back Street. You must see the cabins and the Natives are so friendly." Although both women had been in Tanana for approximately the same amount of time, Anna had been eager and able to explore her new setting more quickly than Ruby, whose primary concern was helping her children adjust to their new home. Also, Anna could not wait to see the homes and meet the families of her school children.

The two new friends ventured forth, both wearing wool headscarves. Ruby was shorter than her companion but was used to keeping up with Elmer, so the two women walked in step with one another. Early snow had already fallen, and frosty vestiges remained on the shadowed areas beneath the trees and on the north side of buildings. In the otherwise clear sky, the clouds reminded Ruby of meringue dollops on her lemon and banana cream pies. Fragrant woodstove smoke added to the satisfaction of walking, as did the sound of crisp leaves rustling from an occasional slight gust of wind. On either side of the rutted road, an assortment of log cabins, outhouses, and dog yards lay hither-and-yon with well-traveled paths running amid scruffy knee-high grass. Occasionally a husky barked when Ruby and Anna passed by, but in general, the half-asleep dogs basked in the sunshine and did no more than raise their heads and open a drowsy eye. The underbrush was turning the spicy colors of ginger, nutmeg, cinnamon, and paprika. Bicycles, dog sleds, and short woodpiles added to the interest. The cabins were well aged. The thick logs implied practicality, not romantic, cute picture-book compositions. The log-hewn Community Hall was common to all rural villages, and as denoted, was for community events. These ranged from Native dances, potlatches,[36] and movies to school programs.

Ruby modeling her new parka

Ruby described her explorations in a letter:

"Sept. 30, 1957

Sat. Anna and I went strolling second street! I wish you could have joined us. We came to the chiefs house and Anna knew him well as he is also the janitor for the school and he now is sick in bed with plursy and flu, so we stopped in to see them and I met the wife and their two children, one the age of Mark and the baby six weeks old. Were my home as simply furnished. Their coffee table consisted of an apple-box, their heating stove was a gas barrel cut in half lengthwise with the roundness to the bottom and a metal sheet put on the open side so that it can be used as a cooking stove too. The baby has a bassinette but also a hammock which is hung cattycorner across the corner and above the bed in which the parents sleep. The baby had cried much until they put that up and now they put her in there and swing her and she is happy. The floor was very rough and dirty but swept, the floor is made of wide old boards."

For Ruby, this initial walk on Back Street was more of a meandering orientation of Tanana, rather than a deliberate visitation; other than the chief's house, she and Anna did not enter homes. The Natives outside watched the twosome, and Anna was quick to wave and call a "hello" or "how are you?"

In one of her letters home, she wrote, *"I am introduced to the natives as 'the doctor's wife.' They respond back with 'Oh! She is.' And, then they break out with a big smile. No other comments. I do not have much contact yet with natives. And Elmer is an old timer here; already they all know him."*

At that moment, the villagers had nothing to go on besides past experiences with other physician's wives, the previous woman doctor,[37] or just good faith after meeting Elmer. It would be later, when Ruby felt comfortable in these new surroundings, that she would engage in more direct exchanges. She would be quick to remember their names, show appreciation for their gifts of sewing or garden vegetables, and respond with pleasant conversations.

It wasn't often Ruby got a respite from parenting or the luxury of basking in a mellow autumn outdoors without keeping a watchful eye on a child. Hence, the time slipped away too quickly.

"Anna, Mark is probably awake from his nap, and Elmer will be ready to get out of the house," said Ruby. She pulled back her headscarf, took a deep breath, and closed her eyes briefly.

Anna, also warmed by the outing, unfastened the top two buttons of her jacket, said formally, "I enjoyed being your guide." They glanced at each other and laughed lightly. "Guess I'd better look over my lesson plans for Monday. I sure love those little kiddos!"

After this get-acquainted outing, Ruby had a better sense of her new home place and felt more comfortable greeting the Natives. She reciprocated their open-door hospitality and, whenever possible, invited them into her home. Just as her perspective of their homes was colored by her culture, so did theirs tint their opinion of hers. "So sad that baby sleeps alone," one woman told her after seeing Mark had a room of his own.

Regardless of the different backgrounds, the women shared in common the care of children and the skill of sewing. As the weeks went by and the interactions increased, Ruby learned about their beadwork and parka assembly. Ruby was a seamstress and handcrafter, too, and the Native women found her to be an eager student. For years, she had designed patterns and sewed clothes for herself and her children, embroidered pillowcases and tea towels, and crocheted pillowcase edges. Within a short time, Ruby would solicit their workmanship and pay them to transform a squirrel fur coat of hers into a parka and add a broad fluffy hood.

Cabin on Back Street

CHAPTER 8

SWEPT OFF HER FEET

Kansas, 1941–1955

SHE WAS CAUTIOUS. He was outgoing. She was seventeen. He was nineteen. It was on a youth retreat in August 1941 that they met for the first time. Ruby shyly found a seat on the school bus that would transport the young people approximately 140 miles from Hillsboro to Enid, Oklahoma. She recognized two Loewen cousins, but otherwise, this was an experience into the unknown. She watched out the window as a fellow with glistening black hair goofed off and seemed always to be joking. He sauntered onto the bus last. Scanning the loaded bus, he spotted the only seat remaining—next to the girl with shoulder-length hair and dimples. After a quick, "Hi, I'm Elmer Gaede," and a returned, "I'm Ruby Leppke," he started clowning around.[38] He knew everyone, and they all responded enthusiastically to his wisecracks. She couldn't believe her good fortune. This handsome young man sat beside her, although he sure paid a lot of attention to the cute redhead a few seats ahead.

There were plenty of other young men for Ruby to check out during the retreat, but she kept her eyes on Elmer. He continually talked to people *and* spent a lot of time with that redhead. To her surprise, on the way back to Hillsboro, the likable Gaede boy chose to sit with her again. She was on cloud nine! For all the hardships he'd experienced as a child, the experiences hadn't eroded his spirit, and he exuded optimism and energy. He told Ruby he wanted to be a radio announcer or an airplane pilot when he grew up. She thought those ideas were "cute and funny" and figured these were youthful ambitions. Actually, she presumed he would be a steady and stable farmer like his forefathers. This Hillsboro high school senior was just the man she wanted.

In the fall of 1942, Elmer enrolled at Tabor College in Hillsboro. Ruby had quit school after her sophomore year and now implored her parents to let her attend the high school at Tabor, which at that time included both high school and college classes. (Her sister Lulu Mae had gone to the public high school in Peabody.) Ruby's paternal grandpa Isaac Leppke offered to pay for any grandchild who wanted to attend Tabor; thus, he paid the $10 tuition for Ruby. Because transportation was another obstacle, Ruby lived with her Leppke grandparents in Hillsboro.[39] Certainly, her motivation was to be nearer her boyfriend, but secondarily, she loved being around her grandparents.

Ruby longed for romance and saw it demonstrated through the tenderness of the aged sweethearts. Grandpa Isaac was hard of hearing, and Grandma Florentine was nearly blind. Grandma spent many hours in her rocking chair, every so often asking in Plautdietsch, "*Wo lange diert daut eha de Leewe Gott komma wort?*" (How long is it going to be until the Lord Jesus will come?) Not expecting a response, she would rock some more. Ruby heard this often. When Grandpa would move slowly in the kitchen and make coffee, Grandma would see his shadow and ask, "*Wer rest de maun?*" (Who is that man?) There would be a brief silence, and then as deaf as he was, Grandpa would recognize her voice and reply, "*Nah Mutta*"

(Now Ma). Her wrinkled face and dull eyes would brighten, "*Oba Foda!*" (Oh Pa!). The sound of his voice and knowing he was nearby was all she needed. At bedtime, he would find her white nightcap and tuck his sweetheart into bed. Ruby basked in the wonder of her grandparent's devotion and believed that growing old with a mate would be a comfort and joy.[40]

Education was not the primary focus of the love-struck young woman, yet she delighted in shared study hall and *studying* in the sunshine of the nearby park. Ruby admitted she had chased the college boy.

What attracted her to him, besides his good looks? For starters, he was of her same familiar Mennonite background, and they shared a common faith in the God of the Bible. Their values, such as service to other people, were mutual too. He participated in Young Ambassadors, a church ministry to the inmates of Marion jail, where he played his accordion and sang in a quartet.

She did not see herself as particularly attractive, and with surprise, gladly received his affirmations that she was pretty. Moreover, she glowed with satisfaction when he told her she would make a good wife, who would raise his children, make his meals, stand by him, and be a companion. Weren't those every young girl's desires? Still, she wondered why he had picked her. He was athletic, and she was not. He swam, ran track, and played golf, softball, and basketball. He also walked upside down on his hands—up steps and off diving boards. She figured he would lose interest in her eventually. But, perhaps it was the homemade ice cream. He did repeatedly tell her, "That's the best strawberry ice cream I've ever had!"

Dating activities were restricted. The Mennonite culture did not allow participating in roller skating, motion pictures, playing cards, bowling, playing pool, or dancing. If a young man had the money, he'd take his girl to the drugstore for soda pop. Elmer didn't have the money. All the same, the blissful pair, who could not get enough of each other, found things to do. They took bobbers and fishing poles to muddy creeks and savored picnic lunches of cold fried chicken in a park. They got around on Elmer's bike, with Ruby balancing and hanging on as best she could on the center bar. Sometimes they joined other couples. The young men, in pressed slacks and buttoned shirts with rolled up sleeves, practiced their musical instruments, and the girls, characteristically wearing home-sewn full-skirted dresses, made homemade ice cream. When the weather kept them indoors, they played Monopoly as a group, or the boys would play Carrom.[41] It really didn't matter what they did; Ruby smiled, Elmer joked, and they laughed often.

That winter, the two sledded in their family's farm pastures and then cozied up to a woodstove in the farmhouse, drinking hot cocoa or eating chili and talking about their future. By springtime, Elmer had saved enough money from finding and selling golf balls from the local golf course to buy an engagement ring. He presented it to Ruby at Marion Park. She was thrilled! Her parents were not. The Gaede family was among the poorest in the community.

During the summer of their engagement, Elmer hired out to farmers. He bucked hay bales and helped thresh wheat during harvest. Ruby worked as a cook in the Marion jail. Money was scarce. Elmer still didn't have a car, so he pedaled his bike to Marion, ten miles one way, to see his bride-to-be. The prospective daughter-in-law delighted in spending time at the Gaede's home. Elmer's mother kept the house neat as a pin, and the standard fare of farm food—fried chicken and fried potatoes—was extra delicious. As poor as they were, the Gaede family was happy, and it just felt good to be there.

Without question, Elmer readily accepted the responsibilities of a husband-to-be. He quit college to earn money so they could get married. First, he got a paper route in Wichita. Then he found work at a dairy farm on the west side of Wichita. Ruby had quit high school and also moved to the big city, where Mennonite girls were hiring on as live-in maids for wealthy homeowners.

After a weekend home in February 1943, he wrote his parents at their farm outside Hillsboro, "*Thank you again for the bother you had with getting me a haircut, having my pants patched, and taking me to the 81 highway … after about a minute wait, the first car, a '42 Buick, came and took me along.*" In that era, hitchhiking was an acceptable, economical, and safe means of transportation.

The military draft for World War II loomed over Elmer's head. Just as many other Mennonites, he was a pacifist and non-combatant. In the same letter, he continued, "'*PREPARE FOR A SHOCK!!!! Uncle Sam is going to be good to you, Elmer!!*' *said Mrs. William[42] as she handed me another classified card from Marion (county seat). They had reconsidered my case after receiving new regulations from the government and had placed me in class IIC.[43] That means as long as I stay on the dairy farm. Ruby was too shocked to say anything when she heard it.*"

This agricultural deferment meant he would not have to enlist in the military as long as he was employed on a farm. As he watched many boys being inducted, he was nervous. He had to keep his job at the dairy. At some point, he would need to repay his obligations to the government in work that qualified as military service, even if it was work as a civilian.

Early marriage

Ruby and Elmer were married on April 16, 1943, in the Ebenfeld Church, outside Hillsboro. Elmer looked unusually serious in his dark suit and narrow tie. Ruby wore a long cream-colored satin dress with a lace bodice and hip-length lace headpiece trailing down her back. She held a bouquet of calla lilies and looked serene and beautiful. Their final hurdle had been to get Elmer's parents to sign the marriage certificate—a requirement since Elmer was only twenty years old. Ruby turned eighteen the following day. Ruby's sister, Margie, was their only attendant.

The new couple claimed Matthew 6:33 as the foundation for their marriage. "But seek ye first the kingdom of God, and His righteousness; and all these things shall be added unto you (King James Version)."

Later, in a letter to his parents, he wrote, "*This last year you have been especially good to me. You have let me leave from home before I was twenty-one and have let me keep the money I've earned. And also of great importance to me is that you gave your consent for me to get married.*" Times were different then.

They embarked on their married life with $200 in savings and purchased the Gaede family Model A Roadster for $75. The canary yellow body with black fenders reminded Ruby of a bumblebee.

Elmer continued his work at the dairy, and the dairy farmer's wife asked Ruby to be their cook. Money continued to be a problem, even with the free room and board, plus a salary of $90 a month between the two of them. They had expected to be able to eat leftovers from the meals Ruby prepared, but somehow the farmer and wife consumed them all. What appeared to be an ingenious means of income turned out to be a disaster. Matters got worse. The man-of-the-house let it be known he preferred the hired girl's cooking to that of his wife's! The wife fired Ruby. Elmer was subsequently let go by the husband.

However, the young couple had basic skills, simple expectations, and each other. All the same, Elmer had to find agricultural work immediately to keep his IIC status. First, they worked for Ruby's parents on their farm. They lived in the cold stonewall washhouse that was built above the storm shelter, off the screened back porch of the two-story white farmhouse. This lasted six weeks. As is typical between generations, the newlyweds were judged as too relaxed and easy-going. Solomon and Bertha grumbled and prodded them to put in longer hours and take more responsibility. Naturally, this mystified Elmer and Ruby. Neither had been coddled, and they knew and understood the definition of farm work.

Still optimistic that they could make ends meet by living with family members, they moved to Elmer's parents' farm.[44] Here, they claimed one bedroom and attempted to make it function as a kitchen too. Expenses were shared but counted out strictly by ounces and pennies. Ruby, who previously adored her mother-in-law, was perplexed by the conflict. Her fondness would rebound after they no longer shared the same roof.

One Sunday afternoon, while sharing just-cranked homemade ice cream, Elmer turned to his father, "You've always talked about going to California; you've wondered what it would be like there. Maybe some kind of work there would suit you better. Why don't you go for a year, see if you like it, and we'll stay on the farm? If you don't like it, you can return."

In the fall of 1944, Henry and Agnes packed up and drove to Reedley, California, located in the fertile San Joaquin Valley. They found employment in the potato and fruit packing sheds. Other Mennonite families had previously discovered that the California climate and conditions were more suitable for their overall welfare. Meanwhile, Elmer and Ruby prospered on the farm. They planted wheat, alfalfa, oats, potatoes, and fruit trees. They also milked cows, raised chickens, and sold chickens and eggs. "*The hens layed 160 eggs,*" wrote Ruby excitedly to her parents-in-law. "*We are so happy here.*"

Their letters to Elmer's parents described their life in detail as that of hard-working farmers who put in fence posts, dealt with damaging windstorms, and fixed broken-down machinery. They were always at the mercy of the weather, gas rationing due to shortages during World War II, and livestock illnesses. Being happy didn't mean carefree; it meant seeing the fruit of their labors and taking satisfaction in their efforts.

Woven into the letter that Ruby and Elmer composed were accounts of cousins and friends dealing with the draft. "*Homer Penner is too tall they can't take him. I always tho't Elmer was tall but he looks like a grasshopper compared to him.*"

In addition to farm work, Ruby found a job in Hillsboro at Vogt's Grocery store, and later, an osteopath doctor asked if she would work for him. She did. She liked to help with medical procedures and deliver babies.

The young husband and wife saved their money and planned to purchase a 160-acre farm of their own, one where they would raise their children and eventually retire.

Life was good. The future was predictable, until Elmer picked up a Mennonite Brethren denominational publication. *The Christian Leader* carried an article about the need for physicians in South America. "I'd like to do that," Elmer announced to his content wife. "My Uncle Menno Gaede, who is now a physician in Reedley, California, once challenged me to become a doctor." Ruby also learned that his Uncle Alvin Gaede was a physician in Bakersfield, California. She was dumbfounded. Why would he want to do that? Her eyebrows arched in surprise, yet she didn't say a word.

She was speechless when he actually pursued this new direction. It was as if he had walked right through the barn, didn't stop to milk the cows, kept walking to Tabor College, where he promptly enrolled. He and Ruby purchased a postage-stamp-sized lot from Ruby's Grandma Leppke on Adams Street, adjacent to the college campus. To their advantage, crop farming and raising livestock weren't Elmer's only skills; he was a jack-of-all-trades and built a simple, white frame house. Now he was a hop, skip, and a jump from his classes.

Their pocketbook took a hit. Elmer had sold the "bumblebee" and purchased a 1947 Fleetline Chevrolet. In addition to that expense, he needed money to continue with school. During the summer break, he and Ruby did as other Tabor students did. Ruby would tell her children later in life,

> "We would drive all day and night to California and work in the potato sheds and fruit canneries. We were trying to get there as fast as we could

and beat the competition for the jobs. One night we were so tired and we were driving alongside a train track. All of a sudden we realized the train that had been to our right side was on our left. We had no idea how we had crossed the tracks. Oh man! We really woke up then!"

After a few semesters at Tabor, Elmer's instructors encouraged him to complete pre-med classes at the University of Kansas campus in Lawrence, Kansas. Once again, the young couple was in transition. They sold their house and moved.

The two years in Lawrence were a blur of Elmer completing college, starting medical school classes, and welcoming their firstborn. Naomi Christine arrived on April 2, 1950, just a few weeks before Elmer and Ruby's seventh wedding anniversary. As usual, their housing arrangement was based on frugality, and they were living in an unfinished upstairs "housekeeping room" with a bathroom shared with another tenant. Given the paper-thin walls, Ruby had her hands full trying to quiet Naomi, who had colic and was a difficult baby. *"She cries from 4 until midnight,"* wrote Ruby to Elmer's parents. Ruby tried her best to quiet the child so that Elmer could get much-needed rest for his classes and late evenings of studies. Sleep-deprived but resolute, Elmer kept his eye on his goal.

No grass grew under this couple's feet. In the late summer of 1951, after completing classes at Lawrence, they packed up their meager belongings and once again moved in with Ruby's folks, Sol and Bertha Leppke, on the Peabody farm. On August 14, 1951, Naomi acquired a sister. Ruth Renee was born in Goessel, Kansas. By mid-September, Elmer had left his little family and enrolled in Medical School at the University of Kansas in Kansas City, Kansas, for a fee of $240. He found lodging with his aunt Malinda (Gaede) Groening and her husband, Ted, while trying to find a suitable place for the rest of his family.

In tiny cursive, Elmer wrote Ruby nearly every day on postcards. Somewhere in the details of his six classes, taking the history of patients, and the cost of books, he noted, *"I'm terribly busy."* Then he would give her an update on his search for housing, *"There is a place, but I'll tell you, it won't meet your wishes entirely ... unfurnished ... concrete floor with linoleum ... will have to paint the walls ... temporary closet in one corner ... laundry done in a bathroom ... livable if we want to make it such."* He concluded on a positive note, such as, *"Malinda treats me like family. The food is swell."*

Eventually, the young family was together and making do in what was not more than a garage. Then medical school friends Harry and Verda Friesen rented a house, which they sub-rented to Elmer and Ruby. "Again, this was such a tiny place and so hot living upstairs. I remember it was so hot one night that I took a sheet and wet it. It wasn't exactly comfortable. We didn't have fans mind you. A city with blacktop stayed hot," Ruby recalled. All the same, they made do, along with other medical students who were in the same boat.

955 W. 42nd St., Kansas City, Missouri

In July of 1952, a thirty-year-old, two-story bungalow across the street came up for sale. Elmer's parents purchased the house as an investment. It was insured for $7,000 for three years at the cost of $70. For $45 a month, Elmer and his family were their first renters. After months and years of odds and ends living situations, they were in a real house, 955 W. 42nd St., Kansas City, Missouri.

"I liked the yard because it had a forsythia bush with yellow blossoms that bloomed early in the spring, and lily of the valley," wrote Ruby in a memory book. "In the dining room was a bay window with flowers. We didn't have a dining room set. I put a bedspread down on the floor to have it warm for Naomi and Ruth to play on and did my ironing there."

Money remained tight. Ruby cleaned house for the Groenings and brought in $5 to $6 each time. Elmer rode his bike to the hospital rather than put gas in the 1947 Chevy—until someone stole his bike. On quick trips to Ruby's parents, they would bring back frozen chicken fryers, sausage, homegrown frozen corn, and garden produce when in season. Ruby added oatmeal or crackers to hamburger to make it last longer. "I had a choice of buying a pound of bologna or a pound of hamburger for our meat for the week," Ruby wrote. It wasn't that they were vegetarians, but meat cost more than fruits and vegetables.

One evening after the girls were in bed, Ruby said to Elmer hesitantly, "Naomi asked for something to eat today ... there was nothing I could give her." Every morsel was accounted for and used for a meal. There were no snacks.

With the backdrop of scraping hard to make ends meet, they were deeply grateful for a couple at the nearby Covenant Church who invited medical students into their larger and comfortable home. "I'll never forget the angel pie with a crust made out of meringue and filled with ice cream," recounted Ruby. "We were so poor, and it was nice to go into that home.

I was glad that you girls were always so good and would stay right beside me and not wander around the house. It was easy to go places."

The church welcomed the medical students and their wives, not only to attend services but for young mothers to find fellowship and support through luncheons and special speakers. Much to Ruby's surprise, she was asked to teach a preschoolers' Sunday school class. Timid as she was, and with a churning stomach, she agreed. Telling Bible stories with a prop of flannel-graph backgrounds and characters laid the groundwork for her to work with children in Alaska.

It was at a ladies' meeting at this church that Ruby listened to the missionary woman from Nome, Alaska. At that point, such a far away, cold, and remote place was as appealing to the Kansas farm girl as living on the moon. Never in a blue moon would she go there. There would be plenty of places in Kansas, or perhaps California where Elmer's parents lived, for her husband to practice medicine.

Life continued like a freight train; well, it was actually passenger train tickets that Elmer and Ruby discussed in back-and-forth letters in June of 1953. Elmer was doing a six-week preceptorship in Scott City, Kansas, and Ruby and the girls were back on the Peabody farm. No wonder Naomi bonded dearly to her Grandma Leppke and forever had a love of little chicks, calves, and fresh cow milk.

Along with details of treating a heart attack patient and a child with a reaction to poison ivy, Elmer wrote Ruby,

"Tonite after Clinic hours one of the flying farmers took me up on his Piper plane for nearly 2 hours. We were in 4 counties and saw alot of area up to 30 miles north and 15 miles south of town. He even let me fly & make turns etc."

When Ruby and the girls arrived on the train for a visit, Elmer wrote to his parents, *"We had an especially enjoyable time … fishing at Dr. Palmer's ranch … the creek was drying up … I went in with my hands and pulled them* (fish) out ... loaded with catfish and carp ... six catfish weighed 45 lbs. ... One evening a businessman took our whole family for an hour airplane ride over the country." Ruby was aware that "doctor's wife" was in her future, but was a "flying doctor" anywhere in that picture? Her reaction was not recorded.

Elmer's time in Scott City flew by, and the family was reunited in their Kansas City home. Ruth's two-year-old independent personality was developing. Ruby wrote Elmer's parents, "*I pick her up to carry her and she says, 'No! Walk.' She rides the trike now and goes so fast that when she makes a turn she falls over.*" No crying was involved. Ruth had the constitution of a hardy little girl, which would serve her well in the future she knew nothing about.

Elmer's next preceptorship was at a mental hospital within driving distance of home, although the preceptors stayed on the campus. As had become customary for Ruby, she packed up the girls to visit their daddy. She included a picnic lunch of bologna sandwiches, pickles, fresh fruit, and a bit of cake. It was a day of sunshine, golf, and more family time pleasures. Ruby wrote Elmer's parents, "We went swimming. Naomi just loves the water. She stands in water up to her neck and then ducks herself clear under. Elmer takes her down the big slide with him and she screams with delight."

The end was finally in sight. Following years of sleepless nights, countless medical cases, a final paper, and studying for the State Board exam, on June 5, 1954, Elmer Gaede, the farm boy, reached his goal of Elmer E. Gaede, MD.

He had not been a straight-A student. He had worked hard for his Bs and Cs. Now all that remained was his internship at the hospital of his choice: Bethany Hospital, Kansas City, Kansas.

Nearing the end of his internship, he inquired about a physician's position with Mennonite Brethren Missions in South America. The available openings were not a suitable match with his level of experience. About the same time, a nurse he worked with mentioned the need for physicians in Alaska. The door of opportunity to the south was closed. Conversely, the door to the north was wide open. Public Health Services in Alaska could use him.

By 1955, Elmer's medical internship was completed, and the repayment of student loans rested on his shoulders. Not only would working for Public Health Services in the Territory of Alaska fulfill his deferred military obligations, but the pay would reduce his student loans more quickly than working in one of the 48 States.

By the third week in June, Elmer and Ruby's household belongings were crated and shipped to Anchorage, Alaska. Within days, Elmer, Ruby, Naomi, and Ruth were loaded into their 1947 snail-shaped, black Fleetline Chevy. After a stop at the Leppke farm, they headed to Reedley, California, to say goodbye to Elmer's family. Who knew when they'd see either of their families again.

No, Ruby never bargained for a life in Alaska, away from her Mennonite family outside the sultry flatlands of Kansas. She had been satisfied with a landscape of barns, silos, windmills, fenced cattle, and wheat fields. Nevertheless, she would stand by the man with the glistening black curls who had not turned into a farmer after all.

CHAPTER 9

THE WILDERNESS WIFE

Tanana, 1957

MALE AND FEMALE ROLES were clear-cut in the 1950s. Elmer, the husband, had the responsibility to mow the lawn, do household repairs, and keep the car in working order. In Tanana, there was no lawn to mow or car to fix. A hospital maintenance man, Pete Miller, took care of repairs on the medical compound. Elmer's domestic jobs were lessened.

For Ruby, "good" mother and wife meant cooking meals; shopping for necessities; cleaning house; keeping the ironing basket empty; braiding her girls' hair; making cupcakes for school events; creating birthday cakes that resembled mountains, hens, houses, or whatever her child desired; and in the best way possible, sewing, finding, or purchasing clothes for her family. Her tasks were not only numerous but made more difficult by the lack of services in the wilderness.

Prior to their departure from Anchorage, and in anticipation of living in the bush, Ruby had calculated how many canned and boxed goods would feed their family for the coming year.[45] From an ordering list, she'd selected items and filled in amounts for Cheerios, Shredded Wheat, and Kix cereal; Cream of Wheat and oatmeal; flour, sugar, Jell-O, Spam,[46] cake mixes, canned peas, corn, pears, peaches, instant potatoes, powdered milk, orange Tang, pork and beans, yellow mustard, rice, laundry detergent, bar soap, and so on. Her order amounted to over one hundred cases of staples. It cost $1,000 and was shipped by railroad from Anchorage to Nenana and then placed on the Yutana river barge to Tanana.

When the supplies arrived on the barge, the food items filled the basement pantry. The girls got a kick out of scrambling up and down the ceiling-high, deep shelves whenever their mother sent them to "go shopping." Occasionally, fresh fruits and vegetables could be purchased at the Northern Commercial Company store—for a pretty penny; or vegetables, such as potatoes, from the goodwill of the villagers.

At one point Ruby wrote Elmer's parents:

"We were given a head of cabbage that was grown here and I did not have a scale to weight it but my guess was that it weighed 10 lbs. And it was delicious, so sweet, crisp and good. We are hoping to make a garden next summer, people here are selling their local potatoes for $6.00 a bu."

Given Ruby's frugal background, she was constantly taken aback at food prices.

```
ALASKA                              STATES

Bananas - 30¢ each                  27¢ for 2 lbs.
Bread - 70¢                         12-14¢
Eggs - $1.25                        49-79¢
Green beans - 2 cans for 75¢
Potatoes - 1 bushel/54 lbs./$6.00   35¢ for 10 lbs.
```

```
Peanut Butter - 29¢
Lettuce - 29¢ for 2 heads
Sugar - 89¢ for 10 lb.
Coffee - 90¢ for 1 lb.
Bacon - 60¢
Hamburger - 56¢ per lb.
Milk - 21¢
```

Ruby's original station in life had *not* equipped her to prepare meals without homegrown produce. More common to her than a pantry of fruits and vegetables in tin cans and grains and puddings in boxes, was a local wealth of meat, vegetables, and fruit. In her growing up years, she walked through the screened porch, under which kittens scrambled in mock fear of the collie dog, out to the homegrown store of groceries. Her hard-heeled shoes clomped on the broad natural-limestone pavers. Contingent on her destination, she carried a tin bucket or a bushel basket. Near the wire gate, which secured the white board fence around the house, her father had planted a rough, but practical, iron-welded boot scraper. The intent was to reduce caked dirt and mud from tracking into the house. Ruby instinctively latched the gate behind her and, depending on the need, walked to the garden, field, washhouse, chicken coop, or barn.

In the damp and cold "dairy section," otherwise known as the washhouse, milk, cream, and butter stayed cool for a short time. The chicken house provided eggs. Produce, such as corn, arrived in the farmyard on flatbeds pulled by a farm truck. Ruby stripped the scratchy husks off the fresh roasting ears, which were later boiled, smothered with golden butter, and speckled with salt and pepper. At other times, Ruby and other apron-covered women sliced corn kernels off the cobs to can or freeze.

In another section of "produce," succulent tomatoes, green beans, and peas in crisp pods waited at her fingertips. Peas were boiled, thickened with a mixture of cream and flour, sweetened with sugar, and blackened with pepper. Small, translucent-skin potatoes, ranging from the size of a thumb to that of a golf ball, were sliced and fried in butter, mashed with cream and butter, or boiled, then fried in butter. Butter and cream were two basics of farm cooking. And, for Ruby's mother, Bertha Leppke, so was black pepper.

In the "meat department," farm stock provided a selection of beef, pork, and chicken. Ground pork sausage was stuffed into the thin tubes of cleaned pig intestines. Nothing was wasted.

This bountiful and assorted harvest was not available to Ruby in Tanana. Cooking required more than following a recipe; it called for substituting ingredients and dreaming up possibilities for different uses of the same item. Canned milk was used instead of cream. Lingonberries, or cranberries, as the Alaskans called them, filled in for raisins. A tablespoon of vinegar was added to a cup of powdered milk for recipes calling for buttermilk or sour milk. Powdered cocoa replaced hard squares of baking chocolate. Canned peas, corn, and green beans were rotated throughout the week. Potato flakes could be whipped into a substance similar to that of mashed potatoes. Powdered eggs, which smelled like sulfur, filled in for real eggs in baked goods. Ruby learned from her missionary friend, Margie Gronning, and Anna that the popular chiffon and sponge cakes, as well as meringue, were not possible with powdered eggs. If real eggs actually showed up in the store, or through the hospital cook's order, the yokes would be deep orange, with barely a jiggle.

Fortunately, the farm girl could still make other desserts that were all the craze: tapioca pudding, vanilla pudding dabbed on top of vanilla wafers (and topped with bananas whenever these randomly showed up), cream puffs with a pudding filling, and Jell-O creations that were acceptable as either a salad or a dessert.

A mere four weeks after Ruby and the children arrived in Tanana, Elmer did his part to add options in the meat department. Ruby wrote home, "*Elmer and Rev. Gronning went duck hunting and they got 4 small ones, moose hunting is definitely easier. As they were sneaking up to the lake they saw three bears on the other side and one wolf and heard him call to his mate. That gets to wild for me but still I went out with Elmer Sunday afternoon (My first time out of Tanana since we came here) we flew out to a lake and scared all the ducks off as we landed so we waited for them. As we krept up on a flock that had returned we came across bear tracks and a place where he had taken his beauty nap. I told Elmer that I would rather eat moose. The ducks were good for variety, the girls will not eat much of the meat.*"

As much as Ruby worried about her husband's flying,[47] she was ecstatic when she heard he was "going to town," which was to Fairbanks. Whenever this happened, Ruby made a list of groceries to bring back: cottage cheese, celery, bananas, store-bought white bread, and a ring of bologna; the latter being Elmer's choice, and something he could be happy to eat in a sandwich, with yellow mustard, every day of his life. Her notes included other items she could not purchase in the village, such as narrow red rickrack, hard sticks of muted colored modeling clay, and birthday cake candles.

In Tanana and other villages, the Montgomery Ward, Sears, and Alden catalogs were the only window-shopping and store-buying possibilities.[48] A remaining option was to request a friend or relative to purchase and mail the desired item to the village. Either way, delivery would be three to four weeks, even if shipped by the most expedient means. She instructed Elmer's parents, "*Just want to make mention that you must mail all packages to us by Parcel Post otherwise all freight goes to Nenana and we wouldn't get it until spring.*" Freight to Nenana would be stored until the Tanana and Yukon River ice went out, usually in late April or early May. Even then, the river had to be free of large ice chunks and debris before the barges would venture out, sometimes as late as June. Hence, all shopping orders required advance planning.

Guessing sizes was an indispensable skill and much more difficult for shoes than for dresses and shirts. As any parent knows, children outgrow shoes frequently. Naomi and Ruth thought nothing unusual about standing on a piece of white typing paper and having their mother draw around one foot, then fold and enclose the outline in a printed catalog order.

Sometimes this conscientious mother was at her wit's end with the size calculations as well as the slowness of delivery. For example, after eagerly waiting for kid's pajamas or flannel shirts for Mark, the order would take five weeks to arrive—and the articles would be too small. Fortunately, Ruth could fit something ordered that ended up being too small for Naomi, although Ruby would have to put up with her oldest daughter's disappointment. This option did not work well for Mark, with the age difference and gender of his sisters. "Too large" wasn't all that frustrating since the children would grow.

Then there were instances when Ruby breathlessly tore open the package and discovered that the long-awaited shirt for Elmer or lacy blouse for her did not look anything like it had in the catalog. How could such a basic order be so difficult to fill? She was beside herself. No wonder she found it easier and less nerve-wracking to sew clothes *when* she could get fabric, which also had to be ordered. Figuring out what an inch-by-inch rendition on a catalog page would actually turn out to be, took a savvy gambler. What size were the flowers? The checks? How true was the red or blue? How thick was the flannel?

In desperation, she wrote requests to Elmer's parents. "*Can you send me four pairs of undershirts with sleeves for the girls ... I could use some quilted dark green fabric for a robe—about three-yards ... Mark dumped out my cardamom spice. Could you include a small box in your next package?*"

Another concern was finding warm enough clothes for toddlers. Ruby's apprehension about the Interior winter was evident when she wrote, "*We have a problem for Mark, they just do not make warm enough clothes for tiny tots in the catalogues so I may venture to make something for him in a parka line. We have the zipper problems here so I will write and ask some one to get us some or maybe I can order them from Sears. I do dread to think of the 40 and 50 below that we have here. I just do not understand how the babies keep from freezing to death in those shabby cabins that people live in here."*

Ruby's comment was not meant to be belittling but was out of genuine concern for the Natives. She was also dismayed about how Roy and Margie lived. "I cannot enjoy our luxurious home when I see how the Gronnings have to live. They would be much warmer in our basement which we do not use but half the space, and so it goes and we ask why must it be so." These observations occurred in early October, not even the dead of winter.

Despite her apprehension about keeping her family warm in the Last Frontier, on an overcast day of 32 degrees, on the first Saturday of October, she organized a picnic.

McDONALD'S
PIKE PLACE MKT. GROCERY INC.
613 WESTERN AVE. — SEATTLE 4, WASH.

August 19, 1957

ANNA BORTEL
Tanana, Alaska

Shipped via ILIAMNA 8/13 Prepaid
Terms Net   Fob Seattle

Qty		Size	Item	Unit	Total
1	only	1#	Calumet Bak Powd	.27	.27
1	"	2#	S. W. Beans	.33	.33
2	only	1#	Cocoanut	.35	.70
5	"	1#	Hills Coffee	1.04	5.20
3	"	2#	Velveta Cheese	1.05	3.15
1	"	1#	Hershey Cocoa	.65	.65
1	"	1#	Nestles Quick	.49	.49
1	"	3#	Oats	.45	.45
1	cs	100/Ind	Kellogg Asst	3.95	3.95
3	only	6 oz	M&M Choc	.29	.87
3	"	6 oz	Hershey Kisses	.29	.87
1	ctn	Asst	Bars	1.10	1.10
1	ctn		GGm	.79	.79
2	only	25#	G. M. Flour	2.65	5.30
2	"		Swans Angel Cake Mix	.55	1.10
2	only		Pills Hot Roll Mix	.30	.60
3	"		Pills Orang Cake Mix	.35	1.05
2	"		Py O My Lemon Mix	.39	.78
2	"		" " Choc Mix	.39	.78
1	only	10#	Dried Apples	5.25	5.25
1	"	4#	Raisins	.78	.78
2	"	12 oz	Black Figs	.29	.58
2	"	1#	Pitted Dates	.39	.78
1	"	16 oz	Marash Cherries	.59	.59
1	"	4#	Albers Flapjack	.59	.59
3	"	8 oz	Minit Tapioca	.29	.87
1	only	48	Kotex	1.49	1.49
3	"	400	Kleenex	.29	.87
6	"	80/s	White Napkins	.15	.90
2	"	12/	Paper Plates	.17	.34
1	"	24	Hot Cups	.53	.53
2	"	12/25	Foil	.33	.66
2	"	25#	Sugar	2.85	5.70
10	only	1#	Brown Sugar	.15	1.50
10	only	1#	Powd Sugar	.15	1.50
2	"	24 oz	GG Swt Pickles	.57	1.14
2	"	24 oz	Nalley Kosher Dills	.41	.82
2	"	11 oz	Hez. Swt Gherkins	.43	;86
2	"	12 oz	Nalley Swt Mix Pickles	.31	.62
3	"	12 oz	Nalley Swt Relish	.29	.87
3	"	3#	Crisco	.99	2.97
1	"	Qt	Peanut Oil	.85	.85
1	"	8 oz	Pepper	.59	.59
1	doz		Tomato soup	1.55	1.55
1	doz		Asst Noodle soup	2.15	2.15
1	doz		Veg-Beef soup	2.15	2.15
1	½doz		Pea Soup	1.65	1.65
1	only	1½	Blue Karo	.27	.27
2	"	1½	Red Karo	.29	.58
	"		P. O. Soap	.10	.60

The single schoolteacher's order of food for one year.
The Gaedes would need more for their family.

Some helpful hints for Ruby, and other wilderness wives.

2. Use wild greens and berries as much as possible because they are often rich in ascorbic acid. Sourdock, fireweed shoots, willow greens, scurvy grass, lambsquarters, rose hips, currants, blueberries, and cloudberries are some of the wild plant sources of vitamin C.

3. Use sprouted beans. The mung beans will sprout in three days if watered and kept in a dark place. Water them several times a day and use the bean sprouts when they are three or four inches long in salads or cooked. Larger beans and soy beans are apt to mold unless the water is treated with one-half teaspoon chlorinated lime to a gallon of water. Rinse well before using sprouts. For sprouting, buy soya beans from seed stores; those sold in grocery stores will not sprout.

4. As a last resort use ascorbic acid tablets of known strength. The daily requirements for ascorbic acid increases from 20 milligrams (mg.) for infants to 75 mg. for adults. A deficiency is indicated if a person bruises easily, gums bleed, and wounds heal slowly.

Dried Fruits and Vegetables Foods which have been dried by modern methods do not require long soaking nor long cooking. The dried vegetables which most readily substitute for the fresh include onions, potatoes, cabbage, carrots, greens, herbs, and sweet potatoes. In almost all cases the manufacturer supplies directions and proportions on the can or package, but as a general guide use one pound of dried in order to produce the equivalent of four pounds of fresh.

Dried Cabbage Soak 10 to 20 minutes. Bring to a boil and cook 10 minutes. Serve creamed or in soup, stew or gravy.

Dried Onions Soak 20 minutes in water to cover. Drain and use as fresh onions to flavor soup, meat, sauces, and salads.

Dried Potatoes
Cube Style—Soak 1 cup potatoes in four cups water for 20 minutes. Bring to a boil and cook 20 minutes longer. Add salt when almost done. Serves six.

Mashed Style—Soak 1 cup potatoes in water to cover for 20 minutes; bring to a boil and cook 20 minutes longer. Add milk and seasonings and beat well or make into soup or croquettes.

Potato Salad—Soak 1 cup cube style 20 minutes; cook 20 to 30 minutes longer. Drain well. Add onion which has been soaked and cooked 15 minutes. Season with vinegar, salt, or salad dressing and scrambled dried egg.

Dried Sweetpotatoes Soak 1 pound dried sweetpotatoes in twice as much water for 20 to 40 minutes. Bring to a boil; cook 30 to 40 minutes until tender and moist. Add salt, pepper, and butter. Serves six as hashed or hash browned.

Dried Soups Commercially mixed soups contain dried vegetables and rice, noodles or macaroni. It is cheaper to mix a soup at home from dried onion, carrots, rice or noodles, and herbs such as parsley, celery tops, bay leaf or other dried herbs.

Dried Fruits Good quality dried fruits include apples, pears, peaches, prunes, apricots, raisins, currants, dates, and figs. Except for ascorbic acid, dried fruits have about the same value as the canned. If cooked properly, the dried products should have good color and flavor, be plump, juicy, and not too sweet nor leathery. Avoid long soaking and overcooking. Most of the dried fruits are packaged in 1 or 2 pound quantities or in large boxes. It is hard to estimate the exact amount of dried fruit. A pound of dried fruit equals approximately 4 pounds or 2 quarts of stewed fruit. Allow ½ to ¾ cup of stewed fruit to a serving.

2.

Cheerfully and practically written suggestions

CHAPTER 10

PICNICS

Tanana, 1957

RECREATING FOND MEMORIES comforted Ruby. Going on a picnic was one of those experiences that brought back the happy feelings of her Kansas home and family. No, the picnics weren't exactly the same in Alaska. Mosquitos, lack of fresh produce, and sandy river shores with skinny black spruce trees added a different dimension from flat prairie land and muddy creeks, yet eating outdoors, and being with the people she loved, was the same, and that's what mattered to her.

Ruby's father, Solomon Leppke, seemed always to be working in the fields—except on Sundays, of course, when the family went to church and parents perhaps took an indulgent afternoon nap. That was the life of the farmer. Therefore, when the family went on a picnic, there was the uncommon pleasure of spending time leisurely with "Daddy," as Ruby still called him. Sure, she worked hours side-by-side with him in the field, barn, and mechanic building, but the tone and relationship felt different on these occasions. He wasn't instructing her what to do, or to hurry, or to pay attention. The role melted into father-daughter affection. Understandably, picnics elicited treasured memories for Ruby.

When Ruby's children were adults, she would recall those times. "My daddy liked to eat near a creek, so we'd try to find one that wasn't dry, and sometimes the grass would be greener and softer along the banks, and there would be trees for shade too." It was obvious that she could still vividly picture those times, feel the sultry summer, and taste the deliciousness of the moment.

"Mom would bring potato salad and cantaloupe. Mom's salad was made with potatoes, onions, and boiled eggs; and then vinegar and sour cream dressing, with some salt and pepper. Mom like to have those potatoes sliced in a certain way, not chunks, but slices since the dressing would marinate better. Sometime we'd have watermelon. Usually zwiebach (Mennonite double-decker yeast buns), potato chips, and pickles. Maybe cabbage slaw. Of course, cold fried chicken. Then for dessert, there would be pies and we'd try to bring Jell-O – if we could keep it chilled. Those were fun times."

One of the first picnics in Tanana was shortly after the Gaede's arrival. Although somewhat spontaneous, at least Ruby had time to stir up, and let rise, yeast dough and had shaped a portion into hot dog buns. If and when the Northern Commercial store carried baked goods, they were many days old and expensive, too, after being purchased in Fairbanks and flown in. While Ruby was baking, Anna contacted the Gronnings; that is, she walked to the mission house. Accumulating ten thousand steps in a day was not challenging in the village.

Elmer brought out the ambulance and gathered up the gang. The shocks were long gone in the old vehicle, and the passengers were tossed uncomfortably around the flat back area. Ruby and Margie tried to keep their young sons from toppling into the cardboard box that was full of hot dogs, potato salad, canned peaches, cupcakes, assorted picnic-makings, and wire clothes hangers that would be untwisted to make hot dog sticks. Baby Bethel hid her face in Margie's shoulder.

The destination was Picnic Point, high on a bluff, about a mile and a half downriver, toward the CAA towers, and near the village dump. The view was unobstructed by any nearby mountains. It opened to a magnificent panorama to the east, past the confluence of the Yukon and Tanana Rivers, south toward Mt. McKinley, and down the Yukon River as it narrowed to the west. A simple two-by-four and plywood table designated the picnic spot and was handy to keep food and paper plates off the ground and out of reach of toddlers' hands. A lone plank and log bench sat off to one side.

Ruby and Anna found enough brush to start a small fire in a rock-encircled shallow pit, and soon a fire crackled. Margie spread out the fixings on the table, minus tomatoes, lettuce, or onions—none of which were obtainable anywhere in the village, not at the hospital kitchen or the Northern Commercial store. Mustard, ketchup, and pickle relish would have to suffice. Naomi and Ruth were instructed to spread a green wool army blanket on the ground for sitting. Elmer and Roy untwisted the coat hangers, and soon the smoke carried the aroma of cooked meat. Mark and Chris Gronning kept wandering toward the bluff's edge, and every adult needed eyes in the back of their head to patrol the twosome. Once the fire was in full flame, Mark changed his course and stubbornly attempted to crawl into the fire. Ruth, ever the little mother, of which he could have used several, did her best to divert the child, but his determination was more than she could handle. His screaming protest annoyed everyone to no end, and finally, his father gave up trying to eat and held him at a safe distance so that he could throw twigs, not himself, into the fire.

The picnic ended when the parents could no longer tolerate two cranky little boys with a sticky mixture of black dirt and white cupcake frosting on their faces. "I can hear naptime coming," said Roy, scooping up Chris in giant arms. Mark grabbed Ruby's glasses when she captured him for the ride home. In more ways than one, she had her hands full with that child. All the same, she had savored the time outdoors with her family and friends.

Picnic at Picnic Point

Later, on another chilly October day when the air smelled like snow, and its denseness seemed to muffle the occasional sounds of a chainsaw ripping into wood or a dog barking, Ruby decided to have another picnic. Elmer could not go on the picnic because he was delivering a baby. With three children, or, more specifically, with one strong-willed toddler, Ruby knew she needed back-up support. She was outnumbered. She scribbled a note on the back of an envelope and called to Ruth, "Please take this to Anna." Within five minutes, Ruth and Anna were both back at the house.

PICNICS

Ruth gently swung a bag of marshmallows, and Anna carried a box of graham crackers and some chocolate bars.

Ruby put other food items into a cardboard box, including matches. Finding coats for the children came next, followed by locating the red wagon. Mark and the box of food went into the wagon, and a regular parade ensued. Naomi jumped and skipped ahead. Ruth insisted on pulling the wagon, even though it was too heavy for her. "I'll do it myself," was still her frequent response, not said loudly but determinedly. She managed well until the entourage started down the gravel, rutted incline to the river, where the bank was cut out in front of the hospital. Ruby and Anna gasped in unison when the wagon started to run over Ruth. Ruth started to cry. The women grabbed the front and back of the wagon to keep everything from tumbling out. Mark squealed in confusion and excitement. Within seconds, everyone and everything arrived safely at the intended destination. For a moment, all was silent, except for the gentle lap-lap of small waves against the flat gray rocks, beaten smooth by the push-pull of the current.

Ruby could have won a fire-starting contest, and in no time, a little campfire warmed the group that chatted happily; at least the side facing the fire was warm. Mooseburger grease dripped off the makeshift grill, and the flames sizzled and spit. The smell of cooking meat and burning wood filled the air. Soot etched Ruby's campfire coffeepot.

The buzz of a "kicker boat"[49] stopped all chatter. The boat came nearer. A huge moose head and rack were visible in the back. "Someone is going to have fresh meat," said Ruby. Her eyes fixed on the sight. It wasn't as though she had not seen a moose or a kicker boat before, but the way she said it indicated she found the sight unusual and even entertaining. Anna looked at her and laughed.

The wilderness woman went back to meal preparations. Ruby smiled as she gently poked the driftwood to keep the small blaze going and carefully turned over the meat; she was truly in her element as an outdoorswoman providing nourishment and pleasure for her family and friends.

The round yeast rolls Ruby had made for sandwiches functioned well as mooseburger buns. Shoestring potato sticks from a can added a salty crunch. Between mustard and the salty sticks, everyone's gloves or mittens were yellow-tipped, except for Mark's, who kept pulling his off. Anna thought this was amusing and her giggling and teasing egged on Mark's obstinacy. Naomi admonished him, "Do not throw your mittens in the river!" Ruth didn't say a word but repeatedly picked up the mittens, shook off the sand, and handed them back to him. This was a hopeless job. Ruby gave up trying to keep the poor child's hands warm and just enjoyed the taste of warm meat on a cold day. "Nothing like a picnic. Best burgers I've ever had," she said.

What was an Alaska picnic without s'mores,[50] or "angels on horseback," as Anna called them? Mark already had his eyes on the rest of the contents in the picnic box and was pulling on the bag of marshmallows. "Remember when you took marshmallows to church?" Anna said to Ruby. They both laughed. Somehow, Ruby had managed to conceal them from Mark, and after the service, showed Margie and Anna. The women giggled and agreed they should toast them in the Gronning's barrel stove. And so they did.

Now at the outdoor picnic, the sky and river merged together in grayness. "Look! It's starting to snow," exclaimed Ruby, with delight. Big flakes floated down, and the ground quickly turned white. Anna and Ruby toasted marshmallows until they were golden, and Ruth had the patience to do so too. Naomi continually set hers on fire. It was not long before Mark not only had red-cold, yellow-smeared fingers but a gooey white marshmallow mustache around his mouth. Anna lifted him up in her arms. "Markie, you take the cake!" Ruby gathered the picnic items and piled them back into the wagon. That signaled the end of *that* picnic, and, although a bit nippy, Ruby rather liked the pre-winter picnic.

In the same way the Bible describes the virtuous woman in Proverbs 31[51], Ruby went about preparing for her family, both in the present and the future; both in practical and fun ways.

"*She selects wool and flax and works with eager hands. She is like the merchant ships, bringing her food from afar. She gets up while it is still dark; she provides food for her family ... She sets about her work vigorously; her arms are strong for her tasks. ... her lamp does not go out at night. In her hand she holds the distaff and grasps the spindle with her fingers. ... When it snows, she has no fear for her household; for all of them are clothed in scarlet. ... She watches over the affairs of her household.*"

Perhaps an Alaska version would speak of river barges, dim winter days, plummeting temperatures, kerosene lamps, packaging moose meat, large pantries in basements, sewing machines poking through softened moose hide, and tacking fur ruffs on parkas. Interestingly enough, this woman of noble character was said to be "worth more than *rubies*" (*Proverbs 31:10, NIV*).

When Ruby had crossed the border into Alaska, she'd entered a rigorous new world, but it was no more daunting than the New World her ancestors had entered. Her mother and the mothers before her knew their roles, had worked alongside their men, held a child on one hip and stirred cabbage borscht with the remaining hand, kept their households clean, and household members fed. Ruby had managed these responsibilities in Kansas and in Anchorage; she would do the same here, in a remote village along the Yukon River. Despite the fact, it still puzzled her how the farm boy she'd flipped head over heels for had flipped her world upside down too.

the BUSH DOCTOR'S WIFE

HINTS FOR THE 1950 HOMEMAKER

DO

Have dinner ready. Freshen your makeup and hair. Be cheerful and interesting.

DON'T

Don't greet your husband with problems about the children or the day. Don't complain if he is late for dinner. Offer to take off his shoes. Speak in a pleasant voice. Listen to him and let him speak first, even though you may have what you think is urgent to tell him.

How did Ruby score?

Her husband did not like to be late for supper and, whenever possible, showed up at 6:00 pm, even if that meant eating in five minutes a meal that had taken Ruby an hour to prepare.

Her husband did not like to take off his shoes too early in the evening. He might be called back to the hospital.

She probably did not look fresh after wrestling Mark out of the bathroom, where he enjoyed putting everything down the toilet.

She did not feel interesting. She felt tired from work. Her husband would not care that the ironing basket was now empty, and she had baked six loaves of bread.

She did not mean to complain but found it necessary to report to her husband that Mark had tried to light matches and had a magnetic attraction to the riverbank—and the river.

PICNICS

She did not want to listen to her husband when she learned he was flying to a downriver village in the morning, and a storm was coming in.

She had yelled at Mark all day, not in a mean way, but for his self-protection. She was not sure she could find her low, soft, pleasant voice.

CHAPTER 11

REACHING ACROSS THE MILES

Tanana, 1957

RUBY WAS ACCUSTOMED to living in close harmony with her Leppke family. She dearly missed the regular get-togethers, the common language, and the shared traditions.[52] Thus, from across the miles that separated her from them, she reached back as best she could and yearned for reciprocation of news.

Ruby described her daily life in weekly handwritten or typed letters mailed to Elmer's family in California, her parents in Kansas, and her sister, Margie, in Oklahoma. This was her only means to stay connected. Holiday and birthday phone calls could not be anticipated. Except for a telephone line between the CAA compound and hospital, and the physician's duplex and hospital, there were no other telephones in the village, and these few lines could not call outside the village. Of course, there were no social media or internet options.

Communication outside the village was conducted by one-way or two-way radio at the CAA airport station or the hospital. The Tanana hospital physician had specific times to contact the schoolteacher or roadhouse innkeeper in various villages to discuss health concerns.

Ruby wrote her family:

"Elmer says, 'This is KIK731, Tanana, standing by for medical traffic, this is KIK731, Tanana, calling Allakaket, do you have any medical traffic, over.' He carries on these kinds of calls with 8 villages in our surrounding area. He does this every week day at 4:30 in the afternoon. I turn on the radio and I can hear him talk but I can not hear the villages reply as this comes back on a different frequency."

This was not a simple matter. The weather could render radio signals to one village impossible. At times, Elmer would call a village in a different geographical area and ask them to try relaying a message down to the one he could not reach from Tanana. Sometimes this worked; other times, he remained at an impasse. All in all, it could be arduous, time-consuming, and frustrating for concerned schoolteachers, innkeepers, and a dedicated physician.

As for Ruby, penmanship was a subject taught in grade school, and the readers of Ruby's letters benefited from her legible writing. Typing was a basic course, most certainly for girls who wanted to get one of the primary, acceptable jobs for women, that of secretary or nurse. Ruby's spelling was another issue. Although she had made straight As in spelling, her letter writing contradicted these high scores; even so, credit could be given that she used phonetic misspellings.

Often, to maximize her limited time, the overly busy mother used carbon paper between sheets of plain paper so her writing would be doubled to the plain paper beneath it; this way, she could send out multiple copies. Any personal or confidential remarks were handwritten in the margins or at the end of the specific letter. The typing ribbon, of inked fabric, came in a combination of black and red. Black was her preferred color unless emphasis was needed. However, when Mark crawled onto her lap and tangled his fingers with hers, the letters would be in black *and* red and interspersed with unnecessary repeated alphabet letters and!!!!!!!!@@@@@.

When Ruby could corner Elmer, he wrote to his parents, also. His scribbling was barely discernible, and he never used a typewriter. Writing had been listed on his report cards as C-, as was drawing, and at times language, English composition, and English literature. Algebra, chemistry, and mathematics were more his capabilities, as was Greek, but not Hebrew. Truthfully, Elmer's writing had probably become poorer over the years, the trait of a physician who had rushed to take notes in medical school. Then he never had adequate time to jot down remarks as he examined a patient—or tried to remember afterward what had been discovered, discussed, or diagnosed. He would have scratched his head in amazement to learn that years later, physicians would dictate voice-recorded notes, which were then transcribed into patient charts by a medical transcriptionist; and even more so, fifty years in the future when health-care providers typed everything into a computer. *That*, though, would require typing, a skill he might not have been able to sit still long enough to learn.

Naomi and Ruth wrote letters, too, and undoubtedly when they received gifts for Christmas or birthdays. Theirs were written in large letters on Big Chief writing tablets. Sometimes they would draw pictures of their Alaska surroundings, such as huskies, river barges, and fish wheels.

Standard purple three-cent stamps carried the news to waiting recipients in seven days; red six-cent airmail stamps speeded the process to four days, depending on the Alaska weather.

One of many letters to Ruby's loved ones. An airmail stamp cost six-cents.

There was no door-to-door mail delivery in Tanana. Mail was delivered to and picked up from the post office. The flat, faux storefront gave the building an appearance of being taller than it actually was, and the letters TANANA had faded over the decades. Elmer took the family mail to the hospital where it was driven in the jeep-ambulance with other mail to the post office, a half-mile into the village center, after which it was driven back past the hospital to the landing field for postal pick-up by an airplane. This was not efficient from a processing perspective, but that was the way it was done.

Four-by-nine-inch envelopes carried the communication southbound where the reader slit open the narrow end with a knife. After Elmer's parents received and read the letter, they passed it along to Elmer's siblings, Harold and Lillian, and their spouses. By the time it had made the rounds, the envelope had frequently served as a grocery or hardware list, telephone notes, general doodling, or sketches that had been part of some explanatory conversation with a family member. In return for Ruby and Elmer's weekly efforts, their parents were faithful letter writers as well.

Ruby did not walk to the post office to get mail; she waited until Elmer brought home letters that had been picked up by one of the hospital staff.

She learned from Anna that if perchance an infrequently subscribed-to periodical attracted the postmaster or mistress's attention, he or she would read the material. Depending on the information gleaned, the postal clerk might discuss it with the recipient when they arrived, or truthfully, with anyone who stopped in for mail. Ruby wasn't sure what to make of this. It seemed a violation of privacy, but at the same time, she was amused, and, in part, she thought it was making good use of the limited reading material in the village.

Tanana Post Office

The mail plane arrived on designated days. Ruby kept track of these vigilantly. She felt anxious and disappointed when there were delays caused by the weather. If her week had been difficult, a single white envelope would lessen her loneliness or discouragement. She looked forward to the handwritten words that felt like a reunion of the soul. She imagined her mother washing supper dishes, wiping her soapy hands on an apron, and sitting at the oilcloth covered kitchen table in the Kansas farmhouse with a lined notepad. Or she could visualize her mother-in-law in her print pullover apron with seam binding around the edges and two flat buttons holding everything in place. Perhaps she had just tightened the last lid on a homemade jelly jar or wrapped a cooled, fresh loaf of bread before sitting at *her* kitchen table in the California bungalow. She, too, was weary from a full day's work, yet motivated by care and concern to communicate with her son and his family in that terribly faraway place known as Alaska.

When Ruby had a newly delivered letter in hand, she tried to put off her eagerness until Mark was taking a nap. Then she would put on the teapot for a cup of Constant Comment tea. Sitting at *her* kitchen table, she would slowly read each handwritten word, warmed by both the sender's love and interest, and the steaming citrus tea. Someone else might not have cared what the wheat prices were in Kansas, how many tenths of an inch of rainfall was measured, or what new piece of equipment had been purchased, but she did.

Especially tantalizing was to read which particular fruit was ripe in California. Recipes were welcome, as was the news of births and birthdays. She appreciated being kept in the loop of celebrations, illnesses, and funerals. When she read that other family members had struggles with potty training, bedtimes, and picky eaters, she sighed with relief that she wasn't the only one. For a woman who had known supportive family ties and frequently shared experiences and holidays with one another, this was like a friendly visit or a hug across the miles.

Understandably, letters were not hurriedly tossed in the trashcan. They were read by Elmer, discussed at the supper table, and reread. By osmosis, Naomi and Ruth kept up with what was happening with their grandparents and cousins. Ruby saved each letter until she wrote back a reply, making sure to address the questions or comments expressed by the sender. All in all, it nurtured the emotional bond across time and distance.

When everyone finished absorbing the news in California, Elmer's mother, Agnes, tucked the letter into a box for safekeeping. Ruby had requested she do so and thought someday a book might be written about their experiences in Alaska.

A blend of journal and newspaper was Ruby's writing style. More often than not, she wrote facts rather than introspections; she shared vexations in a matter-of-fact way, rather than expressing internal struggles or regrets.

"September 25, 1957

We are having colder weather the rain turned into snow and it was a beautiful snow fall, it melted here but up in the mountains it is staying, the ground is freezing and in the shadows the ground stays frozen all day. Sunday morning we had a low of 17 above which was the lowest in the territory. The northern lights are just magnificent here.

Mark gave us a scare Friday morning, I knew he was in the bathroom playing with the water as usual and after a while something urged me to go check on him and I found him with my aspirin bottle and nerve pills, the bottle was empty and wet but I could see white aspirin crumbs on his face and he pointed to his mouth and I was concerned that he had eaten to many. Elmer was out moose hunting and it was time for him to return but I decided not to wait for him so I took Mark to the hospital and the supervising nurse took over. She poured some antidote down Mark and tried to get him to vomit, well I had tried to Mark to vomit here at the home by poking my finger down his throat, and he just does not vomit easy. Finally the nurse put a tube down his nostrols and into his stomach and she rinsed out his stomach and then Elmer returned and by that time Mark was exhausted but they decided to keep him in the hospital to give me some rest!"

At least the hospital was within sprinting distance for these emergencies.

Mark's escapades dominated Ruby's letter writing. In all fairness, Mark consumed much of her daily life, and therefore proportionately filled the pages of her chronicles. Given her play-by-play descriptions, the reader could feel her fatigue and frustration.

"September 1957

Speaking of Mark, he exhausts any bit of energy I have. His favorite entertainment is to go to the bathroom tissue, throw some in the stool then swoosh his hands in the water then he flushes it several times, I'm glad that there is no water bill to pay, the sewege draines into the river so it won't stop up. Next he goes to the airfreshner and tries to drink some of it but since the cap is to hard to take off, he goes to the bathpowder and makes himself smell pretty. I change his clothes about twice a day. He still likes the record player but he is tired of his records so he sneaks into the girls and plays theirs until I discover what has happened.

Elmer and Rev. Gronning got another moose and we have 200# of hamburger. ... I sent Naomi to the store for an onion and they had none."

Reading Ruby's letters required patience. Conceivably her spelling errors were the inability to correct what had been already typed. She also admitted, "I need more typing practice." Perhaps this was the reason for her stingy use of periods and liberal use of commas, which on her keyboard were one finger space apart. On top of this, Mark's inquisitive fingers poked at the keyboard, and his head bobbed in her face. Added to these distractions was a kitchen timer sounding for oatmeal raisin cookies needing to be taken out of the oven and the girls coming home from school—with her oldest ready to launch into minute details of her day.

With an extra-active child, a fast-forward husband, and an oldest daughter who said, "I have so many words!" the bush doctor's wife had mixed feelings of wanting her family around her and sending them off for the day. All in all, this letter ended on a positive note: meat, but no onions, a break from Naomi's chatter when she went on the errand, and her husband's safe return from hunting. The Gaede and Leppke families caught a very long-distance view of life from across the miles.

MORE HINTS FOR THE HOMEMAKER

Plan Ahead
Write out your weekly menu. Shop for staples once a week and fresh fruits and vegetables twice a week.

Ruby ordered a year's worth of staples, purchased expensive fresh produce at the Northern Commercial Company store seldom, sent a grocery list with Elmer when he flew into Fairbanks on business, and made requests to her mother-in-law for dried fruits, nuts, and spices.

Organize Work
Have a weekly plan for laundry, ironing, baking, shopping, housecleaning, mending, gardening, and so on. Let the family help you with setting the

table, washing dishes, and planning parties.

Ruby baked nearly every day to provide bread for sandwiches, hamburgers, and such. Laundry took place when the basket was overflowing—or when there was a warm enough day to hang it on the outdoor clothesline. Ruth liked to wash dishes. Mark liked to wash dishes. He splashed bubbles up to his shoulders and soaked his tummy. He also liked to climb onto the kitchen counter and put his feet, shoes and all, into the dishwater.

Be Comfortable
Wear comfortable shoes and clothes while working. Maintain good posture. This will prevent fatigue.

Ruby wore an apron most of the time—and she was "working" most of the time. She always maintained good posture. This did not prevent the fatigue resulting from barriers to shopping for her family or from chasing a lively and loud toddler.

Refresh Your Spirits
Every morning before you start your day, comb your hair, apply makeup, and even add a bit of cologne. Think happy thoughts about how you are serving your family for their benefit. Have a hobby, perhaps ceramics, cake decorating or flower arranging. Look through magazines for new recipes and house decorating ideas. Try to find a moment to sit down and just relax.

Ruby always powdered her face, applied a touch of rouge, and wore pink lipstick. New recipes. Oh, yes, if only she could find new recipes—that tasted good—for Spam, potato flakes, and the infinite amount of Jell-O she seemed to have ordered. A hobby? She had taken a cake decorating class in Anchorage and could create cakes that looked like a hooped skirt for a doll stuck in the middle, two-story houses, a chicken, and more. She never asked herself if she was "interesting." Somehow that was not one of her personal goals. She desired to be the best mother and wife and meet the needs of all four people. Close her eyes and relax? That was supposed to happen when Mark took his nap, as it had for her when the girls were his age, and all three would curl up on her bed. "Just relax" didn't happen as easily now.

CHAPTER 12

AUTUMN GIVES UP

Tanana, 1957

THE BRIGHT COLORS ON THE HILLSIDES had faded, and the sun rose lower and edged to the south. Frozen ledges formed against the river shoreline and ice cakes hurried down the river. Ruby had never seen the like. In the early stages of freeze-up, the river reminded her of the thick and lumpy sherbet punch she made for ladies' fancy events. To live adjacent to such a broad and turbulent waterway had been an adjustment for the prairie land farm girl. Sometimes she had no words to describe this extreme country.

A month prior, the *Yukon*, *Tanana*, *Taku-Chief*, and *Yutana* river barges had docked in Tanana for the last time of the year and then churned back upriver. They would not return until the next summer.[53] That sealed the end of river transportation and concluded any possibilities for food products to be brought in, other than by air, which was sporadic and expensive. Shipments via the river would have to wait until after breakup.[54]

Temperatures dipped consistently below freezing, and daylight receded by more than six minutes a day, which added up quickly by the end of a week. The feast of fall foliage had dulled to a palette of pale cocoa, cloves, and maple frosting. The energizing sunshine had weakened, in some cases taking with it bright attitudes. Ruby no longer saw villagers picking cranberries and blueberries, or digging end-of-season potatoes, carrots, or turnips from their gardens; neither were they fishing or meandering along the riverbank for an afternoon or after-supper stroll. The chances of having a friend or relative show up in the village were lessened, and the community felt stale from reduced contact with the outside world. Airplanes encountered increasingly bad weather, and mail service became inconsistent. Overall, the village felt smaller with the absence of river barges, limited air traffic, and compressed days. Some of those days felt lifeless from a lack of environmental stimulation.

But then there was the entertainment that seemed to come out of nowhere and would turn into a scandal. Ruby recorded how innocently it started:

"October 8, 1957

I must tell you about Mammie, she is a cat that has been at the school-house for several years and one of these years teachers had her own cat come over on the barge so now Mammie was not going to share the living quarters at the school-house so we were asked if we would like to adopt Mammie, the girls were very crazy about her and Ruth carried her to our place, Ruth struggled and puffed (Mammie weighs at least 10 lbs.) Mammie loved it here and she did not want to go out so I let her stay. At night when I tended Mark I looked for Mammie and here she had gotten on Ruth's bed and was sleeping at her feet, so I took her off and put her back in the living room. Tonite I believe Mammie may have to stay out doors."

This was just the beginning of the Mammie drama, which served as a diversion behind Ruby's growing uneasiness about the winter. Certainly, she had made it through two Alaska winters in Anchorage, yet there she'd had more fully stocked grocery stores, kids' winter hand-me-down clothes from friends at church, a department store, and even the Army Surplus store that carried warm winter gear; granted, it was all in male adult sizes, however, she could rip apart the garments and sew clothes for either herself or the children. But now, she was in a small bush village in the middle of Interior Alaska with basic necessities much farther than a drive across town.

Accordingly, she turned to her family for assistance. She instructed Elmer's parents, *"Just want to make mention that you must (now) mail all packages to us by Parcel Post (since the river is freezing up and the barges aren't running) otherwise all freight goes to Nenana (where the barges pick up mail/freight) and we wouldn't get it until spring."*

Her letters continued with a nervous tone.

"We are doing quite a bit of ordering now mostly more warm clothes and the children's Christmas presents.

I got my first order from Sears and I'm real pleased. Boots for Mark, a Dacron lace table cloth which is just beautiful and practical. Basket for Naomi's bike so that she can run errands for me. Turquoise slippers for me to match the turquoise corduroy house coat that I want to make for me. Long underwear for the girls."

In a similar fashion to a hand reaching out to grab hold of another's, her letters went out frequently and grasped for understanding and support.

"*October 14, 1957*

Monday we were given grouse hen that some of the construction men had shot. I dipped them in milk and then flour and then deep fat fried the chunks and it was very good eating for a change from the moose. It tastes like very mild liver of a chicken and it is on the dry side like wild meats are.

Have I mentioned to you that I am using much of the powdered eggs? It makes the baked foods a bit heavier than fresh eggs, the powdered eggs smell like soy-meal. I don't really see how any of you would enjoy eating with us here, if you come for a visit you might have to bring a case of eggs and a couple gallons of cream and milk and butter. The eggs we had sent in from Fairbanks are so old that the whites run all over the skillet and the yolk is so deep orange that it is nearly thick. I do not eat fried or boiled eggs much we have them in other form.

I find myself very limited in my cooking – moose meat, potatoes and canned vegetables."

Intermingled with her daily responsibilities and adapting to life in the bush were situations completely out of the realm of her thinking. Sometimes, there were no mental hooks on which to hang the incident that burst into her day. For instance, Elmer, as the Medical Officer in Charge of the Tanana Hospital, had unknowingly been conferred by the Natives the position of co-leader, alongside the village chief; with this came the expectation that he would deal with such things as criminal behavior.

"October 16, 1957

Elmer received a letter from the Law that he is to report at court in Fairbanks Nov 13, because of that murder that took place after he first arrived here in Tanana.[55] *I am so happy that he has to go. I am getting a big grocery order ready. I want him to get cottage cheese, and so many other things we do not buy here."*

How did Ruby feel about her husband being pulled into law enforcement? From the number of words allotted to the topic and her elation about the consequences (going grocery shopping in Fairbanks), the reader could only surmise that cooking was more of a concern than her husband's role in law and order.

Added to Ruby's written broadcasts was the reoccurring subject of Mammie, and this was even more sensational than cottage cheese.

"October 14, 1957

To our surprise Mammie is pregnant! And there wasn't suppose to be an eligible male in Tanana. So to add a bit of spice to life here and prove the fact, Naomi suggested that Elmer X-ray her, so that's what he did and five heads and spines showed up on the picture. Mammie is the talk of the town, supposedly has never had kittens before and some even wondered if she flirted with a red fox, we don't think so. We believe some of the construction people must of brought in a cat. According to the size of the skeletons on the X-ray my guess is that she has 3 more weeks to go. We will try to keep her inside as much as possible. Some folks have already spoken for a kitten!"

Ruby, Elmer, Naomi, and Ruth speculated about the outcome of Mammie's choices, as did most everyone in the village. Who would have thought a cat would spark so much life, drama, and conversation into the frozen fall air? And one had to wonder if Sol and Bertha Leppke, sister Margie, Henry and Agnes Gaede, and all the rest of the relatives checked their mailboxes with anticipation of another installment of the sordid Mammie Diaries.

Certainly, Ruby kept her readers in suspense as she jumped from Mammie to other narratives of her daily life as the bush doctor's wife.

Part of preparing for winter meant tucking things in or re-equipping them for winter use. If Ruby had lived in town, that could have meant cleaning a lawnmower, hanging up shovels, raking leaves, mulching outdoor shrubbery, and putting studded tires on a car. Here, the item to *tuck in* was Elmer's airplane, which was still on pontoons by the river. He hadn't had time to put it on wheels and fly it up to the village landing field, and now ice threatened to cluster around the plane's bottom surface. Elmer did not want his J-3 captured in ice or towed downstream. The least he could do was move it nearer the bank, which he could not accomplish by himself.

J-3 on floats before the river freeze-up.

On a cloudy Saturday afternoon, he found Ruby in the sewing room, mending a pair of corduroy jeans. Ruth and Naomi were sitting cross-legged on the heavy wood comforter trunk, delving into the tin button box and trying to organize buttons into similar color piles. Ruth was meticulous in wanting to sort out every button, whereas Naomi had already started stringing beads for a jangling necklace. Mark rotated between picking up buttons and crawling at his mother's feet to help accelerate the sewing machine foot pedal. Without saying a word, Ruby alternated between pulling her persistent son out from beneath her legs and pushing the fabric underneath the moving needle.

"Mark! Leave my buttons alone!" scolded Naomi. Ruth helped him start his own pile. He clutched a fistful of buttons from the prized shiny gold stack.

Footsteps sounded in the stairwell. Mark dropped the buttons on the floor, and his eyes got big, "Daddy?" Elmer rounded the doorway and lifted Mark into the air. Buttons grated between his shoe soles and the hard floor.

Mark giggled. Elmer looked at Ruby. Her eyes didn't leave her task, and the sewing machine hummed steadily. Elmer cleared his throat. "Uh, Ruby, I thought you might like to get some fresh air …"

"Just a minute," she mumbled. Straight pins that she'd just removed from the fabric stuck out from her lips.

"I need to get the plane up closer to the bank."

"Children, go find your coats," she said, tugging the fabric from the machine.

The girls wanted to leave their button piles sorted on top of the trunk rather than put them away. Their mother agreed. They could come back later and play.

Ruby, Naomi, and Ruth wore red jackets and red cotton bandana headscarves tied in small bows beneath their chins. The trio resembled a mother hen with chicks. Mark insisted on wearing his outgrown brown corduroy cap with earflaps. The earflaps could no longer snap, and they waved upward, emphasizing his fat cheeks.

When the family stepped off the front porch, Ruby noticed the uncanny silence. Leaves no longer crackled beneath her footsteps but were frozen together in layered mud-clumps. The sky was dull. Clouds were strewn like quilt batting. No birds chirped. No common sound of a motorboat running full pitch against the river current. Somewhere at the other end of the village, a solitary chainsaw growled and whined. At 4:15 p.m., the sun would soon slip behind the horizon.

The girls interrupted the stillness with their chatter. They were intrigued by the novel frozen river's edge and hurried ahead of their parents down the bank. It wasn't long until the pair found just what they were looking for and started popping thin shelves of ice that were layered above the core and filled with water bubbles. They placed a toe of their boots near the bubbles; then, with pressure and release, they made the water flow back and forth. This fascinated them temporarily, but then they rambunctiously stomped harder and broke the icy film.

Ruth and Naomi on the shoreline of the freezing Yukon River.

Ruby helped Elmer half-carry and half-drag the two-seater aircraft up and out of the ice-fingers' reach. The metal floats on gravel screeched like fingernails on a chalkboard.

Elmer had recently taken Mark up in the airplane, which had been the first time the boy occupied the entire backseat by himself, without sitting on his mother's lap. While his parents maneuvered the plane, Mark jabbered and pointed at the J-3. Whenever he had seen another airplane tied by the river, he could pick out *his* daddy's. He took personal pride in this ownership. Now, his mother told him "no" to flying and to climbing on the large pontoons. The toddler screwed up his face, ready to protest. Before he could throw a fit, his father promised they would take a spin when the plane had wheels.

Ruth tried to distract him. "Mark, come make the ice crack." She reached her hand toward him. He threw his arms in the air but then walked toward her. She showed him where to place his stubby booted feet. As roly-poly as he looked, he wasn't heavy enough, and nothing happened. "Jump," she instructed. He finally accomplished the task. The children laughed hysterically, and the noise sounded extra loud in the otherwise quiet late afternoon. Chances were that if any of them had slipped into the open water, they would have been swept away in the rapid current. Surprisingly, Ruby never wrote of that fearful possibility.

Within a week, she wrote, *"Elmer put his plane on wheels, and now I had that experience too. Changing from floats to wheels is no more effort than changing a tire."*[56] True. All he needed was someone to lift the wing so the axle could be placed on a block. In Anchorage, he had had help from male friends. Here, the bush doctor's wife had just gained a new skill.[57]

Another new skill was to nurse a cat in labor. Although she was an experienced farm girl with animals giving birth left and right, and she'd assisted an osteopathic doctor with human deliveries, she had never assisted in a cat's labor and delivery.

"October 20, 1957

Mammie gave birth to four darling kittens. It took her twelve hours to have those. Since I had never nursed a cat in labor I did not know what to expect but seeing that her behavior was different I kept her in all day. It is a good thing as that evening she was looking for a place to hide, she even wanted to get into our cubbards so I took her to the basement and opened the door to the closet where we have all our heavy winter clothes and she crept into the box that was filled with hard boots and there she had her kittens. She is such a good mother. The girls have named the kittens Spot, Nosey, Yukon, Snowball. The kittens are black and white. Mark loves to see the kittens but he is so rough, he picks it up and holds it gently but when he is through he throws it back in the box."

That wasn't all Mark was up to:

"I sure do not know how to keep Mark occupied, he now pushes any chair to the sink, then works the faucets as he wishes if the chair happens to be a bit low he teeters on that little space in front of the sink on his tummy with his feet in the air. Sometimes he slips and he gets a drink in the sink. He also likes to snoop in the top cubbards and finds candy and any thing spillable is his delight. If my Mom worried about Naomi not talking at two I'm sure you would be about Mark, he says very little that we understand but his gestures make it plain what he wants. We are very thankful that inspite of all his Monkey-business he is irristable, he is keeping his stoutness and looks like he might make a good football player."

A busy boy and a tired mother. Darker days and colder nights. A cat with a mystery story—and kittens. Autumn gave up, but the bush doctor's wife could not.

TANANA CRANBERRY BREAD

```
2 C. flour
1 C. orange juice and rind
1 C. sugar
2 T. boiling water
1½ tsp. baking powder
2 T. melted shortening
1 tsp. soda
1 egg
1 tsp. salt
1½ C. cranberries
1 C. nuts
```

Pour orange juice into cup, add shortening and boiling water to make ¾ cup liquid. Grease bread pan. Let stand 20 minutes before baking.

Bake at 350º for 50 minutes.

(This recipe appeared in the October 1958 issue of *Northern Lights*.)

CHAPTER 13

HALLOWEEN AND OTHER ENTERTAINMENT

Tanana, 1957

SPORADIC RADIO CONNECTIONS brought news, music, and programs, along with distracting background static. Ruby was elated when she was able to hear music on the radio; it gave her a comfortable and familiar feeling of knowing who she was and where she had come from. She sang along with the songs she recognized. Her voice range was broad, and her ear for music innate; she could choose to accompany the radio with soprano, alto, or tenor. It reminded her of singing with her parents and harmonizing in the Mennonite churches in Kansas, where everyone grew up learning singing parts. In addition to words, hymn songbooks were written with musical scores. Thus even people who needed to see the notes could do so and blend their voices with the group around them. Ruby enjoyed singing duets with Elmer too. She would usually take the melody, and he would harmonize with tenor.

She wrote her parents:

"October 20, 1957

Believe it or not as we radioed the other nite we got Delrio, Texas. It was sorta nice to hear their music again. One of the C.A.A. men took a look at our old radio. He put in two new tubes and it works swell in fact we had LA. and San Francisco on last nite. So now can keep up with the rest of the world. The Russian statalite news is interesting"[58]

The radio was not all that important in the summertime when there was the appeal of the outdoors, and the sun roosted high overhead, but as the darkness eroded the daylight, everyone stayed indoors more. For Ruby, radio programs served two purposes: a diversion for her children and good company for herself.

Earlier in the season, the children's energy was used up on riding bikes, making mud pies, accompanying their mother with berry picking, or chasing around the woods. Certainly, the large basement channeled some liveliness, and Naomi and Ruth roller-skated up and down the long hallway. Nevertheless, it was after suppertime until bedtime when it seemed all three wandered around aimlessly, too often, looking for trouble. If the girls were contentedly playing in their rooms with their dolls, then Mark found a reason to be a nuisance. If Mark was content spinning his top or building towers with his blocks, his sisters subtly, but deliberately, set him off. Radio music or programs offered a distraction for everyone.

Unshackled[59] was an evening radio program that the Gaede family, Anna, and some of the nurses listened to regularly, as regularly as they could with the fickle broadcasting reception. It was an award-winning radio drama produced by Pacific Garden Mission in Chicago about real people in real-life stories shackled by wrong choices, selfishness, and alcoholism. The dynamic music, sound effects, and actors captivated the listening audience.

Ruth and Naomi mirrored their mother's excitement. On the scheduled evenings, they raced to the living room Hi-Fi cabinets and hovered at her elbow as she tried to move the dial into an optimal position.

"Mommy, put it on the table. Maybe it will work then," pleaded Naomi.

Truthfully, everyone *did* prefer the radio to be on the kitchen table. If Elmer was home, and there was any homemade ice cream around, he'd head for the refrigerator. The children would reroute from following their mother to tailing their father. Mark did not know what was going on but did not want to be left out, so he stayed under everyone's feet.

"Hurry, Daddy!" said Naomi. "It is almost time."

Five bowls of ice cream were assembled. Mark climbed on his father's lap and dug his spoon into both his and his father's ice cream. The girls leaned on their elbows to get as near as possible to the radio as if they might be able to see inside the radio to view the action. Naomi tried to interact with the characters or interpret to Ruth what the conversation actually meant as if her sister needed her to do that. Ruth put her finger in front of her lips and shushed her. Sometimes the melodramatic background music frightened Mark, and he burst into tears. It was all a bit chaotic; nevertheless, Ruby valued the moments. Her family was around her, and she liked that feeling.

The ending of each episode was the same. The down-and-out character was freed from his or her bondage by finding God, and the listener learned that everyone is hopeless without God. The girls cheered. Mark clapped his hands.

On other evenings, horse neighing and clippity-clop horse hoofs reined in the children's attention to *The Lone Ranger*.[60] Even if they could not always follow the plot, they noisily hummed the background theme music of the "William Tell Overture" and galloped around the living room shouting, "Hi-ho Silver."

There were plenty of evenings when, after all the frantic scurrying for bowls of ice cream, or cereal, or popcorn, the radio simply would not do its part. Ruby fiddled and fiddled with the radio knob. When nothing but the annoying sound of atmospheric or electrical disturbances came through, she felt as if a much-awaited guest had capriciously changed his or her mind.

"Maybe next week," she told the girls. "Why don't you go get Candy Land or Chutes and Ladders?" She tried to put on a cheerful front, but she felt disappointed. It was harder for her on the evenings when Elmer was at the hospital or out of the village. It was nice to have some other presence in the house, and in general, to feel linked with the Outside world. Radio contact accomplished this purpose.

Television broadcasting, on the other hand, was unobtainable in Tanana. To put things in perspective, televisions had only recently become a general public commodity. Most televisions were small. All televisions were in black-and-white only. The Gaedes had been given a five-by-seven-inch model when they lived in Kansas City. Naomi and Ruth had watched *Captain Kangaroo* (introduced in 1955) and *Howdy Doody* (1947).

Here in Tanana, Ruby did not have the opportunity to watch popular daytime soap operas, such as *The Guiding Light*, *Search for Tomorrow*, and *The Edge of Night*, not that she would have had time anyway. She was not one to sit still, and her interest in such things was low. Several years later, when the family moved and viewing was possible, she and Elmer never purchased a television. Frankly, she would have preferred radio music in the background as she went about baking, sewing, ironing, and even letter writing. Consequently, Naomi and Ruth's knowledge of talked-about TV shows, such as *I Love Lucy*, *Father Knows Best*, *Leave it* to Beaver, *Dragnet*, *Truth or Consequences*, and *Gunsmoke*, was practically non-existent. Their only exposure to television was when visiting their grandparents in California.

This media void influenced their awareness of national and world events such as sports, politics, Olympics, and the civil rights movement. When the game Trivial Pursuit would become the rage, none of the Gaedes would be the first pick for any team. They would not know the icons of movies, television, musical productions, sitcoms, or United States' entertainment in general. However, they would be the first ones out the door to tromp in the woods, toast marshmallows over a fire, or ride bikes. They would be fascinated by cloud formations, enthusiastic about digging tunnels in crusted snow, and delighted to pick cranberries. And they would put together jigsaw puzzles.

Chances are, these traits are not unique to Alaskans. They might also be accurate for many families in rural communities where men, women, and children prefer the amusement, natural exercise, and stress management of going to a creek with bare feet and a fishing pole, ice skating on a frozen pond, pitching horseshoes, quilting with a circle of friends, or roasting hot dogs while fireflies dart and sparks jump and fizzle. Ruby was a participant, not an observer. She would have been engaged in these events rather than watching a television series.

By late October, many people in the village were already experiencing winter boredom and grumpiness. They knew the daylight hours would be compressed more and more, and temperatures would drop further. The end was not in sight.

One day after Anna had completed grading papers at school, she pulled on her boots and made her way to Ruby's kitchen. The day was frigid, and even though it smelled and felt like snow, nothing was coming down. Ruby answered the door while still drying her hands on a calico print apron. Her eyes lit up.

"I was hoping it was you," she said. "Come in, come in."

A blue mixing bowl half-floated in the sink of billowing bubbles and traces of the children's snack were still on the table. Ruby reached for the stainless steel teakettle and filled it with water. The gas stove burners lit with a slight puff. Peanut butter cookies with tic-tac-toe marks by a sugared fork were cooling on the short countertop. The house was quieter than usual.

"Where are the children?" asked Anna.

"I should probably check, but it's just so nice to have them out of my hair for a few moments," said Ruby. "Give me a minute, and we will have tea and cookies. She motioned toward a kitchen chair.

Ruby finished washing the baking tins and pulled down shallow dark green Melmac cups. Although Ruby's set was fairly new, the durable dinnerware molded from melamine resin, made by American Cyanamid, had become popular in the 1940s. The friends settled across from each other, munching cookies and sipping hot tea.

"I feel like I'm in a rut," said Ruby with a sigh. "Cleaning house, ironing, chasing after Mark ..."

"Well, what do you think of this?" burst out Anna. "We could have a Hobo Party. One Halloween, while I was teaching in Illinois, I had my teenage Sunday school scholars come to my apartment for a Hobo Party. Previous to their coming, I cooked beef and broth and had it ready so that when they came, I gave them the startling news that they had to go beg for food items to put in the Beggar's Stew. Were they shocked! But off they went."

The women laughed. Ruby's shoulders relaxed, and she leaned toward Anna. "They came back with items for the stew, and we ate it out of tin cans. Then they were to share all the happenings of the past year as their lives as hobos."

As a young girl living during The Great Depression (1929–1939) and the Dust Bowl (1930–1936), Ruby knew about hobos. The majority were men, men without a job, money, or home; men seeking work, food, and shelter. In many cases, they traveled by train, not by purchasing a ticket, but by running alongside, climbing on, and then hiding beneath or on top of a train car.

The party-schemers compared notes on their experiences with hobos. "We lived one mile from the Rock Island train tracks," started Ruby. "Mom didn't just hand out food; she required the hobos to do some kind of work, such as cleaning out the chicken coop."

"We lived near a train track too," said Anna. "Word must have gotten out that Mother would feed anyone who stopped in. She didn't require anything. One time, she gave a man a pair of Daddy's shoes. Always, she would give them a Christian tract that told them about their need for God."

In short order, the party was planned for the following Friday night at the Gaede's. Ruby designed invitations on crinkled brown paper with burnt edges.

Hobo Handouts at Gaede's Back Door
Come in Hobo Garb.
Bum Music and Tramp Pie
Will be served.
Bring two large tin cans for food and drink.

The afternoon of the party, the children did nothing to help their mother, who was trying to create a hobo camp in the basement playroom. Mark snuck upstairs, pushed a chair up to the kitchen sink, and teetered his stomach on the narrow ledge. His feet shot up into the air behind him, and his hands splashed into the sink. He was quickly drenched. Naomi reported this to her mother with all the older sister superiority she could manage, followed by an exaggerated huff. When Ruby scolded him, Mark cried dramatically, but with no sincerity or tears. She found dry clothes and instructed him that he was going downstairs with her to ride on his jumping horse. At the bottom of the stairs, they collided with Ruth, who was trying, unsuccessfully, to keep the curious kittens in their box. Ruby nearly tripped several times in her sprints up and down stairs. Naomi had energy that could have been put to good use; however, most of it was used to run around purposelessly and tattle on Mark.

In the midst of the pandemonium, Ruby created a sad and somber ambiance. She removed half the light bulbs hanging from the basement ceiling and put candles in tin cans. "Why did you do that?" asked Naomi. Ruby struck a match and lit a candle. "See the shadows on the walls? Now go help Ruth get those kittens into the box."

Back upstairs, with a watchful eye on Mark, Ruby stirred cubes of moose meat into bubbling canned vegetable soup. Tea made from mashed cranberries that she and Anna had picked in early fall simmered nearby.

All at once, Elmer dashed through the door. The children lunged at him, and Mark trailed him into the bedroom. "Why is Daddy in a hurry?" asked Naomi. "He's late for the party and is turning into a hobo," said her mother. Moments later, laughter and singing were heard at the backdoor. Roy Gronning removed his heavy parka and sported a shirt-of-many-colors and a red felt cowboy hat. Margie's hat matched Roy's, as well as the many patches she had pinned to her untucked shirt. A large plastic nose disguised Anna, along with a black wrap around her head and white taped glasses. Elmer emerged from the bedroom wearing a mop on his head, as hair, and carrying all his worldly goods in a red bandana on the end of a broken wooden pole. Some hobos had crayon-colored white paper masks that covered their faces. One, in particular, gave the impression of a happy hobo, which was out of character with the otherwise dejected faces.

Hobo Party in the Gaede's basement.

The wayfarers helped Ruby carry food downstairs, and the party commenced. Like everything Ruby cooked up, the Hobo Stew was tasty, and there were no complaints from the hard-luck hobos.

Elmer put on his best image of a forlorn hobo and called a Hobo Yearly Meeting. This started with two songs, "I've Been Working On the Railroad" and "Nobody Knows the Trouble I've Seen." Both were deliberately sung off-pitch and with hobos wiping their eyes on faded bandanas.

"Let's hear about your troubles now," said Elmer, hanging his head and feigning despair. Each person tried to top the other's pathetic account of hopping trains, running from vicious dogs, and raiding garbage cans. Roy received the honor of King of Hobos, and Elmer crowned him with a skullcap he had kept from medical school. Naomi and Ruth pretended to gag, and at the same time, reached to touch the smooth, hard cap. The boisterous fun lasted until late. Ruby was not sure when she had laughed so hard.

The hospital also sponsored a Halloween party for all employees. Ruby was surprised by the entertainment location. She wrote home:

> *"They had a wiener roast in our back yard. It's the first time I ate weeners roasted while standing on three inches of snow. We were all so bundled up we could hardly bend over."*

This might have been a first for Ruby. It would not be the last, and that would be *her* choice, not because she was the doctor's wife and expected to comply with the given activity.

On November 3, 1957, she summarized the first two months in Tanana in a letter to Harry and Verda Friesen, friends during medical school.

> *"The thermometer is hugging 0, we have three inches of snow on the ground. The sun sets after 4:30 and rises after 7:00 so winter is creeping on us fast. The sun now stays low and during its shining time it is so that it shines straight into our windows the north side of our roof doesn't get any sunshine these days.*
>
> *Our home is very roomy, cozy, luxurious, and modernly furnishes. I have automatic washer and dryer, bottle gas stove, electric ref. Plus*

that I teach a Joy-Club (Bible Club) (first and second graders) average attendance of 18. This class meets every Thurs. after school.

We really are experiencing a life more like a general practice, there is hardly an evening that he does not get called to the hospital.

We feel settled by now, we all love Tanana. The girls have suggested that we stay a while. The village is perfect for us. The river which is our front window view is an unexplainable beauty with enormous pieces of ice (like flat barges) flowing down stream, this later jams and becomes solid."

After only three months, she was growing friendships and figuring out how to care for her family's Frontier needs. It was as though she could finally let out her breath, which she had held in so tightly.

CRANBERRY HOBO TEA

```
1 qt. strong tea
1 sm. can frozen orange juice
2-3 qt. water
1 sm. can of pineapple juice
1 C. sugar
1-2 qt. cranberry juice
1 sm. can frozen lemonade
3-4 cinnamon sticks

Simmer for a half hour. Good hot or cold.
```

CHAPTER 14

CHRISTMAS CHILLS AND THRILLS

Tanana, 1957

"SOME DAYS, I feel like I'm barely treading water," exclaimed Ruby to Anna. Anna had come over after grading papers, and the two women sat at the kitchen table. The spicy aroma of molasses crinkle cookies filled the air. Anna took off her glasses and set them on the table to defrost, and Ruby lit the burner under the teakettle. "It's not so much the girls as it is Mark." Ruby brushed cookie crumbs off the table into her folded apron and then into the trashcan.

Anna added her frustrations. "And, children are already in a holiday spirit and eager to spread glitter and glue everywhere, rather than do their arithmetic problems."

The women continued sharing frustrations. After awhile, the kettle whistled, teabags seeped in cups, and the arctic friends were finding support in conversation and warm cookies. Ruby stood up and closed the long drapes. "Do you think it's too early to light the suppertime candle?"

she asked. The sun had gone down some time ago, and no light was visible outside the windows. There were no streetlights, and seldom a vehicle drove by.

Anna nodded. "That would be cheerful." Ruby found the matches, hidden from Mark's curious explorations, lit the thick candle, and continued, "I have to call him 'Mark the Mennis.' When I was in the basement washing room ironing on Friday, Mark put one of the kittens into the dryer and then shut the door. Fortunately, he couldn't reach the controls, but I know for sure if he could have, that kitten would have had a roller-coaster ride it would never forget."

Anna stifled a chuckle. She found Mark amusing and fun; however, she didn't have to live with him day in and day out, as did Ruby.

"It makes no difference to him how he holds the kittens, up-side-down or any way. Naomi just goes into tears when she sees how much they have to tolerate."

The typically talkative teacher stirred her tea and kept listening.

"We put a gate on the door to his room, and my, what a shock that was to him. Now he knows that if he doesn't mind or keeps getting into things, that he will be confined."

All at once, the noise in the bedroom escalated, and the three children rushed into the kitchen. Mark stumbled over himself and climbed onto Anna's lap. As endearing as that appeared, he clutched a paper doll's dress, torn in half. In truth, he was trying to escape from his sisters.

"That was the best dress I ever made!" moaned Naomi.

"What do you have there, little Markie?" said Anna teasingly. The two grinned at each other. Mark knew a refuge when he saw one and nestled into her arms.

Ruby reprimanded the toddler and found more paper for the girls to color and cut more dresses. The girls returned to their room, and Mark stayed on Anna's lap, fidgeting with the remains of the paper dress and edging near her cookie.

"Well, enough on that subject," said Ruby. "You can see what I mean."

The conversation turned to the challenge of finding Christmas gifts to send loved ones when there were no actual shopping opportunities in the village. Both women had done the best they could for the current year, ordering from catalogs; however, Ruby wanted something more personal, or Alaskan, for future giving. She and Anna tossed around ideas.

"Last week, Roy took Elmer and me to the backwoods to find some diamond willow tree branches," shared Ruby.[61] "I have seen the most beautiful candle holders, so maybe by next Christmas, I will have a pair for each family." Anna agreed the holders were unique and lovely. "I'm not sure I'd like to do that myself, though."

"I like working with wood," said Ruby. "My daddy was always whittling something."

"It may be a year out until we really have to think about these things again, but we do have to plan ahead here, regardless," said Anna.

"Not just for Christmas," said Ruby knowingly, as she folded and unfolded the hem of her apron. "Anytime there's a chance to fly into Fairbanks or Anchorage, or you know someone who is, you have to keep a list handy."

One Friday evening after supper and before the children's bedtime, Elmer removed his customary bow tie, cleared his throat, and walked over to Ruby. He knew she did not love to fly, at least not in his small plane, so he said cautiously, "A cargo plane landed today with furniture for the new nurses' quarters. It will be going back empty." He paused at the sounds of children tromping up the basement steps. Naomi and Ruth surged through the door with arms full of kittens. Mark scrambled after them as fast as his nearly two-year-old chubby legs could manage. The kittens, frightened by the mad dash, arrived clawing, yowling, and trying to get loose. Mark half-cried and half-screamed for his sisters to wait for him. The girls shrieked when the kittens scratched their neck and arms. A circus ensued. Day after day, this scene had been replayed.

"I cannot deal with that this moment," said Ruby. She turned her back to the chaos and resumed washing dishes.

Elmer ignored the background fuss as well and cleared his throat again. "So, I was wondering if you'd like to take a vacation to Anchorage. It would be a free ride and save us $200 otherwise."

Ruby thought for a moment about care for the kittens, packing for the short trip, and every other detail that swarmed into her mind. "Well, I think that just might work. And we could take my sewing machine that Mark pushed onto the floor and broke. Surely we can find a repair shop." That settled it. Ruby and the children would leave the next day on the cargo plane, and Elmer would join them later in his own plane.

After dawn the next day, which was around 10:00 a.m., the hospital ambulance delivered them to the airstrip. (Elmer was stitching a cut foot, cut from chopping wood.) Thick clouds clogged the sky, not that the sun would have made much difference. At that time of the year, it was never overhead but peered over the horizon before sliding back down around 2:00 p.m. Ruby wrote home,

> "If it is cloudy you would sleep through the day if it was daylight you were waiting for… and we have almost 4 more weeks to go till the shortest day… Christmas will be dark, but the snow will make it pretty."

The two-engine freight plane was without seats and mostly a shell, with no comforts or much insulation from outside. In addition to the pilot and copilot, two other men were on the plane. Both were thick-bodied and square-jawed. The collars of their heavy jackets were pulled up snuggly around their necks, and plaid caps with earflaps rested just above their eyes. Ruby guessed they might be brothers. They had already found a spot on a pile of tires but got up when she tugged her children up the steps into the plane.

"Could we help you, ma'am?" one asked. The men moved forward to grab her suitcase and steady Mark, who was slipping out of her arms. The other motioned toward a mound of well-used tarps. Like a mother hen, Ruby gathered her brood around her.

The smell of oil was thick, and Ruth stuck her nose in her stuffed kitten's white fur. Ruby felt Naomi shiver next to her. Shortly after takeoff, the copilot walked over to Ruby, slapping his arms and shoulders with his hands, which were tucked into wool gloves. The youngish man was layered in heavy boots, an olive-green army surplus parka, and a winter cap. "I'm sorry, ma'am, but the heat doesn't work."

After he walked back to the cockpit, Naomi turned to her mother, "Why, Mommy? Why doesn't it work"? Ruby shrugged. The small family snuggled together. Ruby tried to distract them by reading a children's book she had brought. Mark had no patience with the story and kept trying to turn the pages.

Twenty minutes later, Ruby heard an engine sputter. Her body tensed, and her eyes reflected her fear to the children. They held perfectly still and looked back and forth at the plane engine, the cockpit, and their mother.

The engine caught again, but Ruby still held her breath. As she kept staring out the window, the prop once again spun to a stop. After a series of these stomach-churning episodes, the copilot once again walked out to

Ruby. "We're going to head to Fairbanks instead of Anchorage. It's shorter. We need to get this thing down as soon as possible."

Outside, the gentle snow had picked up, as had the wind. Ruby strained to see the lights of Fairbanks but could see nothing, even though she felt the plane descending. She watched and waited. All she could see was snow. Suddenly, the remaining plane engine went into full power, and the plane climbed back into the gray sky. Ruby clung to a now fast-asleep toddler and whispered prayers.

"I'm praying too, Mommy," said Naomi. Ruth had buried her face against her sleeping brother. Ruby's stomach hurt. It seemed like an eternity before the plane's wheels touched down, and the lights of the terminal came dimly into view.

The terminal was warm! Ruby was glad for the peanut butter sandwich rolls she had packed, although her stomach did not feel like eating a single bite. She arranged her family in a corner where she had spotted a worn couch and short table. "I'll let you know as soon as the plane is fixed and ready to fly to Anchorage," said the copilot. "I'm sure it will be soon."

Ruby expected otherwise and settled in for a long wait. The children did not wait well, but at least they weren't cold, and they could stretch their legs walking, or in Mark's case, running around. By midnight, the little family had fallen asleep, burrowed together awkwardly on the couch.

At 4:00 a.m., she felt a nudge. "Sorry to disturb you, Mrs. Gaede," said the copilot. "We are ready to go now."

Ruby was ready to get to Anchorage and see her friends, but she was not ready to walk out into the snowy darkness or the icebox of an airplane. Maybe that had been fixed too. She listened carefully to hear both engines shake to a start. Within a half hour of takeoff, it was obvious the heat had not been fixed. Mark was indifferent, and perhaps his plumpness helped him stay warm. He made his way over to the men who had resumed their spot on the tires. "Hey, little guy," said one. "Whatcha doin'?" They seemed to enjoy the diversion and even moved some tires closer to Ruby and the girls. "I think it's somewhere between 10 and 25 below zero outside," one announced. "Probably colder up here." His smile was warm. His face was cold. He pulled the cap flaps over his ears and snapped them under his chin. The small talk helped pass the time and kept Mark entertained. Naomi and Ruth blew frost-smoke into the air and then pushed their faces into their stuffed animals. "We're staying warm, Mommy," Ruth explained.

The plane flew smoothly to Anchorage and arrived at 6:00 a.m. Of all things, one of the men lived near Paul and Irene Carlson, the Anchorage friends Elmer and Ruby had lived with when Elmer served at the Anchorage Native Hospital. Ruby and the children hitched a ride.

"December 4, 1957

We knocked on the door and really surprised Irene, she seemed real happy to see us. I was so terribly tired I laid down on the divan and rested as I talked!! We had breakfast and went to church. (Bethany Baptist.) Everyone was so surprised to see us and it was good to be with them all ... Mark did real well, we were at three different places for the 4 nites. Elmer came Monday nite, I felt so relieved to have him near to share the family responsibility, plus that of traveling. You know I nearly went wild in the stores I felt like I wanted to take the whole store with me, I bought every thing from glue to the dress pattern I was wanting ... we got us a ham and frying chicken for variety ... The trip was my best Christmas present I think."

And, of course, she brought back items on Anna's shopping list.

December continued with programs and get-togethers. The school program was first on the list, and the girls nervously practiced their parts. The program, held in the log Community Hall, was filled to capacity with parents, grandparents, and villagers who just needed a distraction in the winter darkness or a lift for the holidays. Somewhere in a corner, someone coughed intermittently, and a baby cried with the high mew of a newborn. Nonetheless, the spirit was not dampened, and there was much chatter, laughter, pride, and applause. Even Elmer managed to break away from the hospital and take pictures of the girls with his Kodak slide camera.

The girls did their best. Naomi's hair was in pin-curled ringlets, and she glowed with affection as she cradled her favorite blond pig-tailed doll, Betty, who was wrapped in a soft, multi-colored flannel receiving blanket.

Come, my little dolly,
And close your big blue eyes;
Christmas stars are shining
Away up in the skies,

Ruth's verses suited her so perfectly that Ruby and Anna weren't sure she could carry them off. Ruth stood on the stage, slightly swaying from side to side.

I'm just a little tiny tot
I'm bashful as can be, but someone said
Come up here and see what I could see.
I never saw so many folk
I'm feeling kind of queer
Guess I better hurry up and get right out of here.

The audience might have thought Ruth was a good actress; however, when there were bright lights, it *was* her typical behavior to look at the floor and cover her eyes with both hands—as she did then.

Ruby found comfort by mimicking what she imagined her loved ones were baking and what had been family food traditions.

> *"I have been baking all week, I made Mom Leppkes pepernuts, and they taste like they should, surprise. I made date roll candy and Mom Gaedes Christmas black walnut cookies, I try to make as much like being with you all is possible … I also made a cookie Christmas tree 10 inches tall. I believe I will save that for Marks birthday cake (December 27)."*

Caroling was not something she had grown up with, other than singing Christmas carols in church, so now, when she got an invitation to go outdoors and carol, a new tradition was added to the season's celebrations. She wished Elmer could come along, but when the time arrived, he had a woman who had just gone into labor, and he needed to keep watch at the hospital. One of the new nurses who had stated, "not even a team of wild horses could drag her out in that awful cold" agreed to watch the children, so there was nothing to stop Ruby from joining the merry group of hospital personal, CAA employees, and Anna. Ruby was made of sturdy material and stuck her feet into heavy white army "bunny boots" and Elmer's army parka.

Of course, there were no streetlights, and on that particular night the carolers went out, there was not a hint of moonlight to mellow the darkness. In consideration of that, before Thanksgiving, some people in the hospital complex and CAA compound had strung Christmas lights around their windows. This color had a heartening effect, along with flashlights that led the way with friendly circles on the snow.

Ruby wrote home, "*Monday nite I went caroling with a dozen others ages varying from 10 to 47. It was 50 below and we had to watch our noses and lungs so they would not get frost bitten.*"

This was her first below zero caroling adventure, but it would lead to more. At one point in her life, she would carry a cassette player with taped carols, knock on someone's door, turn on the player, and sing Christmas joy. By herself. In the dark. On a frigid night, she would bring cheer, both to others and herself.

Grandma Bertha Leppke sent the youngsters candy and other treats. Naomi snatched the Heath bars and held them above her head. "Mommy, hide these from Mark!" Ruby put them on top of the refrigerator. "Nothing is safe from him," complained Naomi. That was true. He would push a kitchen chair to the kitchen counter, climb on top, and shuffle back and forth to open the upper cabinet doors. The sugar bowl was often his goal. It was a wonder he didn't fall off and crack his head.

Ruth searched the Christmas box for nuts. "No nuts," she said sadly. "Don't worry," encouraged Ruby. "Grandma Gaede in California will send nuts; she always does."

On Christmas morning, Ruby was in rare form. Not only was there the family gift opening, but she was also preparing to have dinner at 1:00 p.m. for the chapel attenders. How she had the energy, with three children and darkness that sapped anyone's vitality, was astonishing. One had to wonder if she was high on Geritol.

After weeks of following their mother around with Christmas catalogs and pointing out the dolls they wanted, both girls found ballerina dolls under the Christmas tree. Naomi's had brown hair with movable ankles, knees, and hips. "I want a doll that can kneel and pray with me," she had told her mother. She named it Kathy. Ruth's had pink hair and without moveable joints. Regardless, she was over the moon to have "Tinker Bell," well, as much "over the moon," as she demonstrated with her natural reserve. Additionally, sometime during the previous days and nights, Ruby had secretively made all their dolls flannel rosebud nighties.

There was more. The children had drawn names with their cousins in Oklahoma and California, and the tearing of wrapping paper continued: paper dolls, storybooks, a Bible game, corduroy jeans, and balloons. Mark ripped the paper off his gifts and busily went to work on his spinning top, Tinkertoys, truck, stuffed pony, and other toys.

Ruby and Elmer had exchanged gifts early in December.

"Elmer and I got our Christmas presents this week. He got me an electric Presto skillet the large size and I just love it. I got him a pair of Eskimo house slippers (they cost $12.00) I wish they were less so we could get you all a pair. I started the girls each a fur coat for their tiny-tears doll."

It was indeed a bonanza Christmas with more gifts from the hospital employees: a Hamilton Beach Osterizer (food blender), three boxes of chocolates and candies, a plate with Alaskan Art to hang on the wall, and a pound each of mocha and Java dinner coffee.

With a top spinning on the kitchen floor, Ruby continued final preparations for the early afternoon festivities. Fortunately, she did not take it upon herself to provide the entire meal, only homemade rolls and pumpkin and pecan pies.

Elmer had rounded up card tables and placed them with metal folding chairs in the living room. Ruby always entertained with a special flair, and in the middle of each table, she placed one of her homemade candles. The core of each candle was red or green wax, and the outsides were knobby whipped white wax on which she'd pressed sequins. The light from the flames made the sequins sparkle like little stars.

The guests arrived with frost-tipped parka ruffs and bursts of cloudy, cold air that met the warmth of the house. With such thick mittens, it was a true feat that any could come carrying favorite Christmas dishes of Jell-O salads, fruitcakes, Swedish meatballs, baked apples, and so on. Mark ran to Anna and babbled that he wanted her zipper. Somehow, the two of them had developed a greeting habit that he unzipped her parka when she came to visit. Elmer went to the front door when he heard more guests outside. Roy was trying to carry baby Bethany up the steps as well as hang on to Chris, who kept slipping. At the same time, several nurses had arrived at the back door. Nearly every adult had pulled a sled with offspring or food, and now the sleds were parked together in an irregular line in the snow. Soon the house buzzed with a mix of adult conversations and the laughs and cries of children.

After the meal, the gaiety continued with adult games. Anna and Roy loved Scrabble, and someone had managed to order the newest game on the market, Spill and Spell. Card tables were rearranged to accommodate everyone's interests. Christmas carols played on the phonograph in the cabinets along the living room wall.

In the middle of the noisy adult conversations and the nostalgic holiday music, Mark flipped his own records of Bible stories on the child-size record player he and Chris Gronning had pushed under one of the tables. Noah's Ark animals bleated with Baby Jesus's stable animals. This combination didn't occupy Mark's full attention, and he beat intermittently on his new xylophone.

"Ruby, he'll be in a rhythm band someday," Anna quipped. "Perhaps, he's destined to be a musician."

Ruby retorted, "Well, it is better than flushing socks down the toilet or climbing into my dishwater feet first."

As the first four months in the village rolled toward a new year, Ruby found herself moving beyond mere coping to finding pleasures in unexpected places, such as a grove of diamond willow and singing Christmas carols on a frozen night. At the same time, during this season, in contrast to her typically stoic reporting style of letter writing, her heartfelt feelings emerged.

In a letter to her parents and sister Margie, she wrote, "*How we would like to be with you at Christmas, it seems that during this time we especially like to be with loved ones.*" Much later, in a memory book she noted, "I liked Tanana, but sometimes Kansas seemed so far away."

BLACK WALNUT CHRISTMAS SUGAR COOKIES

(Grandma Agnes Ediger Gaede)

1½ C. sugar
1 ts. soda
1/4 C. shortening
4 ts. baking powder
2 eggs
1/4 ts. salt
1 C. sour cream
1 pkg black walnuts
3½ to 4 C. flour
1 ts. vanilla

Cover dough and chill. Roll out not too thin. Cut into large circles, size of regular tin can. Bake at 400 degrees for 10 minutes or until golden. Ice with powdered sugar and sprinkle with green and red sugar.

CHAPTER 15

THE NEW YEAR STARTS WITH A BANG

Tanana, 1958

THE YEAR WAS WINDING DOWN, as were the many holiday festivities for which Ruby had planned and prepared. She had energetically entertained people, dealt with long dark nights with mere glimpses of sun during the day, and so far kept her children warm in the frozen Interior of Alaska. Last on the list was Mark's second birthday, December 27.

The little kid was grumpy and for good enough reason. He walked around crying and rubbing his ears, all the while coughing with a hacking croup. Ruby could not keep up with his runny nose. She herself was not feeling at her top mothering capability and was suffering from a head cold. Both mother and son felt miserable.

Ruby would have preferred to be in bed rather than making supper, and more so with Mark underfoot and whining. She could not take a step forward or backward without bumping into him. All the same, the macaroni and cheese casserole with toasted, buttered breadcrumbs on top needed to go into the oven. She shooed him back as she pulled down the oven door to light the pilot light, which required turning on the gas and touching a lit match to the igniter. What happened next terrified them both. She wrote home:

> "As I was making supper I lite the oven and Mark was right there and shut it (gas) off so I reached down to light it right away again and we had an explosion. I think of the song, 'some through the water some through the fire some through the blood.' [62] Well the Lord did help me through the fire. I was in the middle of the explosion it all happens so fast, Mark was beside me blown down on the floor and he was frightened and I felt as though I was on fire, I felt my hair and it was singed badly my face burned so badly, I'm glad the girls were at the table playing and I screamed for Naomi to run to the hospital for Elmer. He came and brought salve, Furacin (a topical cream for second and third degree burns), and we put it on all the burned places, my nose hurt so and my right hand. Elmer did such a good job of treating me, and the pain was gone the next day. I wore a glove over the Band-Aids on my right hand. This is the second of Jan. and my hand has nearly pealed, and my nose has a new layer of skin, my chin and neck are in the process and I have no scars, the burns weren't deep. So we have much to be thankful for."

Who knows if the casserole was baked or if she put it into the refrigerator for the following night's supper, or if the scare shocked the croup out of Mark. Perhaps Ruby figured the oven explosion was enough use of matches and didn't want to light even two candles for Mark's birthday, which would not actually be noticed since his "cake" was a cookie Christmas tree she had made earlier. With Mark improvising his own, there was no need for fireworks or firecrackers to start the New Year.

The Native village culture was new to Ruby and Elmer, but not to the Arctic Missions' missionaries, Roy and Margie; thus, when the couples got together, sooner or later, something came up about a customary tradition or practice; this led to questions, answers, and suppositions. Now a potlatch was being planned for New Year's Eve. The Natives held potlatches for holidays and life events such as funerals—the latter of which included gift giving. This would be Anna's first potlatch, too. She and Ruby pondered how to proceed in their arrangements. Margie was helpful.

"You need to bring your own plates, bowls, and silverware," she instructed them. "And a paring knife to cut the meat off the moose bones." Then she started to laugh. "You'll be surprised at the 'tables' or lack of! It's a real picnic."

Ruby and Anna glanced at each other curiously and then at Margie, but Margie's gleaming eyes kept the mystery. "Let's go together," said Ruby to Anna.

By this time, Anna had moved from the school teacherage into a vacant apartment in the CAA compound, which was in the opposite direction of the Community Hall where the potlatch was to be held. The Gaede's duplex was between the two. "Yes," agreed Anna. "I'll stop by."

Margie was a talker, and even though she wouldn't completely spill the beans, she couldn't help but tease. "The rough wood floor will be scrubbed."

Ruby and Anna figured that was a clue but didn't know how it fit in.

When the evening arrived, Ruby pulled out a cardboard box and filled it with their durable dinnerware, along with silverware and paper napkins.

She had not been told anything about beverages, so she filled two quart jars with water and added small green plastic glasses to the assortment.

Naomi and Ruth tied on their mukluks, which had soft, tanned moose-hide soles, rabbit trimmings, and corduroy sleeves for the strips of moose hide that pulled snuggly around their lower legs. Mark did not want to be left out and struggled to put one arm in his parka sleeve. The girls had red-fox-fur ruffs around their hoods, but Mark only had a white wooly rim around his.

Anna tapped on the door and walked in with a dazzle of fresh snow filtering around her. "Oh boy!" she said, giving a giant shudder. "It is truly Seward's Icebox." Her eyes glistened from the cold.

Outside, Elmer put Mark and the box on the sled. It was too cold to run, much less walk quickly, and the group bobbed along slowly, following the bouncing beacon of the flashlight; bouncing because Naomi and Ruth had begged to carry it and took turns making wild and racing lights hither and yon, not at all useful to guide the group. Anna's flashlight was the serious escort. Beneath a canopy of sparkling stars, the adults speculated what the evening would bring.

As they neared the Community Hall, the stillness was interrupted by the voices of other villagers. People recognized the doctor and teacher and greeted them reservedly, but warmly. Decorations had not been taken down from the school Christmas program, and red and green crepe paper streamers and bells still drooped from the low ceiling. Large pinecones with silver glitter hung together loosely with wire attachments in front of the few single-pane windows that were completed frosted with icy ferns and lace. Bare light bulbs dangled from the ceiling and were attached by cords to coils of electrical cable looped over a large nail and onto a wood post on the wall. The room smelled of wood smoke, wet fur, overly warm bodies, and cooking meat.

THE NEW YEAR STARTS WITH A BANG

In unison, Elmer, Ruby, and Anna wiped off their cold-fogged glasses and surveyed the situation. Sure enough. What Margie had said about a "picnic" was somewhat true. There were no tables. Across the room, Margie stood up and waved with a napkin, much like an announcer starting a race with a flag.

Ruby tried to describe the setting in a way her parents could visualize it:

"They had two wood burning gas barrels for stoves in the building. The guests who arrived first were seated on the benches along the walls. The latecomers sat on the floor about 5 feet from the benches and faced those on the benches. Children crouched on the floor on both sides. We arrived late so sat on the floor."

A white oilcloth with small bunches of pink and yellow flowers spanned the distance between the people sitting on the benches and the adults and children gathered on the floor. Ruby's initial reaction was that *this* was the table, and she settled her family to the side of the four-foot runner.

Naomi and Ruth chattered with classmates. Elmer and Roy talked hunting. "Having an airplane sure helps getting a moose," said Elmer. The robust Scandinavian agreed. Small beads of sweat moistened his receding hairline. The room was heating up.

Ruby's conversation with Margie and Anna stopped when she looked up to see men with their mukluks on walking down the middle of the oilcloth carrying containers filled with moose soup. The astonished look on Ruby's face was priceless. "Yes, they walk on this!" Margie laughed. "I wanted to surprise you." Once Ruby regained her composure, she said, "Yes, a picnic." Anna giggled, "I have to get a picture of this." She beckoned nearby schoolchildren to smile for her.

Potlatch in Tanana Community Hall with oilcloth runner

The soup of moose meat, canned vegetables, and elbow macaroni was ladled from either a sawed-off square, five-gallon tin Blazo gas can or what Ruby described as "a boiler we used to feed livestock from on the farm." As cumbersome as these were, and as delicately as the servers had to maneuver around kids, bowls, and other items on the oilcloth runner, everyone was served without an incident. The soup was rich, but as Margie suggested, "You might want to bring a salt shaker next time."

Following the soup, the servers came through with roughly cut hunks of meat, often attached to bone. The server cut these into smaller portions for children and likewise for some of the women. All the same, eating the meat required two hands since the portions were the size of a man's fist, and no one gave a thought to placing the chunk on a plate and cutting it into bite sizes. Ruby's jaw dropped as she watched people put the large piece to their mouths, grab hold with their teeth, and then use a pocketknife or paring-size knife to cut the piece off the bone.

"This is so dangerous!" she whispered to Anna.

"Truly an art," said Anna.

Ruby expected that at any moment, someone would cut off a lip, pierce a cheek, or injure him or herself in some other fashion. Fortunately, none of this happened, not that there wasn't a doctor on call, and sitting nearby potential victims.

Next came large thick, round saltless crackers. Sailor Boy Pilot Bread was, and is, a staple of Alaska villages. Some people claim the northland variety of hardtack has a shelf life of eternity. For partakers who have not grown up on this dry, fairly tasteless product, there is no pleasure. For those who have, they tell stories and give recipes for all the uses: teething babies are calmed; peanut butter or smoked salmon spread on the hardy wafer are common; and, since it will never go rancid, hunters and trappers throw it in their backpacks.

Ruby was encouraged when she saw the servers walking down the "table" plopping globs of butter into empty soup bowls to use on the crackers.

The many-course meal did not end here. Hot tea, Juicy Fruit chewing gum, cigarettes, and canned fruit cocktail filled any space a tummy might still have.

"Where did all this food come from?" asked Ruby, shifting her position on the floor and repositioning the pile of coats nearby.

"The general store provides most of it," said Margie. "Except, of course, the meat, which the men hunt and donate."

Mark and Chris bobbed between their daddies and Anna until they became threats to any half-full bowl or cup.

"Time to go," said Roy, capturing his son with an outstretched arm.

Accordingly, this ended Ruby's immersion into a common village tradition, one for which she now knew to pack along a salt shaker and paring knife, and, if she didn't want to sit *on* the "table," to arrive earlier and find space on a bench.

Daylight hours, or minutes, were increasing ever so slightly. Ruby was heartened all the same. *"We have sunrise at 10:15 am and sunset at 2:00 pm,"* she wrote home. She also added, *"We hit 15 degrees above zero and it really felt like spring!"*

The reality was that it was still very much winter and that it was a *dark* winter at that. Despite that, the children were undeterred by either the dark or the cold and begged to go outdoors. Mark attempted to ride, push, and pull his tricycle on the semi-shoveled sidewalk between the Gaede duplex and the hospital. He was determined to make the three-wheeled vehicle move at his command. Even though he would throw back his parka-hooded-head and scream, he would not give up. As long as he screamed and stayed within the confines of the snow-ridge along the sidewalk, Ruby would not lose him in the darkness. At least she did not have to worry about him crossing the road and falling into the river. In that respect, the frozen river offered security.

Naomi and Ruth did not scream. They, along with other children on the medical compound, burrowed in the snow, piled up the snow, dragged shovels out to the snow, and built igloo-looking crusty snow forts. Ruby could see them out the kitchen window within a rim of light showering down from a compound lamppost and hear their play-filled sounds through the thin windows.

She used this time alone in the house to jot a letter to family, iron Elmer's shirts, or look over recipes shared by Anna or Margie. Taking a nap or totally relaxing was out of the question. She knew that at any moment, one of the children would push through the door and announce that she or he needed to use the bathroom or have some other reason to re-enter her immediate world.

No doubt, Mark kept her on her toes, and she could never let down her guard. A few days into the New Year, Ruby was stacking freshly washed towels in the bathroom linen closet when she heard the scratchy sound of a match being lit. She opened the bathroom door to find Mark sitting on the rug in the hallway with a tiny blaze in his hand. Seeing his mother and hearing her yell his name, he dropped the match on the rug. Ruby stomped out the small flame and shook her son by the shoulders until his teeth chattered. She marched him over to his room and up went the gate. She thanked the good Lord she had been nearby and not down in the basement and that she had managed to keep him alive for the first two years of his life.

Whereas Anna thought he had a propensity for music, Ruby wondered if the little pyromaniac would be a firefighter. Certainly, he would make a good detective since no matter where anything was hidden or thought to be out of his reach; he could find it: the sugar bowl, the girls' paper dolls, ink pens, postage stamps, and matches. If the two-year-old could have verbalized what he would like to become, it would probably have been an airplane pilot or hunter—like his daddy. As it turned out, his love of fire was never extinguished, whether it was a campfire or an autumn burn pile.

FIREWORKS OF ANOTHER KIND

Both the United States and the Soviet Union started satellite development shortly after World War II. On January 31, 1958, approximately four months after The Soviet Union had launched Sputnik 1, the United States launched its first satellite, Explorer 1. The Space Age had officially begun.

CHAPTER 16

HIGH SOCIETY IN THE ARCTIC

January, 1958

IN THE DEEP WINTER DARKNESS, the hospital employees craved variety and stimulation. They worked and ate at the hospital and lived collectively in adjacent quarters. Conflicts between people were exacerbated by the continuous proximity, and more so when there were limited opportunities to get *out*, whatever that might mean in a community without amenities and with dead-end roads. Where could anyone have gone? The small window of daylight over the noon hour curtailed anything more than a quick walk along the riverbank in the otherwise darkness-draped day. There were, all the same, those hardy souls who could not resist a walk beneath the spotlight of an enormous moon or under the waving blue, red, or green Northern Lights. These splendid experiences in themselves could be rejuvenating.

As Medical Officer in Charge of the hospital, Elmer's responsibilities included social activities for the employees. He could not take his employees to ballgames, live performances, or hire a band for entertainment. He could not provide day passes to an amusement park or a museum, but he did what he could to combat the melancholy. Often he ordered movies that came on 16 mm film and were coiled into round reels contained in flat, circular metal containers, fourteen inches in diameter. These films were threaded into a projector and held in place by the perforations along the sides. His selections represented his educational inclination and ranged from *The Ways of the Navajos* to *Giant of the North* to *The Living Desert*. The last of which terrified Naomi and gave her nightmares about the enormous sand-colored spiders scurrying across the desert.

Elmer accepted some input from his employees for films but carefully monitored their selection. Sometimes he would ask Ruby for her opinion. Her personal preferences would have been those with a religious base or of interest to her children, such as *A Man Called Peter*, *Heidi*, or *Hansel and Gretel*. Neither Ruby nor Elmer referred to these motion pictures as "movies" since going to a theater where movies were shown was forbidden by their Mennonite upbringing. Instead, they referred to them as "films," which was accurate, indeed.

Whereas Elmer strove to be an activities director for the hospital personnel, Ruby did her part to support the existing social structures. She was an inherent hostess and loved to cook and bake, use special tableware, and pull out her white lace tablecloth. Her hand went up when it came to volunteering for school treats, refreshments for a baby shower, or planning a birthday party. Her skills extended beyond the actual preparing of food to creative and humorous party games, imaginative party favors, and exquisite table decorations—the last being subject to last-minute changes since there was no local dime store, and she had to use, reuse, or reinvent what was on hand.

Not long after Ruby had settled into Tanana, she had written home expressing her pleasure at hosting her first social gathering.

"October 29, 1956

This is Monday morning and I am baking, washing and cleaning house and trying to get this letter off. I bake every other day. Tomorrow nite I have the Womens Society group here so I want my house clean and I plan to bake Swedish cardamom bread. I will slice it, spread it with butter and put eyes nose and mouth with lifesavers, then I will make cranberry tea for the drink. The tea is served hot and is fun to have this time of the year.

This Sunday we are entertaining all those that come to our church. I plan to have Tamale pie, lemon lime Jello with grapefruit (canned) in it, hot rolls, pickles and angel food cake."

Now in January, she offered again to host the Women's Society.

The Women's Society was a sophisticated name for a sewing circle. The CAA wives had started it prior to Ruby and Anna's arrival, and some of the nurses and attended. The Native women were welcome but typically declined. Certainly, everyone would have appreciated and benefited from learning their skills in beadwork on mittens, slippers, and hair clips. The group usually rounded out at eight women since not everyone attended every time. There was a perception of "getting out" since the location changed each time, and members looked forward to fancy refreshments prepared by the hostess.

And so on this evening, in the middle of the Alaska Territory, with temperatures stuck at 40° below zero, Ruby was carefully dressed in a body-hugging beige knit suit. Her crystal bead necklace and narrow silver belt reflected the flickering light from candles on the kitchen and the coffee tables.

In the background, coffee percolated noisily and filled the house with a welcoming aroma. On the kitchen table, Ruby carefully arranged clear glass luncheon plates that had a ring insert for a matching teacup. A cut-glass bowl held sugar cubes. Evaporated canned milk filled a matching creamer. The tiny creampuffs she had made in the morning were filled with tuna salad. Pickles and black olives were arranged in a divided relish plate. A small arrangement of pink plastic roses added color. For a moment, she stepped back to survey the scene and smiled. Then her mind abruptly focused on the relish plate. Mark loved pickles and *thought* he loved olives; however, after chewing on them, he would run to the bathroom and spit them into the bathtub. Ruby took a deep breath, cast that image aside, and straightened a corner of the tablecloth.

Right on time, the women started to arrive from their quarter- to half-mile walk in the hostile cold and darkness. After tromping through the snow, they tugged off their boots and slipped into fashionable high heels, all the while greeting one another pleasantly before milling around the kitchen.

Ruby and Anna did their best to maintain the 1950s cultural dress expectations; however, when Ruby and her family lived in Anchorage, prior to Tanana, she shopped at the Army Surplus store. In Tanana, the Gronnings received boxes and cardboard barrels of clothes sent from churches. (Thus, referred to as "missionary barrels.") Margie would invite Anna and Ruby over to sift through the articles.

After the New Year, Anna began sewing wool slacks to replace her school teaching dresses, and Ruby adopted the same mode when she left the house. She continued to outfit Naomi and Ruth in dresses or jumpers for school or church, however, with corduroy elastic-waist pants pulled beneath and long johns underneath the pants.

Yet, when Ruby entertained, she greeted guests in the expected 1950s attire.

"Look what Ruby made this time!" exclaimed Jessie, a plump blonde woman with her hands placed dramatically on her hips.

"We are so lucky to have you in the Society," said Alice, the kindhearted receptionist at the hospital. Her white hair cascaded around her face, and when she smiled, as she often did, she looked like an angel.

"I'm not sure I can top this," said Anna in a stage whisper.

Ruby blushed and brushed off the compliments. "Would you like tea or coffee?" She filled delicate cups with their choices.

The group meandered into the living room and pulled out knitting, embroidery, hemming, and mending projects. Gracefully the women crossed their legs, endured the bump of the garters holding up their nylon hose, and continued chatting. Conversation ranged from books they had read—and were willing to share—to guess-what-I-heard village news, to offering trades on yellow cake mix or cherry Jell-O resulting from an over-estimation of their year's order of food.

As was typical, new recipes for moose, ptarmigan, or rabbit were discussed. Finding variety in menus required ingenuity. One could not just walk into a grocery store and easily select chicken drumsticks, pork chops, or beef ribs. Unless someone shot wild game, menus revolved only around what was canned or dehydrated.

"Moose meat is a welcome change from the usual chopped Spam and canned chicken, isn't it?" commented Betty, whose husband was with the CAA. The spritely woman brought a spark to the group with her positive spirit.

"Duck can be a real treat," Anna suggested. "Doc and Roy Gronning went hunting and brought back some ducks. They shared them with me. I used the gizzards, liver, and hearts to make soup and stuffed the ducks for dinner."

Ruby added enthusiastically, "If you dip any kind of meat into flour, and deep-fat fry it, it will usually be good ... and make gravy ... you know how anything wild will be a bit dry ... yes, gravy fixes that too."

"Mmm. I can just taste the gravy," said Betty. "Did you serve this on rice or mashed potatoes?" ("Mashed potatoes" meaning dried potato flakes in a box and whipped up with hot water and a touch of salt.)

Before Ruby could answer, Carol, a plain-faced, athletically built woman whose husband also worked for the CAA, deliberately set aside her mending, took a deep breath, and completely changed the subject. "Guess what? I finally did it!" She paused to watch the women's faces. "I soloed yesterday!"

In detail, Carol described her trepidation and exhilaration of the grand finale of her flying lessons.

Ruby whispered to Anna, who sat beside her, "I really *should* take flying lessons. I'm just not interested. I'm too scared.[63]

When Carol breathlessly finished her story, Alice set down her shiny knitting needles and started to clap her hands. Soon, the room was filled with cheers, followed by questions and more conversation.

After a while, cream puffs and more coffee were consumed, and some projects were even completed. Jessie held up a mitten. "Ta-da!" Somehow, that was the signal to end the evening. Reluctantly each woman put down her stitching undertaking.

"You can come to my house next month," Margie volunteered. "I have a great dessert recipe to try, and I even have all the ingredients."

"That's terrific!" said Betty. "Having all the ingredients" was significant to anyone living in the village.

One by one, the women slipped off their pumps and pulled on heavy winter footwear. Bulky coats covered their dresses. Wool mufflers were pulled up over their mouths and their noses. No one would have guessed that minutes before, these women, who were now cocooned in wool and fur, had looked as elegant and dressy as any lady at a concert in a large metropolis in moderate climes. Alaskan women were truly a blend of femininity and durability.

FASHION IN THE 1950S

```
Being pretty and feminine was presumed. Women were
expected to be impeccably dressed and groomed when
in public and when their spouse was at home. No
T-shirts or denim jeans at home or in the yard. When
leaving the house, if even to go grocery shopping
women should have on a dress, with matching shoes,
belt, and handbag. For church or an entertainment
function, coordinated gloves and hat should mix in
with the attire.

Long narrow skirts and full billowing ones that
reached mid-calf were the trend. Regardless of
skirt style, nipped waistlines and tight bodices
were emphasized. Most women were slim in the 1950s;
regardless, tight-fitting undergarments were
necessary to achieve a sleek, hourglass figure.
Fancy collars and large buttons added to the décor.

Cotton was often used for daywear and wool for the
evening or outside the home activities. Tweed fabric
```

covered storefront mannequins and was displayed in fall season catalogs. All these fabrics required careful ironing. Synthetic fabrics had recently entered the market, and polyester and rayon were used to make women's blouses and dresses.

In 1957, the "sack dress" appeared. The completely loose garment destroyed the emphasis on the waist entirely and set the mode for the 1960s sheath dress.

CHAPTER 17

CENSUS TAKING

Tanana, 1958

ELMER WAS INTERESTED IN the basic demographics of his patients. He wanted Ruby and Anna to take a census of the village and had mentioned this to them at the New Year's Eve potlatch. Anna was eager because this would give her background information about her students, plus she was fundamentally curious as well as attentive to the people around her. At first, Ruby dragged her feet, and her mind was abuzz with questions: Who will watch the children? What if people think we are nosey? Will it be safe? Anna, however, was like a dog team at the starting line and ready to mush onto the trail. They settled on a Saturday when Elmer was in the village, and no obstetric patients were due.

It would not be an early start. The January sun would not bravely scale the winter sky until around 10:30 a.m. On this day, it brought with it a welcome warm spell of only minus 6 degrees. Anna walked slowly to the Gaede's duplex, gazing across the frozen Yukon to the island a half-mile away and enjoying the clouds of snow that bloomed and faded around her ankles with each footfall. Her reverie ended when she stepped through the common entry of the duplex. A mass of meowing black-and-white fur zoomed through her legs, followed by Mark, scrambling from the basement as fast as he could go. His determined look let her know his pursuit would not easily be stopped. Ruth chased after Mark. Tears streamed down her face. "Mommy! Mommy!"

Suddenly the door into the living quarters jerked open. When Naomi saw what was happening, she let go of the door and braced herself against the kitchen cabinets. "Mark! Stop chasing the kittens!" Caught in the middle, Anna realized that instead of one fur ball, there were four kittens, all yowling and racing into the house.

By this time, Ruby had reached the door and tried to tackle Mark. He eluded her grasp and slid across the kitchen floor on his stocking feet. Anna followed the mayhem. Naomi and Ruth ran about helter-skelter into the living room, trying to pry the kittens off the couch and drapes. Eventually, Ruby captured Mark and sentenced him to his bedroom behind the gate. Naomi and Ruth subdued the kittens and begged their mother to let them return them to the basement. Ruby, however, was at her wit's end and directed them to deposit the wild cats outdoors. Now!

Anna viewed the scene as comical but knew better than to open her mouth.

The girls disappeared into their room.

"I have had it with those kittens," said Ruby, nearly in tears. "They do not want to stay in the laundry area, and when I take them outside, they just sit on the steps and whine pitifully." It took a few minutes for her to gather her wits about her. Anna let the monologue be and did not step into the conversation. In silence, Ruby walked to the coat closet.

"I am leaving," she said to Elmer, who appeared out of nowhere.

Once out the door, she continued to Anna, "He thinks he's going to work on his Sunday school lesson. That will be if Mark's not annoying the girls and trying to get their marbles, or if he doesn't play with the oven controls and blow someone up. I'm still trying to grow back my eyebrows."

"Let me see," said Anna, stopping. "Your eyebrows do not look bad."

Ruby reached up to trace her eyebrows with a gloved finger, and the two resumed walking.

"As for marbles," continued Anna. "I contend with them at school. "I'm not sure how that fad got started. And in winter, mind you. Can they shoot marbles in the snow? No. What happens in the classroom when they drop them? They all roll to the center of the room because the floor slopes. After awhile, it just gets on my nerves."

Ruby appeared not to hear. "I don't know if it would help if Mark could talk. I would worry that he is so slow, but Naomi was slow too. Well, he does repeat after me, 'I'm mama's sweetheart, I'm daddy's big boy, I'm Naomi's lover, and I'm Ruth's Chubby Chub.'"

"And, he can say, 'Annie, down,' so he can pull down my parka zipper!" Anna laughed proudly. She got such a bang out of him.

Ruby wasn't finished. "If that's not enough, he doesn't want to take naps anymore. Imagine. My sakes! He's only two years old. The girls took naps with me until they were four. They just curled up and went to sleep. No struggle."

"Who wouldn't want a nap?" said Anna, grasping at some conciliatory response.

"At least we stumbled upon something that works—sometimes. Oftentimes, Elmer comes home for lunch. When he does, after he eats, he sits and reads for a short while before returning to the hospital. I tell Mark, 'Read your airplane magazine with Daddy.' So, he crawls up on the armrests on Elmer's chair and pages through the magazines. Sometimes they talk. Elmer is teaching him flying terms and has promised to get him an airplane when he graduates. Graduates from high school? From diapers? Ha! After twenty minutes, he's relaxed for a nap, and Elmer leaves the house."

That image made Ruby smile. She took some deep breaths and turned toward Anna. "I guess I can stop harping on all that now." The chilly sunshine seemed to clear her head.

She opened a notebook awkwardly with her dense wool gloves to show Anna the categories for the census. In addition to name, birth date and place, nationality, and education, Elmer wanted them to tabulate who had been in for X-rays or had associated with people who had tuberculosis.

Anna nodded her head. "This will be helpful. Really, Ruby, I cannot imagine how you can get anything done besides bridling Mark." Indeed, he was often like an earthquake registering a ten on the Richter scale.

The census takers decided to canvas Back Street first, then later go to the CAA camp, and last of all, the medical compound. Ruby shook off the frustration of her frantic morning and quickened her pace. They bounded onto the porch of the first log cabin, tapped the snow off their feet, and knocked sharply on the wide, split log door. A young Native woman unlatched the door. Her face was as golden brown as the moose hide that was draped across a nearby chair. When she saw the teacher and doctor's wife, she smiled and urged them to come inside. The cabin consisted of two tiny rooms. Sunshine shone through gingham curtains, and a teakettle whistled on the woodstove. The floor still retained some soap bubbles and puddles from its recent scrubbing. Two preschool and several early grade school children played on a bed that was rumpled with sleeping bags.

"Miss Bortel, why are you here?" The grade-schoolers waved at Anna and squatted on the end of the bed nearest her. Not only did children sleep in the same room, but they also slept together in one bed.

Anna explained that the project was to find the number of people in the village and to write down information. This satisfied the children, and they returned to playing with wooden blocks.

The woman answered the questions easily, and the pleasant experience spurred Ruby and Anna onward. Fortunately, they had not stopped at the second cabin for their initial contact. When they knocked, the door opened a crack, and a woman peeked out with a scowl. Her uneven dark hair fell into her eyes, and she held a child on her hip. The child whimpered. Ruby wished she could remove the child's filthy T-shirt and find warm soapy water. Standing in the shadow of the porch roof, the two census takers shivered. Anna asked the questions, and Ruby jotted down the answers. Then they thanked the woman, stepped into the sunlight, and gasped fresh air.

"I am concerned about her," said Ruby.

Anna agreed.

Now they did not know what to expect. A large weathered wood structure with a peaked tin roof was next. A well-traveled trail ran through the snow to an attached lean-to door. Anna removed her mitten and knocked loudly. Inside, slow solid footsteps were heard coming to the door. Warily, the women looked at each other. A tall, attractive older man with a shock of salt-and-pepper hair gradually opened the door. To their relief, he smiled and motioned for them to come in and sit down in his orderly front room. His accent, which they discovered was Norwegian, made him difficult to understand; nonetheless, within minutes, they were clinging to every syllable, transfixed by his tale.

Tom Tryland was eighty-three years old. As a young man, he had traveled from Norway to Illinois, and after several years of college, had trekked north to Dawson in the Yukon Territory for the Gold Rush in 1899. He had seen his share of gains and losses; even now, he hoped for another gold strike. It was as though he had stepped out of an adventure storybook, and when the census questionnaire ended, Ruby stood up reluctantly, eager for more stories and not eager to leave the pleasant warmth of the cabin.

The afternoon went on, and Ruby's notes stretched into pages. Each cabin contained its own unusual history. One woman was confined to a wheelchair and living with her brother—when she was not in the hospital. She had had several strokes. Several women didn't know the ages of their husbands. Some elderly Natives could not remember their birth dates. They tried to deduce them from an event in the village or a season.

Premature dusk settled onto the village, bringing with it a lavender glow and descending temperatures. Ruby counted the number of cabins they had surveyed, "Twenty-three cabins and only one more to go on this side of Back Street."

"Let's hope for the best," said Anna.

No light shone from the windows of this last cabin. "Maybe they are just not home," Ruby murmured nervously. "Maybe we could include this one in next Saturday's outing."

Anna didn't reply and continued down the narrow snowpacked trail. As always, Ruby followed. Anna raised her hand and knocked confidently. The door grated against the wood floor. Anna let out her breath noticeably and exclaimed. "Oh, you are Walter's mother!" The woman smiled and invited them into the dark cabin. With the steep kerosene prices, the villagers often waited for complete darkness before lighting their lamps. Not wanting to cause any obligation, Ruby held the census notebook close to her face and tried to record the information. All the same, visibility rendered this impossible.

"Oh, let me light a match," the woman responded graciously.

Ruby hurried to jot down the data before the match burned the woman's fingers or the notebook.

"Thank you so much," said Ruby.

"Tell Walter I'll see him on Monday," added Anna.

Ruby stepped off the porch with a smile on her face. She tucked her pencil into a pocket and stuck the notepad under her arm.

As they walked home, Anna's thoughts circled back to the beginning of their venture. "You really need to find homes for those kittens," she said. "Whatever happened to all the people who said they wanted one?"

"For some reason, they are now as scarce as hen's teeth," replied Ruby. "One excuse after another. I do need to get rid of at least two, to begin with, the two Naomi and Ruth haven't claimed, even though they are as wild as the barn cats we had in Kansas. I'm not sure they will make good pets."

The census team had completed a day's work, that is, as much "day" as the Arctic sun would allow them. In a village of approximately three hundred people, ninety-six had been accounted for that day. Except for a very few, the highest level of education achieved was probably second grade.[64] The census team would take on the other areas at a later time: the hospital personal, ministers, CAA personnel, and White Alice employees. The demographics were mixed in this Interior Alaskan village.

"Man alive, what a day this has been," burst out Anna.

"Yes, indeed," agreed Ruby. "Why don't you come over for hot cocoa? By the way, I wonder who will have the tallest tales to tell—Elmer or the two of us!"

Anna turned to Ruby. "That may depend on Mark and the cats."

CHAPTER 18

VALENTINE'S DAY AND A LITTLE SWEETHEART

Tanana, 1958

RUBY'S EYES WANDERED LAZILY over the scene outside the large living room window and toward the river. She smiled. The February sun shone low over the southern horizon and reflected through the thick three and four-foot icicles, hanging like stalactites along the roofline and blocking her view in a delightful way. The glow and gleam of these natural suncatchers added brilliance to her otherwise black-and-white winter world. When an unexpected wind stirred the freshly fallen snow, snowflakes jumped up and danced in all directions. As much as she loved the outdoors, the sunshine at these temperatures was mean-natured, teasing a person to go outside, but once outside, releasing a death-grip of 40 to 50° below zero temperatures. Ruby was not tempted. She was satisfied to observe the beauty from inside, where it was warm.

The smell of yeast bread permeated the house and wrapped the family in a cozy aromatic blanket. The bread was still in the yeast cans and sweating, as Ruby called it. At some point, she had started using large 48-ounce aluminum yeast cans for baking. Like puffy, round hairdos, the bread tops rose above the cans. Even when she smeared oleo[65] inside the cans before plopping in the dough, the finished product would sometimes stick to the ridges within the can. She learned if she let the hot bread remain in the cans and "sweat" for a short time, it would come out more easily, although her children were nagging her to take it out sooner, so they could have it as dessert for their lunch.

The children finished their sandwiches and small glasses of Tang. Mark had not spilled his. His father had kept his eye on him, for which Ruby was grateful. Elmer, an easy man to feed, had not tarried with his bologna sandwich, coated in mustard, and enjoyed with a large dill pickle. He could have eaten the same thing every day. Since she was tending the bread and making Jell-O at the same time, she did not sit down for lunch; instead, she anticipated nibbling on the first slice out of a can.

Elmer wiped his mouth with a napkin, cleared his throat, and stood up. "I need to organize my hunting gear."

Ruby nodded and picked up his lunch plate.

"Daddy, Daddy!" Mark called, sliding off his highchair to tag along to the basement.

"How's my big boy?" said Elmer, picking the tyke up under the armpits and swinging him over his head.

Mark shrieked with excitement and dug his pudgy fingers into his father's well-oiled curly hair.

"Are you going to fly Daddy's airplane when you grow up? Now watch your head." Elmer ducked under the doorway and headed down the stairs.

At least the extra kittens were gone, and the two remaining had settled down: Ruth's mostly white one with a spot or two of gray, Yukon, and Naomi's black-and-white one, Nosey. The ambushes had ended, and Ruby could do her laundry without their sudden attacks at her ankles. She was glad to be rid of at least part of the literal kit and caboodle.

"Let's make valentines," said Naomi to Ruth. They turned to their mother for approval.

"Yes, that is a good idea," Ruby responded. "Find your supplies."

The girls sat at the kitchen table with sheets of red and pink construction paper. Silently, they cut hearts from the folded seams of the paper. Their snub-nosed scissors made a muffled crunching sound. The oven's heat filled the kitchen, and Ruth took off her flannel shirt and sat in her white undershirt with lace along the shoulder straps. Her naturally curly hair coiled around the edges of her face. Naomi draped herself on her chair, with one leg tucked beneath her and the other standing on the floor.

At that moment, Ruby couldn't want for more. Her family was fed, the house smelled of baking, her husband was home, and her children were not quarreling.

The phone rang. The phone line was only connected to the hospital, so she knew Dr. Gaede was needed. "Well, shoot," she said.

Naomi and Ruth kept their heads down, but, just as children often do, they echoed her words. "Shoot. Shoot," they chanted in up and down unison.

Ruby called Elmer and eavesdropped on the conversation. With only Elmer's comments to go on, she gathered someone was hemorrhaging. Just the previous week, she had written home:

> "Three of the latest deliveries have hemorrhaged badly and so he has had to give them transfusions, this is a bit of a problem here, it is seldom that the natives give blood but the construction and C.A.A. men have volunteered beautifully and we are thankful for that. I believe I have

mentioned that the O.B.s like to come in quite a bit early as that gives them a little rest from their little tribe. Elmer gets many of the single girls from Fairbanks that when they are due, some of these girls keep their babies and some don't and let them go out for adoption."

Elmer left, and Mark wanted to know what the girls were doing. He climbed back into his highchair and snatched the glue bottle, sticking the squirting end into his mouth. Apparently, he liked the taste. He proceeded to put glue on his fingers and lick them. Unperturbed, Naomi pulled the bottle away. His attention shifted to the white paper doilies the girls planned to use as lace on their valentines. There was enough glue on his fingers that when he touched a doily, it stuck. Rather than annoy him, the toddler found this fascinating. In their own ways, the threesome stayed busy.

Even though Ruby always had something to do, such as ironing, mending, writing letters, baking bread, and more, making her family comfortable and welcoming people in her home were more important—and satisfying. Therefore, when she heard a tap at the door and found Anna standing in the entry, she was pleased. The schoolteacher looked as though she had spent the day fighting with a chalk eraser. She was dusted in snow from her parka hood to her mukluks. Frankly, pink chalk dust could have livened her naturally pale face.

"*Na oba!*"[66] Ruby exclaimed in Plautdietsch. "What are you doing outside today?"

"I was restless—needed to get out. It's cold enough to freeze my toes off, but at least there's not six or more feet of snow here, like when I taught in Valdez," said Anna, finding the bright side.

Anna's coat was so frozen that even after she hung it over a chair, the snow was reluctant to melt. She walked around, patting the dampness off her face and holding her hands near the stovetop where Ruby had turned the gas on high beneath the teapot.

Out of the corner of her eye, Ruby watched Mark squirm off his chair and disappear into his bedroom. Seconds later, he galloped into the living room with a Davy Crockett raccoon cap on his head, worn backward, his xylophone in one hand, a tiny piano dragging from the other, and a mallet between his teeth. Conversation stopped when he crumpled on the floor at their feet and beat madly on the colored metal keys of the xylophone and then the plastic ones of the piano. His head nodded to the music.

"Markie!" shouted Anna over the din. "You should be in our Jamboree!"

Ruby let out a half-laugh. "I guess he adds life and sound to the long winter."

"So did the cats," replied Anna with a chuckle.

The racket made conversation near to impossible, and simultaneously mother and teacher picked up their cups of tea and found a corner of the kitchen table that was not covered with Naomi and Ruth's valentine making.

Anna continued. "What a jolly time we had at the last Jamboree with the Gronnings. We really made some lively music!"

Shortly after Ruby and Elmer had arrived in Tanana, they initiated what Anna referred to as "Jamborees." On these evenings, musicians at the chapel, who played an assortment of instruments by ear or by notes, got together and produced a semblance of harmony, as well as much laughter. Elmer and Anna both played accordion, and when two weren't needed, Anna pulled out her ukulele. Ruby was the sole mandolin player, although when she and Elmer sang duets, she played piano or a pump organ. Anna could play the pump organ as well, which she did for school programs.

Margie adapted to the need of the situation with either the piano or autoharp. Other people added their talents.

This idea had roots in Ruby's growing up when family members and cousins would gather on a weekend night and make music. No card playing. No television. No movies. They made music. Her father, Sol, played cornet, harmonica, violin, and mandolin. Her mother, Bertha, from the Litke family, was born with music in her DNA. The Litkes were known for being musicians, not professionals, but having a strong showing at church and community events. In Bertha's case, she "just heard it" and didn't necessarily need notes to tease music out of an accordion, piano, banjo, mandolin, or autoharp. Mandolin seemed to be a common instrument in the family and community, and both Ruby and her brother, Wilbur, picked music and harmony out of the strings.

Ruby and Anna's moods had lightened at the remarks about Mark's music and the cat frenzy, and now their reflections on the recent Jamboree set the stage for other incidents that struck their funny bone.

"Usually we all know where to start if someone says 'key of G' or 'key of C' … but … remember … how on that one song … we all started in a different key?" Anna laughed and gasped between words.

Mark stopped his one-boy-band to stare at her.

"Well, at least we had the same tempo," Ruby said, trying to find the positive.

To anyone else, the glimpse into the Jamboree would have been ever so slightly amusing, but for Anna and Ruby, it was as though the musical dynamic of crescendo had been added to their recount. Their laughter escalated.

"Mommy's out of control," whispered Naomi to Ruth.

"She and Miss Bortel are silly," said Ruth.

Coughing to catch her breath, Anna took off her glasses to wipe her eyes that were squinting tears.

Ruby doubled up and could hardly speak. "I'm not sure why that seems so funny," said Ruby, taking a gulp of air and relaxing back into her chair. "But it sure felt good to laugh."

Anna regained her composure and appraised Naomi and Ruth's valentines. "You know, Ruby, the girls have each other, but Mark …"

Ruby interrupted her, "What would I do with two Marks?"

That was an image neither could comprehend.

"Well," said Anna. "I guess I'd better go home. Even though it stays light until almost 4:30."

"Not like you can wait until it warms up," stated Ruby matter-of-factly. Anna got out of her chair, reached for her coat, and walked to the door.

Ruth mumbled to Naomi. "She would have to stay here until Easter for it to warm up."

"She could sleep in the playroom," said Naomi without hesitation.

Ruth cupped her hands over Naomi's ear, "On the jumping bed? We could jump on her."

Naomi, surprised by her sister's naughty comment, put her hand over her mouth. The girls giggled.

After Anna left, Ruby felt somewhat guilty. What Anna did not know was that Ruby and Elmer *had* talked about a companion for Mark. Over the past months, they had had conversations such as this:

Elmer: Maybe Mark needs a playmate, and he wouldn't get into so much trouble and be so much work for you.

Ruby: Well, maybe. Naomi and Ruth *are* terrific companions for each other.

Silence.

Ruby: I do not want to get pregnant again. Not again. I am finished.

Silence:

Elmer: (Speaking slowly) Maybe we could adopt a Native baby.

Ruby: (Controlled exasperation on her face and in her voice) You are gone so much, and I don't think I could manage four children on my own. It's not as though Mom, Margie, or other family members are nearby to be physically supportive. I'm the one … (her voice trailed away).

And then a certain unmarried woman in the village was pregnant. Dora Tooyak was not an Athabascan Indian from Tanana. She was an Inupiaq Eskimo from Point Hope, a coastal whaling village near the top of Alaska. She was far from her tribe. The short, round-faced woman had confided to Dr. Gaede, that she already had a two-year-old, and even though she very much wanted to keep this second child, she didn't know how she could support two children. All the same, she didn't want this baby to go to just any home. Her family doctor, Elmer, heard how heartbreaking the decision was to give up her baby. Unlike the other Native women who believed they could not influence the adoption of their child, this woman had the courage to try to influence the decision. She asked if he knew a good Christian home for her baby. He promised he would see what he could do.

Until Dora had approached him, Elmer had dropped the subject with Ruby. And so it had been that after supper one evening when the children were playing, and the house was quiet, but not too quiet, that he thought it a good idea to help Ruby dry dishes. First, he put a hand on her shoulder. "You're really getting the hang of cooking moose," he said. "Those fried minute steaks were nice and tasty. Mmm." She thanked him and handed him an embroidered tea towel for drying the dishes. He paid no attention to the design on the towel: a day of the week and a farm animal. Ruby, not knowing what to expect, asked him about Valentine's activities and décor at the hospital and with the staff.

After the dishes were dried, Elmer finally broached the subject. "Ruby, there is a patient who is having a baby and plans to put it up for adoption."

He cleared his throat, which was a consistent and characteristic trait, and continued. "I was wondering if this might be the baby God has for us."

Without looking at him or saying a word, Ruby took the damp tea towel and hung it over the oven handle to dry, pulled out a kitchen table chair, and sat down. Her fingers twisted a section of the apron on her lap.

At that time, many White folks wanted to adopt Native babies, especially Eskimo babies, because they were characteristically round and plump, thus deemed "cuter" than the Indian babies that were lankier. Given this popularity, two military families in Fairbanks were on the list for Dora's unborn baby.

After a heavy silence, she met his gaze. "Well, tell me more about this woman. And we wouldn't know if it would be a boy or a girl. Does that matter? If Mark has a brother or a sister? I thought we wanted a boy."

Ruby's eyes never left his until they finished a back-and-forth discussion. Then she folded her hands, closed her eyes momentarily, and said, "But, Elmer, the baby is already spoken for."

They agreed on three things: a) it didn't matter if the child was a boy or a girl, b) they would not talk to anyone about the matter, and c) they needed Divine Intervention to make this come about.

The baby was born on February 4, 1958. Her mother named the brown-skinned infant with black hair and chubby cheeks, Pearl Marie. How hard it must have been to know she would say goodbye to the flesh of her flesh, the tiny human she had carried close to her heart for nine months; harder still, not to know who would raise her beloved child. Would she fit in with their family? Would they raise her as their own? Would she have plenty to eat? Education? Would they tell her where she had come from? The tribe in Point Hope?

After the adoption, Ruby revealed, in carbon-copied typed letters to their loved ones, how everything had transpired.

> *"Elmer and I each pondered the idea in our hearts and never brought it to the surface until December. So we discussed it and prayed about it and in January talked to the girls about it. We were considering ½ Eskimo and ½ white baby boy. When the mother of this baby came to Tanana to wait her time of delivery, Elmer got the information that this baby would go out for adoption so we prayed and prayed. The baby was born while Elmer was in Manly Hot Springs on an emergency trip, the nurse delivered her, and it was a girl, so what should we do we prayed and then started from the legal end. Many of the babies are spoken for even before delivery. So we asked God to put something in the way if it was not His will for us to have this baby. The same that we wrote the Welfare office the psychiatrist came here and we consulted him concerning adoption, from all angles. He talked to the mother and checked the baby and said that both showed above average intelligence and he said he would talk to the man in charge at the Welfare office in Fairbanks. When the Welfare found out that we were interested they sent us all the papers and told us to go ahead, but that the procedure was a little different than they ideally handle adoptions."*

The practice of adopting Native babies into White families in the 1950s would change in 1978 when the Indian Child Welfare Act (ICWA) was established. From that time forth, the adoptive placement of an Alaskan Native child would first give preference to a member of the child's extended family; second, to other members of the child's tribe; or third, other Native families. White families could not expect just to sign up and easily adopt.

However, this law was not in place in 1958, and Dora had not chosen to contact a family member or another Native family. And, the Office of Children's Services (OCS) had not been challenged in their decisions of how and to whom Native babies were adopted. At this point, Dora, Elmer, and Ruby were stepping into uncharted territory. When Elmer told Dora that he and his wife were interested in loving and raising her child, she beamed. Tears ran down her cheeks. She felt relieved and so very grateful.

As agreeable as the three were, their desires weren't enough. There was red tape to work through, and more so since this baby was already assigned to one of the two families in waiting. But Elmer knew the system, and so did the psychologist involved in the placement, and they both offered their support. The psychologist wrote a letter to the OCS confirming and encouraging the mother's decision.

Ruby continued her news release:

> "We had quite a time to keep the secret from the nurses as they kept wondering why Elmer did not send the baby on to Fairbanks as all other adoptions and my going in to see the baby did not help the situation. So the Saturday that we signed the papers we decided to make a formal announcement and we asked Rev. Gronnings, and Anna the teacher to have Sunday nite dinner as guests at the hospital dining room. There we ate and just before dessert Elmer told them that it was time to let the cat out of the bag and he pulled a fluffy stuffed kitten out of a bag which had a card on it telling that we had adopted baby Mishal."

No legal action could be taken on the adoption until ten days after the birth. Accordingly, it turned out, and wonderfully so, on February 14,

Valentine's Day, Ruby and Elmer signed the papers and gave Pearl Marie the name of Mishal Rose. Ruby wrote, "*If you check your Bibles you will see the name means Prayer.*" The middle name, Rose, was for the nurse who had delivered her.

The announcement in the hospital dining room put everyone into a happy uproar. The previous mundane chitchat exploded into unrestrained congratulations and glee.

Anna was slightly miffed that she had missed any clues. When she quizzed Ruby about having baby bottles, blankets, and such for this new addition, Ruby admitted she had ordered those things and hidden them carefully—from not only Anna, who frequented their house, but the children as well. "You really know how to keep a secret, don't you, Ruthie," said Anna, squeezing her arm lightly. "And, Markie, you are going to have a sister to play with." She tickled his tummy, and he chortled.

Roy smiled and shook Elmer's hand firmly. "Congratulations, Doc." Elmer couldn't stop grinning. Margie happily hugged Ruby. "Ruby, you don't have to recover from labor and delivery. This should all be fun." Ruby blinked back a few tears and, with an uneasy smile, said, "I hope so. I trust God it will be so. As soon as she was born, I visited her in the hospital and tried to imagine that she would be in our family." Her fingers fidgeted with her skirt. "I'm most concerned about how Mark will respond. He is so used to much of my attention…" Her voice faded. Margie wrapped her arm around Ruby's shoulder. Ever the optimistic, she said, "Give it time. It will all work out."

Ruth sneaked behind her father's back, got hold of the paper sack, pulled out *her* white stuffed cat, stuck her nose in the white fur, and then cuddled it under her arm. Naomi, who knew about the announcement, had been so edgy with anticipation during the meal, she had nearly driven her mother crazy by sliding on and off the metal folding chair at the table. Now she jumped out of her seat and hopped up and down.

The nurses were elated, especially Rose Schuking, who had delivered the baby. "I had no idea this was to be the doctor's baby!" said the quiet, obviously capable woman. "I was concerned when the mother went into labor, and Dr. Gaede was out of the village, but everything went smoothly." Like most of the nurses, she was in her twenties and from the States. Like them, she had had little or no idea what adventures would come her way when she had signed up with Public Health.

Not only was everyone happy for the doctor and his wife, equally uplifting was the fresh news that filled their minds and conversations with something other than worn-out talk and stale topics.

Word about the doctor's family adopting the baby traveled around the village as fast as if someone had struck gold. Within short notice, the village chief, Alfred Grant, arrived at the Gaede's duplex. The thin Athabascan Indian with straight black hair and a sparse mustache walked forthwith into the kitchen where the family was eating Sunday dinner. Elmer paused with fork midair. Ruth dropped the bread she had been buttering. Mark stopped jabbering. "Dr. Gaede," the chief said. "This is good you adopt that baby." He pointed to Mishal, who was asleep on Ruby's lap. That was pretty much it. Elmer stood up, held out his hand, and thanked him. Ruby invited him to join them for the meal. The chief smiled, nodded his head several times, and backed out of the kitchen.

"That was so nice of him," said Ruby.

"Yes, it means a lot to have that acceptance and approval by the Natives, and especially the chief," replied Elmer. "Maybe it's because we somewhat got acquainted when I took him caribou hunting. Well, I probably scared him half to death when the airplane ski came loose and hung straight down, and we expected to make a crash landing."

Ruby glanced back down at her plate. She thought to herself, "That was an odd way to build a relationship."

Naomi filled in the awkward pause, "I guess he likes us anyway."

Ruth threw her arms into the air and added her two cents' worth: "He thinks we are going to be a good family for baby Mishal." A big smile covered her face. "And we are!" When she realized how boldly she had spoken, she crossed her arms in front of her and ducked her head.

Mark beat his spoon on the table and tried to reach the mashed potatoes.

Ruby wondered what she had gotten herself into.

Anna couldn't miss an opportunity to throw a party, and before the cat-out-of-the-bag evening had ended, she had pulled together like-minded nurses to plan a baby shower. The planners and attenders extended to the Women's Sewing Club members. The hospital chef pored through cookbooks for a suitable baby shower cake. Anna signed up to make individual Jell-O molds. She also airmailed her mother asking for baby shower party games.

Thirty-five women gathered for the celebration in semi-dress-up attire: solid-colored, narrow-skirted jumpers with white, puffy-sleeved cotton blouses; dark wool slacks with waist-length, button-down plaid sweaters; and slacks topped with shirts that had fancy ties or wrapped collars. Pearl necklaces and bracelets showed up as well. Once again, this garb was as out of place as parka and mukluks on a Hawaiian island. In truth, getting dressed up was half the fun.

Naomi and Ruth were the only children included. Most of the time, they stayed out of the way, although they snooped around the refreshment table. They cheered for both teams in the diaper-the-baby relay and played with their bubblegum-pink and sunshine-yellow plastic pop beads. The beads had a knob on one side and a hole on the other. The beads "popped" when the connecting knob was pushed into or pulled out of the opening. Ruby only allowed the girls to play with these when Mark was not around. Of course, he would have swallowed a bead, put it up his nose, stuck it in his ear, or tossed it in the toilet. There was no need to encourage that risk, even if the hospital was right next door.

That was not her worry now. She was caught up in the moment with the hospital dining room buzzing with compliments on impressive attire, game competition between teams and individuals, and the expressed enjoyment of the food and pink punch.

Women had been hard-pressed to find baby gifts on short notice. Miraculously they showed up with an astonishing array of baby items: a pink- and-yellow crocheted shawl, two baby blankets, a diaper bag, seven dresses, three sleeping bag sleepers, four soft knit nighties, one dozen flannel diapers, lacy rubber pants, beaded moose-skin slippers made by one of the Native women, bibbed slacks with a white blouse and two sweaters, and $3 in a nice envelope. The merriment invaded the oppressive and intimidating world of ice and darkness. Every woman who had participated left with the energy and glow of a bonfire.

As if that wasn't enough, Ruby received another mental health booster to pull her toward the hope of spring. Bethany Baptist, the church that the Gaedes had attended in Anchorage, wanted to join in with the joy. Unbeknownst to Ruby, the women's group brought unwrapped baby gifts to their monthly meeting, showed them to one another, and then packed them into a box. They didn't stop there. They served traditional baby shower fare of cake, nuts in tiny paper cups, and punch, along with fancy pastel paper plates and napkins. A napkin and a nut-cup, to be pressed into Mishal's baby book, were tucked among the gifts.

When the unexpected box arrived and was opened, Ruby's face beamed with pleasure. The girls repeatedly squealed at the assortment of frilly dresses, snuggly sweaters, more fancy plastic diaper-pants to go over the cloth diapers, diaper pins with Disney Land characters on the heads, and even little black patent leather shoes with teeny straps. Baby Mishal would be dressed for a month of Sundays in the cutest dresses of nylon and lace that anyone had ever seen, and especially so in the middle of Alaska.

Whether the name of Pearl Marie or Mishal Rose, gems or flowers, Ruby was the mother to a precious sweetheart of a child who became hers on Valentine's Day.

Mishal's Baby Dedication at the Arctic Missions Chapel in Tanana.

VALENTINE'S DAY AND A LITTLE SWEETHEART

Mukluk Telegraph

THE MUKLUK TELEGRAPH

July 1958
Volume II, Number 2
Reporter for Anchorage Native Services Hospital
(Dolorous Byrnes):

Nurses Needed

You are all probably aware of the great need for Registered Nurses in all of our hospitals. Your help in recruiting would be greatly appreciated. Write to all your friends who are Registered Nurses and ask them to write to the Area Office, Box 7-741, Anchorage, Alaska, Attention: Nurse Officer, and we will be glad to send them all the necessary information concerning nursing in Alaska. Nurses hired in the States will have their transportation paid from their place of residence to Alaska at Government expense.

CHAPTER 19

IGLOOS AND POLAR BEARS

Tanana and Point Hope, 1958

MARK NO LONGER HELD CENTER STAGE. Mishal claimed the spotlight. Now Mark had competition for Ruby's everyday time and, so to speak, "media" time via Ruby's reports to her and Elmer's families.

> "Mark is excepting her nicely and I let him help me bath her! He puts the oil on her head and back and he is very gentle with her which looks strange for him as boisterous as he is … I am not losing any more sleep than before we had her and it is so good to have my normal strength as with the others the recuperating (after birth) was such a struggle … Elmer calls her **his** baby.
>
> She is a dream baby, she eats at 10:30 in the eve, cries for 10 minutes and then sleeps til 6 or 7 in the morn, I just cannot believe it. I am

making her a scrap book or baby book and I went to the lady who did my parka and asked her for some caribou skin to use for the outer cover and sometime when we have native in the hospital that sews beads I will have her sew the name and Tanana on the cover.

I never had a book for Mark so I am making his cover with the bark of a Birch tree and the ties will be caribou skin. Mark is such a good boy he sleeps good at nights and plays well as long as the girls are not at home, when they are here he wants to be where they are and they don't want him all the time."

That wasn't all this special baby was about to receive. "Grandma" Elia[67] demonstrated her acceptance of Ruby and Elmer as parents of a Native baby by including Mishal in the circle of babies she bequeathed her trademark "Grandma Elia slippers." The slippers were made from moose skin, with straps extending from the back of the foot around the ankle and attached with a hook-and-eye fastener. Typical of the village beadwork, on the top of the slipper was a wild rose; in this instance, a pink rose with a yellow center and green leaves. Tiny goldish-copper beads were stitched around the opening of the slipper and along the strap. No hole in the bead could be perceived, and they appeared more like tiny gold nuggets. Indeed, Mishal was an adored baby by everyone in the village.

It was the first of March. Mishal was a month old. If only momentarily, temperatures rose to 37°, and Ruby declared it a heat wave. People were sweating in their parkas. Fourteen hours of sunlight added to the glimpses of spring. "Pussy willows will burst out soon," announced Margie. The soft little gray knobs had a musky scent of their own and were regarded with cheer as much as smiling yellow daffodils in the States. Certainly, temperatures could still plunge, and snowstorms roll in, but essentially, Ruby had made it through her first Interior Alaska winter with her family fed and clothed and her mental health intact.

During this time, Elmer had somehow gotten it into his head that he needed to shoot a polar bear. He became obsessed with this idea and mentioned it to everyone around him. His eyes gleamed when Leonard Lane said, "Dr. Gaede. I have gone polar bear hunting many times. I will be your guide."

Leonard, an unusually tall Inupiaq Eskimo with a broad face, wide nose, heavy eyebrows, and a faint mustache, worked for Elmer at the hospital in the maintenance department. He had grown up living a traditional Native lifestyle of hunting and fishing. He could read the weather, sky, and ice. Coincidentally, he was from Point Hope, the same village and tribe of Dora's, Mishal's birth mother.

Leonard was much bulkier than Elmer. It would be an extremely tight fit for him in the cocoon of Elmer's tiny J-3. On the other hand, the benefit of his size was sheer muscle strength. If Elmer needed to be dragged or carried to safety, Leonard could bully his way through whatever obstacle prevailed.

Of course, Elmer was optimistic that nothing like that would happen, even though he was taking his plane farther north than he had ever been and across more remote country. If they were to go down due to weather or mechanical problems, the chances of being rescued were as likely as finding a needle in a haystack. Elmer knew about haystacks; he was a farm kid. He knew about needles, which he used to sew up people. Nevertheless, he trusted his mosquito-sized aircraft, and he was depending on the large Eskimo to be his guide. With all that bright hope, he had never been to Point Hope.

Point Hope, a village on the top of Alaska, barely hangs onto a finger of coastal land along the Chuckchi Sea. It is reportedly one of the oldest continuously occupied areas in North America. The low-lying whaling village has been washed out repeatedly, and storms still taunt it unremittingly. If Elmer desired "more of Alaska's Frontier," he was about to get it.

In preparation, and per Leonard's suggestion, Elmer and Leonard set a time to cut blocks of snow from the crusty, wind-whipped snow packed against the riverbank. Teaching Elmer how to build an igloo was Leonard's goal. The Inupiaq Eskimos used the word igloo or *uglu* to describe their subterranean dwellings made of driftwood, sod, or whalebone, which, in wintertime and covered with snow, truly looked like stereotypical igloos. Actual domed ice structures were constructed only for temporary or emergency use. The polar bear hunt Elmer and Leonard anticipated could very well demand this knowledge and readiness.

On the igloo-building day, the snow glistened with the desire to melt; yet the river remained solidly frozen. The weather was comfortable enough that Leonard's heavy army-green parka was not zipped all the way to the top, although his hood remained over his short black hair. No mukluks today. He had on green leather boots. Elmer wore a similar parka and also had black hair; however, that is where the resemblance stopped.

Ruby and the three oldest children walked down the draw in front of the hospital to watch the construction. Mishal was asleep in her crib, and Ruby felt comfortable leaving her alone. She could quickly go back to check on her or send one of the girls.

Anything having to do with the river, riverbank, Elmer's plane tied on the river shoreline, making homemade ice cream along the river, throwing rocks into the river, or clambering around on the ice upheavals on the frozen river drew Mark like a magnet. Now he ran, stumbled, fell, picked himself up, and ran some more until he saw Elmer and Leonard. "Daddy, Daddy!" he called.

Naomi and Ruth followed with their mother. The twosome looked like Bobbsey twins. "Ruth, now we will see how real Eskimos live," Naomi informed Ruth. Ruth believed her. Once at the igloo construction site, they stood in expectation.

"It's kinda warm to make snow blocks," said Leonard. He pressed his hand against the riverbank snow. "They will melt."

"Well … let's try anyway," insisted Elmer. "Just in case."

Leonard agreed reluctantly. "Yes, it will not be this warm where we are going. We could make an igloo there if we need to."

"Winter Survival" class started. Elmer studied Leonard's use of a shovel to carve the blocks. Leonard cut and placed several blocks. "Now you try, Doc," he said. Elmer awkwardly dug the shovel into the snowbank. He would have been more comfortable shoveling manure out of a barn.

Leonard Lane constructing the igloo.

The base of the igloo was an approximately six-foot circle with rectangle snow blocks. The next row was made of square blocks that were tilted slightly toward the center. As the rows progressed, the blocks became smaller and more off-center. The finished height was not quite six feet, with a doorway only large enough for one man to squirm inside on his belly. Ruby had no idea how the two hunters would both fit inside if need be. Most certainly, they would have to curl up. Were they expecting close contact and body heat to save them?

Naomi and Ruth did not tell their mother they anticipated using the igloo as a playhouse once the experiment was over. Ruby, however, heard them chattering excitedly, and not too discreetly, and put two-and-two together. She let them dream. In reality, there was no way she would allow that, no matter if the ice was frozen solid at this time of the year. She might have had eyes in the back of her head, as mothers tend to have, but not over the riverbank.

Preparation for the hunt had already been underway when Mishal joined the Gaede family. It was then that Leonard had started hanging out at the house, eating cookies, drinking coffee, teasing the girls, and poring over aviation charts with Elmer. Conversations became more intense as the deadline for departure approached. "I need to figure out a better way to keep the fuel oil warm if we are forced down," said Elmer, deep in thought. They brainstormed options and what was available. Weight was a critical factor, and they had to make decisions about food, clothing, and tools for repairs. Unquestionably, they would need the small Coleman stove, no matter what. It could warm oil or heat water for tea.

Ruby walked in and out of the kitchen and listened to parts of the conversation. "How do you find a white bear on white ice?" she asked, carrying Mishal in one arm and shaking a bottle of Foremost powdered milk formula with the other.

Leonard swung around in his chair with Mark on one knee, "You can see their shadow, and they really aren't white. They are yellow against the snow."

Ruby pondered that for a while.

"Let's look over our gear one more time," said Elmer. He was a man of lists and careful planning. Conversely, this life in Alaska demanded that people take chances and improvise. Elmer was good at improvising, and he did his share of flying by the seat of his pants. The more he would live in Alaska, the more chances he would take. He would think of them as "calculated" chances.

The men got up, Leonard thanked Ruby for the cookies, and Mark tailed the hunters to the hunting closet. While they spread gear on the bed in the playroom, Mark ran around with his Ping-Pong ball gun and shot at the concrete walls. The balls ricocheted here and there. Mark laughed loudly.

On Saturday, March 8, the hunters soared off into the crystal clear dawn. A 20–30 mph tailwind pushed them down the wellmarked course of the Yukon River. The start of the venture would be familiar to Elmer.

It had been too early and cold for Ruby to bundle up four children and watch the excited hunters take off, although Mark had awakened just before Elmer left the house. "Come back, Daddy," he had said mournfully. Ruby heard the plane take off and said a prayer for the hunters' safety.

People asked Ruby how she felt about her husband's flying. She always responded, "I just have to trust God." She tried. All the same, her body did not care what she told it. Within the day, her stomach was in a knot, and she had lost her appetite. She expected, with dread, that soon she would have a bladder infection. For some reason, this occurred every time Elmer left the village for several days of medical trips.

Why should Ruby have been anxious? This was not his first hunt. He had taken that same airplane to hunt moose, black bear, and a grizzly. Once again, he had a buddy. He had always returned. He had experience. That, actually, was the reason she was anxious. He had a history of close calls.

Ruby and Elmer had arrived in Anchorage in the summer of 1955. By the summer of 1956, Elmer had achieved his floatplane rating on the colorful Piper J-3; this followed with wintertime flying on skis. Ruby did not care that his instructor passed him, and he had received his pilot's license. She would have preferred seeing him on a tractor seat in a flat Kansas wheat field than in the Alaska skies, flying over water and into mountains. My goodness! It was only a two-seater and only had a 75 hp engine. It was tiny, so very tiny in the huge Alaska wilderness. And why did he need to hunt moose and bear? Shooting those pesky jackrabbits in Kansas made sense. Risking one's life as he did here did not.

First, there had been Elmer's inaugural moose hunt. In November. In freezing winter weather. At least he had taken his buddy, Paul Carlson, not that he was a pilot who could help out. The two flew across Cook Inlet to the Kenai Peninsula, spotted a bull moose and landed, or, more accurately, skied across an icy lake. Yet, when the airplane skis touched down on the glare-ice lake, it did not stop. It shot across the lake until it bounced sharply into the snowpacked edge on the other side.

Of course, she should have been thrilled they were okay, but still, why did they have to take the chance? That was not all. There was more and more. Getting snowed in and not being able to return home. No radio in his airplane to call for help. The Air Force rescue planes finally spotted him, and the story ended happily. Happily, that Elmer and Paul returned safely. Happily, because Elmer had gotten his moose. Ruby's stomach was not happy—even if the moose meat tasted delicious.

Then there had been the grizzly bear hunt. Well, she did not want to think about the overloaded plane and what transpired between the hunt and the return home. That meat did not even taste good. It reminded her of greasy, gristly bad pork. No, those were her husband's adventures and the tales he recounted proudly and with much enthusiasm to their dinner guests, while she put out plates of lemon meringue pie—and smiled sweetly.

After Elmer left, Ruby was not entirely alone with her four children. She assured her mother, "*Anna Bortel has been staying with us most of the time Elmer has been away and is very jolly and an inspiration to all of us.*"

Anna had come over midmorning with a small bag. "What is in there?" Naomi asked presumptuously. Ruby shushed her daughter.

"Well, my pajamas, robe, slippers, toothbrush…" Anna said. Makeup was not important to her. She had simple needs and adjusted well to Alaska's camping out-like living environment. She leaned down and opened the contents. "… and books and cranberry nut bread and…" Anna pulled out the items of interest.

Mark stuck one short leg down over the couch and then the other and ran toward the action. He had been busy examining Mishal, who Ruby had rolled in a flannel blanket and brought into the living room. The baby had been half-asleep, her almond brown eyes opening and closing lazily. Mark had poked her gently in the mouth. She half-heartedly sucked on his finger. He snickered. Ruth hovered nearby and guarded Mishal from Mark's prodding, although she, too, found Mishal's infant reflexes entertaining.

Ruby was grateful for Anna's offer to stay with her. The children got along well with Anna, and she shouldered part of Ruby's parenting load. Anna rocked Mishal when she cried and kept Mark out of the kitchen while Ruby was making supper. Naomi and Ruth brought out Candy Land, a new board game designed as entertainment for children with polio and had recently come out for public purchase. During the school days,

Anna and the girls were gone, but it was the evenings when tasks piled together and multiplied—baths, bedtime snacks, bedtime stories, and so on—when she appreciated another adult's presence.

Mark refused to accept his daddy's absence, and for as much as Anna sweet-talked him, he would not bring her a storybook or look at any book she had brought with her. "Daddy! Daddy!" he sobbed. And then he threw himself on the floor and thrashed his legs and arms in all directions. Anna relinquished him to Ruby, who, with much struggle, convinced him to cuddle up to her and read one book. Ruby's soft voice settled the little boy, who, with a final deep inhale and exhale, let go of his battle, and slumped against her, with eyes closed.

After the girls said their prayers and were snuggled into bed, Ruby and Anna could relax.

"I don't know how Naomi and Ruth can sleep comfortably," remarked Anna. "They lie in the middle of their beds absolutely straight with their dolls and stuffed animals beside them on their narrow beds."

"At least they shouldn't get cold," said Ruby.

Anna started grading papers with her sharp red pencil, and Ruby puttered about picking up toys from the living room and snack bowls from the kitchen table.

Later, when they were warmed from leisurely soaks in the bathtub and Ruby was in her pretty, soft flannel nightgown with lace around the gathered bib and sleeve edges, and Anna in her unadorned flannel pajamas, Ruby began talking. The lights were out in the bedroom, but Ruby's mind was alive and roaming. Typically, when Elmer was away from the village and Anna spent the night, the two women chatted and giggled like teenagers. That was not the case this time. Although Anna was quite a talker and storyteller, she had the sense to listen.

The somewhat stream of consciousness conversation started with how financially strapped Ruby and Elmer had been after they were married, had children, and were in school. Gas was cheap enough that they could afford to drive back to the Peabody farm. Ruby's parents, Sol and Bertha, shared what they had of fryer chickens, eggs, canned fruit, and any produce. "I don't know what we would have done without my parents," said Ruby appreciatively. "We were so poor." This led to reoccurring self-deprecation. "I feel so inferior to Elmer. I didn't even finish high school, and he is a doctor."

"Come now, Ruby," encouraged Anna. "Look at all the things you can do." Anna listed as many as she could come up with, cooking, baking cream puffs, and deep-frying maple rolls—besides the basic breads and cookies, creating birthday cakes without any recipe, organizing get-togethers, singing duets with Elmer. "It's not all about education. You are a good wife and mother too."

Truly, in that day and age, it was not about education. For a woman, it was about being a good wife and mother.

Ruby did not reply. Her eyes were open, and she seemed to search for an answer somewhere in the black corners of the room. "Elmer spends so much money on that airplane, not just the purchase and the lessons, but gasoline and repairs. He would say he uses the plane to get us meat, but sometimes he flies just to fly." She paused for a moment. "It does not seem right. Why shouldn't I have some equal money to spend as I want?"

Anna did not ask what Ruby would spend money on if she had it, nor did Ruby volunteer that information. There really wasn't anything to purchase in the village. Anna wondered what she would order from the catalog.

Before drifting off to sleep, Ruby murmured, "I just wish he would not have gone into medicine but stayed on the farm."

Elmer had left on Saturday. Now it was Wednesday. Ruby kneaded bread dough and tried to figure out when she should worry seriously. She watched the weather but had no idea what it was like where he was, way up north, along the forsaken coastline. Had all gone well, and they were cutting up meat with Leonard's relatives in Point Hope? Had Leonard wanted to stay longer to visit with his family? Or, had they gotten caught on an ice floe moving out to sea? Had they fallen through a split in the ice? Were they in a snow-block igloo?

The bread was more than adequately kneaded by the time she shaped it into loaves and roughly put it into pans. She sighed loudly, dropped her hands to her side, and then wiped her fingers on her apron.

The girls felt their mother's tension and stayed out from underfoot. When Mishal cried, they rushed to her crib and tried to comfort her. "Mommy, I'll give her a bottle," offered Ruth. For all Mark's wiggles, he stood still on the couch, looking out the window and searching the sky for his daddy's airplane. "Daddy land," he whined. He did this repeatedly.

With false cheerfulness, Ruby told the children, "Daddy will be home any day. He is probably safe at a missionary or schoolteacher's house. God will take care of him."

She said these things to convince them, even if it didn't convince her. The gloomy images in her mind spilled over like lava from a volcano: a crashed airplane, her husband frozen to death, or eaten by a bear. Terrible things. Outcomes that left her husbandless and with four children. Once again, she compared Alaska to Kansas. If he were flying in Kansas and made an emergency landing, it would be in a pasture, wheat field, cornfield, or even a road. A farmer would see him and come out with his tractor and pull the plane to safety. Or, if it was in a Kansas whiteout, he could find a fence and follow it to a house or barn.

The ruminations tired her.

Airplanes came and went over Tanana and usually landed on the airstrip that she could see behind the house. She knew the specific drone and buzz of Elmer's plane and listened closely. Maybe she had missed it. Maybe she had been running bath water for Mark or Mishal. Maybe her husband would come walking through the door.

Finally, at Friday noon, six days after the hunters had departed, she heard the buzz of the J-3. "Mark, Daddy is going to land," she shouted. The tyke ran for his parka. "Go to Daddy!"

Yes, they had had trouble. They had been caught in a whiteout and been forced down. They had not built an igloo, but they had slept in the J-3, not exactly with first-class leg space, while waiting out the storm. Elmer thought best not to tell her every little detail all at once; instead, he told her that he had met Mishal's grandmother, Beatrice Tooyak, a large woman in a dark calico *kuspuk* worn over her fur parka. No, he had not revealed to Beatrice that her grandchild was now in the Gaede family. Confidentiality took precedence.

As always, he brought back souvenirs. Once the bearskin and hunting gear were unloaded, and Elmer had taken a bath and changed clothes, and the girls were home from school; he carefully unwrapped items and told the story of each. He had two pairs of sun or snow glasses to protect eyes from snow blindness. These were made from polished caribou hooves and had narrow slits in the middle from which to see out. A strip of caribou skin fastened the glasses around the person's head. Mark ran out of the room when Elmer pulled out a mask made from whalebone. The surface was rough, nearly black, and had white eyes. Ruby was most interested in a watchband made from squares of ivory and attached to one another with white elastic.

Ruby's report to her family didn't convey any of the emotions she had experienced. Her letter was back to normal and about the unusual and wonderful sights in Alaska.

> *"I wish you could have seen the northern lights last nite, the most glorious sight to behold. They were of red rays which is rare and occurs only once in several years. The rays began at the horizon of the North, South, East and West, and tapering to a point at the middle of the sky just center right above us. It is magnificent and one can not help but praise the Lord of creation."*

In her 1958 Christmas letter, her March entry was also without drama. She left it to Elmer to turn the frightening, to her, polar bear hunt into a full-blown book chapter, years later, in *Alaska Bush Pilot Doctor*. A book that was true to facts, non-fiction, but would read like fiction.

CHRISTMAS LETTER 1958

"March 8 Elmer left for a Polar Bear Hunt at Point Hope. He took an employee from our hospital who is a native Eskimo from Point Hope. Elmer used our J-3 plane on skis for the hunt along the Arctic. They flew over the ice and some water up to the International Date Line. The trophy was a beautiful 8 1/3 foot polar bear. Upon their return they got caught in two blizzards that forced them down for two nights."

DEPARTMENT OF HEALTH, EDUCATION, AND WELFARE

Wage and Salary Schedules -
Prevailing Rate System Jobs
April 1, 1958

Job Title	Hourly Rate
Carpenter	$4.30
Carpenter-trainee (Native)	3.33
Churn Drill Operator	4.25
Electrician	4.80
Forman Carpenter	4.65
Foreman Laborer	3.25
Foreman, Mixed Gang	5.00
Laborer	2.90
Laborer Leadman	3.00
Lineman	4.80
Locksmith	4.12
Mechanic, Heavy Duty	4.39
Operator, General	4.31
Painter	3.83
Plumber-Steamfitter	4.75
Truck Driver (Up to 10 T)	3.86

CHAPTER 20

CARING FOR ONE ANOTHER

Tanana, Ruby, Kokrines, Birches 1958

WHEN ELMER, RUBY, AND MARK left the house and walked to the J-3, tied down on the frozen river shoreline, the clock hands indicated 8:00 a.m. This was Ruby's first trip to visit a missionary family downriver. The only way to do that at this time of the year was to fly unless she had wanted to go by dogsled, which was possible but not desirable—or fast.

On this mid-March morning, the snow, which turned to slushy mud during the day, was still frozen from the nighttime temperatures. The river would remain solid for quite some time yet. It was difficult to know what to wear for footgear; mukluks would get wet from the melting snow, but they didn't slip like a rubber-soled boot on the re-frozen icy surface. Ruby decided on mukluks, and Elmer wore rubber boots.

A hospital maintenance man kept Elmer's airplane parking area cleared, as well as the makeshift runway on the river itself. Throughout the winter, Ruby and the children had knelt on the couch in the living room and stared over its back when the enormous CAT rumbled out onto the ice. "Is the ice strong enough?" The girls always asked. No one else seemed concerned, and never did the CAT break through or exhibit any signs of danger.

Ruby started to climb into the backseat of the J-3. Her short stature required extra effort, and it did not help that she had dressed particularly warmly beneath her squirrel fur parka. She peered inside the cabin and pulled the seatbelts to the side of the seat. As she placed her right foot on the high step and stretched upward for the cross member above the front seat, Mark grabbed her remaining leg. She had just given a bounce to achieve her grasp and was thrown off balance. "Mush, mommy," he said impatiently. The Natives told their dogs and children to mush, meaning "hurry along," and Mark had added that word to his small vocabulary. Elmer restrained the pouting toddler while Ruby lifted her left leg, dragged it above the fourteen-inch threshold and behind her, and plopped onto the seat.

Mark became frantic about getting to go along and was about to flail against the fuselage when Elmer lifted him onto Ruby's lap. The little guy clapped his mittens and waved his head to and fro in excitement. His ruddy cheeks pressed against the sides of his red parka hood. Ruby dodged his head and held onto her glasses. Elmer handed her a heavy blanket to tuck around herself and Mark and then climbed into the front seat. Ruby wondered how Leonard had ever fit, and even spent two nights, in the plane. He and Elmer must have been desperate.

Anna had volunteered to stay with the girls and actually seemed to look forward to it. "We're going to make a cake, and do puzzles, go to the chapel, love and cuddle Mishal, and see how many cute dresses we can put on her. Are you sure you want to take Markie with you?" she said breathlessly.

"Anna, I know you think Mark is so cute," said Ruby, touching Anna's forearm gently. "But, I will not leave him with you. He sneaks the girls' crayons and colors on the walls. He tries to sneak the girls' cats into his bed at night too. When they scratch him, he yells at them to 'mush along.' They are supposed to stay in the basement at night."

"Okay, okay." Anna had accepted that the three girls would be plenty to take charge of.

Ruby had added, "Besides, you can imagine the fit he would throw if he saw both Elmer and me leaving in the plane."

That was true. Mark frequently begged, sobbed, and hurled himself on the ground when he saw Elmer making preparations to go flying without him.

Shortly after takeoff, the stringy, meringue-like clouds were true to their nature, and the air was turbulent. That, plus the faint smell of gasoline on the chamois cloth Elmer carried in the area behind the passenger seat, caused Ruby's stomach to turn slightly. She buried her nose in Mark's hair until he bounced around excessively; then, she pulled up her green wool muffler around her face to weaken the stomach-churning odor. As annoying as Mark's enthusiasm was, he functioned as a body-warmer, and she wrapped her arms around him, not unlike a straightjacket. Elmer was warm in the front seat. Unfortunately, the airplane's heater could not force much warmth to the backseat. The cold air outside gave no hint of springtime, and the plexiglass windows were frosty.

The destination was to the village of Ruby, one hundred miles downriver, where Arctic Missions' missionaries, Russ and Freda Arnold, lived. Elmer had met them several times on medical trips.

Originally, Koyukon Athabascans, who came and went with the seasonal migrations of fish and wild game, had inhabited the village. Then, as the result of a gold rush in 1911, an actual village, named Ruby, for the red rock on the riverbank, was established. Given its function as a supply post, the population jumped to several thousand. As in many places in Alaska, the Gold Rush was short lived, and by 1918, the town was in decline. A fire in 1929 destroyed many of the businesses and a flood in 1931 took out what was left of buildings on the riverfront. After World War II, the village was practically a ghost town until Natives from the village of Kokrines, approximately thirty miles upriver, moved in to take advantage of the abandoned houses.

When Elmer had given his wife the history of the village, she had brushed him off. She was more interested in what it was like currently and what that meant in terms of support and services for the Arnolds, especially Freda.

In 1958, the village of Ruby was smaller than Tanana, with only 120 people compared to Tanana's 300. Of that number, about twenty were White folks, including the Arnolds, a teacher couple, and several old sourdoughs[68] who had been miners and trappers. There was a post office, a grocery store, and a roadhouse—operated by Mamie Olsen. The Arnolds held church services in their home, and there was a Catholic church as well. This compilation was rich in comparison to the village of Kokrines, where Elmer and Ruby would stop on their way home.

Whenever a plane landed in a village, people came out to see who had arrived, inquire as to news they might have, and check on passengers, mail, airfreight, or whatever. In this case, they knew Dr. Gaede from previous medical field trips, and they unreservedly asked him questions about friends and relatives upriver. After satisfying their curiosity, Ruby and Mark climbed into a pickup with a driver, and Elmer hopped onto the tailgate with two other men.

The Arnolds lived in a small one-bedroom frame house. There was an outhouse a distance away and a fenced area with clues as to a summer vegetable garden. Husky dogs curled contentedly on top of their houses. Their only greeting was a yawn or shifting position.

Russ was tall, dark-haired, and fit, most likely from chopping wood, hauling water, managing a dog team, and dressing out eight-hundred-pound moose. His eyes twinkled with the love of life and with what he was doing with his life. Freda's soft brown hair curled over her high forehead, and she had an embracing smile.

The Arnolds cordially invited the Gaedes inside, where a wood-burning barrel stove took the chill out of the compact living room. Four little faces appeared from a back room.

"We always have Native children running in and out of our house," said Freda, motioning the children to welcome Mark. "My children think the more, the merrier."

Russ introduced the towheads: Darris, age six; Sondra, four; Barry, three; and Lynda, one-and-a-half.

Ruby made a mental note of their sizes and ages for future hand-me-downs of clothes or toys. Mark was slow to warm up and fidgeted on Ruby's lap until the children's toys and laughter lured him to the bedroom. Ruby listened for any squabbles; hearing none, she settled back on a couch to learn about the Arnolds' life and ministry along the Yukon.

True to her nature and her concern for others, especially mothers and wives, Ruby wanted to know about Freda's conveniences for daily living. The Arnolds had no running water. However, they had electricity from a light plant operated by Jack Koski, who sold the power he generated. An outhouse took care of bathroom needs, and water was packed (hauled) from a spring behind the village in five-gallon Blazo gas cans. Freda showed Ruby the fifty-gallon oil drum that sat at the end of the kitchen and collected their water supply.

"In winter, when there is snow, we use our dogsled, and we can load six cans of water," said Freda. "Later in the year, we use the jeep for transportation."[69]

After a while, and with the conversation still flowing, Ruby and Freda fixed a simple supper. Ruby swallowed in anticipation when she watched Freda pull out smoked salmon strips. That was a delicacy Ruby had taken to when Native friends first offered it to her. Freda set out Pilot Bread crackers[70] and cheese.

"That's my favorite combination," she remarked.

The teapot whistled, and Freda called in the children and men.

The supper table was a hubbub of children laughing and talking, and the adults trying to carry on a conversation. Freda refilled water glasses and teacups and replenished crackers. Ruby thought of the effort it required to provide drinking water and thought twice before accepting a refill.

To corral children for bedtime took some doing. The Arnold children were tucked into the one bedroom, and the adults, and Mark, slept on the two sofas in the living room, which pulled out into hide-a-beds. Mark giggled and wiggled at the good luck of a slumber party with his parents.

The details Ruby wrote about this trip were sandwiched between real-time activities.

> "Stayed over night, brought items, such as cinnamon rolls, sweaters the girls had outgrown, a book. ... On our way back we stopped at Kokrine and visited the Arctic missionaries (Larry and Maxine Scripter), Elmer found them, especially her down in spirits and in need of medical care so she will come in here (Tanana) for a check up."

CARING FOR ONE ANOTHER

This first trip added even more incentive for Ruby to pursue an ongoing connection with missionary wives and to encourage them in their daily and spiritual lives. She reflected how she, Anna, and Margie stuck together for their mental health. How comforting it was to be able to talk to someone who had some concept of what "back home" was and who during holidays shared similar traditions and recipes.

Within a few weeks, Ruby continued her missionary story:

"Elmer went out on a field trip last Wed. noon, he went to Kaltag, Koyukuk, Nulato, and Kokrines. At Kokrines he picked up a missionary wife and brought her here for a rest and medical check, she is 3 mths preg. And the plane ride was rough as it was windy. Kokrines was 2 hs. flying with a head wind. You can't imagine how poor Mrs. Scripture (Scripter - missionary wife) looked and felt. She has a bad case of cabin fever. It is hard for her to live the extremely primitive life and longs for intellectual stimulation ... only 35 other people, mail delivered only every two weeks. Boy – 11, Girl – 6, Girl – 2 ...We had her stay here, of course, and she talked constantly and I enjoyed it as she gave us some real insight into her life."

Ruby wished the entire Scripter family could get out of the Bush for a short while, and her attitude toward what she perceived as Elmer's airplane fixation started to change. She reframed the flying object as a means to provide care and service to the missionaries.

"We have previously felt the urge and after talking to Mrs. Scripture we see the need for visitation to the missionaries here in Alaska and to fly them out from their village to some other place for refreshment. So we are wondering if the Lord would have us get a 4-seater in order

for Elmer to use it in this manner. It would also give us a chance as a family to fly and visit more."

Truthfully, the missionaries' hardships were not that much different from that of the Natives, and it was not as though the Natives were untouched by the winter stress and work. Life was just plain tough. Ruby observed how Roy and the other men packed water from the river for drinking, bathing, and other uses. In the winter, they kept a deep hole cleared in the river ice, pulled up water with a bucket, and carried water up to their houses in two five-gallon Blazo gas cans, attached with wire to a wooden yoke across their shoulders. Of course, the water had to be boiled for purification and warmth for bathing, doing laundry, and washing dishes. Talking a hot shower on a winter morning of 40° below zero did not happen.

Margie had told Ruby with a chuckle, "We arrived in Tanana over two years ago, January of 1955. The reality of 50° below zero welcomed us! It was hard to have a two-month-old son and no indoor plumbing."

Ruby was speechless at both the facts and the nonchalance in Margie's voice.

Now Margie had two children. She was still washing diapers—without running water— and keeping little kids clean. Decades later, some villages would have a central washhouse with laundry services and showers, yet at this point, except for the CAA and medical compound, everyone in Tanana struggled together. Even under those circumstances, Ruby had a hard time imagining Margie being depressed. The small woman had a large capacity for finding the humor in a situation as well as focusing on other people, whose needs she perceived as greater than hers.

When Ruby's contemplations spilled over to Anna, the schoolteacher replied, "I thought the Natives would be used to it, and that, perhaps, we would get used to it too, but not after talking to some of the mothers of my students. That's just the way it is up here."

Ruby had to admit: she could not change the weather, living conditions, mail service, or village activities.

After church one Sunday, while Elmer and Roy were stuck in a conversation on hunting, and the children were playing noisily around the metal folding chairs, Ruby, Anna, and Margie clustered around the wood-burning barrel stove, and Ruby again mentioned her concern. Margie was quick to give her opinion. "We knew it wouldn't be easy. One thing that is an enormous boost is to have Christian fellowship. Within Tanana, there are a number of individuals with the common belief in Jesus Christ, so we find comfort and encouragement from one another. We pray together when life gets hard and trust God to be there for us."

"I'm not sure that is the case in those little villages with so few people," said Anna.

As practical as Ruby was in tending physical needs, the spiritual element *was* the bottom line. Everything considered, Ruby wasn't sure what she would do without Arctic Missions' presence in the village.

On a 20° warm and windless Saturday, when Ruby was in her baking routine and the children were indoors warming up and letting their mittens dry, she heard the front door into the arctic entry open, followed by a quick tap on the interior door, and then Anna's excited voice.

"Ruby!" Anna announced. "A group of us just got back from tromping on the river! Not on the runway part, but the uncleared part. It was so rough. The snow makes everything look soft and puffy, but the river ice did not freeze smoothly. The lumps of ice are pushed against each other until locked in, at all angles."

It was clear; Anna was not prone to cabin fever. She didn't stay long enough in her "cabin." She was always out exploring with nurse friends, no matter the temperature, which at this time, was warmer and with long daylight hours, not hot by any means, but comfortable enough to push back one's parka hood and breathe deeply without one's nose hairs stiffening and causing pain.

Mark ran to Anna, jabbering. Anna knelt down, caught her breath, and sniffed the yeasty air. "What's your mama baking?" she asked Mark.

He did not answer.

"Crescent rolls for Sunday dinner," replied Ruby. Ruby's apron was once again decorated with flour, and even Mishal, who was now sleeping in her arms, had a dusting of flour on her rosy cheeks.

Anna continued, "Well, I knew that about the river ice, and I'd been out there before, but I guess it's still a novelty, and it just seemed like another world. And today, the snow was sparkling in the sunshine, and so white with the blue sky above."

The timer jangled, and Mark scurried to the oven and patted the door. Naomi and Ruth, who were at the kitchen table, turned around expectantly. Ruby passed Mishal to Anna and bent down to pull out the rolls. Anna gently examined the latest frilly dress Mishal had on and commented on how picture-perfect the child looked. Naomi dodged her mother and opened the refrigerator to find the oleo.

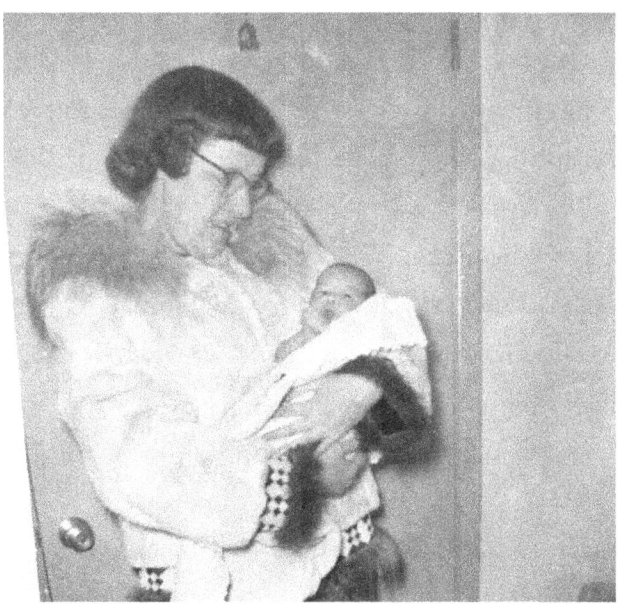
Anna Bortel holding Mishal.

"Get jelly too," urged Ruth. Fortunately, Ruby had ordered adequate grape jelly in her first year's food order.

Ruby put together a plate of warm rolls for Anna and herself, and they moved into the living room. Mishal's head fell limply against Anna's chest, and the baby slept through the noise and jostling.

Naomi and Ruth prepared their snack, licked jelly and oleo off their fingers that had slid off the warm rolls, and returned to making play food out of a mixture of flour, salt, and food coloring. Their hair had grown out, and they both wore braids "like the other girls." When they leaned over the table, a braid would swing forward. The girls batted the nuisance aside and cut pretend plates, twice the size of a half-dollar, out of the cardboard backs of their Big Chief tablets. Their menus included mashed potatoes, moose roast, and peas. Some bland-looking mixture was in a many-sided flat bowl. Was it oatmeal? Cream of Wheat?

"This is a drumstick!" Naomi announced emphatically. She held a tiny plate with a thick, elongated strip of salty dough above her head as if to show an audience. Her actual audience was Ruth and Mark, and Mark didn't care; he just wanted to stick his fingers in it and taste it. Of course, Naomi and Ruth had already done that. "Icky," said Ruth, shaking her head.

Ruby settled herself on a chair across from the couch where Anna sat with Mishal lying beside her. "It is time to think about ordering next year's groceries. I did a good job last year, especially since it was my first time. Everything is lasting well, and some items we will have enough for next year, such as dark wheat flour."

Anna responded, "I do need to come up with something different for next year."

Ruby agreed. "I am so tired of the same menu every day and every week: moose meat, potatoes, and canned vegetables. No one complains, but every day, corn, creamed corn, peas, or green beans? The creamed corn? Now that's a joke. Just mushy, lumpy soup. Nothing like what I had at home. Oh my! We would stand in the yard, shuck corn, cut the kernels off, and then cook them fresh. Mmm … add some cream, a bit of sugar, flour, and salt, and stir it all together. Yes, siree! You can't beat that for good cooking!"

"Even a good ol' Piggly Wiggly grocery store would be a thrill," said Anna with a dramatic exhale.

Mark darted over to show Anna the tiny cardboard bowl of Kix he had made. She pretended to nibble on the cereal. "Yummy," she said. He hopped back to the table with a silly grin.

"I'm going to grow my own vegetables next year," said Ruby, her eyes shining in anticipation. The farm girl in her was waiting to get out.

"Did you know that Lewis supplies the Northern Commercial Store with produce from his garden?" replied Anna. "I heard he cut a twelve-pound cabbage into chunks and sold the pieces for fifty cents per pound!"

"Some patient gave Elmer a smaller head," said Ruby. "I made it last a month—borscht, coleslaw, and just plain cooked. So good."

The women laughed. They concluded their grocery shopping discussion with the agreement to check with each other before putting in their food orders. Perhaps one or the other would have extra items she could share. They would work together.

Naomi had eavesdropped on her mother and schoolteacher. "Ruth," she whispered. "Which do you like best of the food we eat at school?"

Even though the government food subsidies were specifically for the Native students, Florence Feldkirchner, head teacher, instructed Anna to distribute the items to all the children. Subsidies varied from month to month and did not provide complete meals.

Ruth thought for a moment. "The graham crackers and cooked dried apricots. The apricots aren't as good as the ones Grandma Gaede sends us from California, though."

"Sometimes I like the tomato juice, and sometimes I don't," said Naomi. "I like the yellow cheese, and I like it when Miss Bortel puts snow in the powdered milk."

"The hot cocoa is okay," added Ruth. "But not as good as Mommy's."

Years before, the government had also provided thick, chewable, quarter-size vitamins. By the time Naomi and Ruth were in the Tanana Day School, the oversized bottles had become covered with dust. Naomi found the stale taste and chalky texture fascinating and choked them down thoughtfully. Ruth begged her mother not to make her take them. Ruby had no difficulty assuring her she need not take them; there were plenty of new and better vitamins at the hospital that Ruth's daddy could bring home.

Ruby's apron accompanied her daily. The oven seldom sat vacant. On weekends, the kitchen table rarely seated the family only. Mrs. Scripter was the current guest. Elmer had brought her back to Tanana for prenatal care, as well as emotional and mental care by Ruby. Ruby was just the antidote for the missionary woman.

Maxine Scripter was a pretty woman with a fair complexion, curly dark hair, medium height, glasses, and a pleasant smile. Ruby admired her red coat. The missionary woman was like a shaken pop bottle with the top just flipped off. Fizz everywhere. She talked and talked to Ruby. Ruby nodded sympathetically and in agreement. They drank hot tea and sat at the kitchen table while comparing notes on child-raising and baby formulas. Ruby learned the personalities of the Scripter children and the backgrounds of Maxine's parents. There was no end to questions back and forth.

"How do you do that?" asked Ruby when Maxine told her about homeschooling her two older children.[71]

"Just one more thing," replied Maxine shrugging one shoulder and minimizing the effort.

"I could never do that," said Ruby. "I didn't really like school myself anyway, except geography."

She contemplated the issue in silence. Then, since isolation was a topic woven throughout their conversations, and reading was one way to combat that seclusion, she brought up the subject of books.

"How do you get reading material? There are no libraries in these villages, and who do you have to share books with you?"

Maxine gave a half-laugh. "My family back home sends me books, but that's about it. They are heavy to pack along in the small bush planes, so I can't bring much back with me when we do get out of the village and to Fairbanks."

Ruby mentioned several Christian books that had roused her attitude and faith and went to look for them. In her excitement to be an encourager in this way, she scribbled a note to order more, such as *Never a Dull Moment* by Eugenia Price; *How to Rear a Happy Christian Family* by Charles Farah; *Handfuls of Purpose* by Mrs. Charles Cowman; *Nervous Christian* by Dr. Little and Theodore Epp; and *Mental Health for Christian Living* by C. B. Eavey.

Indeed, Ruby fed Maxine's body, soul, and spirit, and as simple and repetitive as Ruby believed her meal-making had become, Maxine savored the fresh carrots and apples Ruby managed to find in the hospital kitchen and reveled in meals other than moose and rice. Just having someone else figure out what to cook, and actually do the cooking, was a gift in itself for the wife and mother. Even more, running water, indoor plumbing, and a hot soak in the bathtub were luxuries out of this world. Maxine was ever so grateful for her retreat, yet with her children at home in Kokrines, as well as Easter the next day, it came quickly to an end. Ruby described the culmination and transition:

> "We packed and I mean packed Mrs. Scripter in the back of our plane with cartons of eggs all over the place plus other food items that were given her by kind people here, it was very windy but they safely got on their way. Elmer had clinic at Kokrines during the stay at the Scripture home and then he left for Birches where he picked up Mrs. Johnson and their two children and packed them on the back seat."

Birches was not a village. It was the name given to a CAA station and the CAA white frame house along the Yukon River where the Johnsons lived. Harold Johnson was large-boned and bulky with a square face and black wavy hair. Unlike Elmer, he was not quick on his feet and tended to shuffle. He seemed to have trouble adapting to changes and when things did not go according to his plans. Given the randomness of weather and Alaska schedules, he probably found life in the Interior difficult at times.

Vera stood tall beside her husband at a slender five feet eleven. She had delicate features and was even-tempered and soft-spoken. She secured her shoulder-length brown hair behind her neck with a large barrette. Chances are, she was the one who oiled the track when Harold had difficulty changing his plans.

The couple had adopted two children at the same time, and now both were around age three. Barbara, half-Athabascan Indian and half-White, could often be found on her daddy's lap or running to him with a toy. David was from a White couple.

When Elmer had flown the Johnson family to Tanana for a Sunday service, or when Ruby had flown to Birches with him for a quick visit, she had observed how nicely the children played together and obeyed their parents; she thought how easy they were compared to Mark.

Bringing the family to Tanana for Easter was an experience of its own. Ruby never missed recording these dramas, and Elmer never missed relating them in full detail:

"They left Birches at 7:00, it was not very windy there but as they approached Tanana it got very windy. It was so windy here and the surface looked so bad and it was getting quite dark that I told the girls that I did not expect our daddy to return tonight and 15 minutes later he landed. The river is just like glass and the plane with skis just slides all over the place and has quite a struggle when it is windy but all went safe again and we were so thankful."

Thankfully, Ruby had a clothes dryer, and the bedsheets Mrs. Scripter had slept on were washed and dried before Vera and the children arrived to spend the night.

Laundry, baking and cooking, and hospitality all rolled together in Ruby's life. She wrote home: *"I plan to have a Polar bear feast Fri. nite plus game nite and we are going to have Easter breakfast here for those that attend the chapel."*

Even though Ruby hadn't anticipated Mrs. Scripter showing up for a medical checkup and layover, she had fortunately planned ahead for Easter.

> *"I got an order from Sears with some of their sale items and Mark got his first white dress shirt. Ruth got some white sandals which she will wear at Easter, Naomi got black patent slippers. We will have snow on the ground yet but the children like to act like you do in civilization."*

Mishal had plenty of "Easter" clothes from the extensive baby gifts she had received; in fact, every day, she looked like Easter.

The weather and environment relinquished no clues that it was the Easter season. No tulips, early green shoots of grass, lambs frolicking, or snow-free yards to hide Easter eggs. Most likely, the girls would wear their new shoes for Easter breakfast at the Gaede home and then carry them to the chapel and wear them inside only. Winter footwear was still needed outdoors.

The logistics of air and accommodations could have been staggering; however, Ruby and Elmer were not unlike a team of farm horses, pulling hard, pulling together. Ruby held down the home front, and Elmer flew back to Birches to get Harold Johnson.

> *"In the morning, (Easter) Elmer went back for Mr. Johnson so that he could be here for Easter breakfast. They got back at 8:30 and we*

had breakfast at 8:45, with 13 adults and 13 children. I made Easter baskets with grapefruits cut in half – 14 grapefruit cost us $5.99, we had bacon, eggs, rolls, ryebread and bran-muffins. I used a paper bunny which I put in the grapefruit basket for place cards. Every one went to S.S. and church and I stayed home. The Johnsons were here for the rest of the meals during the day plus the night. Monday morn Mr. Johnson flew to Fairbanks to get his new family plane, the Johnsons are moving to Bettles. Monday at 5:30 Elmer flew Mrs. Johnson and the children home to Birches."

With her household down to a population of the basic six, Ruby pulled on her apron and returned to laundry, ironing, restocking her pantry with more homemade baked bread, and eating leftovers.

The whirlwind activities of March into mid-April, with planned and unplanned occurrences and caring for one another, continued into the following months. Whirlwinds were normal. On the other hand, earthquakes were not.

APRONS

Ruby grew up in a time when aprons were used to protect the dress beneath it. During the Depression, when money was tight, women didn't have many dresses. Even without that major impact on the economy, washing clothes was a complicated and arduous task, and it was easier and quicker to wash an apron.

Aprons had many practical uses:

CARING FOR ONE ANOTHER

- Grabbing something out of the oven or carrying a hot dish to the kitchen table.

- Carrying eggs from a chicken coop.

- Carrying carrots, tomatoes, and other vegetables from the garden.

- Bringing in kindling and corncobs to start a fire in the kitchen stove.

- Wiping hands when working.

- Wiping a child's perspiring forehead.

- Wiping a child's dirty face.

- Drying tears.

- Doing a quick dusting when someone drove up the road to the house unexpectedly.

- Holding clothespins while hanging just-washed clothes on the clothesline.

- Catching crumbs brushed off a table or countertop and then emptying them into a trash can.

Aprons for regular, daily work were one piece and covered the front of the body, from neck to knees. The design was loose for easy movement. Scrap fabric and flour sacks were inexpensive materials; otherwise, popular patterns were gingham checks and small floral calico. A bit of rickrack or seam binding added some color. Fancy "tea aprons" were used for entertaining guests. These were tied around the waist and gathered.

In the 1940s, the apron was a symbol of the perfect housewife. It evoked warm images of mothers and grandmothers cooking, working in the kitchen, holidays, and family.

In the 1960s, when laborsaving devices became available for housework and cooking, the apron was no longer something to wear proudly. Women started to view their status as more than homemakers and, thus, abandoned their aprons. Aprons then symbolized grandmothers or women who were not keeping up with the times.

More recently, the many cooking shows on television have created an upsurge in aprons. Home cooking is popular, as are aprons. Colorful and fancy aprons can be purchased at craft fairs, stores specializing in housewares, and boutiques.

Women are not the only ones who have worn aprons. Men have worn aprons when working in culinary venues, blacksmith shops, gardening, and grilling. Ruby's father, Solomon Leppke, had a simple blue denim apron when he took up whittling in his 80s.

Today, aprons continue to serve some of the same decades-long purposes, along with:

- Protecting your favorite T-shirt from bleach when cleaning.

- Wiping your hands when repotting a plant.

- Cleaning up a spill when cooking.

- Keeping jeans clean when polishing shoes.

CHAPTER 21

RUMBLES OF CHANGE

Tanana, 1958

RUBY KNEW ABOUT TORNADOES, dust storms, swarms of grasshoppers, lightning and thunder, and hailstorms. She did not know about earthquakes, nor did she like them. She did not like the rattling of silverware in the drawers or end tables dancing.

"April 8, 1958 -

We had a severe earthquake early Monday morning. I was just warming the bottle for Mishal at 6:30 and the house began to shake, I hung on to a chair and kept wondering when it would die down, but instead it increased, my heart started beating fast and I prayed that the Lord would keep all safe, then there was another tremor ½ hour later, I thought Elmer was shaking the bed ... I had to laugh at Margie Gronning she said she hadn't even noticed as she just took for granted that Rev. was rolling over in bed. If you could see those two you would laugh too as she is only about 4 ft tall and he is 6 ft and they have a real soft innerspring mattress with a cheap springs and I can imagine poor Margie always sleeps on the hillside."

Within twenty-four hours, Ruby had experienced sixteen noticeable tremors, each one as unnerving as the one before, even though no damage was evident inside or outside the house. All the same, Ruby was on edge.

"We have had a frightening amount of earthquakes last week. The natives say that never before have they experienced such here. Radio reports say that one of the centers was located at Mt. McKinley where a crack that formed was 40 ft. wide and a mile long. We have had at least 4 to 6 tremers every day since the major shake … it reminds me of the scripture passage which reminds us of the later days that we shall have increase of earthquakes."

When she managed to move on to the next subject, the topic was about Mark:

"Mark is so cute and his disposition is so much better. He calls the plane daddy's and mine plane … he loves to sing, his favorites are "Jesus loves me" and that is all he says of that song, then I heard him singing "Fishers of men", he does that like this 'huh, huh, huh, huh, fishers of me, and he has the tune right for that, too. Just yesterday he sang 'A sunbeam, a sunbeam and he got part of that tune right too."

It was on one of those days, when Mark had just gotten up from a nap and was singing that the girls surged through the door from school.

Oftentimes, they dawdled, but not on this day.

"Mommy, Mommy!" Naomi shouted before she even had her head into the kitchen. Ruby, who had just opened the refrigerator beside the door, stood right in front of her, and they nearly collided, as did Ruth, who was directly behind Naomi.

"Monday will be our last day of school," Naomi announced loudly.

"Probably," Ruth corrected her cautiously.

"The earthquakes condemned the school!" continued Naomi.

"The men from Juneau condemned the school because of the earthquake," clarified Ruth.

This caught Ruby off guard. It was six weeks until school was to be out. The girls were doing well in school, but what now? Was their coursework actually completed? It was like another earthquake. Tanana Day School wasn't the only one shut down by the officials from Juneau. The school at Stevens Village was closed as well. What would every other mother do now? Granted, missionary women in more remote areas of Alaska taught their children school year-round. They used the Calvert Curriculum.[72] In spite of that, Ruby had no interest in teaching her children schoolwork. She would have preferred to teach them how to crochet, build a bookshelf, or plant potatoes.

A day later, Ruby waved down Anna when she saw her walking rapidly from school to her CAA apartment. "How do I do this?" she asked Anna.

"Ruby," Anna said impatiently. "The girls have workbooks. You just have to help them with those. It's not that hard." Anna kept marching down the road, her shoulders forward and head down.

Even though Ruby was fair to good in arithmetic, she was not keen on teaching it, and for sure not writing stories. Anna was unsympathetic, and Ruby's fretfulness showed itself in a letter: *"Last week we had usual routine for me plus trying to have the girls finish their workbooks. I do not enjoy it as*

I'm much to busy and for the first time in my life I'm a bushel basket behind with my ironing." Ruby was much more concerned about being a good wife and having the ironing done than being a schoolteacher.

Yes, Anna had been brusque. Her teaching job had just fallen through the cracks. A new school *was* to be built in Tanana; however, it would not be possible to have it constructed until January or so. She couldn't just hang around and wait. She had to have an income and a place to live. She heard there was an opening at Bettles where the Johnsons were moving. Yet, it wasn't just about finding a job; she loved living in Tanana. Ideas, facts, and options were flying around in her head, as well as communication literally flying in from the Juneau Territorial Education Department. What was *she* supposed to do? At this time, she had no reserve to come alongside Ruby and carry any of her distress too.

There seemed to be upheaval everywhere. Anna didn't know where she would go next. Elmer was downriver in Galena and would probably spend the night there. Ruby was buried in workbooks and ironing, and she was not prepared for one more thing to shake her world.

In the evening, she and the children went to the Gronnings for what Ruby expected would be regular Bible study and prayer. To her surprise, there was a birthday cake waiting for her. Roy, Margie, Anna, Alice (the receptionist at the hospital), and several Native women sang "Happy Birthday" and pulled out small gifts. Margie lit the candles on the yellow sheet cake, and Ruby blew them out in one extended puff. The birthday girl relaxed and immersed herself in the moment with the happiness of friends and fellowship. At 9:15 p.m., she prepared to go home. She wrestled down Mark, who was busy building and knocking down block structures with

Chris Gronning, put him in the red wagon, and prepared to walk home.

"Mark, make room for baby Mishal," she said.

Ruby swaddled Mishal in one of the crocheted blankets from the baby shower.

"My baby," said Mark patting her head gently.

The road still had patches of slush and mud; nevertheless, Ruth insisted on pulling her two younger siblings. On the other hand, Naomi insisted on carrying the oversized flashlight, which she used as a searchlight into the darkness for whatever she discerned to be of interest or threat. The road and ruts in front of them were not her priority, much to the frustration of Ruth, who was trying to see where to walk. As the cluster slipped along, the distant drone of a small airplane approaching caught Ruby's attention. Was it planning to land? There were no lights on the Tanana airstrip and, of course, not on the plowed river area.

She spent half a page in her next letter describing her fright.

"I heard some native boys say 'that is the doctors plane and so I asked them if I had understood them right and they said yes that the doctor. I grabbed the wagon from Ruth and started running so hard and my chest hurt, and told the children to hurry, and I was praying out loud. I saw that some one had built two fires on the river so that the pilot could see to land, I just couldn't believe that Elmer would fly in such darkness, the children and I dashed home and I ran to the hospital and couldn't find Elmer so I ran down to the river to see if it was really our plane and sure enough so I knew he was in the hospital with an emergency,

After awhile Elmer came to the house and explained that in the afternoon they had gotten in a little boy 2 ½ that was very sick and the nurses did not think he would live so they communicated with C.A.A.

here to call Galena and notify Dr. Gaede that we had an emergency here. Well Elmer figured he could barely make it which he did, he worked with the baby throughout the nite, the baby died at 5:00 in the morning. ... During that trip Elmer riped his one ski open and Leonard helped him fix it."

Once again, her farm boy turned pilot had tested the limits of flight. Did he not consider her concern? What would she do without him? Her imagination went wild with "what ifs" —if the plane had crashed upon landing and she would have found him dead inside; if the Natives had not done what they knew to do in such a situation. Did he disregard her concern? Then again, perhaps it was not that at all. Perhaps it was his dedication to his patients, saving lives, and confidence in his flying ability. She tried to understand the man but sometimes came up with no good reason.

And so it went.

Near the end of April, the temperatures rose above freezing, and more than sixteen hours of sunlight brightened Ruby's world. The daylight and dry weather eliminated the mud; now, the children played in the dirt. Ruby was relieved to have three of her children out from underfoot, but there was a downside with that. She wrote her mother:

"The children live outdoors, Mark wouldn't even eat breakfast this morning he just wanted to go out doors. He was in all last week because of his cold. Since we have no grass around the house just dirty dust and the house and children get so filthy dirty."

And, as if the actual mud wasn't gone, the girls started into mud pie making with a passion. They carried large tin cans with dirt and other cans with water and mixed the mess together. At this time of year, there wasn't much to decorate their pies besides pebbles, and their pies did not bake as fast as they desired. After a while, they gave up, carted their dolls outside in strollers, and pushed them up and down the short stretches of sidewalk within the medical compound. Mark rode his tricycle singing behind his sisters. Every now and then, Ruby looked out the window to check on her offspring. She frowned at Naomi's short corduroy pants that reached above her white, sockless ankles. There was no more hem to let out, and the knees were threadbare. They would not make it to Ruth as hand-me-downs. To her advantage, neither of the girls was into clothing styles.

The upside of the pleasant weather was that Ruby could wholeheartedly get back into her wiener-roasting mode. One Saturday, and in a gay mood, she snuggled Mishal into the wagon with hot dogs, homemade buns, mustard, and pickle relish. Ruth, the dedicated wagon puller, seized the handle. It was a rough start when Mark tried to push the wagon and ran it into Ruth's shins. Ruth cried. Naomi tried to restrain Mark, and the yelling started. Not to have her happy day quashed, Ruby calmly but firmly took hold of the handle and shushed the children, who considered it wise not to argue with their mother, and assembled themselves into a duckling-like procession behind her.

Her brood followed her down the riverbank in front of the hospital and a short distance from Elmer's airplane. "Daddy and mine plane," Mark said happily. The river remained frozen, although gray river rocks poked through the frozen snow on the shore. The older children viewed these as missiles to be launched onto the river ice.

Ruby started a fire, and just on cue, Elmer strode down the incline with his white medical jacket flapping.

"I think things are under control now," he said, referring to the emergency that had shown up. Hot dog roasting was not entirely under control. Mark insisted on poking the clothes-hanger-hot-dog-stick into the hot dog through the middle, rather than the long way, causing it to dangle precariously. Ruby left him to his father and pulled out a bottle of milk for Mishal. Mark responded better to his father anyway. Naomi and Ruth discussed how they liked their hot dogs.

"I like mine kind of black," said Naomi. "With lots of mustard."

"I don't," said Ruth. She carefully turned hers on the bouncing clothes hanger.

The girls continued chattering. Mark's hot dog now had flaky gray ash on either end, from flopping onto a smoldering branch. The little scientist picked at it and, with big breaths, tried to blow it off. No need for fancy toys, the kid was immersed in his own world of wonder. Mishal lay quietly in the wagon with her brown eyes blinking in the sunshine. Ruby and Elmer saw no need for parenting that day and struck up their own conversation.

"The river ice has moved out at Fairbanks and Nenana," said Elmer. "We're next."

Ruby shielded her eyes with one hand and looked across the expanse of the river. "I wonder what it will be like. I can't imagine a half-mile of ice moving. I hope we aren't asleep when it happens."

"One of my patients told me we will either hear the ice grinding or the hospital blowing its whistle, so everyone knows," answered Elmer. "I guess I'd better change the J-3 off skis and onto wheels and fly it over to the airstrip."

Within a few days, the ice went out. Ruby could hardly find words to describe the spectacular event in her May 1, 1958 letter.

> "Yesterday it first started to move in one large mass, can you imagine a mass a ½ mile long and a ½ mile wide moving at once, it is a thrilling wonder. It moved for about a ½ hour and then it jammed and this morning at 6:00 it again moved and the large mass moved out and we will have a couple days of mammoth ice pieces all very close together covering the entire top surface of the river."

In her 1958 Christmas letter, she would add more details.

> "The last of April we had the privilege to see the spectacular break up of the Yukon. We made some good movies and hope that some day we might show you those pictures. After the ice moves out the river is very high and timber and trash fills the surface of the river, this is 'hayday' for the natives and whites that use wood for fuel. A long grapple is used to catch the logs that run along or near the shores."

The Yukon River breaking up in front of Tanana in 1957.

Within a week, the river crept up the banks and overshadowed the springtime exhilaration. For such matters, Ruby sought out Native friends to explain the phenomenon. "Elmer," she said after supper when the children were outside playing again. "Rosalie told me that it wasn't unknown that the ice could jam around a corner and a village could be flooded." She looked out the living room window nervously; her fingers thrummed the edge of her apron. All Elmer said was, "Not recently that I know of." That did not give her peace of mind.[73] She was frighteningly aware of how close her home was to the threat.

Each morning when Ruby got up, she checked the river. Once the water level receded, she relaxed and fully embraced summertime in the Interior.

It was as though all things had come to life after the solid, white stillness of the river had disappeared. The continual motion of the fast-flowing river brought energy, as did the long daylight hours. Whereas the darkness and cold had imprisoned the village world, now young and old were enlivened to be outdoors past the 9:45 p.m. sunset, which would get even later. The sun rose around 4:30 a.m.; despite that, it was typical for the Natives to stay up late and then sleep into the morning, or just go until they dropped, sleep a few hours, and keep going. It was a short, summer manic dance. Ruby, a night owl herself, had difficulty requiring the children to come in at their usual bedtime.

The "home school" threatened to collapse. Ruby wrote, "*About the time we sit down to do reading and arithmetic, there is a knock on the door and when I visit the girls do not do their work very well.*"

Some of the knocks on the door were Anna's, who dropped in two to three times a day to chat and have a cup of tea with Ruby. She had tidied up her responsibilities at Tanana Day School and was waiting to fly to her home in Ohio. Given her acceptance of her situation, she was back to her affable self, and she even took a few moments to answer Ruby's questions about the girls' workbooks. "*She is just like a sister to me and how I will miss her,*" Ruby wrote her mother.

The house had a greasy-good aroma of fried minute steaks, moose, of course. Ruby had perfected these by pounding them thin, dipping them flour, frying them quickly in oil, and then baking them with a scant bit of water. Wild meat was so dry it needed water, broth, or bacon grease, the latter of which she did not come across often.

Elmer came through the door precisely at 6:00 p.m., suppertime, and lifted his nose in the air like a scent-seeking dog. "Sure smells good," he said, walking to the bathroom to wash up.

The children gathered at the table, and as soon as their father reappeared and their mother sat down, Mark burst out, "God is good."

Naomi and Ruth looked at their parents, then bowed their heads and started the mealtime prayer they were trying to teach their little brother.

> *"God is great and God is good.*
> *And we thank Him for our food.*
> *By His hand we all are fed,*
> *Give us Lord our daily bread.*
> *Amen."*

Mark managed some of the words. To his mother's relief, his vocabulary and sentence making had finally come together.

Ruby got up several times to get what she had forgotten to put on the table, and the girls busily smooshed craters into their instant mashed potatoes. They filled these reservoirs with dark, rich gravy and then plopped in pale, canned peas. Their mother did not like them to play with their food; yet, at this moment, she let them continue and brought up the subject of school to Elmer.

"Elmer, will we need to order school supplies for the fall semester? What will the other parents do? I just can't see …"

Still looking at his plate and forking in his supper, Elmer interrupted, "I talked to Mr. Isaac today. You know, from the Education Office in Juneau. Anna was there too. The decision about school is up to the chief, the CAA manager, and me—as the Public Health Officer. We have a plan."

Ruby dropped her hands to her lap and stared at him. The girls continued to make craters and dabbed pieces of steak into the gravy puddles. The next day's letter included this account:

> "*Mr. Isaac from Juneau came here to check on Anna and the school and Elmer told him that we absolutely had to have a school in Sept. so they looked at possibilities and it seems that we will have school in quansit huts, army equipment, until the new school is finished in Dec. sometime Not only that but Elmer said that we wanted Anna to stay here to teach and so Mr. Isaac asked Anna if she would come back in fall and she says "If I have a place to live" so it is up to the Hospital and C.A.A to provide housing for the teachers until they can live in the quarters attached to the school house. They are planning a three room school which will mean that we will have two other new teachers, which we imagine will be a teaching couple.*"[74]

Ruby was utterly flabbergasted. She had recently hosted a going away party for Anna, and the Gaede house had overflowed with eighteen adults and seventeen children. Some of the nurses had finagled a twenty-pound beef roast from Fairbanks, which was a jaw-dropping, mouth-watering treat for those who pretty much ate wild game all the time. Ruby had frosted a large, rectangle-layered cake with tiny yellow flowers, surrounding cursive frosting, "God Bless Anna."

Now, as if she had been carrying a heavy bag of potatoes, a huge weight had been lifted from Ruby's shoulders. She would not have to teach her children school, and Anna would remain her face-to-face friend. Earthquakes? She had no confidence that those would subside; all the same, her heart was lighter as she contemplated putting in her first garden and seeing loved ones during the summer.

EARTHQUAKES IN ALASKA

Alaska sits along the Ring of Fire. The Pacific Ring of Fire is a region around the Pacific Ocean where there are active tectonic plates and deep ocean troughs that set off volcanoes and earthquakes. Ninety percent of the world's earthquakes, 81 percent of the world's strongest earthquakes, and approximately 75 percent of the world's volcanoes occur within the Ring of Fire.

In 1964, when the strongest earthquake recorded in North America (9.2) took place, Ruby and her family lived on their Gaede-Eighty homestead outside Soldotna, Alaska. None of the family was injured, and the structures on the homestead remained intact. This story is told in Alaska Bush Pilot Doctor by Naomi Gaede Penner.

In 2018, a 7.0 earthquake shook the homestead again. The family and buildings again remained safe and sound.

Earthquakes have not increased over the decades. Alaska typically has around fifty thousand earthquakes a year, some of which are barely or not noticeable. The perception that they are increasing is due to nearly-instant global communication with visual awareness of the destruction and lives lost; as well as when earthquakes hit heavily populated areas, the impact is greater.

CHAPTER 22

THE HAPPY DAYS OF SUMMER

Tanana, 1958

SOFT SPRING TEMPERATURES and fresh blue skies filled with fluffy mashed potato-like clouds introduced Ruby to her first summer in Tanana. She was immersed in her favorite things, the warmth of sunshine on her face and arms, making music, spending time with her husband, digging in the dirt and making things grow, happy children, and picnics. She smiled often.

Music had been a part of her life growing up, in her early marriage, and now, here in Tanana. Whether vocal or instrumental, it gave her pleasure. At this moment, there were special services at the Arctic Missions Chapel that included music.

In the first part of May, Ruby wrote:

"We had a nice program in our chapel last night we had an orchestra – Elmer the accordion, Anna the Uke, Mrs. Gronning the string harp,

and I the mandolin. We also sang the song "Where Could I Go." We had quite a few natives attend as we had advertised the program. The natives seem to enjoy the loudspeaking system which is used for Evening Vespers every eve from 6:30 till 7:30."

Shortly after Ruby and Elmer had arrived in Tanana and started attending church at the Arctic Missions Chapel, they had sung duets together or trios with Anna. Practicing the music, standing beside her husband, laughing at their mistakes, and trying again, brought a feeling of closeness and intimacy to Ruby that often seemed so elusive. She craved time with Elmer, who put medicine and activities first.

If she could have had it her way, she would have sat leisurely with her husband and chatted over a cup of cocoa or a bowl of popcorn, perhaps reminisce about their home in Kansas, or chuckle over how Ruth had gotten Mishal to squeal in pleasure, or discuss a book she had recently read. Leisure with him did not happen. She always felt so hurried at mealtimes to get food on the table, monitor the children's eating behavior, and listen for Mishal's cries. She would start a conversation with her husband, and then the phone would ring, and he would answer, "Dr. Gaede." Yes, the "doctor" came before "husband." Or, he would eat hurriedly and want to take a spin in his airplane, or need to clean his hunting guns, or whatever. Admittedly, sometimes, they did talk, not that they actually sat down. More often, it was when he dried dishes. Given all that, making music with her husband filled some emotional gaps in her heart and reminded her of when they first fell in love.

By mid-May, the river had settled down to an everyday invigorating motion without the threat of climbing to her doorstep. The lack of crisis allowed her to observe the river with fascination, not fear.

> "The river has quitened down with only a few ice chunks here and there floating along as graceful swans, the birds are praising God with their beautiful songs and as the song goes – 'The birds up in the tree tops sing their song – so why shouldn't I, why shouldn't you praise him too.'
>
> The barges are beginning to run, they have the following names, Tanana, Yukon, Taku-Chief and Yutana. These barges carry a tremendous amount of supplies for all the villages along the Yukon and up the Koyukuk river. They provide the stores with their goods and individuals who order staple goods for the year. Construction Co.s have their machinery and supplies transported in this manner. One of these barges has a bright orange stern wheel. These are strictly freight and not passenger boats."

Now that the barges were chugging and churning on the river highway, it was time for Ruby to pull together the loose ends of her next year's food order. After going through her first experience of estimating supplies for a year and seeing what she had over-purchased or run out of, she was better equipped to plan for this second year.[75]

> "We finally got our groc order made up for next winter. It comes to $900.00 with out the freight. There were a couple items that we could not get the brand we wanted from this co. so we will order that from Anchorage."

Food consumed so much thought and conversation. On the Kansas farm, the talk was of the two-tenths inch of rain in the wheat fields or how many eggs the chickens were producing; here, alternate food sources were the topic of her letters.

> *"We had cold weather last week even some snow and freezing weather. I cannot imagine that the wheat is heading in Okla. at Margie's. Sunday it is a bit warmer and we are sitting in the sun to absorb its healthful sources. There are good fish in the river, they call them white fish[76] and they are delicious they can not get them fast enough with the hook so they use a net."*

In Alaska, there were always wild game and fish as food staples. Ruby adapted well and didn't hesitate to try what the land and water offered; in spite of that, there were those foods that were familiar, and at times, she craved. When Elmer was headed to Fairbanks, her uneasiness about his flying was set aside. She anticipated his shopping at actual grocery stores, with a variety and availability of non-canned and non-powdered items.

> *"Elmer is flying our plane into Fairbanks next week for a medical convention. He shall bring back some fresh foods and potatoes we are plum out even of powdered ones. I'm hungry for fried potatoes. We also need baby food for Mishal. She is on cereal, applesauce, tomatoes juice and strained pork."*

The good wife had sent along her grocery list, yet, her husband brought back even more than she had imagined—like icing on a cake.

> *"Elmer bought $70 worth of groceries and sent them here airfreight as it was much more than he could bring. He bought bananas and you should have seen Ruth she says "Oh it's a long time since I had*

bananas" Naomi asked for a loaf of boughten bread and she got her wish so she stuffed herself. I asked for cottage cheese and potatoes I hadn't had fried potatoes for 3 weeks and boy did they taste good Then as he came home on our plane last night at 7:30 he brought the girls each a nice ball for bouncing, a rubber rose with a bulb that you squeeze and a worm comes out, and a fire fly (sparkler). Mark got a little airplane of course, one where the props turn."

Ruby beamed more than if he had brought her a bouquet of flowers, a box of chocolates, or fine jewelry.

After his return, Elmer put the plane on floats, which was his preferred mode of flying in the summer. It was the safest way too. Alaska was filled with lakes and rivers, and he always had a place to land if there were an engine failure or weather obstructions. Here, with his first early summer on the Yukon River, perhaps he was premature in his timing.

"Elmer got the plane on floats again but there is so much timber running on the river that it is rather dangerous flying. Rev. Gronning catches the timber with a long hook and pulls it on the beach, this is their next winters fuel."

The door of winter had closed, and one would think the ambitious summer sun would be endless. Yet the Natives and old-timers, although reveling in the warmth and daylight, knew they could not while the time away; they needed to keep an eye toward the next winter.

Life and light were everywhere, and Ruby caught the Alaska summer fever. The outdoors lured her away from household tasks and convinced her to turn a blind eye to ironing and mending. Hanging laundry, however, was another thing. It was a legitimate reason to skip dusting the bookcases or even sewing.

She had always hung wet laundry outdoors on a clothesline or, in Anchorage, in the winter, all around the house. Not until she had moved to Tanana had she experienced the winter luxury of an automatic clothes dryer. She had to admit that towels were softer when fluffed and dried automatically, and with Mishal in diapers, the dryer was a bonus. At any rate, there was nothing like sun-dried sheets and pillowcases. And, again, there was the pleasure of feeling the sun on her cheeks and a breeze through her hair.

A shared clothesline was in the middle of the medical compound. Mark thought of the blowing sheets as a tent and ran giggling through them with his dirty hands outstretched. "Go ride your trike," Ruby told him, catching him by the shoulders and directing him out of the fabric tunnel.

Ruby got her hands dirty too. She put seeds in the ground and watched life rise from her efforts. She learned quickly that the dirt around the compound was dusty sand rather than rich loam with nutrients.

"You should see our house plants grow, we have not darkness anymore. At midnight it starts to dawn and so light that I feel like working. Last week while Elmer was away I never once went to bed before midnite. I got a skirt and blouse made plus some mending for a change.

I made some small flower beds, had to haul good dirt from the woods now the cats think its such a nice soft place to dig. We also put out 6 tomatoe plants and some cabbage, the natives say the tomatoes will not do as well as they need a hot house. Tomorrow I will put out a few carrots, beans, onions, radishes and leaf lettuce."

Within a month, the Land of the Midnight Sun rewarded Ruby with radishes and leaf lettuce.

"It gives such a nice taste in the mouth," said Ruby of both. After months of meals with predominantly canned and powdered products, the snap of teeth biting into a radish was delightful, as was the sharp flavor.

"That lettuce gets stuck in my throat," said Naomi. She choked and made a face. When her mother tore it into small pieces and laced it with canned evaporated milk, a bit of sugar, and even sliced hard-boiled eggs, she would think differently.

The girls danced with joy when their mother told them she was going to build them a playhouse. It was her idea, not theirs.

Ruby snooped around and inquired about scrap plywood behind the hospital. After getting approval, she dragged sections back to the duplex, measured and sawed, attached large pieces to two-by-fours, and rhythmically pounded in nails. Some pieces were not whole, and she turned the cuts into openings for odd-shaped windows. All this was secured to a quarter-inch plywood floor. The roof was slightly peaked, although perhaps not waterproof. That would have to be tested. She even fashioned short, narrow bunk beds that were structurally sound enough for the girls to lie on.

> *"We are having very comfortable temperatures of 60 to 70 during the daytime, nites are cooler … The girls love the outdoors and spend much time in the playhouse which I have not finished yet. I need to put the door on paint it and put in some shelves for them … Mark loves the*

out doors and plays nice with the children he usually is their baby and gets all the wagon rides. He loves Mishal and calls her his baby sister. He never touches her things and is never jealous when I hold her."

Ruby's years spent working alongside her father on the farm paid off, and she capably constructed a playhouse with what was at hand and with every piece carefully joined and leveled, which was more than what she could credit Elmer.

"He builds things like a doctor and thinks if a piece of wood doesn't completely match up that it will heal together, like skin," she told Anna with exasperation.

Even before Ruby had put on a door, the girls were ready to move in.

"Ruth, let's take our dishes into the playhouse," said Naomi, gathering pink and lime-green plastic doll dishes.

The playhouse entertained the girls, even on rainy days, and they invited Mark to come in for tea parties and sit on the lower bunk. The roof passed the test, and they all stayed dry, although mud was tracked in both directions with their frequent trips to and from the house to get Cheerios or use the bathroom.

After Ruby cut a piece of plywood to fit the door opening and had located two sets of hinges, Naomi daringly suggested she and Ruth spend the night in the playhouse.

"We can lock the hook," she said. "We will be safe."

It was light most of the night, so they stuck pieces of fabric over one moon-shaped and one triangle-shaped window. In their pajamas, they lay straight on the narrow hard bunks, each with a wool blanket. Ruth fell asleep, but Naomi did not. In the distance, she heard a CAT rumbling. Was it coming closer? What if it bulldozed over the small playhouse? It seemed to be getting nearer.

"Ruth, are you awake?" she whispered loudly.

No reply.

After a while, Naomi slid down from the top bunk, nudged Ruth awake, and declared the mosquitos were too bad to spend the night in the playhouse. The girls stumbled into the house, roused Ruby, and climbed into their beds—with their multitude of stuffed animals and dolls.

Naomi wasn't the only one who had been frightened. Mark had persistent issues as well.

> *"He is so easily frightened and he will say "I'm scared". He does not like to hear the wash machine vibrate, he is afraid of reflections on the ceiling and went into histerics at the first bugs that were out this spring he is getting used to then as he sees the girls play with the flies."*

And so Ruby was back to writing about her children.

> *"Now I will answer some of your questions which I have neglected. You ask about Mishal, she is ½ Eskimo & ½ White. Adopting babies here really is just as difficult as the states there are many of the army couples that want to adopt. You have to be a resident before the welfare will let you adopt. Elmer found that the welfare in Fairbanks had a special place for Mishal but since we were here and had our hands on the baby they dropped her papers like a hot potatoe, so again it makes me feel that God wanted us to have her. So it would be rather difficult for us to help someone in the states to get one of these babies."*

Ruby seized the invitation to both "get out of town" and go on a picnic with the Gronnings and Anna, who had not yet left for the summer. She bustled around the kitchen and put together a potato salad with the potatoes Elmer had brought from Fairbanks, baked hamburger buns, and found a can of shoestring potato sticks in the basement pantry. The girls pulled on shorts, and Ruby grabbed a light jacket. This would be Mishal's first boat ride. Mark put his face in front of hers and said, "Baby go on boat ride." Ruby climbed into the boat, anticipating gaiety and carefreeness.

Once on the island, Naomi and Ruth took off their shoes, ran in the sand, and walked toe-heel on the stout driftwood logs, which were sun-bleached gray and weathered smooth. Mark and Chris Gronning scooped and shoveled sand out of and into holes. Margie took off her shoes and sat beside the busy toddlers, curling and uncurling her toes in the abrasive sand. The campfire crackled from dripping mooseburger grease, and a lazy smoke plume drifted into the sky. The mooseburgers were the best ever. Time stood still, and like a Kansas sunflower, Ruby turned her face to the sun and closed her eyes. Elmer leaned back on a nearby log and talked to Roy and Anna. Every now and then, he laughed—a sound that hugged Ruby's soul. Water lapped at the beach. An outboard motorboat reverberated as it clawed its way up the river in the swift current. The children played happily without quarreling. It was a perfect day.

After some time, a cloud passed over the sun. Anna reached for her headscarf. A breeze rustled the picnic baskets. Ruby and Margie pulled on their jackets. The lazy conversation quickened.

"Let get this fire put out," said Roy, picking up a bucket yet walking unhurriedly to the shoreline.

Elmer looked at the sky. Ever the pilot watching the weather, he gathered up picnic baskets and followed Roy to the water's edge where the boat was secured.

Ruby told the rest of the story in her next day's letter:

"Last Thursday we had a hamburger fry with Gronnings, Rev. Gronning took us with his motor boat across the river to a sand bar, he made two trips as we were 5 adults (with Anna) and 5 children. We were having a perfectly good time and as we finished our supper the wind turned and the water got choppy we casually packed and started back we were much to loaded with the first load and most of us got pretty wet as the front of the boat went into the waves and splashed us and got water into the boat. It was a bit frightening and Elmer and Naomi stayed behind on the beach and Rev. Gronning had trouble with the motor as he was returning to get them and it took a half hour longer than it should have and Elmer was wondering if maybe we had been capsized. But all came out well."

Ruby ended the letter to Elmer's parents with this request:

"Mom could we ask you to please save our letters, it's not impossible that some day we might try to write a book and we keep no diary and the letters could serve as one. Thanks!"

What a wise woman.

THE PROPER WAY TO HANG CLOTHES ON A CLOTHESLINE

1. Wash the clotheslines before pinning on clothes. Birds enjoyed sitting on these lines, and there were dust and weather elements that dirtied them. Walk the entire length with a damp cloth held tightly around each line.

2. Shake out each clothes item before hanging it. This will minimize the wrinkles.

3. Be efficient with the use of clothespins by pinning items side-to-side whenever possible.

4. Hang socks by the toes, not the tops.

5. Hang slacks by the bottom cuffs with the inside seams together, not by the waistbands.

6. Hang shirts from the shoulders or tails. Either area will retain pin marks that will need to be ironed out; however, the shirttails are tucked into slacks, so the marks will not be noticed.

7. Hang sheets and towels on the outside lines so "unmentionables" will be hidden in the middle.

8. Fold dried clothes as you remove them from the clothesline. This will help smooth out wrinkles.

9. Towels tend to be stiff and crunchy if dried on a clothesline. If a dryer is available, take down towels while slightly damp and fluff them in a dryer.

10. Hang out clothes regardless of the temperature. If the clothes don't sun-dry, they will freeze-dry.

CHAPTER 23

THE REVOLVING DOOR OF HOSPITALITY

Tanana, 1958

THE JARRING AND SHAKING of earthquakes started with the sound of distant thunder. Ruby's mind no longer registered a question mark when she heard the sound. She knew what it was, and adrenalin raced through her body. She especially hated earthquakes when she was taking a bath in the bathtub. The soap slithering from the soap dish into the tub was one thing, and it was plenty unnerving to find oneself surrounded by mini-tidal waves; however, most disturbing was the vulnerable feeling of being unclothed in what could be an emergency.

The bathtub was about to become an issue for other reasons. Tanana had no hotel, bed-and-breakfast, or youth hostel. There were no accommodations at the CAA campus or medical compound for out-of-village guests, other than Public Health officials who could stay in a room at the hospital and eat their meals in the staff dining room. More typically, though, the officials expected Elmer, the Medical Officer in Charge, to entertain them during their stay.

In the summer of 1958, the Gaede home, with its three bedrooms, one bathroom, small kitchenette table, and basement playroom with double bed, was a magnet for missionaries, loved ones, and officials. No one looked at an online schedule to see if rooms or table space were available; they just arrived according to their own schedules and needs.

On the first of June, a Public Health official flew in. Ruby spent the day cleaning house, baking uniformly shaped yeast rolls and a pie, setting a pretty table, and preparing, as always, a tantalizing meal. Elmer pulled out movies from his polar bear hunt, set up his Kodak projector, and tacked a sheet to one wall for a screen.

A few days later, Mr. and Mrs. Jim Orr, neighbors from Anchorage, and their bubbly seventeen-year-old daughter, Judy, flew in for a few hours. Both Elmer and Ruby were delighted to see their familiar faces. On his first bear hunt, Elmer had taken Jim. Jim was built like a football player. His physique and doggedness offered what any hunter would want in a partner, and more so for Elmer, who was a novice. Jim could have packed out both Elmer and a hindquarter of a moose if it came down to that.

Mrs. Orr had been the welcoming mat Ruby needed when she had left her Kansas homeland and arrived in the Alaska Territory in the summer of 1955. Mrs. Orr had taught Ruby how to shop for bargains in Anchorage and how to make use of the abundant rhubarb that flourished in many Alaska yards. Although rhubarb is not native to Alaska, once started, it grows like a weed; Alaska cookbooks are devoted to cooking the red or green sour stalks; over time, Ruby perfected her signature rhubarb cherry pie.

After a quick lunch and while Elmer was walking the Orrs around the village and giving them a tour of the medical complex, more guests arrived.

Roy and Margie Gronning had arranged for Rev. Kenneth and Vivian Hughes to come for Daily Vacation Bible School (DVBS), which was held for schoolchildren during a week in June. Margie had explained the concept to Ruby and was definitely gung ho about the action songs, Bible stories, crafts, puppets, and so on. The two women worked out the details and decided the couple would stay in the Gaede's basement and eat breakfast and some suppers with the Gaedes.

When Elmer and Ruby first met the Hugheses, Ken shook their hands firmly and immediately started talking. He overflowed with vitality. His eyes didn't miss a thing and seemed always wanting to smile. The forty-eight-year-old man with sandy hair had a slight build. Vivian was a head shorter than her husband, with dark hair pulled back, dark eyes, and dimples framing a pleasant smile.

Ruby described the couple to her parents:

"The Hughs have been such a blessing to us, they came to Alaska the day after they were married as missionaries, they have been here 24 years. They look so young and yet she had 5 babies only 2 living children she is R.H. neg. they founded Lazy Mt. Childrens Home. This is also with Arctic Missions. They have now 50 mouths that are fed in that home. Their children are now married and partly supporting their parents as they will now homestead near palmer, build their own cabin and clear 10 acres. Then they will go out to the various villages here where Artic missionaries are and hold evangelistic meetings and refresh missionaries. This of course thrills us as we saw such a need for the work."

Roy and Margie knew the Hugheses from Lazy Mountain Children's Home, located outside Palmer, Alaska, where Roy and Margie had worked prior to Tanana. Starting in the 1930s, children's homes sprung up throughout Alaska.[77] The organizations took in orphans or children under other needful circumstances. A number were homeless due to parents having or dying from tuberculosis, which was rampant in Alaska. It was also during the Depression when jobs were scarce, and parents couldn't provide. Some children were just dropped off on the front steps of the orphanages. People made hard decisions. Although any child was accepted, the majority were Natives.

One evening at the supper table, after the three oldest children had been excused to play outdoors and Mishal was content in Elmer's arms with her bottle, Ruby asked Ken and Vivian what had prompted them to start the Lazy Mountain Children's Home.

Ken took a deep breath and began. "In 1936, I traveled through Valdez and met Blanche Nason, a missionary who had started El Nathan orphanage..."

"That's where Anna Bortel, the school teacher here, worked when she first came to Alaska!" interrupted Ruby excitedly. "I so wish she were here to talk to you. She's home in Ohio for the summer."

Alaska is a huge territory. However, many of the missionary undertakings at that time were closely linked. It was not uncommon for someone in one part of the state to know of another person in a far corner elsewhere. Perhaps they had crossed paths at a missions' conference, teachers' convention, or even in a grocery store aisle or around a table of clothing in an Army Surplus store when they dropped into Fairbanks or Anchorage for supplies.

"Please go on," Ruby said, gesturing with an open hand.

"We got along well, and her mission endeavor appealed to me," said Ken. "A year later, Louise Johnson, another missionary, who had become the director of El Nathan, contacted us about helping."

He paused a moment to look at Vivian. "We liked the idea."

"So, we packed up our children and belongings and moved the following year," said Vivian smiling back at Ken and squeezing his arm.

Ruby stood up, refilled coffee cups, and asked if anyone wanted more pie. No takers. She untied her apron and sat back down.

"Vivian and I had tossed around the idea of starting a sister home to El Nathan, some place in a farm-like setting," continued Ken.

Vivian interjected, "We had lived in the Matanuska Valley, Palmer, when it was first colonized in the mid-30s, you know, the experimental farming colony—where people had been shipped up from the States. Those poor people thought they would have a promised land and get on their feet during the Depression, but the Territory of Alaska was anything but a land of milk and honey. If you can imagine, they were living in tents."

Ruby remembered the Matanuska Maid dairy products in the stores in Anchorage, with the logo of a young female ice skater with a profuse parka hood ruff. A number of the colonists had purchased cows and produced milk, if not honey.

Elmer leaned forward when the talk of a farm was introduced. He jostled Mishal's bottle. Her sleepy eyes popped open, and she kicked her legs in protest. On his hunting trips, Elmer had flown over that area and observed with interest the hay fields, red barns, and cattle.

The story continued, and as it turned out, in 1946, forty acres of land was donated for that specific purpose, three miles east of Palmer, Alaska, on Lazy Mountain. Palmer was the setting the Hugheses had imagined and had talked to God about. Ken described the arduous work of putting in a road and clearing land, obtaining Quonset huts for dormitories, and other details of making a habitable place for children and workers.[78]

Vivian interjected amusing paragraph-long stories about her involvement with cooking kettles of oatmeal and soup, trying to find enough bedding to keep everyone warm in the drafty tent-like Quonset huts,[79] and so on. They were probably more amusing now than when they actually happened, although the spirit of the Hugheses suggested they could tackle anything.

And so the week went by with Naomi and Ruth walking to the Arctic Missions Chapel for DVBS, where twenty-five of their classmates attended. Each day the girls returned singing, their favorite song being "Stop and Let Me Tell You." Whenever they sang, "stop," they pushed out their hands in front of them. During the actual DVBS singing, Margie or Vivian held up a red stop sign, not that any of the Native kids had ever seen one to understand its significance. Before the first day had ended, the girls pressed Mark into singing most of the song. He sang on perfect pitch and punched his fist into the air when he came to "stop."

Before the Hugheses flew home to Palmer, Ken helped Elmer with a new addition to the family.

Ruby wrote:

"Now for the real news. God certainly can do anything but fail, and do far above that which we think. You know while Elmer was in Fairbanks several weeks ago, he spotted a Family Cruiser (PA-14) and he told a broker there that that was a plane he would like to have. There wasn't a sign of the plane ever being up for sale and last week Elmer got a letter from the broker saying that plane was for sale and the price is reasonable for Alaska. So Saturday Rev. Hughes flew Elmer to Fairbanks (Elmer's J-3 airplane was on floats so he would not have been able to land in Fairbanks, whereas Ken's plane was on wheels) and they looked the plane over again and it looked extra good and so now we have a Family Cruiser. Elmer did not bring the plane here as he will need instructions ... The plane is red with beige trim, on wheels only and we of course will get skiis for it for the winter. The plane has

a radio in in which is a luxery for us, it has a 115 hr pr motor, it is upholstered nicely."

The purchase of a new airplane meant selling his other plane, the J-3 that Elmer had learned to fly in, in Anchorage. Unlike most pilot wannabes, he had taken lessons on the landing gear of floats rather than on wheels; thus, his lessons on taking off and landing were more rigid, and even more harrowing, than if he had learned in the traditional manner and sequence. The J-3 had made it possible for him to hunt moose, black bear, grizzly bear, polar bear, and sheep. It had been his companion for house calls up and down the Yukon River. Mark, an Alaskan man in the making, had peered out the windows of the J-3 and gotten his start in flying in that small plane.

Before the Hugheses had arrived, Elmer had written concluding remarks about his cherished airplane; cherished in the nostalgic sense that someone else might feel about a prized car, truck, bicycle, boat, or horse.

> *"We certainly are reluctant to sell our float plane so we're using it as much as possible now. … Today Ruby, Ruth, and I flew to Kokrines downriver and spent the afternoon with missionary Scriptures. We went pike fishing. I caught 8 or 9 measuring 24-36 inches. … I saw several of the Indians with medical problems. We got back to Tanana at 10:00 pm – the sun was still fairly high and it was perfectly quiet without any turbulence. Ruby and Ruth really enjoyed the trip."*

Elmer sold the Piper J-3 to a friend in Anchorage—and noted, "I got nearly as much as what I paid for it two years ago."

Several weeks after the purchase of the broad-winged Family Cruiser, Elmer completed the necessary training to fly the larger plane and flew it home from Fairbanks.

As anxious as Ruby was about her husband's flying, her letter home showed unusual elation, and she wrote in detail about the arrival.

> "Our biggest thrill last week was the fact that Elmer got our Family Cruiser and we all had our first ride yesterday afternoon and was Ruth thrilled, she shows little excitement ordinarily but she was so excited about daddy having a bigger plane and us flying as a family she jumped all over the place. Mishal had her first plane ride and loved it, Naomi, Mark, Ruth sit in the back bench seat and the rest of us in the front. Elmer had a radio on the plane which will help him fly the beam, he also has lights, starter and those things seem like a luxery as the other plane had none of those."

It was noteworthy to mention Ruth's behavior. Whereas Naomi would unabashedly express emotion, Ruth was not only reluctant to do so, but almost apologetic.

With bedsheets freshly washed and hanging on the clothesline in preparation for the next guests, Ruby found time to take a day trip down the Yukon River to visit Russ and Freda Arnold again.

> "Sat. mid-morn we got up and went to Ruby (village.) I had baked buns for a hamburger fry and two pies, deep-fried maple rolls, and made a batch of veg. soup. We took our entire family … our new plane is on wheels and the villages have something of a dirt landing strip."

How she managed to bake, fry, and cook in such short order was anyone's guess.

Shortly after their arrival, Russ had a campfire crackling for the hamburger fry. It was a perfect day to be outdoors. Ruffles of clouds added texture to the broad blue sky, and the sun stood tall and proud, unlike in the winter when it hung sheepishly over the horizon. Wisps of smoke punctuated the clear air in a friendly way. Freda and Ruby wore sleeveless blouses, and Freda's full skirt swayed gently in the pleasant breeze. Little Sondra ran around in a red print jumper with a white puffy-sleeved blouse. She looked like any child at a city playground in the 1950s. The children darted in and out of the picnic area, asked when they could eat, and gathered pinecones to toss into the fire—and at each other.

Although the purpose of this jaunt was strictly to encourage the Arnolds, medical talk worked its way into Elmer and Russ's conversations about hunting and fishing.

"Well, that boy had cut himself on something under the water, I don't know what. I did know I needed to get it cleaned up and stitched up right away."

"Are you sure it's only first aid you know?" asked Elmer with a grin. "I may need to make referrals to you!"

The men laughed.

Elmer paused for a minute. "Say, the next time I hold clinic here, I'll teach you how to give injections. That would help us both, plus help the Native people."

Russ nodded in agreement.

Ruby and Freda discussed food ordering and meat preservation.

"Just like you, we order our year's food supply from Anchorage," said Freda. "Like yours, it comes in on the barges. We always order enough cases of whole canned chicken and tuna fish to have on hand."

Russ looked up from adorning his hamburger with mustard and added, "We eat salmon, moose, and local berries too. I imagine you've become accustomed to all that as well."

Ruby was familiar with cutting up and packaging moose with Elmer, and together taking it to the large walk-in freezer locker at the hospital. She wondered what the Arnold's did for meat preservation.

"I hunt moose in the fall, when it's cold, and hang the quarters over there." Russ motioned to a ramshackle building that was either a large shed or had been someone's small house. At this stage of its life, the definition was indiscernible. "Of course, everything remains frozen during the winter months. When we run low, we bring in a quarter to thaw, package it, and put it out in the arctic entry."

Freda added, "I often can moose too. We also dry and smoke fish like the Natives do."

Later on, Ruby would experiment and do well with canning moose.

Russ kept up a steady dialog with Elmer. He wanted to put a barrel stove in the dirt-floor basement and fashion a means to get more heat upstairs. He and Elmer brainstormed methods. Elmer was a problem solver and one to take stock of what was around him for use or re-invention. Russ also planned to dig a well so they could have water directly into the house and not stored in a barrel.

Even with the children running to a parent for this and that, there were no lengthy interruptions for the adults. Mishal squirmed on a blanket on the ground, trying to reach the other children. Every now and then, she shrieked in frustration; otherwise, she did not demand attention. The other children played nicely, occasionally sneaking a maple roll and dividing it among themselves. The brown maple frosting on their chins and cheeks gave away their furtiveness.

All at once, Elmer looked at this wristwatch. "Guess we'd better head back," he said abruptly, clearing his throat.

Freda brought outside a basin of water for the children to wash their hands and faces.

THE REVOLVING DOOR OF HOSPITALITY

The last-minute conversation included exchanging what each had to do the following day for their worship services. Ruby and Elmer would be singing a duet and needed at least twenty minutes to choose a song and rehearse. Russ would be putting together a Bible lesson. Before sorting out their children and going their own way, the adults stood in a small circle and said short prayers for one another. Ruby's heart was blessed by the fellowship with these new friends, and she looked forward to the next time they would meet. Elmer's purchase of a larger plane was already making these connections easier.

Upon her return, without taking a day off or a complaint, or spending a day at a beauty spa, or even a quick nap, Ruby thought ahead to her next visitors. She wondered how she could make their stay more pleasant by fixing up the basement to welcome both overnight guests and playing children.

> *"I am cleaning the basement this week and will probably paint the concrete walls of the large playroom as we will let the missionaries from Kokrines (Scripters) live in that area until Elmer's folks come and then they should be ready to leave, she is coming here to have a baby and she is bring the entire family with her, they have three other children and our children will enjoy the playmates. The only way out of Kokrines now is boat and float plane so now we have decided that Elmer will meet them at Ruby and fly them in here with the family plane."*

Yes, more family members were to arrive along with everyone else. The girls marked off calendar days until Grandma and Grandpa Gaede would arrive from Reedley, California.

"They will bring me nuts," said Ruth confidently to Naomi. "Almonds."
"They will bring me dried peaches," replied Naomi.
The girls held hands and danced in a circle.

MAPLE ROLLS/LONG JOHNS

Ruby L. Gaede

Prepare yeast dough as for cinnamon rolls.
Knead until smooth.
Let rise in a covered bowl until double in size, about an hour.

Roll out dough to ¼-inch thick.
Cut into rectangles of approximately 2-by-4 inches.
Let rise until nearly double.

While waiting for rolls to rise, pour cooking oil into an electric frying pan or deep fryer to 3 ½ or so inches deep. Heat to 375 or 400 degrees.

Fry dough rectangles until golden on both sides. Remove and place on a paper towel on a cookie sheet.

Let cool to room temperature.

Mix icing. Apply icing.

Icing
Make a basic white frosting with oleo or butter, powdered sugar, and milk. Add maple flavoring.

CHAPTER 24

LOVED ONES AND MORE

Tanana, 1958

WHEN NAOMI HAD VISITED her Leppke grandparents in Peabody, Kansas, she had loved the flat, circular merry-go-round at the Peabody Park. After she had secured herself between the grab bar spokes extending from the middle, she had shouted to her father to run along the side and push. "Faster, Daddy, faster!" Ruby's months of July and August were much like that merry-go-round, although she wasn't shouting for anyone to make it go faster. If it wasn't guests practically flying to her doorsteps, she was out the door flying in Elmer's airplane. Who knew how many fish she fried, sheets she washed, or loaves of bread she baked? She didn't keep track. She didn't complain either.

Trips to visit missionaries weren't the only bait that snared her into Elmer's airplane.

> "July 7, 1958 Yesterday for the first time, I begged Elmer to take me fishing so we went with the float plane, sat down on the Yukon near the mouth of a creek, where Elmer and Leonard had gotten some Shee fish and Pike just Fri nite. We were there 15 minutes and the wind whipped up so I suggested we go to our plane so that it would not brake away from its flimsy anchor, we took off and boy was it turbulent we took off for home and by that time the river was choppy. The Shee fish are some of the best eating fish in Alaska, I much prefer it to Salmon an they are really mostly nearer the coast. When Leonard and Elmer returned with the 8½ lb, one smaller fish Thurs night at midnight, I had to get out of bed and fry them some fish. I did not mind one bit as that was Leonard's farewell party! He left the next morning for Point Barrow."

In contrast to Elmer, who, like an Alaskan volcano, had erupted with enthusiasm after his first visit to Tanana, it had taken Ruby much longer. Yet, she had done it. Now she could exuberantly enjoy life, even if it was somewhat like a Kansas tornado.

> "We had a very nice 4th of July, had lunch with the Gronnings I took a tuna dish, cabbage salad and pies over, that afternoon the village had planned races, such as sack races, running, bike races and egg races, I got second prize in carring an egg from in front of the store to the front of the Parish hall. Elmer got first prize in the broad jump he got $5.00, I got $3.00. The villagers were very surprised that Elmer was athletic. They thought he was a 'pamper child.'"

Fourth of July race in Tanana. Ruby Gaede is the woman on the far left, half-way back in the picture.

On July 19, Elmer flew Maxine Scripter and her two girls, Nancy and Shirley, in from Kokrines. That same day, Rev. Larry Scripter and son Bobby started upriver to Tanana in Larry's motorboat. The entire family would stay in the Gaede's basement playroom until Maxine delivered her fourth child.

Larry was of average height with dark hair and glasses. His skin was tanned from time spent outdoors. Just like Russ Arnold, he carried no extra weight. His son Bobby was the spitting image of him with the same oval face and slim build, although fair-skinned like his mother. Shirley's dark curls bounced around her pretty face. The Gaede and Scripter children were stair-stepped in ages: Bobby (eleven), Naomi (eight), Ruth (almost seven), Shirley (six), Mark (two-and-a-half), Nancy (two-and-a-half), and

Mishal (five months). That made ten people around the kitchen table, not counting baby Mishal, and ten people using the bathroom.

Kids were underfoot everywhere. They ran up and down the basement stairs. Ruby and Maxine shooed the children outdoors. Kids dashed out the front door and returned through the back. Ruby repeatedly said, "Shut the door. Don't let the mosquitos in." Orange and grape juice spilled on the table—and off the table. Rice Krispies crackled beneath feet. Peanut butter made doorknobs sticky and slippery. Maxine encouraged Bobby to follow his father down to help Roy Gronning chop wood or make repairs.

"I'm sure he could use your help doing something, anything, just go and find out."

She also wondered if walking more would start her contractions and get this fourth child on its way. She volunteered to accompany Mark and Nancy to the hospital playground. She would have volunteered to weed Ruby's large garden; however, stooping over was out of the question.

As if in a timed race, Naomi and Ruth rode their bikes to the playground and around the hospital circle drive. They did nothing to avoid the shallow mud puddles. They didn't even raise their feet off the pedals and glide through. At least they were sockless. Shirley made mud pies in the playhouse. In most cases, the babble inside and outside the house was that of busy children finding their own harmless amusement.

By bedtime, every child needed a bath in the one bathroom; they almost had to draw straws for who could use it next. Ruby thought it would save time to put Naomi and Ruth in the tub at the same time. That was a logical thought if the girls had not used the simple bathtub as a water park. They hooted and splashed. Perhaps they were having too much fun.

"Time's up," called Ruby through the door.

On August 4, Elmer flew to Fairbanks, a one-and-a-half-hour flight, to pick up Arnold and Mary (Ediger) Leppke, who had driven up the Alcan Highway from North Dakota. Arnold was Ruby's father's cousin, and Mary was one of Elmer's mother's six sisters. This marriage was nothing out of the ordinary in Mennonite communities, and it reduced introductions at family reunions.

Prior to their arrival, Uncle Arnold wrote Elmer in a panic, "I cannot find the road from Fairbanks to Tanana on my map!" There was none. Fairbanks was the final road destination at that time, and even sixty-some years later, there would not be a road into Tanana.

Arnold was definitely a go-getter. Driving up the dusty, gravel, uncivilized Alcan Highway to see his relatives was nothing; after all, he was made of stock that had come over on the ship from Ukraine with other Mennonite families. He didn't need coddling either. The people of the dirt and land, who were subject to weather determining their farming fate, could deal with about anything. In this case, that meant flying in a small airplane to a place inaccessible by roads and eating moose meat. "What are we doing first?" he asked Elmer after an initial handshake.

The girls stared at Mary, who was eleven years younger than their Grandma Agnes Gaede. Whereas Grandma Gaede wore her hair pulled close to her head, Mary let her dark curls flutter around her face. She smiled more often than her older sister, not that Grandma Gaede was unfriendly; Agnes was more quiet, observant, and serious. In spite of that, both sisters were short and sturdy and had square jaws. Without needing to be asked, both blended easily into the tasks at hand.

Uncle Arnold and Aunt Mary slept in the girls' room. The girls slept on the floor in Mark's room, except for one night when Naomi persuaded her mother that there should be a kids' slumber party in the living room. Ruby gave in. What difference would it make? Life was not normal at the moment. The sun interfered with sleep anyway. School was not in session. The only person on any schedule was Elmer, although he was running a minimal appointment book, and instead, gave everyone flights in his new plane and took the men and Bobby fishing.

The slumber party did not include Mark, Mishal, or Nancy. It did include Bobby teaching the girls pig Latin, a made-up language game. Naomi took to it immediately; unfortunately, she was more fluent in it than the three years of German she would take in college,

With Arnold and Mary, twelve people crowded around the table and a card table. Twelve adults and children used the one bathroom. Twelve people needed clothes washed, including a baby in diapers. Twelve individuals went on a picnic. Every day, Ruby baked sandwich bread, dinner rolls, hamburger and hot dog buns, or pies. Aunt Mary rolled up her sleeves, buttoned on an apron, and busied herself with rising yeast, meal preparations, a pastry cloth—and quieted Mishal's cries for food. Within all this commotion, Ruby wrote, "This is more fun than I have had in three years."

She also apologized, "*I seem to be lagging behind in correspondence*" This was amidst other sentences, such as, "*The children are having a wonderful time,*" "*We are a bit lazy in the morning and don't eat breakfast until 9:00 or 9:30,*" and "*Elmer took Roy Gronning, Larry Scripter and Uncle Arnold fishing. They got a 11 lb Pike and Elmer got a fish hook in his ear, so they broke it off with a plires and when they got back he had the dentist remove it,*" and "*Mrs. Scripter still has not had her baby.*"

As much as Uncle Arnold and Aunt Mary wanted to stay longer, there were more sightseeing spots on their list; and as much as Ruby had enjoyed seeing relatives and sharing her Alaska life with them, and speaking with them the Plautdietsch of her childhood, she was beginning to wonder where she would put more people when Elmer's parents would arrive. Perhaps stash all the kids in the playhouse? That was a silly thought and totally unrealistic. On August 10, six days after their arrival, Elmer flew Arnold and Mary Leppke back to Fairbanks, where they continued to explore Alaska—by car.

On August 13, Mrs. Scripter had a baby boy. That same evening, Ruby admitted she was tired. Yes, indeed. That same evening, Elmer made preparations to fly his plane to Fairbanks the next day to pick up his parents.

The wake-up smell of coffee wafted from the kitchen. Even when she wasn't ready for a conversation, Ruby made sure her aluminum percolator was going for her guests. There were no sounds of children anywhere, which is a mother's early morning simple pleasure when she is trying to apply lipstick, prepare breakfast, and do another load of laundry.

Elmer walked into the kitchen with his shirt half-buttoned. He nodded at Mr. Scripter, who was at the table drinking coffee. The window drapes were pulled back, and the sun was up and ready for the day, although slightly filtered through sketches of clouds in a muted blue sky.

Even though Ruby's in-laws weren't expected to arrive in Fairbanks until 4:30 p.m., Elmer had factored in plenty of time to get them in his Family Cruiser and maybe even catch a ride into town and pick up additional groceries.

"I'll make rounds at the hospital and check on Maxine before I go," he said to Larry.

In short order, Elmer was putting miles and memories on the new airplane.

Ruby, the girls, and Mark listened for the sound of the Family Cruiser returning from Fairbanks. Ruby was indoors changing sheets, doing last-minute ironing, and making a simple soup for supper. Soup could be reheated as needed since who knew when Elmer and his parents would actually arrive.

Naomi stuck her head in the door, jumped on one foot, and called impatiently, "What time is it?" This was the umpteenth time she had done that. Ruby so wished that girl could tell time. She had tried to explain the position and significance of the hands on the clock but without success. Perhaps Naomi would learn that the coming year, in third grade.

The next time Ruby looked out the window, she saw Mark standing in the middle of Front Street, facing east with his hands shading his eyes. Ruby ran out, locked her fingers around his arm, and scolded him. "You may stand on the front steps, but not in the street!" He sat down in a huff. Naomi and Ruth were just as antsy. Once their mother was back in the house, they all stood in the street.

"We're older," said Naomi. "We can move if a truck comes."

There were no cars in the village, only pickup trucks, and those were few and far between on the road.

Finally, the far-away hum of an airplane was heard. When it came closer, they saw it was red.

"Daddy, Daddy, Daddy," the threesome shouted.

"Grandma, Grandpa, Grandma, Grandpa!" Naomi and Ruth chanted. Mark did not know what a grandpa or grandma was. He stared at the girls and resumed shouting for his daddy.

"Hurry, hurry," said Ruby, flinging open the front door with Mishal under one arm. The child's bare legs dangled beneath her nylon full-skirted dress.

Elmer had arranged for Ruby to drive the hospital ambulance-jeep to the airstrip, so his parents' luggage could more easily be brought back to the house. The girls pulled and pushed Mark into the front bench seat, and Ruby handed off Mishal to Naomi. Without ado, Ruby put one foot on the brake, pushed in the clutch, started the engine, and shifted into gear. The four children held on to whatever they could. They arrived at the airstrip seconds later, followed by a swirl of silty sand.

Henry Gaede was already climbing out of the airplane's front seat. His brown taupe suit was only slightly wrinkled. There was no doubt he and Elmer were father and son: same forehead, black wavy hair, and prominent ears. Like his son, Henry was a picture taker, and his brown Kodak camera case was strapped over one shoulder. Elmer exited the plane next. Together, the men assisted Agnes Gaede from the confined backseat. This was not easy. She was wearing a dress, as would any woman in the 1950s that was traveling. "Turn around, Mom," Elmer instructed her. As modestly as possible, she backed down to the ground using the single metal step bar. She made it. After all, at one time in her life, she had climbed on and off a tractor, and she hadn't worn overalls either.

Agnes stood for a moment and smoothed down her teal dress with its broad white collar and white buttons to the waist. She was a model of fashion with accessories of a pearl necklace, a black close-fitting hat with a small-netted veil, and a small black handbag. Already, her short black pumps were dusty gray.

Naomi and Ruth rushed toward their grandparents, who embraced them fondly. Mark had seen his grandparents once when he was one-and-a-half years old. He ignored the strangers. Patting an airplane tire, he pulled on his father's pant leg. "Daddy, go for a ride?"

Grandma Agnes took one look at Mishal and gathered her into her arms, arms that were used to holding babies. She relinquished the child for a mere moment when she strained to pull herself into the front seat of the ambulance and then reached for the baby again. Ruby and the other three children crawled into the back and sat on a wool army blanket. Grandpa Henry climbed in beside Agnes, and Elmer drove them back to the house. Like a tour guide, he told them about the CAA housing campus, the island across the Yukon River, and every building in the medical compound.

In consideration of the Gaede family's initial reunion, Larry Scripter and his three children were at the Gronnings for supper. Ruby warmed up soup, and the girls hovered around their grandparents to see what was inside their suitcases. Prior to their departure from California, Elmer had requested his parents bring fruit, cucumbers, and "good" bologna. Ruby asked for rubber gloves for washing dishes, dill seed and parsley for making borscht, and little socks for Mishal. Courageously, Ruth had made her wishes known. "Maybe they can bring a watermelon. Just a little one."

There was no watermelon in the large suitcase; nevertheless, there were small toys, nuts, dried and fresh fruit, cucumbers, and a ring of "good" bologna.

Before the girls' bedtime, and after Grandma had rocked Mishal to sleep, Agnes followed the girls into Mark's bedroom where they still had mats on the floor, since their grandparents would now sleep in the girls' room, just as Arnold and Mary had.

"See, Grandma," said Naomi. "This is Betty doll, Kathy the ballerina, and Pete. Mommy made Pete." Pete was a floppy doll made of white terry cloth, an embroidered face, and yellow yarn hair.

Her grandmother made complimentary noises about her dolls.

"And what do we have here?" asked Agnes of Ruth.

"This is Puff. And this is another Puff," said Ruth timidly. Ever since she was a preschooler, Ruth had attached herself to white stuffed-animal cats, all named "Puff."

That set the tone for Grandma Gaede's visit, and the girls often ran to her with, "Come, let me show you this."

Breakfast progressed a bit slowly with the Scripter family integrated into the mix, and the three oldest Scripter children reticent about meeting more new people. Ruby was glad to hand off Mishal to her mother-in-law while she kept homemade raisin bread jumping in and out of the toaster. Mishal bobbed owl-eyed over her grandmother's shoulders. Living in a revolving-door household would become customary for her. At one point, Ruby had to mix more powdered milk for additional bowls of cereal. The thin milk had a slightly blue tint and always tasted better if made overnight and left to sit in the refrigerator. That morning, however, no one seemed to care, certainly not the children. For them, this was normal.

Henry didn't hesitate to get acquainted with Larry. Fishing was a common topic of interest.

"You'll have to come to visit us in Kokrines," said Larry enthusiastically. "I'll show you real Alaska fishing!"

Henry was ready to go.

Elmer interrupted. "That sounds good, but for now, I think Mom wants to check out the hospital and our garden."

Indeed, Agnes did. Not only were her arms made to hold babies, but as a teenaged girl, she had helped deliver them. Back then, physicians were not always available, and it wasn't unusual for babies to be welcomed into the world with the help of aunties or midwives.

Elmer introduced his parents to the hospital receptionists, who sat at metal desks behind heavy, steel-gray Royal typewriters, striking them loud and fast, then zinging the carriage across for another line. Their desks were covered with manila filing folders.

The hospital wards were painted bright white and smelled of Lysol bleach. Nursed carried themselves with an air of efficiency in their white starched dresses, white caps, white hose, and white shoes. Henry and Agnes peeked cautiously through open doors to see patients in tall, white, metal-pipe framed beds. In the nursery, babies basked in bassinets, wrapped in either pink or blue blankets. Agnes questioned the lack of incubators for babies born prematurely. Elmer shook his head and sighed. "No, not in this remote outpost." Throughout the coming days, Elmer's mother would repeat how proud she was of him for becoming a doctor and then quiz him as to the symptoms, prognosis, and risks for tuberculosis, as well as about the most typical medical cases he saw at the hospital. She was a serious woman, most likely smart enough that if her place in life had allowed, she would have become a physician herself, or at least a nurse.

Agnes was equally interested in the large vegetable gardens beside the hospital. She had a green thumb and in California produced giant balls of pink, blue, and purple hydrangea flowers, as well as sago palms; the latter of which she gifted to family, friends, and neighbors. Although the sun still made Ruby turn her face toward it and soak in its rays, in mid-August, there were hints of frost on the Tanana gardens, and harvest time was in motion. Mark waded into the garden with his grandparents. The green bean bushes touched his elbows, and the big balls of cabbage reached his thighs. He stood out like a stop sign in his red jacket, red pants, and tight-fitting, red cap that buckled beneath his chin. Grandma added color in her red and navy plaid flannel skirt and Elmer's red plaid wool jacket. A tangle of yellow sweet peas and orange and pink poppies grew sporadically through Ruby's merry mini-farm. Grandpa snapped pictures from all angles.

Agnes and Henry Gaede with Mishal in the garden, between Front Street and the Yukon River, with the C.A.A. behind them.

Elmer turned over his parents to Ruby when a fish cleaning accident came in. After living nearly a year in Tanana and seeing it from one end to the other, Ruby was a savvy guide. Without hesitation, she escorted her in-laws to the Native part of the village to see salmon on drying racks. The racks were made of thick spruce poles set in the ground with cross poles between them at the height of about six feet. After the salmon were gutted, their heads and backbones were removed, leaving two slabs of meat joined at the tail. This connecting piece made it easy to string them on the cross pieces, where they would cure in the sun. The fish were slashed diagonally to facilitate drying. There was no protection from the elements. Ravens bounced along the poles and squawked. The noontime sun was warm, and the odor of fish was strong. Mark batted at the flies. "Stinky," he said, shaking his head. The salmon that had been hanging for some time were dark red and had the slight stiff curl of dead leaves, while those caught more recently were bright oily red.

Henry and Agnes Gaede with Mark in front of fish racks.

The next day was damp with dishwater gray skies. This time, Ruth volunteered to watch Mishal while her mother took her grandparents on another tour. Even if only seven years old, Ruth considered herself capable of caring for babies. Ruby agreed this would work during Mishal's naptime. Naomi would stay at home, too, and if there was a need, she could go to the hospital to get their father or someone on staff.

Ruby guided her in-laws to visit Grandma Elia and explained to Henry and Agnes that the Native woman was "grandma" to everyone, and made her unique design of beaded moose-skin moccasins for virtually every baby born in the village. They were curious to meet her.

The gentle rain had calmed the dust, and in its place, there was mud. Agnes wore clear plastic galoshes over her shoes. Ruby carried a heavy army-surplus, green raincoat. Mark stomped in the puddles with his knee-high black rubber boots and reached out to the tall grass that lined the vehicle-wide path called Back Street. "Diamonds," he said. The air was clean and sweet and enhanced more so by the fragrance of blue-gray smoke rising above the tin roofs.

Many of the cabins reflected years of additions with different pitches of tin roofs. Often, a bicycle leaned beside the front door, typically with a basket on the handlebars to transport items from the store or post office. Grandma Elia's house was no different. Ruby knocked on the door and the old Native woman, with history written on her face, opened the door slowly. When she saw Ruby, she smiled, and her dark eyes brightened. "Oh!" she said, wrapping her sweater more tightly around her as she stepped out the door.

Ruby introduced her parents-in-law and asked if they could see her handiwork. Grandma Elia turned back inside and returned with several moccasins. Henry and Agnes caressed the soft moose skin and remarked about the careful and colorful beadwork, all tightly sewn together in flower patterns. Agnes had done plenty of handwork with needle and thread, yarns, and so forth; however, this craft required dexterity unfamiliar to her. Grandma Elia said little, just smiled, and commented with a few yeses and uh-huhs. Henry talked enough for everyone.

After the village tour, Agnes said in Plautdietsch to Ruby and then later to Elmer, "*Jauma lied* (pitiful people)!" She could not imagine living in those simple conditions. She did not know how they survived a winter. She just shook her head with concern.

The Gaede house started to clear out, and Ruby found a moment to write her mother:

> "On August 19, Rev. Scripter loaded his boat and he and Bobby took off for home. Three days later Elmer and dad Gaede flew Mrs.

Scripter, the two girls, and baby – only 7 days old. Elmer landed on sandbar across the river from Kokrines. The cruiser is now on wheels. Rev. Scripter came with his motorboat and taxied the family to their pioneer home."

Once again, Ruby washed and hung out sheets from the basement bed. Grandpa and Grandma moved downstairs, and Naomi and Ruth returned to their bedroom.

The kitchen table held only eight now, including Mishal, whom Grandma Gaede nestled into her ample lap and snuck bits of food into the six-month-old's baby-bird eager mouth.

"Mom, you don't have to hold her," maintained Ruby. "You can put her in the Teeter-Babe." The yellow and white floor-level bouncing seat with a tray was nearby; all the same, Grandma refused to relinquish the child. As young as she was, Mishal probably knew she had a good thing going with this grandmother.

Elmer hastily downed his supper in case he would be called out for an emergency. Wiping his mouth on a napkin, he settled back into his chair while everyone else continued eating.

"Dad, Mom, you've got to go to one of our terrific tourist attractions," he said with a laugh. "The dump."

His parents looked at him quizzically.

"Yes! Let's go to the dump," said Naomi and Ruth readily.

Naomi put her hand over Ruth's mouth and whispered loudly, "Don't tell them. Let it be a surprise."

After supper, the family drove in the ambulance several miles south, where the dump marked the end of the road. The dump sat high on a bluff overlooking the Yukon River and was actually a spectacular viewpoint for the massive river, the island in its middle, and the flats beyond it. The area around the dump was thick with spruce, birch, and aspen trees, along with dense undergrowth. Who knew what the darkness held.

Just as Elmer had anticipated, several black bears were foraging. Out of the corner of his eye, he saw a red fox creep toward the garbage, all the while keeping its eyes on the bear. Everyone watched silently for the drama. Slyly the fox snuck in, grabbed a bite, and darted back into the bushes. It did this repeatedly, and the girls guessed how close to the bears it would venture. Elmer and his father stuck their heads and cameras out either side of the ambulance side windows. The bears did not seem to care about the fox, the ambulance, the audience, or the view. They waddled around in their smorgasbord and pawed at chunks and piles of this and that.

After awhile, Mark grew restless and noisy, and Mishal started to cry.

"The outing is over. Time to go home," stated Elmer.

"Tomorrow, we will pick blueberries and make a pie," announced Ruby.

Every day was packed with new experiences. Agnes was game for anything, although she didn't express her interest as vigorously as did her husband. When asked if she wanted to do something, she would answer with a simple "yes." No big grin like Henry.

And so it was one morning after Elmer had delivered a past due maternity patient, and he was eating cold cereal and warm cinnamon rolls dripping with frosting, that he proposed to his parents a previously discussed opportunity.

"I can now leave the village for a bit longer, so what if you fly to Kokrines with me tomorrow?"

The idea was to help Larry Scripter get a moose. It would be easier for him to fly with Elmer and spot a moose from the air than to wander around in the woods by foot, hoping to run into the wilderness meat department. The plan was for Henry to accompany the hunters and Agnes to stay with Maxine and the children. This would give both Elmer's parents insight into the village life of missionaries.

Ruby's first thoughts were food preparation, not only for the three in her family who were going on the trip but for the Scripter family as well. After all, Maxine's new baby was scarcely two weeks old. How tired Maxine must be with caring for three other children and most likely being up at night with the baby.

Naomi and Ruth put on too-large aprons and glued themselves to Grandma's elbows as she rolled out molasses crinkle cookie dough. Sugary smells filled the kitchen, and when the cookies came out of the oven, Ruth spotted one she judged was "kind of" crumbled and needed to be eaten right then and there.

Ruby ground up leftover moose roast, mixed in sweet pickle relish, Miracle Whip, and several dabs of yellow mustard. She sampled it and added a dash more pepper and salt. Finally, it met her standards. This would be sandwich spread for the brown bread she had already made.

Next came a quick and easy soup recipe: browned moose hamburger, tomato juice, rice, and assorted vegetables. Ruby tripled the recipe so there would be some for the Scripters, some for supper that night, and some for the following day.

The next morning, Elmer loaded up his airplane with the food goodies, his parents, and his .300 magnum hunting rifle. Agnes climbed slowly into the backseat, wearing a brown cotton dress, heavy hose, and sensible, sturdy shoes. She mumbled about being dressed too casually to visit the missionaries. Henry nimbly followed Elmer into the plane. His khaki slacks had crisply ironed creases down the center of each leg, and his buttoned khaki shirt matched perfectly. He most likely would not be featured in the *Alaska*

Sportsman magazine. There was no doubt in the minds of Henry and Agnes that just because they were in the middle of Alaska, along the Yukon River, and going to a remote village with only thirty-some people, that they should not dress properly for a visit.

As it turned out, the hunters didn't spot any moose; however, Grandma Agnes got to hold another baby and give Maxine some reprieve from managing so many needs.

Regardless of the unsuccessful hunt, Larry was as good as his word and took the Californians fishing. Along the Yukon River shoreline, numerous enormous logs had come to rest on their wild ride down the river after breakup. They had been torn off their precarious, cliffhanging positions over the river, and chunks of ice had grabbed them, carrying them along in the motley parade down to the sea. Some of the trees had jumped off the fast track and onto a shoreline or sandbar. Along the way, they had bared their branches and, after a number of seasons, were bleached gray. At this stage, they made natural resting spots for a jacket, lunch, or fishing pole.

As a kid, Henry had caught catfish by hand in the muddy Kansas creeks. However, these Alaska fish were a completely different story, a true fisherman's story that didn't need exaggeration. And, Agnes didn't intend to be a bystander. She rolled up the sleeves of her pink sweater, poked her nose in the tackle box, and in no time was casting off. She was no pansy; even so, the first bite caught her off guard and knocked her off-balance. She pursed her lips resolutely and dug in her heels, literally.

"Hang on, Mom!" shouted Elmer. He reached over, steadied her, and played the fish. When all was said and done, the fish was over thigh-high against her.

"Hmm. Let me try again," she said, with a sparkle in her eyes.

Henry and Agnes kept reeling in the pike, ranging from eleven to sixteen pounds, until they had over twelve on a line. Henry laughed heartily, and Agnes even chuckled a bit.

"Mother," said Henry to his wife, "You will have a lot of backseat company."

The fishermen and woman finally called it a day. They left some fish with the Scripters, gave several to a Native man who had helped them, and stashed the rest into the airplane. Before taking off, Henry and Agnes shook hands with Larry and Maxine and thanked them for adding to their Alaska pleasure.

Sunday. Sunday church. Sunday church clothes. Walking a half-mile to the Arctic Missions Chapel. No second thoughts on any of these things. One could have thought the fancy folks were showing off, or perhaps getting ready to set foot on a Rose Parade float and wave their hands sideways at the crowd, all the while smiling brightly; but, no, they knew the standards for churchgoing, and there was no compromising. Not like it was a sin not to dress up for church. It was a matter of respect for God.

And God's splendor in His creation was evident everywhere. The enormous blue sky held quilt-batting clouds, and the sun glinted off the new, silver corrugated metal roof on the Northern Consolidated Company building. Wild grass still showed vibrant green life. The Yukon River had thrashed itself clean of mud and at this end of summer was running a near turquoise hue.

As could be expected, Elmer set the pace toward the chapel, taking long steps alongside his father and pulling the red wagon with Mishal inside.

The baby didn't seem to mind the uncushioned ride, although every now and then, her legs kicked straight up in the air. Both men marched at a pace where their wide-striped neckties fluttered against their chests.

Ruby walked confidently in her high heels and dainty pink nylon dress. The cape-collar around her shoulders floated up and down in the breeze. Short white gloves and a white pillbox hat finished off her churchgoing attire. Of course, Ruby's mother-in-law was in fine fashion as well.

The girls ran ahead in matching full-length dress coats. Naomi's was navy, Ruth's was red, and both had wide, circular collars and only a button or two on top.

"Wait! Wait!" called Mark, dodging between the two groups of his family. If he would make it to the chapel without skinning his knees was nothing to bet on. All the same, he looked dapper in his gray suit with shorts.

Ruby and Elmer had warned his parents that the church was not much more than a lean-to shed and about the size of a large single-car garage. Of course, there were no church pews, only tan metal folding chairs that scraped noisily against the floor when bumped or moved.

Naomi and Ruth smiled from ear-to-ear when they walked behind their grandparents on the narrow boardwalk up to the door. Elmer introduced his parents to the Gronnings, several nurses, Grandpa Sam, who was the Native "grandpa" to the Gronning's children, and others in attendance. In every case, Henry shook their hands, and both he and Agnes politely responded with, "How do you do?" and "Pleased to meet you." Truly, they were pleased. They looked both young and old people in the eye and had a kind comment for each.

The hymns were familiar to the Gaede grandparents, and they settled into the service as comfortably as regular attenders. Afterward, they stayed to chat with the other twenty-five or so people.

Sunday dinner was enhanced by the garden harvest. Naturally, there was a moose roast with gravy, but unlike during the winter, when mashed potatoes came out of a box and were fluffed with hot water, there were real potatoes to mash. No canned vegetables either; real cauliflower with melted Velveeta cheese sauce. Of course, there was pie. "Just one more blueberry pie before we leave?" Henry had requested. So it was.

Somewhere amid being a cook, nanny, housecleaner, tour guide, and near interrogator of her in-laws about the relatives in California—questioned in Plautdietsch—Ruby managed to write a few lines to her parents:

"*Anna Bortel returned the 25th with no place to stay as the construction men are in the old school (a new school is under construction but will not be completed until Jan – 59).*"

Anna arrived three days before Elmer's parents left. She stayed in the girls' room and slept in one of the single beds; the girls slept head to toe in the other.

"*Our play room is vacant and she will stay here and eat with us. The second female teacher, Harriet Amundson, will come in a week and stay downstairs, too. We don't know how long.*"

It would be another five weeks before it was just the six of them.

LOVED ONES AND MORE

IT WENT WITHOUT SAYING

Men took off their caps and hats in buildings, when the National Anthem was played, and most certainly in church.

People looked one another in the eye and greeted them with "How do you do?" and "Pleased to meet you." Never did they say, "Hey" or do fist bumps.

"Yes sir," "Yes ma'am," and "Yes miss," were courtesies and signs of respect, and in no way demeaning.

Handshakes, typically the right hand, were used when greeting another person and were given by all, even children. A handshake on a business deal meant something; it was a promise as good as if it were in writing.

Men gave up their seats in a meeting area or bus for a woman, an elderly person of either gender, or a person with an assistance device, such as a cane or crutches.

"Bread and Butter" notes were short, written letters of appreciation to the host and hostess following an act of hospitality, such as dinner at someone's home.

Sundays were the day of rest from work, whether or not the person went to church.

Churchgoers traditionally wore their "Sunday Best" clothes—nicer clothes than what was worn every day. The attitude of wearing "Sunday Best" was that of reverence in the house of worship.

Sunday noontime dinner went beyond a noontime lunch of sandwiches. For many in mid-west farming communities. Sunday dinner was beef roast with carrots or fried chicken, mashed potatoes, gravy, homemade rolls, salads, or vegetables that were in season. Of course, there was dessert.

Little League or such sports games were not scheduled on Sunday.

Stores were closed on Sundays, and "Blue Laws" were in effect and still are in some states. Also known as Sunday laws, these laws are designed to restrict or ban some or all Sunday activities for religious reasons, particularly to promote the observance of a day of worship or rest.

CHAPTER 25

SUMMER'S END

Tanana, 1958

COLD RAIN PELTED AGAINST THE WINDOW. Mark begged to go outdoors anyway. His mother told him no. He sneaked out. Within minutes, he returned with a telltale path of muddy footprints. Ruby scolded him and cleaned up the floor. The busy boy climbed onto the couch and followed the rain trails on the windowpane. Fingers of rain. Fingers of a little boy. A smudged window.

Aspen trees were turning a rich gold. The moisture enhanced the intensity of the brilliant hue, and the trees along the river cast a rippling reflection on the water. Soon their leaves would shimmer goodbyes before dropping to the ground. The fresh smell of rain and the pungent aroma of damp and dying vegetation mingled with the smoke of cabin woodstoves. It was a cozy aroma with only the need of coffee percolating in the background and a good book to make it a perfect occasion.

The September 1958 Public Health Service's *The Mukluk Telegraph* (Volume II, Number 4) painted a similar picture:

```
Cranberry and blueberry picking is being indulged
in by hospital personnel and villagers alike. At
the nurses' quarters on a morning now and then
can be detected the delicious aroma of blueberry
muffins - real yummy!

Tanana and vicinity is wearing lovely fall colors
and since last month the Northern Lights have been
streaking white in the sky, and all of nature is
turning now in its annual cycle to the older part
of the year, leaving us still a bit nostalgic about
the beautiful green summer that we have enjoyed
so much.
```

Ruby's parents-in-law had been gone only ten days, and since then, sunny days had been rare. Ruby was grateful for the pleasant times they had experienced weather-wise. The first week in September, she announced to them in a letter, "*I had to take in all our garden as we have had frost every nite for the past week.*" Her first Alaska garden had done its best to please her, and indeed it had satisfied her during the abbreviated growing season.

The Gaede family's tanned faces gave evidence of the canopy of sunshine and warmth during the long days of the short summer; yet at that moment, their sunny brown legs and arms were concealed beneath corduroy pants, long-sleeved shirts, and sweaters. "*It is definitely fall,*" Ruby continued in her letter. "*Trees are yellow and the girls are not in pedal pushers[80] or barefoot anymore, I am pulling out our woolens.*" Flannel felt comfy. Wool itched.

When a dry day slipped into the autumn weather pattern, Ruby hastily put together provisions of hot dogs, homemade buns, and other items for a spontaneous picnic on the river beach. She never complained about the work this required. She never tired of fixing a fire or eating the standard picnic fare, even when the temperatures dropped. Campfires and hot dogs would leave an indelible memory on her children; the smell and sound of a smoky, popping fire would transport them back to those moments of her unconcealed satisfaction, as well as their own contentment and pleasure in her company.

Undeniably, Ruby's life revolved around cooking and baking. Those elements were blended with hospitality and keeping watch over her children. And, whenever there was a special event, Ruby's contribution would often be a highlight. Take, for instance, the shower for Gronnings' third child.

> *"Tonite we have a shower at Tessy Williams at C.A.A. I'm making a cake for refreshments, I made angle food and put a large blue candle in the middle with pastel ribbons streaming around it, then using miniature umbrellas at spots around the cake, the 7 minute icing is blue too."*

On the home front, Ruby bemoaned that Mishal was growing up so quickly. As busy as the mother of four was, she didn't slack off in documenting Mishal's growing up incidents, even though in many families, by the time child number two, three, and for sure, four, comes along, records of new teeth, learning to crawl, and first words are slim pickings. A mother of such a brood does not have much time to record anything except a grocery list.

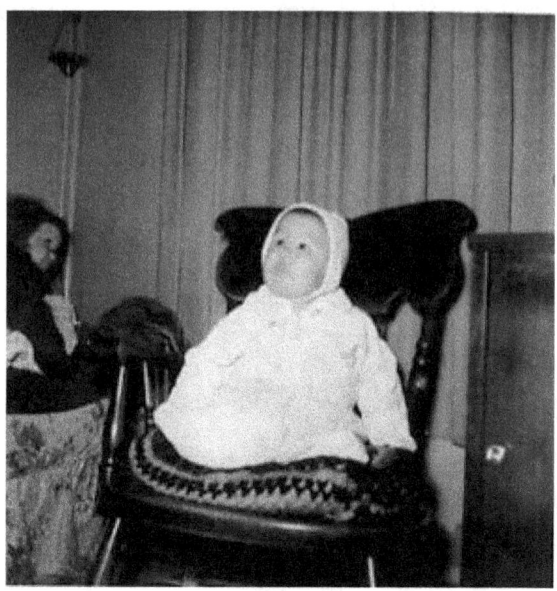

Mishal, six-and-a-half months on a rocker at the Gronning's house.

"(Six months) Mishal now sits in the yellow and white teeter-babe, often playing with her hands. She drools like everything and has 6 teeth. She gets on her knees then her tip toes and makes an arch, she seems to like that. She fell off the divan the other day and she felt very insulted to think her little world is not flat. She is cutting her naps very short now and that means more waking and fussing time, she gets tired of one place very quickly. She screams for food when we sit at the table, she misses grandma Gaede as she always took her on her lap and fed her as she ate."

The change of seasons heralded a new school year. In late spring of 1958, after the school building had been condemned as too dangerous for inhabitants, Elmer had worked with Robert Isaac, Administrative

Assistant for the Territorial Board of Education in Juneau, Alaska, along with the village chief, and people at the FAA to figure out how to continue school that fall. It was decided to borrow Quonset huts, also called shelter wells, from the White Alice site, on the hill, six or seven miles behind the village. The twenty-foot, semi-cylindrical, army-green canvas Quonsets had been used off and on as barracks for the White Alice defense employees. There were no windows except for those in the doors at each end. They smelled musty, a bit like wool socks that had never fully dried, and of lingering cigarette smoke. In late summer, these huts were dragged to the area beside the old Tanana Day School. Four were to be used as classrooms and an office.

The *Northern Lights* documented the beginning of the unusual 1958-year.

OCTOBER ISSUE (1958)

Editor: John Hawkins

Reporters:

Town News - Andrew Kennedy

Hospital - Rebecca Swenson

C.A.A. - Helena Wheeler

School - Larry Grant

MEET THE TEACHERS

Miss Harriet Amundson is from McGregor, Minnesota and is a graduate of Greenville College, Greenville, Illinois. She thinks winters will be like winters in Minn. She teaches 3rd and 4th grades during the day and works on school stoves in the evening.

Mr. Herman Romer is from Bethel, Alaska. Mr. Romer attended school in Texas and is a graduate of the University of Alaska. Mr. Romer teaches the upper grades during the day and works on the school stoves in the evening.

Miss Anna Bortel is from Bowling Green, Ohio. Miss Bortel teaches 1st and 2nd grades, is Head Teacher, and works on school stoves in the evening.

The name of the school is The Tanana Territorial School. The boys and girls go to school in (Quonset) hunts and some call them dog houses. There are three of these huts for school.

FIRST AND SECOND GRADE NEWS

Our favorite nursery rhyme is "Hickety Pickety."

THIRD AND FOURTH GRADE NEWS

We have new books and desks this year, but we will not use the desks till we get in our new school. The girls have been playing marbles and the boys playing football but sometimes the boys play marbles too. In Health we learned about keeping our hands clean and not to spit at each other.

UPPER GRADE NEWS

The school huts were banked with mud about a week ago. Philip Kennedy banked it with a payloader. He banked all five huts after Mrs. Gaede, Miss Amundson and Miss Bortel nailed old roofing sheets around the bottom of them.

VILLAGE NEWS

```
Many of the Tanana men are employed at the new
school. Mr. Smith is to be thanked for all his
hard work on the shelter wells - that goes for his
wife's help too! The C.A.A. made it possible for
us to have electrical lights by hooking us up to
the hospital lines.
```

Naomi and Ruth loved school and their teachers. Naomi had Miss Amundson. The fresh out of college young woman was large-boned and thickset, with brunette shoulder-length hair pulled back from her forehead and held in a clip, high on the back of her head. She smiled cautiously and was initially slow to warm up to adults; however, later on, her sense of humor emerged and helped her endure the unusual teaching circumstances of the fall of 1959. She had grown up on a farm. Over time she would demonstrate the resilience and no-shirking strength that most farm kids learn from an early age. Ruby had no trouble striking up a conversation with her on topics familiar to agricultural life: crops, equipment, weather, animals, and so on. She was familiar with the cold of a northern state, and Alaska would be no surprise to her.

After the previous year, Ruth had become accustomed to Anna Bortel. She was no longer put off by Miss Bortel's unreserved passion for education and children. There were no tears or hesitation this year.

Every morning, the girls bounded out the door with their long braids swinging over their shoulders; the rubber band on the end of each braid was covered by a small colorful barrette. They wholeheartedly embraced the day.

In contrast, Ruby viewed the school situation as pathetic. She commented to Elmer that the children would all need glasses after studying in the pathetic stark light of the bare, hanging light bulbs. Anna commented to Ruby, with a chuckle, that the teachers and students would feel like moles, living in the dark tunnels. Whereas Anna was glad to have a place to teach, Ruby was glad she did not have to teach her girls from the workbooks. In that sense, they were two very happy people.

Two more Quonsets were to be brought down later for the schoolteachers. It was for this reason, the immediate lack of accommodations for Anna and the new female teacher, that the two were living temporarily in the Gaede's basement, even though Herman Romer was allowed to stay in the old school, which was partially torn down.

The slender Yupik Eskimo dressed carefully in slacks and a button-down shirt. His straight, black hair was trimmed short in a crew cut, and he wore black-rimmed glasses. He flashed a smile easily, often over his shoulder and looking back at a person, which regularly elicited laughter. He had an immediate following from the children, and he was well suited to teach the older grades of five through eight. Within a short time, he would also teach math to some of the adults.

In the beginning, Ruby's optimistic and kind spirit took precedence over her desire to have a normal family life: that of two adults and four children sharing one bathroom and sitting around the table for meals. "*We are enjoying the teachers (living with us), they make it more work but they help with the dishes and are good company when Elmer is gone.*"

Shortly after this statement, however, Ruby's letters hinted at fatigue from the weeks and months of hospitality:

> "*They tease Mark and he does not like that … It appears they will have to stay downstairs with us for quite some time yet. We are charging them*

a reasonable amount for meals, but no room price … we so wish that the teachers would live by themselves it would be better for them and for our family but it is working out ok, yet it teaches us to get along with people."

Who could blame her for her honesty? She was ready to walk freely through her house without wondering whom she might run into, in the middle of the night, in the bathroom or the kitchen.

As if it wasn't enough to have unusual circumstances within her house, the hospital maintenance supervisor decided the hot water pipes needed to be replaced in the two duplexes on the medical compound. Why? Ruby did not know. To do so, eight-foot deep ditches were dug from the hospital to the Gaede's duplex. The ditches were just off the back concrete porch and steps and convenient for the children to access. Some areas of the ditches were slightly, and temporarily, backfilled; after school, the children immediately climbed down into those. Naomi's head poked out, but Mark's could not be seen, not even with his bright red cap. When he wanted out of the dirt confinement, he flapped his arms above his head and yelled, "Out! Out!" His sisters boosted him up and out. Soon other children showed up and, undeterred by the cold dampness of the pit, clambered into the remarkable new entertainment center as well.

The ground was sandy and easy to dig into with metal spoons and sticks. The frequent rain gave it a perfect consistency to hold its shape when carved. The young "construction" crew carved vertical roadways into the sides of the ditches and drove small cars in the tiers of a road system. It was a tight fit in the narrow space, and it worked best if every worker remained in the same place and did not try to pass the others. With teamwork, they extended the roads and relayed vehicles from one end or level to the other. Shouts and laughter rose from the trenches. When there was silence, Ruby hoped there had not been a cave-in.

"Mommy, Mommy! Naomi is stuck in the ditch," shouted Ruth. As if Ruby didn't have her mind on sixteen concerns already, Naomi had ridden Mark's oversized tricycle into a section of the ditch. The ditch wasn't wide enough for the trike to completely fall in, and Naomi was strung up partly on the trike and partly hanging upside down. She screamed and cried. Truly, she found herself in a pickle. Ruth, short as she was, pressed her lips together, and with a little grunt, pulled herself out of the ditch and ran into the house.

"*Mien kind, mien kind* (my child, my child)," exclaimed Ruby. She had been peeling potatoes for supper and walked out the door wiping her hands on her apron. It took her a minute to figure out which to grab first, a skinny arm or a skinny leg.

Naomi, amid the silence and stares of the other children, dramatically carried on. Whatever had possessed that girl to ride Mark's trike, and more so, into the ditch? Her knees stuck up above the handlebars, and in no way did she fit. After getting Naomi into the bathtub to soak her bruises, the frazzled mother pulled out the bike, checked for bent spokes, and admonished everyone within hearing distance not to ride tricycles or bicycles around the ditch, even if the sidewalk ran parallel to it.

That wasn't the end of it. So that the hospital duplexes could have hot water during construction, the hot water pipes were temporarily run above ground, about thirty inches high. This opportunity was not unnoticed by Naomi. "Ruth, we can fry mud pies." The girls went to work mixing mud pancakes into just the right consistency so they wouldn't ooze and drip off the round pipes. After trial and error, and with triumphant grins, they concocted a recipe for muddy dough that attached itself to the pipes and sizzled into smoothly baked concave breakfast fare.

Ruby didn't know which was worse: the deep, wet ditches or the unprotected boiling hot pipes. Both hazards seduced her children, and both were in what could have been referred to as her backyard. In either case, by suppertime, every child was covered from head to toe with dirt or mud. Ruby stood her three on the porch stoop and made them take off shoes and socks and empty their jacket pockets. There was no thought of possibly wearing clothes two days in a row. Ruby did a load of whites and a load of darks every day.

Naomi wasn't the only child needing attention. Take, for example, when Elmer thought it was time for Ruth's two front teeth to come out. Seeing the need for tooth extractions among the Natives, Elmer had found and read several books, and, when the itinerant dentist for the Natives was not around, had taken up dentistry. He had pulled Naomi's two front teeth when they were loose, and now, per the developmental timetable, it was appropriate to pull Ruth's. The teeth were not normal in shape and when Dr. Tom McQueen, the official dentist, came through, Elmer showed him Ruth's gums and how no other teeth seemed to be protruding to fill the gap.

"*What a shock*," wrote Ruby. "*The dentist thinks she probably will not get permanent teeth since her baby teeth were malformed so we will have to think about a bridge for her as it does handicap her speech and pronunciation, so the next time we go to Fairbanks we will have a thorough check as this dentist is not suppose to treat whites.*"

As it turned out, Ruth never did get a bridge, she learned how to talk without an impediment, and the remaining bottom teeth somewhat closed the gap.

There were other health concerns that affected the family as well. "Margaret does not cover her mouth when she coughs," Ruth informed her mother. Margaret was a girl suspected of having tuberculosis. The highly contagious disease was transmitted through saliva, and both adults and children were instructed sternly not to spit on the ground, or anywhere else, and to cough and sneeze into disposable tissues. "Maybe she forgot. Please tell her kindly, to use the tissue box that Miss Bortel has in your classroom," replied Ruby. Washing her hands afterward should have been a second step for Freda; however, such a health measure was hard to come by in the Quonsets without running water.

Mark had his issues too. He consumed more than his share of letter-writing space.

> "Mark is by my side all the time, when I bake bread he is there stirring, when I wash dishes he rinses and dries them, when I sew he is there adjusting the machine pulling threads and what have you. He requires 3 times the amount of discipline that the girls did. He hates sleeping alone and tries to sneak into one of our beds, usually Ruth's, although he says often, "Naomi broke my heart." As soon as I am out of sight, he calls, "Mommy, where are you?" When I ask him what he is afraid of, he says, "Earthquakes and bears.""

Life became somewhat easier at the end of September.

> "We are back to being just our family now. First time since July. The younger teacher (Harriet Amundson) misses Mark and Mishal so much, and seems lost. She really did seem to enjoy family life here."

Most certainly, Ruby had gotten to know Naomi's teacher, Harriet Amundson; and this was important to the child's mother. In consideration of that, one can imagine Ruby heaving a sigh of relief, throwing the guest bedsheets into the washing machine, and later, not remaking the bed. Enough was enough.

<u>ALASKA'S TEACHER DILEMMA TODAY</u>

Teachers continue to be needed in Alaska. In particular, there is a shortage of math, science, social studies, and special education teachers.

Teaching in much of Alaska is a challenge. It is important for teacher candidates to educate themselves so as to find a good match for both professional skills and personal lifestyle requirements. To do so, potential teachers must familiarize themselves with Alaska's history, people groups, climate, and, in many cases, village lifestyle. They must be aware of the differences in school populations. High schools in Anchorage, the largest city in Alaska, may have two thousand students, whereas in Interior Alaska or coastal villages there may be twenty or fewer students. At these smaller schools, a teacher may be required to teach a variety of grade levels and subjects.

Some teachers' spouses refuse to accompany them to Alaska. This may have to do with a spouse's job being elsewhere or his/her resistance to living in a remote, cold, isolated, and small community.

Fifty percent of new teachers quit within five years.

CHAPTER 26

RUBY THE HUNTER

Tanana, 1958

DREARY GRAY SKIES with thin drizzle dimmed the memory of the high summer sun. Berry foliage darkened daily, from bright red to crimson and purple-burgundy. The grass around the lakes and swamps turned rusty-orange. Chainsaws buzzed by woodpiles. A sense of urgency filled the air; the urgency to prepare for the swiftly approaching winter, even though it was only the middle of September. Then there was the urgency of bull moose to fight other bulls to mate the cow moose, which were not certain they wanted the wild, dramatic seasonal attention of the bulls. Urgent hunters needed to provide for their families, which included hunting for the moose. Adrenalin. Testosterone. Nervousness. Excitement.

Elmer loved nothing better than to hunt unless it was to fly—or practice medicine. Now he was ready for moose hunting. He had cleaned his .300 magnum and 30.06 rifles. His hunting knife was sharpened. His gear was sorted and ready. And, unlike most of the other people in the village, he had an airplane, which greatly increases a hunter's success.

The Natives depended on moose meat for their winter grocery supply, and hunting wasn't for the thrill of the kill or a trophy. In most cases, the men walked into the woods to see what they could scare up, unsure if they were far or near from their goal. Elmer recognized their predicament and was generous with his time and aviation gas to assist whenever he could.

First, he took out Pete Miller, the hospital maintenance man. It had been a terrible day with heavy rain and wind.

"Can't you wait to see if it will clear up tomorrow?" Ruby asked, kneading the palms of her hands together and trying to catch his eye. "No," he replied without looking at her. "This is moose hunting season. They like this weather. They won't be as cautious as usual. They will be out challenging each other and following the cows."

Pete and Elmer brought back a moose before the day was over. Both men were soaked to the bone. Both were as thrilled as little boys catching their first fish or shooting their first rabbit.

Next up was Roy Gronning. He and Elmer took off into an unsettled, restless sky with low-hanging clouds and an undefined horizon. As soon as the Family Cruiser was in the air, clouds bunched against the windows with only fleeting patches of visibility below. At only several hundred feet above the ground, Elmer circled back to the airstrip to land, meanwhile getting a dim bird's-eye view of everything beneath him. As he did, he spotted a moose three-fourth's of a mile off the end of the airstrip and near the road to the village dump. "Hey, Roy!" he yelled. "This could be easier than we expected."

The men traded the airplane for the hospital dump truck, and Ruby told the rest of the story in her family letter:

"They drove the truck as far as they could go and then hiked into the woods and after awhile they listened and heard the moose come

towards them, the wind in their favor when the moose got real close Rev. G plunked him with one shot, it was a 900 lb. bull. It took them all day to get it in and of course I did not know where they really were and so I always wonder if every thing is alright. This is the 3rd one he has helped get."

In quick succession, there was another hunt, and Ruby reported, *"Elmer just informed me that he and Leonard Lane, the Eskimo who helped him get the polar bear, shot another moose."*

Elmer spared no details of his adventures, which were often told as bedtime stories to his children, around the kitchen table, usually while they ate chocolate pudding, homemade ice cream, or a bowl of cold cereal. Ruby felt proud of her husband's successes and that he helped other men. He was the hunter. She was content as the gatherer of wild berries and harvester of the vegetable garden.

Her hunter-husband visualized her in a grander scheme. He wanted her to go with him, not only to accompany him but to shoot a moose herself. He tossed out the idea. The idea got as much traction as trying to stop his airplane on glare ice. He schemed up ways to tear down her resistance. He dried dishes after supper. He reasoned with her and reminded her what a strong farm girl she was. He solved the problem of what to do with the children. "The new Mennonite nurse, Olga Neufeld, can watch Mark and Mishal, and then Anna and Harriet can come over after school is out."

For a while, it was as though he was talking to a wall, yet, he was as determined as a salmon swimming upstream to spawn. His good deeds, solutions to her obstacles, and persuasive confidence in her ability to actually shoot a moose frayed her resolve. In this instance, what worked against her was her desire to be a good wife and please her husband.

"Okay," she said wearily one evening, following another pep talk. "I'll go with you. Perhaps we should do some target shooting first."

That they did after work the next day. She was a good shot. She kept her eyes open even though the tremendous boom of the rifle jarred her entire body. She braced herself well for the recoil and did not fall backward. After each shot, she inhaled the acrid smell of the gunpowder and observed the warmth of the gun barrel. Her husband cleared his throat, squeezed her shoulder, and said, "You're ready."

By this time, Ruby was quite a savvy Alaskan woman and knew how to dress for the outdoors, which was not that much different than for her chilly-day hot dog roasts or berry picking. In this case, however, she needed better footgear. Between the two of them, they found boots that were waterproof and tall enough to manage at least some marshy terrain. Just like her husband, she had an army surplus coat, albeit a size too large. A green wool muffler was added to the assemblage, not for fashion, but to keep the chill from traveling down her neck. The rosy lipstick? Well, for her, that was standard, no matter the circumstance.

As could be expected, her letters described this wild experience in the Last Frontier.

"We have been out nearly every night this week moose hunting. Last night we spotted two bulls with large racks so we landed on a sand bar and started hiking through the woods. It got dark on us and we got a bit confused as to direction but the Lord brought us out near the same place we had entered the woods. When we get to heaven I will ask the Lord why we did not get to the moose. I feel it was devine guidance, as Elmer has never gotten confused in the woods before. It scared me

a bit and I hardly have the nerve to hunt moose again until I can get one on the sand bar, which is impossible."

Remarkably, this initiation did not completely ground her from taking off for another hunt. Elmer most likely was amazed himself. He didn't even have to dry more suppertime dishes. She just dried out her wet clothes and looked at him expectantly. Away they went.

"Last Wednesday night he took me out and we spotted a bull just across the river from this village so we landed on a sandbar and found ourselves in a bit of soup as the sand was not dry enough but we ignored that and hiked to find the moose and to our dismay we could not cross a small stream of water so back to the plane we go and we pushed it out of the soft sand on higher ground and take off to spot something better along the Yukon. 35 miles down river we spotted one on a sand bar, we flew low and sure enough he has a small rack, we landed and started firing, I always shoot first and Elmer after mine, I was so excited the gun did not even hurt my shoulder but my ears stopped up from all the noise, we hurt the mooses back leg and he took off faster than we would follow.

We hunted for a while but couldn't find a thing. Back to the plane we go, it is now 5:50 and as we started back for home and decided to see if the first bull was still in the original spot and he was! Elmer looked for a better place to land so that we could cross the stream, he found a strip of sandbar that was good but it was such a long way to hike but hike we must!

After I thought my legs would come off with woods to go through, high meadow grass (always hoping a bear was there taking a nap), swamp to cross, we finally got close to where we thought he should be, we smelled moose, Elmer called him by rubbing a small (piece of moose) rack across some trees and sure enough we hear the same type of noise a bit farther away (bulls act that way during rutting (mating) season) so we crept along the low brush along the meadow around another bend and then Elmer backed up (he always is the trail blazer) and says there he is and there he was all 900 lbs of him slowly meandering our way to see who was calling him. I says 'Hope he doesn't charge,' Elmer says 'SHOOT.' I was so tired I could not fully appreciate it all and it thrills me more as I recall the incident as I write this. There the monster was sprawled out. Elmer looked at his watch and it was 5:00 and not long till sunset. We did not skin him since it was so late but Elmer just gutted him and left him on him on the ground for the nite in the freezing temperatures.

Then we marked our trail back to the plane with toilet paper and we took a short cut from the way we came I and we had a 45 minute hike back to the plane and got home by 6:30. Boy, how hot coffee hit the spot. I wished I could do it over again when I wasn't so tired.

The next morning Elmer got up at 6:00 and Rev. Gronning helped him skin, pack out and fly in the meat. It took them till 1:00 noon. Then Leonard and Elmer went back to get the head and rack and if it is possible, we will have it mounted! Of all things, while they were working, what did they see but two more bulls so Leonard plunked one and they had to pack that one out, they scared the other one away as we just can not use any more moose meat. We plan to share some with the school teachers and probably furnish some for the Village Potlach at Christmas time."

Ruby's first moose

She had done it. Moose hunting season was over for her. Well, all except picking hair off the raw moose quarters, cutting up the meat, and determining what would be roasts, little minute steaks, or mooseburger. She knew the process. In Anchorage, after Elmer's first moose hunt, she had learned about packaging the meat tightly in slick, white freezer paper. The packages were labeled for an easy selection later. Was this process difficult? No. Tedious? A bit. However, it came with the satisfaction of standing beside her husband and working as a team; it was a rare and special occasion where her husband wasn't off tending medical emergencies or pushing the limits of his curiosity. She had him to herself. They recounted the hunt. They laughed. They wondered aloud what their families would think when they received her letter describing the event. Her emotional reservoir was filled with happiness.

After all was said and done, the meal provisions of her moose were stacked in the large hospital freezer, along with her husband's. Soon after, and many times after that, she would pull out a package of steaks, pound them for supper, dip them in flour, sprinkle on salt and pepper, fry them in oil until the outsides were crispy and the insides tender, and marvel at her amazing accomplishment. Her husband had been right: the bush doctor's wife could shoot a moose.[81]

The *Northern Lights* newspaper credited her husband for his successes but said nothing of hers. The write-up demonstrated his virility as the bush doctor.

HOSPITAL NEWS

> After shooting a moose and spending 4 hours packing the meat to a sandbar on which his plane was resting, Dr. Gaede spent the night in a sleeping bag only to get up the next morning and fly the meat to the airport and then haul it back and forth to the hospital. But the exercise didn't hurt him for the next day he was to be found playing basketball.

Perhaps a write-up about the doctor's wife would have been something like this:

HOMEFRONT NEWS

> After following her husband and wandering around in the woods, pushing through tall grass, stumbling across soggy marshes, surviving frightening landings and takeoffs on sandbars, and being overcome with fatigue, Ruby Gaede held her ground against a charging 900-pound bull moose, which she downed with her first shot. This was her first moose hunt. But the experience didn't hurt her.

The next week she was found making Christmas gifts of aluminum trays with Alaskan scenes sketched on them and the edges uniformly bent up and crimped like a piecrust; as well as melting, tinting, and forming candles, complete with white whipped wax and adorned with sparkling sequins.

Ruby's moose head returns home.

THE INCREDIBLE JOURNEY OF THE MOOSE HEAD

In the fall of 1959, the moose-head mount was sent to Ruby's parents, Solomon and Bertha (Litke) Leppke, in Peabody, Kansas. Later, it was transferred to Elmer's parents in Reedley, California. In a third move, it resided at Elmer's brother, Harold Gaede's, in Fresno, California.

Several years after Harold died (2011), his wife, Marianna, decided to move to a retirement community. The moose would not be moving with her. She and her family decided it should be returned to the Elmer and Ruby Gaede family on the Gaede-80 homestead, outside Soldotna, Alaska.

The relocation could not happen with a quick trip to UPS, a large priority mailing box, or FedEx; in fact, nothing about this relocation would be easy. The moose head was put into a custom-made wood box that measured fifty-seven inches wide, sixty-five inches tall, and sixty-one inches high and took up space equivalent to one-and-a-half pallets. This Alaska-sized box was loaded onto Wanda and Dan Doerksen's eighteen-wheeler fruit truck, which for many summers had been driven up the Alaska-Canada (Alcan) Highway, with driving times of four to five days, to provide California fresh fruit to Alaskans, in particular, peaches.

On June 29, 2015, the truck headed north with Ruby's moose head, surrounded by cherries, berries, oranges, and other fruit. On July 6, 2015, Elmer and Ruby's son, Mark, met the truck in Anchorage, loaded the crate onto his utility trailer, and hauled the moose two-and-a-half hours back to the Gaede homestead, outside Soldotna. Fifty-seven years later, the moose was back in its natural habitat, most likely needing to reacclimatize after being in warmer climes for decades.

"Mom's Moose" now overwhelms the stairwell in Naomi's cabin on the Gaede homestead and overwhelms the Gaede children with pride and satisfaction when they view it. For Naomi, it symbolizes the substance of the woman before her, and that as her daughter, she carries that gene of grit within her.

CHAPTER 27

EVERYDAY LIFE: MUKLUKS AND MOLASSES BREAD

Tanana, 1958

EVEN THOUGH RUBY HAD GONE through the cycle and seasons of one year in an Alaskan Native village, some aspects of living in Interior Alaska were still novel to her and, as such, mysterious and remarkable. The first of October, she got out of bed and matter-of-factly went to pull back the living room window drapes. The house was quiet, and she enjoyed what would probably be only a few moments to herself. Her terry robe, which was wrapped snuggly around her, showed the wear and tear of middle-of-the-night responses to Mishal's feedings and burps, Mark's nighttime fears and tears, and drips of early morning coffee. She surveyed the scene outside the window and pushed her hands into the worn-soft pockets—before her was true tranquility. A smile eased slowly across her face. Without moving, she stared out the window.

The girls' laughter burst her bubble of solitude. Slowly, she turned and walked to their bedroom. "Girls, there is a surprise for you."

Naomi and Ruth jumped off their beds where they had been noiselessly playing with Betty, Tinkerbell, Susie Lou Anna, and other dolls, and raced each other to the front room window. They hopped onto the couch in front of the window. "Snow!" they shouted. Real snow of four to five inches, not merely a teaser, covered the ground, and more was floating down in thick feathery flakes. Mother and daughters gazed out the window as if mesmerized.

It wasn't as though Ruby hadn't seen snow in Kansas; however, it was different here. Here the snow played against the vastness of the scene before her and offered silent beauty. Of equal appeal, she could stay indoors and observe and appreciate the grandeur. The circumstances were not the same when she was growing up. In Kansas, snow was frequently accompanied by wind and dared her, and every farmer's family, to struggle against its force to gather eggs, milk cows, find springtime calves, and secure barn doors. On this day, however, she did not have to go outside; she could savor the drama of nature and thank the Creator for creating snow.

"What happened to the island?" whispered Naomi.

The frosty particles blurred the horizon and moved like a sweeping curtain, sometimes allowing the darkness of the distant island to appear, and at other moments, making it disappear as if an illusion. Between the far-off island and the road in front of the house, the always-hurried river rushed noiselessly, and the snow began to dance wildly against the windowpane, soundlessly. It was as if a black-and-white silent movie played outside the window.

Naomi's question hung in the air.

Ruth's perspective was on a spiritual level. "Oh, goodie! That's just what I was praying for." She bounced with her knees on the couch cushions.

EVERYDAY LIFE: MUKLUKS AND MOLASSES BREAD

The reverie of the first snow was over and everyday commotion set in. "Hurray, hurray!" shouted Naomi. "Now we can wear our mukluks. Mommy, where are they?" She threw her hands in the air.

The mukluks fit like a boot and were a combination of soft mooseskin soles and rabbit fur that extended up the ankle about six inches. A red corduroy sleeve encircled the top. Within it was braided red and green yarn, which drew the mukluk securely around the lower part of their legs. Rough moose skin was cut into two strips and attached to either side of the soles. It was pulled across the top of the foot, crisscrossed, and tied behind the ankle.

Naomi thrashed around in the hall coat closet and emerged with her pair. "I hope they still fit," said her mother, who reluctantly let go of the "First Snow" picture before her.

Mark heard the commotion and called from his bedroom, "Mommy, Mommy." He crawled over the railing of his crib and landed with a thump on the floor, followed by pattering feet.

Ruby turned on the gas stove and placed the coffee pot on the back burner; within a few minutes, the water started to boil and spurt up through the glass tube in the middle to the clear glass knob on the lid, after which it receded to the bottom. The process was repeated and repeated with a soft pulsing sound. What had been clear water turned to tantalizing coffee-brown, with a delicious aroma.

Trying to gather two rambunctious girls to the table for breakfast before school was like trying to capture feral barn cats. And, while the snow may have been quiet and unhurried, the sight of it infused the girls with super-abundant morning energy. They sprang on and off their chairs, with one leg on and one leg off, one knee on and one knee off. Ruth's buttered raisin bread toast nearly flipped off her plate. They prattled on and on about what they would do at recess and after school. Maybe they would play Duck, Duck, Goose. Maybe make snow angels. Maybe … the list went on and on. Mark added to the morning melee. First, he complained about his tummy hurting, and then he spilled his grape juice. Mishal cried from her crib in the bedroom because she was hungry, wet, and left out.

Ruby was pulled in four directions. To get the girls out the door would reduce the pandemonium. Once they finished breakfast, she urged them to hurry along and tie their mukluks. Finally, she hugged them goodbye and sent them on their way. She could hear elated shouts as they kicked up the snow in front of them.

The refreshed landscape outside invigorated her too. The wet, gloomy days that typified moose season were over, and now the brightness of snow would hide the dark ground, dress the naked tree branches, and revitalize the shadowy forests. It already covered the wet dirt that filled the hot water pipe trenches, and it thwarted any plans for mud pie making. The house would be cleaner, albeit still with footprints; wet, white ones, but not sandy tracks that Ruby practically shoveled out in dustpans.

Mark was as wild as a sled dog raring for a race. He acted as if this would be the last snow for the rest of his life. Didn't he know he would have at least seven more months of snowmen, snow forts, sledding, and sliding? Truly, throughout their lives, Mark, Ruth, and Naomi would behave as their mother did that morning when she opened the window drapes and reveled at the first snow.

As soon as the girls were gone, he pulled his red parka off the coat hook and stuck his head in the closet to scrounge for his boots. He crawled around in his one-piece pajama that included footies, making little grunts.

Mishal shrieked. She still had not been included. Ruby gave her a bottle and focused on Mark. Getting his pajamas off and daytime clothes on reminded her of how Ruth and Naomi tried to put doll clothes on their cats: a leg in the armhole, a shirt on backward, buttons misplaced in holes, and an all in all sweat-producing struggle.

EVERYDAY LIFE: MUKLUKS AND MOLASSES BREAD

None too soon, Mark was ready. He yanked at the silverware drawer. "Spoon, Mommy," he demanded. He clutched a large spoon in one mittened hand, waved with the other, and scooted on his behind down the snow-covered steps. Elmer had left for the hospital earlier than usual, and by this time, the tracks of his black zippered galoshes were long gone. Just like a wiped clean chalkboard, Mark was now the first to leave a mark on the puffy white blanket. His mother peeked out the kitchen window to see where he was headed and saw him plop down on his knees and toss spoonfuls of snow in the air. Snowflakes already covered his parka hood.

Ruby assumed he would stay busy for a while and proceeded to get dressed and make the bed. The house was warm, even with the snow outside. Numerous times, she had thanked God she didn't live in a log cabin that relied on a wood stove for heat or that she didn't live in a Quonset hut with persnickety oil stoves, as did the schoolteachers.

Next up was dressing Mishal, which was much like clothing a doll. Ruby enjoyed choosing among the selection of cute dresses that friends and family continued to send. Even though winter's face was outside her windows, Ruby picked a pink dress with layers of gathering and slipped it over Mishal's tiny, short-sleeved cotton undershirt. There were no disposable diapers, and a plastic pull-on pant covered the cloth ones. Mishal's weren't basic; they came in pastel colors with rows of lace, which flounced when she moved about in what would be referred to in the future as a yoga "downward-facing dog" pose. She preferred this mode of hands and toes, rather than crawling on hands and knees. The girls called her "Fancy Pants" when her little bottom bopped as she moved in this position.

The not-fun part was trying to put something on her feet. Mishal kicked her legs like a galloping horse, and even when her mother did secure a foot, the child curled her toes, making it impossible to fit her foot into a regular toddler's leather shoe. Fortunately, soft moose-skin slipper-booties went on easily.

Eventually, what had turned into a tug-of-war between mother and child was over. Mishal beamed at her mother and made babbling baby sounds. Ruby smiled back affectionately and studied this delightful surprise in her life, truly a gift from God. In contrast to the other Native babies who were born with thick shocks of straight, black hair, Mishal's was coming in slowly and in dark brown waves that would grow into curls. She was irresistible, and when the schoolteachers or other guests came over, she never lacked attention. At this moment, Ruby expected to dote on the child herself and perhaps even enjoy a second cup of coffee. Her anticipation was short-lived.

Mark banged on the back door and yelled for his trike. Ruby placed Mishal in the Teeter-Babe. Recently, she had informed her loved ones that, *"She goes in with a few toys tied on so they don't drop to the floor all the time. You know this is T.B. (tuberculosis) country and the floor is full of germs."*

The trike was in the basement, where Mark had ridden it the day before. Ruby retrieved it and, without donning a coat, carried it out to the snow-covered sidewalk. "There you go. Have fun." She returned inside and rubbed her hands and arms to warm them before once again picking up Mishal.

Mark did have fun until he drove off the sidewalk into a depression over the recently backfilled trench for hot water pipes, where he tipped his trike, fell head over heels, and planted his face in the snow. The little snowman showed up at the door, crying, "I'm through. I'm through. It's not fair." Both phrases were the latest additions to his vocabulary. Ruby unzipped and removed his parka. He bit at his mittens to get them off and kicked loose his boots. She pulled off his puffy snow pants. The snow shaken off his garments started to melt and form little puddles. The boy's cheeks were as rosy as his red parka and his hands ice-cold blue. His mother held his hands in hers and asked if he would like to help her bake. In reply, he pushed a kitchen table chair to the kitchen counter.

EVERYDAY LIFE: MUKLUKS AND MOLASSES BREAD

Together mother and son stirred up molasses bread. Mark stood on his tiptoes and cracked the eggs. He was happy. Ruby was happy. Mishal was not happy. Ruby gave her a change of scenery and placed her in the playpen, where she pulled herself up, hung on to the sides and jumped, jabbered contentedly, and then screeched because she didn't know how to sit back down. Ruby's hands were covered in flour, and Mark had more than just his hands thoroughly dusted with the white stuff. "Just a minute, Mishal," she said in a singsong voice. "Mommy's coming." Ruby kneaded the large clump of dough rhythmically. Mark poked, prodded, and patted his little glob. When the task was completed to Ruby's satisfaction, she returned hers to the mixing bowl and covered it with a plastic cap with elastic around the edges. Mark placed what was left of his in a small soup bowl. A telltale sign of his dough sampling hung on the corner of a lower lip.

The house now smelled of coffee, toast, warm yeast dough, and a tinge of molasses. Within two hours, sliced brown bread, soft on the inside, crusty on the outside, and spread with oleo, would enhance the appeal of the first day of snow.

Mishal's patience had been spent, and tears streamed down her cheeks. She didn't care if her mother had flour on her hands, or that her brother wanted more juice, or anything else. Ruby turned her full attention to the child and tried to show her how to sit down. Mishal did not care to learn. She reached up her hands for her mother to take her out of her confinement. Ruby picked up the child and told her how precious she was. Mishal relaxed and squirmed deeper into her mother's arms.

Mark had no consideration for the mother-daughter bonding. He tugged at his mother's leg and shouted, "Outside!" His outdoor clothes were still damp. It was only 10:00 a.m.

On October 20, Ruby pulled back the living room curtains and, again, stood for a moment without moving, taking in the next sign of the change of seasons. Then, she walked to the girls' bedroom. "Girls, I have another surprise for you."

Teddy bears and other stuffed animals flew hither and yon as the girls slid off their beds and chased each other to the front room window. They observed the scene before them and immediately started to confer. "The river is frozen," said Naomi emphatically.

"I don't think we should walk on it yet," replied Ruth cautiously, shaking her head.

"It is not smooth," added Naomi. "It is lumpy. We cannot ice skate on it."

For days prior, the temperatures had dipped to minus 10 degrees, and ice cakes had formed, floating down the river like small granular pancakes. Over time, they increased in size to gigantic flapjacks. Eventually, the icebergs had attached themselves to one another, making even larger floating masses, and even rowdily climbed on top of the other. Overnight, they had wedged themselves together, not letting any other formations get past, and jammed the flowing river from side to side. Nothing moved.

"It must be winter now," responded Ruth.

Yes, it was winter. And this year, Ruby was confidently embracing the season.

"We had another nice week with mostly sunshine and crisp weather, the girls are iceskating on the road just in front of our house, the snow is packed so nicely. I have been taking Mark and Mishal out each day for a sled ride and at the same time go visiting for an hour at someones

place, I did this right after lunch and then we come back and take naps. Mishal now has a cold and is cutting her 8th tooth and Mark is hoarse so I guess this week I will stay in more.

Last Wed. forenoon we visited Ruth's class room and Mark was with me and we had such a nice time. Thur. we visited Naomi's room (tent) and I mean the teachers do such a good job under such difficult situations. The lighting is terrible inside."

It was a tradition to answer letters on Sunday afternoons. Ruby responded to questions about the children and Elmer's work, commented on news about farming, relatives, the weather, and provided updates on the latest events in her life. Understandably, at times, she needed a break from organizing her thoughts and typing letters. Such was the case on November 9, 1958, when Elmer took his turn and wrote to his brother, who would then pass the letter to other family members. Elmer did not type letters, as did Ruby. He scribbled in stereotypical "doctor" style.

"Dear Harold and all,

Ruby insists it's my turn to write so I'll give her a rest. There's not much new since our last letter. We're bedding down for winter. It's been below freezing since the last week of September and it's steadily going down. This morning it was minus 25 degrees. It only warmed up to minus 16 degrees this afternoon so we were lazy and stayed indoors to read and be with the children. The sun set was a few minutes after 3:00 pm today we have sunrise about 8:30.

Friday evening the hospital had a highly successful iceskating party on the river ice close to the hospital. We shoveled the snow from a large area so we had a very smooth skating area. We had two large fires and served coffee and hotdogs. I estimate that about 60 people came.

The red fox which Ruby previously mentioned is still as friendly as ever and plays by our sidewalk and steps.

The girls and I had a lot of fun yesterday using our toboggan to do down the ramp near the hospital – going onto the river. As soon as we get more snow we'll make a small ski run. We've had about 12 inches snow so far but it settled down to about 6 inches."

Within a few days, Ruby continued on the same theme:

"We had chilly 30 below during several of our days last week. We have had much snow some of it drifted yesterday but today it is falling by the bushels and is mild and just falling gently. Our maintenance man is out on the river with the snow cat clearing a 1800 foot runway for the ski planes to land.

Our daylight is getting very scarce, sometimes I feel like I'm related to the bear as I want to sleep more when it is dark."

Ruby got her weather-watching attentiveness from her father. Every night before going to bed, Solomon Leppke, would step outside and check the sky, stars, and clouds; he would consciously feel for wind or humidity and then return inside and give his prediction for the next day's weather.

Weather was a compass for his decision-making, and in another way, a fickle dictator. Farmers prayed, often. After seeds were planted, they hoped for rain. Later, they grumbled when it was too muddy to get farm equipment into the fields and harvest crops. Then there was anxiety about a possible drought. There was always trepidation about hail. When signs of a blizzard were approaching, they anxiously sought out and herded livestock to shelter. Temperatures seemed too hot or too cold. Ruby and Elmer had always been tuned in to the weather. Thus, Ruby's parents gave weather reports in their letters, and Ruby understood the unwritten concern, joy, or reality of their newscasts.

In Alaska, the weather had everything to do with Elmer's choices to fly or not to fly. Rain, fog, and snow affected visibility. Would ice form on the wings? Were temperatures so below the zero mark that engine oil would congeal in his airplane and need to be brought in and heated on top of the kitchen stove? What was the forecast? When did he need to change the airplane from floats to wheels or skis? When Elmer wrote letters, he filled plenty of space with weather observations.

For Ruby, the immediate or expected elements of weather directed her on how to dress the children. Which items should she order and when? Catalog orders took three weeks to arrive. Was she ahead or behind in doing so? The weather prompted her to sew sun tops or wool slacks for herself, cotton sundresses or flannel jumpers for the girls. When the seasons changed, she conducted inventories. Were there enough woolies in the house for each child, and the right size? Weather determined if rubber boots for mud and puddles were a suitable choice or if it was time for mukluks on the snow. Ruby's eye, mind, and typewriter all had to do with the weather.

Thus was Ruby's everyday life; opening the shades in the morning and observing the weather, managing giggling girls, chasing a toddler who flushed a single red wool sock down the toilet and leaving the other a useless orphan, and trying to keep a lively baby, who was ready to use her hands and feet to explore the world, off the floor.

```
                    THE MUKLUK TELEGRAPH

                         July-1958
                      Volume II, Number 2
                   (World Health Organization)

                   Tuberculosis - a turning point

   Tuberculosis is killing relatively fewer people
   each year. Nevertheless, tuberculosis is still the
   greatest killer of all infectious and parasitic
   diseases, and in North America, Europe and
   Australia, it accounts for three-fourths of all
   deaths from diseases occurring after age 15.
```

In 1955, a turning point was reached in the world outlook on tuberculosis, with the advent of new drugs promising a revolution in the management of the disease.

CHAPTER 28

THE HAPPIEST CHRISTMAS EVER

Tanana, 1958

CRACKS ZIGZAGGED THROUGH the purple-black ice beneath the girls' feet. "Spooky," said Naomi, in a solemn voice. "I wonder how far down it is frozen."

The girls had put on their ice skates and managed to walk from the house, over the riverbank, to the area on the river that had been cleared for ice-skating. Neither girl was chubby; however, they waddled in their thick snow pants and heavy canvas parkas. Their fox fur ruffs swayed around their faces, and at times, nearly obscured Ruth's. She bent over, smoothed the shiny ice surface with her mittens, and stared. "I don't see any water moving."

Like a red beach ball, Mark tumbled down the riverbank and caught up with his sisters. He looked from one sister to the other, observed their attentiveness to the ice, and put his face down on it. When he sat up, his eyelashes and lips were fluffy with snow. Ruth dusted him off gently.

Shortly thereafter, Ruby arrived with a cardboard box of wood and twigs lashed to the red sled. Her black rabbit fur parka reached to mid-thigh. She planned to make a fire to warm chilly fingers and toes in the 20°, which was a heat wave compared to the previous days of below zero temperatures.

Those nippy temperatures were not favorable for teaching in a Quonset hut, as the *Northern Lights* reported.

<u>THIRD AND FOURTH GRADES</u>

```
The stove went out and we had to go to school in
the teacher's house (Quonset) for three days. The
new school is half-way finished.
```

Ruth and Naomi in front of a school Quonset Hut.

Naomi had thought it was fun. Yes, perhaps fun for her, but for the teachers it was one more hurdle in trying to maintain an environment conducive to learning. Their tent-home was filled with a table for eating, beds, two clothes dressers, makeshift spaces for closets, and an area for preparing meals. There was no room to move in desks. "We sat on the teachers' beds and the floor," Naomi had explained. She had taken it in stride. Despite the unusual, unpredictable, and at times rigorous conditions in the huts, both she and Ruth had made the honor roll for the first six weeks of school.

Now, Naomi was caught up with the phenomenon of the frozen river. It wasn't as though it was her first experience with a frozen river. All the same, she nervously asked her mother, "How deep is the ice?" She had watched the hospital CAT clearing the ice for her father's airplane to land. Certainly, the ice had to be strong enough to hold up a group of children on ice skates.

Ruby crouched over the sled with her back toward her daughter. "The Natives will know. Reverend Gronning will know. They get water from the river and have to keep water holes open. The colder the temperatures, the thicker and deeper the ice gets—maybe six feet or more—maybe. And, the holes have to be wide enough to get a bucket down."

That seemed to assure Naomi. She pushed off on her skates and plunged through short drifts, which had formed overnight when the wind had suddenly danced over the ice. In other spots, the ice had been brushed clean by the same gusts. At 2:15 p.m., horizon-level dusky sunlight filtered through a layer of thin afternoon clouds. Now in late November, it was as if the sun was too lazy to stretch beyond the treetops and, like bears, preferred to hibernate until spring.

Ruth and Mark chased after their sister. Mark ran behind in his boots, calling, "Wait! Wait!" Children's laughter echoed ahead of them, where youngsters in colorful parkas sledded down the riverbank on pieces of cardboard. The frolicking children added the only color to the otherwise black-and-white landscape. In the distance, a lone hunter with a gun over his shoulder made his way slowly across the river, up, down, and around frost heaves and pressure ridges toward the island, most likely to shoot rabbits.

Ruby set about starting a fire. She crumpled paper, added twigs, and carefully laid short pieces of wood across the kindling. As much as she wanted to take her time and savor the exhilarating fragrance of fresh air mixed with wood smoke, Mishal was napping in the house, and there was only so much time for outdoor pleasure.

Naomi and Ruth were out of school for a short Thanksgiving break and had been at each other's throats. Their mother had urged them to play outdoors. She was relieved they had come up with something to use up their energy, and, in this case, she found it easy to join them.

Naomi and Ruth noticed the bright fire and smoke spiraling upwards and zoomed back. Each sister held one of Mark's arms, and together they pulled him on his stomach. The scratchy sound of razor-sharp blades filled the air. He slid easily on the slick surface. They laughed with amusement, and Mark's grin spread into the sides of his tightly tied parka hood. "Faster!" he shouted. Every time he opened his mouth, he caught a puff of snow. This did not faze him. They delivered him to the fire, where Ruby held out her arm so he wouldn't topple into the short flames. His blue eyes watered from the kicked up snow that had whipped into his face.

The girls panted from the exertion and tried to catch their breath while laughing and talking. They stooped over the crackling and popping kid-sized fire, held their hands over the warmth, and watched the caked snow on their mittens melt quickly. All in all, it was a peaceful scene with a content mother and happy children.

"You need ice skates on your bike," said Ruth, nudging Naomi.

Of all things, the day before, Naomi had decided to ride her bike in the snow. The bike was actually too big, and she could not sit on the seat, so she pedaled standing up. She rode around the hospital circle drive until one of the tires slipped on the ice, and she crashed down to the frozen ground. Not only did she come home bruised but also indignant. How could that have happened? Ruby bit her tongue. She had warned her. Ruth kept her mouth shut too. She had refused to join her older sister. "Too risky," she had said, refusing to be persuaded to try out Naomi's winter sport.

Aside from the girls' constant bickering, the Thanksgiving holiday and subsequent goings-on had infused a positive spirit into the everyday routine and the start of the holiday season. The school put on a program at the Community Hall, and there were services at the Episcopal Church and Arctic Missions Chapel. Ruby, Anna, and Margie chatted at these events and compared notes on holiday preparations.

"It wasn't easy," said Anna, finding a moment when students weren't hanging on her arms and wanting to tell her this and that. "But I managed to order gifts for all my family and in time to mail them out. But, trying to find boxes to mail them in? You know what that's like. Such is the life here." She lifted and dropped her shoulders in resignation and laughed.

Margie wasn't concerned about sending gifts. "I'm trying to find something for Grandpa Sam."

The older Native man with a crinkled face and kind eyes babysat the Gronning children as needed. He was trustworthy and dependable, regularly attended the services at the chapel, and was friendly to everyone. All in all, he was irreplaceable in the Gronning's life, and they valued him as a part of their family.

Ruby and Anna brainstormed with her. Wool socks? Knit mittens? A soft muffler for his neck? A hunting knife? The choices depended on availability at the Northern Commercial Store, or the time it took to order something, have it sent to the village, and the cost. The Gronnings had barely enough income to support themselves, much less to spend on others. That didn't stop Margie though. "Maybe I'll bake him something," she concluded, "Maybe cookies with mint chocolate chips."

Margie was famous for those unusual chips. Sometimes after evening church, she melted them into powdered milk to make hot chocolate. No one had ever tasted that kind of cocoa before, and they sipped it slowly. In most cases, they concluded they liked it.

Then, Ruby described her gifts of homemade candles and baked goods.

"You are so creative and good at handmade things," said Margie, shaking her head. "I don't know how you do it or have the time."

Ruby paused before responding and then said hesitantly, "I have time-saving luxuries … unlike you, I have a clothes dryer and running water." She stopped and gazed into Margie's eyes. "That's a big deal: running water. I don't have to use my time heating water for cooking or washing dishes or bathing or …"

Her voice drifted off, and she turned to Anna. "Oh, you're in the same boat now, too, aren't you? No running water in your Quonsets. And even when you haul it in, there is no guarantee your stove will be working so you can heat it."

She felt guilty for her conveniences, and her fingers fidgeted. "You girls have it so rough."

The awkward silence held for only a moment.

"Miss Bortel, guess what?" A little boy with tousled black hair and sweat on his forehead, from chasing around the room, reached for Anna to bend down. "I have a secret."

At that same time, Mark and Chris came running and wrapped themselves around their mother's legs, each playing peek-a-boo and knocking the women this way and that. In the jostling, Mishal, who was working on her walking skills, lost her grasp on a folding chair and collapsed to the floor. She glared at her brother.

"Is it time to go home?" asked Naomi, with Ruth in tow. They had finished chatting with friends and had their parkas draped over their arms. All in all, the conversation with the three adult friends was over.

Since Elmer had been called to the hospital, Ruby was left to gather her brood, put on their coats, and load Mark and Mishal onto the sled. The older girls helped suit up the younger two children. Just when Ruby thought she was on the home stretch, they started arguing about whose turn it was to hold the flashlight. It was enough for Ruby to pull the sled in the snow; she didn't have the energy to settle the dispute about the flashlight. She marched along, straining her eyes to see cabin lights along Back Street and then the light pole by the hospital. After she got everyone inside, there would still be snack time, bath time, and bedtime for four children.

The hospital prepared a fancy Thanksgiving banquet for the employees. The blended scents of baked turkey, hot-out-of-the-oven, homemade cloverleaf dinner rolls, and the sweetness of pies greeted the Gaedes in the hallway, even before they pushed open the dining room double doors.

"Oh, is that broccoli or cauliflower that I smell?" said Ruby, lifting her nose and sniffing the air. Either vegetable would be a treat. Any vegetable that didn't come out of a can was a rarity.

The girls walked around the room looking at brown, yellow, and orange decorations of cornucopias, scarecrows, and pumpkins on the walls and tables.

"Maybe we can make a scarecrow when we get home," said Naomi.

"We have construction paper, and Mommy has yarn."

Ruth nodded in agreement.

The staff paid special attention to the Gaede children, and the children generally anticipated these events, whether a meal, program, or a film. Mishal batted her brown eyes and looked enticing in her frilly white dress, which appeared even brighter against her dark skin. Nurses and secretaries passed her around, although, at this age, she would have preferred hanging onto the chairs or crawling on the linoleum floor. Mark sported a brown-and-gold bowtie against his white shirt, and his beatific smile belied his orneriness. Naomi and Ruth were a pretty pair in their matching blue plaid flannel jumpers and black patent shoes with white anklets. They sidled up to their favorite nurses with whom they occasionally visited at the nursing quarters.

The nurses didn't have toys; nevertheless, their jewelry boxes, which held sparkling and shiny treasures of bracelets and necklaces, enchanted the girls, and the women allowed them to spread the valuables carefully on the bedcovers. Ruby and Elmer's background forbade earrings. This made them even more attractive to the girls, who furtively screwed or snapped the backs closed over their earlobes. They stood in front of the nurses' dressing mirrors, admired the glitter, and pretended they were queens.

"When are you coming to see me?" asked Martha, a trim, blonde-haired nurse. She was spending her first Christmas away from her family in Boston, and her husband had refused to join her in the northland, which was not all that unusual for nurses or schoolteachers in Alaska.

The girls glanced at each other. "We will ask Mommy," said Naomi.

Before they could do so, the evening was formally called to order with a request for Dr. Gaede to bless the food. Naomi and Ruth found their places at the long banquet table, slid onto the metal folding chairs, and tucked their feet behind the chair rungs. They both eyed the cloverleaf rolls in front of them before bowing their heads for the prayer. Although their mother was a bread and yeast roll maker, she seldom made those kinds of rolls, which were so much fun to pull apart into three pieces.

Celebrating at the hospital and letting the staff prepare and host the feast was a relief to Ruby; although she commented to herself that she could have made better gravy, and the crusts were a bit thick on the pumpkin pies. Even so, she complimented the cooks and appreciated the work they had gone to. She understood the planning it had taken to secure the necessary ingredients from Fairbanks. In fact, there had been a fresh salad with lettuce, cucumbers, and celery. She had savored the crunchy texture in her mouth.

Ruby had much to accomplish before Christmas. *"I spent most of my time getting our Christmas letters hectographed, about 60, and some doll clothes made,"* she wrote home.

The hectograph was used by the schoolteachers to duplicate worksheets for the students. It involved a master copy pressed onto a gelatin pad on which duplicator spirit was applied. Often, the printed results turned out purple.

Ruby did not use patterns for doll clothes. She combined ideas in her mind with scrap fabric, bits of rickrack and lace, tiny buttons, and snaps. She could effortlessly gather skirts, add a piece of fur to a corduroy coat, or even make a raincoat. The girls could get snoopy, so the seamstress had to be stealthy for these Christmas gifts.

Candle making and baking added to the regular chores of housecleaning, laundry, and cooking. *"I baked fruit cakes and made candles for 3 missionaries down river. I made 36 candles. I made breads (scruddle) and shared it,"* she continued.

This year, she had a better understanding of what the missionaries needed and more ably put together boxes to bring them cheer and possibly some merriment too.

In the background of Ruby's Mrs. Claus workshop, Mishal joined Mark in vying for their mother's attention.

"Mishal is a busy body she objects to the play pen after 4:00 afternoon as she wishes to join the family and do some cavorting around the house. Last week one night she was down on the floor and the hall door was left open and she was down the steps (to the basement) on the first landing before I even knew what was going on, I heard her screaming and I heard thump thump. She walks along the walls and furniture and she goes to the cook stove and pulls on the oven door and lands on her back. Her mouth is as full as a vacuum sweeper, everything from marbles to string. Mark spends much time with clay, pounding it with his toy hammer, and with imaginary moose hunts."

As she sewed, baked, and stepped around two little busybodies, she traveled back in time to her childhood Christmases on the farm in Kansas. Making *pfeffernusse* (peppernuts) was a tradition that her grandparents had carried along from Ukraine/South Russia. *Pfeffer* was a word referring to spices; in actuality, the nut-sized cookies should have been called spice nuts. Each family seemed to have its own version of the small, round, typically hard, nickel- to dime-sized cookies. Ingredients included variations of molasses, cinnamon, cloves, licorice-tasting anise, brown sugar, finely chopped nuts, and sour milk. Truthfully, the *pfeffernusse* had origins broader than that of Mennonites from Russia; in the 1550s in the Netherlands, from where many Mennonites had migrated to Poland and then Russia, there was a history of button-sized cookies of similar recipes.

And, even farther-reaching, the Danes and other Scandinavians had their recipes for the holiday cookies too.

When Ruby stirred up a batch of the sticky cookie dough, Naomi, Ruth, and Mark showed up to nibble but didn't have the patience to cut the many thin rolls into round pieces. It was a fairly tedious process; one made easier and faster with many hands. Ruby wished for the companionship of her mother, sisters, and aunts. She missed the nonchalant conversations about child-raising, canning tomatoes, and new quilt patterns. Until she had moved to Alaska, every holiday was an assumed gathering with familiar foods and routines, and the combined efforts of many layers of relatives, all of whom spoke the same language, held the same values, knew the same hardships, and worshipped the same God. The experiences and preparations for special days were different now, and she reached out in an emotional way to find comfort and connectedness by making traditional recipes.

Ruby also thought of the simplicity and gratitude of her early Christmases. Gifts were unpretentious, and by some standards, commonplace. She remembered the excitement of finding Christmas gifts of an orange, uncracked nuts, and red, white, and green hard ribbon candy. Other gifts were practical and usually homemade: a new apron sewn from calico or a flour sack, an embroidered hankie with crocheted edges, or a bookmark crafted from a wide ribbon. The men might get work gloves or a pair of socks for outdoor boots. To put these modest gifts in context, she had grown up in the Depression and World War II, when many people struggled to provide basic food and shelter for their families, which were presents in themselves.

"I finally got my turquoise, corduroy, Chinese style house coat made," she announced in a letter written over the holidays. Now she could hark and herald the morning news from her living room window in fancy apparel.

The school Christmas program was one occasion when the entire village showed up for entertainment, Natives, non-Natives, hospital employees, and FAA staff. Ruby provided a general description of the evening.

> *"The School Program was last Friday nite and the program was good but the audience was so noisy that the children could not be heard, the place was jammed and I mean jammed."*

Another evening, the Gaedes invited the teachers over for supper.
"Ah! It's warm in here," said Harriet Amundson, flinging off her coat.
Anna burst her bubble of blitheness, with a tense reminder, "You know we will have to watch the time, and someone will need to go back and bang on the oil lines to be sure we have heat for the night."
Naomi and Ruth had returned from school the previous week and surged through the door with the announcement that there was no school. "The lines are frozen!"
Ruby's heart went out to the teachers, and she had explained their plight to her parents.

> *"We are having very cold weather 50 below and our poor school teachers are about to freeze up. The oil gets to thick to run and the oil burners go out. The pipes in the old school are breaking so that previous source of running water is no longer available."*

The fuel lines were too narrow, and the oil kept freezing, shutting off the stoves. Anna was the lead teacher, and managing facilities was a big item on her list of responsibilities. Harriet and Herman, the other teachers, didn't complain about the unusual hardship; however, at times, their bright-eyed youthfulness just needed to be directed. After all, they were only in their early twenties, whereas Anna was in her thirties.

It wasn't only the adults who noticed the cold in the huts; students were aware of it too. The December *Northern Lights* included it as important news:

```
We have just come back from Thanksgiving vacation.
Now it is a little cold in the huts. At recess time
we play football. We have 10 minute recess and 20
minute P.E.

Herman Romer, our teacher, broke his glasses. One
rim was gone so he sent away for another side. He
broke it when he was playing football. He got the
other piece back today.
```

As Ruby put the finishing touches on the meal, Elmer asked Herman how he had managed without glasses. Herman described how he had tried to finagle pieces of wire, tape, and other materials to hold them in place. Trial and error. As usual, his good humor prevailed and brought a chuckle to everyone. Mark didn't know what everyone was laughing about, but stood up, opened his mouth to the ceiling, and haw-hawed.

Ruby had prepared a moose roast from the moose she had shot. She proudly mentioned this to them. They applauded her, and she blushed. When they had offered to bring something to contribute to dinner, she had almost scolded them. "Please, no! I don't know how you manage for just yourselves."

"Ha!" said Harriet with a giggle. "We could have brought potatoes or carrots. They were trying to freeze in the lower cupboard, so we turned the oven on low, opened the door, and put them on that. They are still useable."

"Your floor is that cold? Things freeze on it?" Ruby reached out and put an arm around her.

"We certainly aren't running around barefoot," she replied, extending her legs and wiggling her toes.

The roast, mashed potatoes and gravy, canned peas, and Jell-O salad tasted extra good to everyone. To the teachers because it was something they couldn't concoct in their current living situations, and to Ruby because she envisioned their circumstances.

Before the evening was over, Herman surprised the children with gifts.

"He gave Mishal a teddy bear, Mark a delta winged jet bomber. The girls got a lovely china tea set and how the children have played, we ate our evening meal with the tea set, how some day we shall recall these precious times with the children."

Elmer wrote about the continued festivities arranged by the hospital. By no means could the employees complain about a lack of holiday spirit or the absence of Christmas joy and cheer.

"We had a good turnout to our hospital Christmas party, 45 people. The children, played games, had a story, song, and had a prosperous visit by Santa. On Wednesday evening we had a large group gather for our hospital Christmas eve. dinner.

At some point, I want to show the film "Heidi" to our personnel.

After that we opened our gifts and then went to the community hall where the school teacher and I showed 8 mm movies of the community activities. I also showed the polar bear hunt film. Various gifts were then passed out by the chief. One of the Indian elderly women gave me a beautiful pair of fur mittens made from lynx and beaver."

As if all this wasn't enough, the Gaedes put on Christmas dinner for a group of friends. Elmer continued:

"On Christmas day we had a crowd of 16 for the noon meal. There were 3 natives. We ate half of our 34 ½ lb turkey. In the afternoon and evening we played games."

Ruby filled in more particulars:

"We had 16 at our tables for Christmas dinner, Anna made dessert which helped a lot and Mrs. Gronning made cranberry salad. Our meat was turkey and was it delicious. I made a cornmeal dressing. If I had had the convenience of a real store, I would have bought and made baked apples with red hots."

In her after-Christmas letters, Ruby thanked every family member specifically for what he and she had given to the family. She also recounted the gift-giving within their immediate family.

"Elmer got the girls each a wrist watch and Mark he got a 4 motor miniature passenger plane the props all turn. The girls and I got Elmer a hunting knife, a miniature airplane motors for cuff links and a propeller for a neck tie clasp. Elmer got me a reversible corduroy jumper and blouse. I got my first frilly petticoat. I call it my "silly." I *do feel a bit silly wearing it, but the girls say I look 10 years younger so maybe its OK!"*

Then she added a P.S. *"I finally got my turquoise, corduroy, Chinese style house coat made."* Now she could hark and herald the morning news from her living room window in fancy apparel.

She didn't mention that she had used leftover turquoise corduroy from her new housecoat to make Naomi's Betty doll a parka with rabbit trim around the hood; or that both the girls' Madame Alexander and Jill dolls had raincoats out of yellow print plastic; and their Tiny Tears dolls now had white eyelet pinafores over red-and-white checked dresses.

If Ruby would have used Christmas songs to tell her story, it might have gone something like this: It was a Silent Night as we walked to the chapel, and Oh, a Holy Night too; and not only a *single* star announcing Christ's birth, but a massive canopy of stars twinkling above us, and after our New Year's Eve party, we walked home Upon a Midnight Clear.

The Gaede's letters from 1958 ended with two very different proclamations:

1. This is the happiest Christmas ever.

2. Elmer's contract here in Tanana expires Aug-59.

THE HAPPIEST CHRISTMAS EVER

THE CHRISTMAS SEAL CAMPAIGN

December 1958

This will be held next Tuesday. The school children will be selling the seals the cost is $1, for 100 seals and the money is used in helping to fight the dread disease of tuberculosis, which is still Alaska's most serious Public Health problem.

While we are speaking of tuberculosis, HAVE YOU GOTTEN A CHEST X-RAY WITHIN THE LAST SIX MONTHS? Be smart! It's better to be safe than sorry.

(The first Christmas seals were created in Denmark in 1904 when a Danish postal clerk, Einar Holbøll, was looking for a way to raise money to help children with tuberculosis. Although placed on mail during the Christmas season, they are not actual postage stamps.)

CHAPTER 29

FINDING BRIGHTNESS IN THE DARKNESS

Tanana, 1959

RUBY DID NOT MENTION STATEHOOD in any of her letters; even so, that's how the New Year started. The cover page of the *Northern Lights* was printed on gold paper, with an outline of Alaska; in the center was a star inscribed with "49th State." Alaska became a state on January 3, 1959.

The Roving Reporter, Marshall Smith, a student, interviewed people and recorded their mixed responses:

```
Anne Inge (Episcopal Priest, Cole Inge's wife) - "I
think it is terrific."
Mrs. Benson - "I'm looking for a lot of improvements
for Alaska through Statehood."
Mr. Thompson - "No comment."
Hardy Peters - "I think it is o.k."
Rod Nickovitch - "I don't know."
```

With those brief comments on the historical event, the school paper turned its attention to recaps of Christmas activities, the new Tanana Chief (Alfred Grant), dog race winners,[82] the weather, and the new school. An entire page was devoted to Dr. Gaede's editorial on what contributed to good health, such as a balanced diet, not smoking, and the harm of "strong drink."

The first and second grades were excited about the much-anticipated opening of the new school.

```
We are glad the new school windows came. We will
be happy when we move into the new school. We will
have a big room and we will have new desks. We won't
mark on our news desks.
```

- ```
  We will drink from water fountains in the hall.
  We won't need cups.
  ```
- ```
  We will have indoor toilets that flush. We will
  learn how to flush them.
  ```

The third and fourth grades were keenly aware of the specifics of the progress.

- ```
  The windows for the new school came January 12.
  ```
- ```
  We couldn't get water from the old school because
  the pipes froze. Miss Amundson had to get water
  from the hospital.
  ```
- ```
  We have had bum attendance the past three weeks.
  Naomi Gaede was the only one that wasn't absent
  or tardy.
  ```

The upper grades thoroughly recalled the Christmas parties and programs, and just as the other grades, brought to attention the school facility situation:
  ```

```
School was let out one day and a half because it
was too cold and the oil lines were frozen. The
teachers couldn't get the fire started in the
stoves.
```

And what was the weather? Linda Wheeler slipped in her short article.

```
It has been very cold here in Tanana these days.
Most of the children go to school now. There were
some children not in school because of the coldness.
The coldest lately was forty-nine below and the
warmest was nine below.
```

For Ruby, life went on as usual, with local activities, amusements, and concerns, and, amazingly, without mention of the dramatically low temperatures coupled with lack of sunshine. Sometimes, she looked repeatedly at the temperature gauge outside her kitchen window to confirm that what she thought she had seen had actually been registered. Time and again, she said under her breath and shaking her head, "I don't believe it."

The bottomless winter challenged anyone to leave their homes, which in turn affected the core of people's well-being. Due to the lack of mental, social, or physical stimulation, conversations often become stagnant, and people were prone to depression, lethargy, and squabbling. Like balloons, with the air popped out of them, many people felt deflated, energy-depleted, and lifeless. The holidays had carried energy and motivation, but now, the perpetual darkness and cold suffocated motivation to interact with others or do anything at all.

Ruby hadn't noticed this syndrome in Anchorage when Elmer had been stationed there. However, the city had streetlights, the buzz of traffic, stores for actual shopping, and even the treat of an ice cream cone or a meal out, if so desired or afforded. It was different in Tanana, less motion, fewer places to visit, no newness.

When she did feel a twinge of downheartedness, she compared her circumstances to those of the missionaries and scolded herself. With a population of three hundred, Tanana could be perceived as lively and robust. The missionaries' villages contained only twenty-five to one hundred people, many who were just trying to keep wood in the stove, water fetched from a hole in the river ice, wild meat on the table, and warm clothes sewn for themselves and their family. No one had time to think up a diversion for laughter or intellectual inspiration. Unlike in Tanana, their winter would feel heavier and longer.

With this in the background of her life, Ruby wrote cheerily about the start of the New Year:

"We had a nice New Year. The eve we went to the Chapel, had a short service after which we had a smorgasbord and played games till almost midnight. We slept till nearly noon the next morn.

I went to check on the school teachers as it was 50 below and their oil burners just would not burn as the oil gets to thick to run. They were so tired as they had been up most of the night to hook up light bulbs along the oil lines. I had bacon and eggs with them at 1:00. For supper we had the 3 teachers come over plus Wally the lab tech … Ruth did not have school on Friday as the stove in their tent was clogged with soot. Anna cleaned it out and she looked like a chimney cleaner after she got through she came over for a cup of tea. Friday afternoon I helped Anna sweep and scrub that tent so now she hopes to have school tomorrow."

FINDING BRIGHTNESS IN THE DARKNESS

In an otherwise slow-slogging snowy-cold month, the FAA provided unexpected interest, in a sad and Alaska-reality way.

> *"Last Friday nite the 3 teachers and I went to C.A.A. to look at some household goods a young fella has to get rid of as his wife refuses to come here and is going to divorce him. I bought 6 pieces of copper pans, an electric alarm, 8 clear glass fancy tumblers, an electric coffee pot (not working to well) plus a lot of little items. We all seemed hilarious as we each grabbed the items that interested us and Anna remarked, "What a diversion for Tanana!" and the fella says, "for you, yes" and we felt ashamed to think that it was so much fun for us and to him it probably tore out his heart."*

The FAA funneled some mental health nourishment into the village. Its employees flew in and out and had radio contact with other sites up and down the river. In both ways, the employees acquired information that could be brought up over a cup of coffee at the hospital or sitting next to someone at their children's school program; conversational material that went beyond a recent hunter's success, speculation on the weather, mending traps, or the need to cut more firewood.

The smaller villages did not have FAA stations or regular airplane service. It could be weeks between mail, and there was no reason for visitors to drop in. There were no unusual faces or thought-provoking perspectives. There was no one to incite a good, healing belly laugh. Whereas in Tanana, there was regular air service and subsequently, news, like a gulp of fresh air, arrived through people coming in and out on scheduled flights. Specialized medical personnel, such as the regional dentist or surgeon, showed up, ate in the hospital dining hall, and enlivened the ordinary and repeated topics with their experiences and contacts outside Tanana.

The Public Health hospital also generated activity, which pried people out of their houses. The employees took part in special meals, movies, and events for its employees; and, it didn't stop there. The fact that the hospital CAT cleared ice ridges off a section of the river so anyone interested could ice skate was a conversation starter, relationship builder, and a source of humor; laughter indeed being good medicine.

The school newspaper reported:

<u>SPORTS NEWS AND HIGHLIGHTS</u>

```
WELL, ice skating is the rage. So many people are
happily nursing sore arms and legs. They are making
a skating rink at the hospital. It is as much fun
to watch skaters as it is to be one. Some of the
beginners need double-bladed skates. But, after all
is said and done, skating is a nice sport.

There have been several skiers out on the hill in
front of the hospital - no broken legs yet.
```

Elmer loved ice skating and had brought along his hockey skates from Kansas. Perhaps he had instigated the ice rink. In a similar fashion, he may have introduced skiing down the riverbank ramp onto the river. Somewhere in the hospital, he had discovered long, broad, light-green wooden skis. Without poles, he boldly carved a wide-legged trail through the powdered-sugar snow. Indeed he was a sight in his army surplus hooded parka, cap with wooly earflaps, and arms outstretched to maintain balance. His enthusiastic chuckle cut into the hushed air and was punctuated with "YAH-haaaa," a carryover from country music popular in the 1930s.

The hospital staff spawned more ideas.

> "Friday night the hospital employees had game night and they invited
> C.A.A. and the fellas on the hill ("White Alice" communications) so

there was a good turnout. The games played were in the new nurses unit, the children were supervised downstairs and the adults were upstairs and the adult games were scrabble, Parcheesi, Monopoly, spill and spell, and we brought caroms."

What Ruby didn't describe, and what apparently did not overwhelm her, was the preparation it required to attend these social events. It wasn't as though she could casually stroll out the door, unhindered. At temperatures of minus 30°, minus 40°, minus 50°, and lower yet, she had to dress strategically. How much additional time did it take to put on boots or mukluks and wrap a wool muffler not only around her neck, but fashion it over her face and tuck it just under her glasses? Even with that prevention, she knew her eyes would water in the cold, and her nostrils would burn with each breath. Should she start getting ready ten minutes early? Or would she need more?

What if the children were going too? The girls could dress themselves in outerwear; however, she would have to capture Mishal and Mark, find misplaced mittens, struggle to get Mishal's kicking feet into mukluks and squish Mark into the snow pants he was outgrowing. And then Mark would shout, "Potty!" Would Elmer be around to help? Most likely not. Was it worth it to drag this entourage out into the brittle air? Was it worth fifteen or more minutes? It would have been easier to say, "Forget it."

At any rate, the Frontier Woman, who sang Christmas carols in 40° below, took her kids ice-skating in the light of midday dusk, and looked out her window to a real-life shaken-up snow globe, was compelled to go outside, and partake in the available goings-on. So she went into the frost-sparkled moonlight and tromped down the connecting hospital sidewalk, tunneled with glistening snowbanks on either side.

Shortly after the hospital game night, she ventured out again.

"Sat. night I had the privilege to go out with the girls! We had a pizza pie supper at Mary Ellens, Anna Bortel made it, I furnished the moose burger and root beer for floats. There were five of us and after eating we played scrabble – had we not talked so much we might have played two games but as it was we just did one."

The ultimate delight and indulgence in Ruby's life was a root beer float. Finding root beer for this occasion took specific sleuthing. Perhaps there were brown bottles hidden away in the hospital kitchen, saved for a special occasion. Wherever they were, Ruby tracked them down. Keeping the root beer and the ice cream cold was no problem.

Toward the end of January, Reverend Ken Hughes flew into Tanana in his Family Cruiser. During his week of special preaching services at the Arctic Missions Chapel, he flew to Kochrines to bring back Mrs. Scripter and her four children. Unquestionably, they were cramped in the four-seater plane. Undoubtedly, Mrs. Scripter was overjoyed to come to a big village with fresh conversations, running water at the Gaede's home, and spiritual refreshment at the preaching services. The Gaede's basement playroom and long hallway, where the Gaede girls roller-skated, were like a mother's dream for her children.

Ruby's only comment, understated, was, *"They all stayed here, so I was a bit busy with extra cooking and meetings each night, but we had a wonderful time."*

Extra cooking? Possibly in quantity; otherwise, she did her usual cooking and baking. Ruby never gave a second thought of, "Should I bake bread, or not?" The scent of freshly baked bread greeted them at the door like a warm hug of welcome.

Behind all these comings and goings, Ruby was indeed busy. Tucked inside her letters were snippets about her children:

"Mishal sure is a busybody these days she can a real terror when not restricted. She eats the dirt in the flower plants, into all the wastebaskets, finds every small particle of dirt on the floor, the other day Ruth pulled a thumb-tack out of her mouth, we call her the vacuum sweeper. She is cutting molar. She loves her foods, just to see how much she could eat I let her all she wanted and it was two cans of Jr. baby foods. I just let have green veg and meat and ½ can fruit and she screams for more but I give her the bottle and she is satisfied. We are letting her have her own time at learning to walk, she does well along furniture and she had taken a step towards us, the girls are looking forward to her Birthday. Time has gone so fast with her."

A few days later, on February 1, she wrote that Mishal was walking:

"The greatest achievement in our family last week was Mishal learned to walk. She didn't even take steps until last week and by Sat. she could take 6 steps, she enjoys it so much but occasionally she lands on a toy and really has a tough landing but it does not discourage her she cries and starts in again. We must get some movies of her walking."

Mishal, God's gift to the Gaedes, turned one year old on February 4, 1959.

Rev. Ken Hughes left. The Scripters left. January raced past. Ruby's social calendar remained full: *"Tonight Margie Gronning has sewing club. A week*

from tonight I have a shower for one of our employees that adopted a native baby."

All these events, the FAA, hospital, school, and church brought people out of their winter cocoons, forced them to mingle with one another, and sent them away with laughter, insights, and different subjects to muse upon.

Ruby didn't flounder in the interminable winter. She found and focused on the beauty around her. Trees wearing jackets of snow. The Northern Lights in their silent wild activity of neon green, pink, and blue banners. River snow whipped into seven-minute frosting peaks. Windows were fuzzy with frost. And, icicles, like sun-catchers, hanging in front of her large windows.

"It is a beautiful morning," she wrote. *"Ruth remarked how light it was when we started to school.*[83] *Clear, crisp with a 20 below, Mt. McKinley can be seen to the south of us."*

Brightness in the darkness.

FINDING BRIGHTNESS IN THE DARKNESS

TANANA

COUNCIL NEWS

Council Meeting, January 17, 1959, 3:00 P.M. (with representatives from Hospital & CAA, H&O, the Episcopal Church and Tanana Chapel.)

Chief Alfred Grant opened the meeting for community problems and suggestions. The subject of electricity was brought up first. Mr. Slagle of Nenana has corresponded with Coleman about installing electricity for the town. We agreed to write again to Mr. Slagle to ask for more details.

- - - - - - - - - - -

Someone suggested the possibility of having a small sawmill here for the use of the people in building future homes, etc. It was agreed that the matter should be looked into. - - - - - - - - -
Next suggestion: possibility of having a telephone for the people of the town where they could get at it in case of an emergency. A discussion followed concerning fire signals for the town. Plans were made to get with the Hospital and CAA on the signals.

- - - - - - - - - -

It was brought up that our roads are in bad shape. Discussion followed on different ways to improve the roads. It was agreed that on large projects like this the workers should be paid. The suggestion was made to put everything that needed doing, the material required, the measurements etc. down on paper and present this to whomever is asked to do the job.

- - - - - - - - - -

The Council has made plans to raffle off different articles for the needy people here who are hard up for food, money, etc. - - - - - -

The Council is really going to try to make this a better community, Pasco said. Anybody who has suggestions about improving our town is free to do so at any time. These suggestions will be worked over in Council Meetings and taken up with the community.

- - - - - - -

Just for the record the Council appointed someone to write off and find out what our powers as a Council have, what are our town limits, and are our laws considered legal.

- - - - - - - -

A nice suggestion was made as to how we could get wood for the community in the future in a very short time. Have men volunteer to work shifts during driftwood time and working together, some in boats, some on the bank, some cutting & hauling we could get plenty of wood for the next winter for the Hall.

- - - - - - - -

The Chief reminded everyone that the whole town, CAA & Hospital included, the men on the site, too, were invited to participate in all community activities.

- - - - - - - -

The meeting was adjourned.

- - - - - - - -

Results of the next meeting were: All proceeds from the door prizes of the 17th and the 31st will be donated to the March of Dimes.

- - - - - -

The Woman's Club agreed to give half of the bingo proceeds to The March of Dimes, and the other half will go to the Community fund. This is excluding the profits of bingo games of the 5th & 19th. All coffee sales funds go into the community bank. So lets help with both drives.

Tanana Town Council News, January 1959

CHAPTER 30

KEEPING THE PACE, NOT FROZEN IN PLACE

Tanana, 1959

"February started with snow every day. It is so beautiful now and the snow is deep. Our temperatures came up as high as 30 (above zero) and we felt like we're in the banana belt. We had wind some days so there are some nice drifts for the children to play in and on. They have very much fun sliding down the river banks which are pretty good height."

This was Ruby's newscast to her loved ones on February 2, 1959.

"With no consideration that temperatures were below zero the children did not think twice about going out to play. In fact, they acted as if they had been caged up for months."

"You have to finish breakfast first," said their mother. Mark stirred his milk and Rice Krispies vigorously and then laid his head on top of his bowl until his ear skimmed the liquid. Ruth had told him she could hear "snap, crackle, and pop."

"You jokes?" he questioned her. He swirled his spoon again, and milk sloshed onto the table. Now his curiosity was turning to frustration.

"Just eat it so we can go outside," said Naomi. He lifted the bowl with both hands and slurped the contents slowly.

None too fast for their mother, the three left the table. Naomi and Ruth pulled up snow pants, tugged on mukluks, slipped their arms into their parkas, and guided the braided yarn harnesses holding their mooseskin mittens over their heads. Everything had to go on in the right order.

"Wait! Wait!" shouted Mark, sitting on the floor with snow pants wrapped around his ankles. He didn't want help, yet he could not manage all the parts and pieces of the preparation. At long last, he was bundled up and ready to go.

In three-fold merriment and all wearing red winter-gear, they trundled across Front Street to join other children from the medical compound. The wind had whipped the snow-coated riverbank into a children's playground slipper slide, and in a jumble, they disappeared over the edge. Over and over, they crawled back up, and only after barely catching their breath, slid down again and again.

Knowing her three would not wander away, Ruby started dragging around the Electrolux canister vacuum. Occasionally she looked out the front window. The sight of exuberant children warmed her heart. She thought of the rare occasions her father would take time out from work to pull her on a sled drawn by a horse through a field. Even now, she could feel the pleasure and serenity of gliding over the snow, her cheeks turning red from the nipping cold, and the horse snorting steam into the sullen

Kansas air. Sometimes she would sit; other times, she would lie on her stomach, the snow bursting onto her face as the runners cut through the powder. Moments of play were rare in her childhood, and she wanted her children to have plenty of childhood play.

Mishal was definitely having an enviable childhood. Ruby's fascination with her had not ebbed since the moment the infant had entered the Gaede home. Ruby recorded through letters her progress and her propensities.

> *"Our baby Mishal is one year old. She seems so little but oh so much energy. She takes a book and tries to sing. I was in the basement tending laundry and when I came up she was unpacking a cubbard and found an open pkg of coconut and scattered it with canned goods. … She throws everything into the bathtub. She is doing so many cute things. She puts her hand to her mouth and pats it and says ahhhhhh! She is constantly on the exploring rampage and checks under the stove and ref. for particles of food and popcorn, and garbage! Every time we turn around we have to check her mouth. At prayer time during meals she is so noisy so we have been saying shhhhh, and now she puts her pointer finger in her mouth and says shhhhhh."*

After some time, the older children burst rowdily through the door with a mini-blizzard of snow flying off their clothes. They tossed back their parka hoods, their faces gleaming with exhilaration. Damp curls pressed against Ruth and Mark's heads. Mishal toddled over wide-legged, squatted, picked up the snow on the floor, and immediately put it in her mouth.

"Mommy," Naomi called toward the kitchen. "It was so fun, and we held arms and went down together." She ran her fingers through her moist bangs until they stood out like a short brim of a baseball cap. "And then we crashed into Cindy, but she wasn't hurt, and then there was a dog …

and did you know there is a path through the pressure ridges toward the island ... we should hike there."

Naomi liked nothing better than a hike, in the woods, across the frozen Yukon River, or berry-picking; in contrast to Ruth, "who does not like hiking as her legs are short." It wouldn't be long before Mark would like hiking too; however, at this moment, he just wanted to be heard.

The youngster flung his mittens at his oldest sister. "Let me talk!"

Ruby rounded the corner, rolling a peanut butter cookie ball in her hands. All quarreling ended, and a chorus of "cookies" broke out. Peace prevailed.

The older girls sat at the kitchen table with red and pink construction paper. Elmer's Glue, scissors, and crayons completed their array of materials. This year, Grandma Leppke had sent them store-bought Valentines, so instead of creating their own, they were making "mailboxes" for the Valentines they would collect at school. They folded, not quite in half, 20-by-12-inch heavy, cream-colored paper, and stapled the sides together to form a pocket. Then they printed their names in large red crayon letters across the top. Naomi decorated hers with six double-layered red and white construction paper hearts—most of which had "I love you" printed in red or black crayon. One small heart read "U 4 Me."

Their little sister wanted to help make Valentines. She tugged on their legs and hopped, her feet never leaving the ground. When all else failed, she shrieked annoyingly.

"Mishal!" said Naomi, banging her fist on the table. "Find something to do."

Ruth's tender heart couldn't stand the distress. Ruby had written to relatives that, "*Ruth is still my patient little helper, she feeds Mishal, she loves babies*." Now Ruth tried to pull Mishal onto her lap. Within a second, both girls toppled over, Ruth's body making an *A* over Mishal's. The young child's eyes opened wide in surprise, and then she rolled over on her back and giggled. Ruth giggled, too, and curled up beside Mishal. Naomi sighed. She had a mission to complete. Eventually, the Valentines were fashioned and addressed to classmates.

Naomi had her turn to giggle the next day when her third-grade class, along with the fourth graders, had a Valentine's party with cake, sandwiches, and Kool-Aid. She wore red corduroy pants and a red sweater, along with red barrettes on the end of her braids, which she often swung side to side for amusement. When she and Chris Sommer were named the queen and king, a silly grin spread across her face from dimple to dimple. She had a crush on the quiet Athabascan Indian boy with red, curly hair, freckles, and big brown eyes. As the two passed out Valentines, Chris said little. Naomi walked beside him, looking at him out of the corner of her eyes. She swallowed hard and tried not to giggle nervously. She wondered if anyone could hear her heart beating like a drum.

Ruth had asked her mother for red, satin ribbon bows on her braids; otherwise, she did not preen, as did Naomi. Whereas Naomi rushed home and gushed out that she and Chris had been queen and king, Ruth's report was matter-of-fact.

"We dropped our Valentines into a mail slot," she said. "Then, the post-people called out, 'mail' for one of the boys or girls, and that kid went to get their Valentine. It kinda took a long time, but the post office booth looked nice. It was made out of cardboard, and it was fun."

The setting for these parties was the new school. Aside from the Open House and Dedication, the Valentine parties were the first events to mark the long-awaited transition.

Twelve days earlier, on February 2, 1959, the students had carried their books and school supplies from the Quonsets to the new school, and with awe and quiet twitters of excitement, put them into new desks, in one of the three rooms: first and second grades, third and fourth grades, and fifth through eighth. They were like moles coming out from underground and now blinded by bright lights, big windows, and shiny linoleum. They shrugged off coats and sweaters that had been survival gear in the gloomy, heat-deprived huts.

The *Northern Lights* school paper featured a rough sketch of the building on the front cover, and inside, the Roving Reporter asked the teachers and students what they thought.

```
Vernon Nusunginya: It was kind of bum (not good)
over in the tents.

Diane Miller: Our room is pretty and our stoves
don't go out.

Clarence Estes: The blackboards are bigger.

Gary Hayward: It's nice and warm.

Frieda Swenson: It was dark in the tents but it's
nice and light here.

Edward Elia: We don't have to go out to the bathroom.

Mr. Romer: A very nice and modern building. An
improvement for both teachers and students.

Miss Amundson: Very nice. I hope we can keep it
that way.

Miss Bortel: It's a dream come true! I'm tired of
oil stoves.
```

KEEPING THE PACE, NOT FROZEN IN PLACE

Marshall Smith, the student editor of the *Northern Lights*, expounded:

```
HOW I CAN MAKE TANANA SCHOOL A GOOD SCHOOL

Tanana School is a good school, but if we work to
make it better it could be the best in Alaska.

A new school can be new for years or it can be old
and dirty in a few weeks. It is up to the students.
A clean school is more pleasant to go to than a
dirty school. Our desks which are so new can soon
be ruined.

Not only the school but the school grounds should
be kept clean. They should not look like a dump,
and some schools are almost that.

Just as you can dirty the walls with writing, you
can dirty the air with foul talk. This means a lot
for a better school. What you learn now will last
you all your life. Remember, school is no better
than its students. So if we try Tanana School can
be the best in Alaska.
```

In her spacious and comfortable classroom, Naomi truly had been able to show off her carefully chosen red attire for the Valentine party and not have it cloaked under her customary parka, albeit that was appropriately red as well. Now, coat hooks lined the hallway and were actually necessary.

Naptime for Mark and Mishal was approaching, and Ruby anticipated a rest from her daily chores. It would feel good to get off her feet, let her shoulders sink into the bed mattress, draw a blanket up to her ears, and let out a long, tightly held breath. Perhaps, she could even catch fifteen minutes of shut-eye. And then, again, perhaps this repose would only be a dream. She described in detail the nightmare that ensued.

> "Last Wednesday afternoon just as I was resting with Mark I heard a knock at the door and I was about to ignore it when something urged me to answer it and there were two little girls 4 and 6 trying to tell me something about a plane and smoke. I finally suspicioned it might be our plane."

In less than 30°, Ruby dashed on a snow-packed sidewalk to the hospital. As she ran, she clutched her unzipped coat around her and clopped as quickly as possible in her untied boots.

> "As I walked toward the hospital I saw smoke coming from where our plane is parked. I ran to the hospital to hunt Elmer up and he dashed to the plane and the maintenance man ran with the fire extinguishers and the fire was put out.
>
> Elmer heats the engine with two large light bulbs plus wrapping the whole motor with canvas and insulation. Questioning the children I found out these two girls and another child had played near the extension cord which lead to the plane and by tripping over it broke the bulbs and then of course a short. The wind was in a good direction and blew the fire away from the plane or it would have been an expensive damage but after checking and cleaning it all up Elmer just needs a paint job on all the cowling, maybe $100 worth of expense. We were so glad these girls came and told us, unlike the other child who ran home."

Plans for a nap were one thing. Plans for the future were another. Starting in February, her letters had snatches of change dropped between news events. "We will let you in our latest news," she wrote. "We will be moving to the states this summer. Our first choice is Minnesota and if that is not the place for us I know God will let us know. We are glad we can leave the details to him."

Ruby's party planning was well thought out, down to the literal nuts and bolts of fun details. Her special touches added a spark of energy and freshness to the everlasting winter.

> "Tuesday night I had the shower for the folks that adopted a Indian baby, 17 women came out and it was a snowy night. I served tiny cream puffs filled with tuna salad, a triangle cracker with liverwurst (I forgot to put the olives on!) and icecream-cake sandwiches. I made nut cups with material pinned to make a tiny diaper and then dipped into melted paraffin and shaped it as it dried to be an open diaper to hold nuts. I folded napkins to look like kimono-sacks. Our first game was Spill and Spell but could spell only baby items. Another game we had two sides and with the lights turned out they had to pin and unpin a diaper on a doll and see which side would win. We also played snatches of nursery rhymes (from the childrens records) and they had to guess which was being played. The lady got many nice gifts."

Close on the heels of this over-the-top social event was more meal-planning and hospitality. "Friday night we entertained a Miss Mathews from the Anchorage office who is a nursing authority, and Tom McQueen the dentist, and our nursing supervisor. Then the two women teachers came and other people walked in and we had a jolly time." She enjoyed it all, all without a convenience store to pick up last-minute food items or a dishwasher for the cleanup afterward.

March came in like a polar bear, with 30° below zero and more snow. Ruby referred to this as, *"We had another nice week,"* and went on to tell about Easter, and not one of yellow and purple crocuses or cuddly baby chicks. *"I made my Easter suit out of the navy blue checked, I did not have a pattern but I borrowed a neighbor lady dress suit that I like and made a pattern off it. I love to sew and it is a real relaxation for me."* Later in the month, she would add, *"This is the first Easter that the children won't be wearing new clothes, perhaps we can learn the true meaning of Easter."* Despite the lack of Easter apparel and fuzzy chicks, the Gaede children were ecstatic when the teachers brought back Easter candy from Fairbanks, where they had attended a conference. The candy had frozen, so all the better they had not brought back daffodils.

When Elmer added his two cents' worth in a letter. His comments underscored the wintery weather, as well as the uncertainty of their relocation.

> *"It's 5 ½ months now since the temperature has been above 32 degrees. Ice is about 40 inches thick on the river and with about 24 inches of snow. We're not certain at all about rotating to the States since there has been quite some difficulty keeping doctors here in Alaska. We may not know until a month ahead. If we rotate I may sell our plane."*

Before signing off and licking the envelope, Ruby added, *"Elmer's work is still varied and he gets to visit quite a few villages for medical work. It is very handy to fly with our plane since many places have only plane service once a week. There is about two feet of snow on the level so it'll be probably late April before we see the ground. Moose are in great abundance near by and the caribou have moved within about 70 miles from here. Beaver trapping now in full swing the villagers are busy with their dogsleds both for their traplines and for practice for the big dogsled races in about six weeks. We are all busy getting ready for spring."*

At this point, "spring" did not seem right around the corner; although, one had to admire Ruby's sunny optimism. For those five-plus months, and even now, she had kept up the pace of social life and daily parenting and never got frozen in a snowbank, an igloo, or a Quonset hut, or sent to the Funny Farm.

```
            DEDICATION PROGRAM

         TANANA SCHOOL - FEB. 15, 1959


    Flag Procession and Pledge
       Flag bearers: Chris Sommer & Sally Woods
    Invocation: Coleman Inge
    Girls Chorus:
       "Tanana Song"
       "Going over Jordan"
    "How I Can Help Make Tanana School A Good School"
       Winning essay by Marshall Smith
    "Looking Back"
       Brief school history of Tanana by Anna Bortel
    Greeting from the Village Chief: Alfred Grant
    "Looking Forward"
       Dedicatory Sermon by Roy Gronning
    Girls Chorus:
       "We Would Be Building"
    Benediction: Coleman Inge
```

```
We wish to thank the Council for donating paper
cups and letting us use the coffee urn. We thank
CAA, Tanana Chapel, and the hospital for the use of
folding chairs. We also thank those who sent cookie
and we appreciate the help of Mrs. Roberts, Mrs.
Nusunginya and Mrs. Gaede in serving.
```

- Chris Sommer became an electrician and the village chief in Galena, Alaska, downriver of Tanana.
- Sally Woods's family moved to Manley Hot Springs. After she graduated from high school, she achieved a master's degree in Special Education. Her master's thesis was, "How Alaska Natives Learn and Changes to Alaska Education that Would Ensure Success." She married Albert Kookesh, who became an Alaska State Senator. They are the proprietors of the Kootznoohoo Inlet Lodge, in Angoon, Alaska.

Sally wrote the foreword to *'A' is for Alaska: Teacher to the Territory* by Naomi Gaede Penner.

CHAPTER 31

UP IN THE AIR

Tanana, 1959

THE YUKON RIVER remained frozen in place. Front Street alternated between slush at midday and icy ruts at night, and the puffy whiteness in the woods was still willing and able to swallow up small children. Even so, March introduced the freshness and excitement of spring. Pink and purple tulips did not spring up; however, pungent-smelling, gray, furry pussy willows did. The girls delighted in sticking them against their noses and rubbing their nubby ends against their cheeks. "They're like little kittens," remarked Ruth.

At school, the second-grade class had planted flower seeds in tin cans and decorated their room with hand-colored and cut construction paper birds, flowers, and lambs.

The first Tanana Parent Teacher Association came to life, and even though Ruby had no assurance her family would be in Tanana the following school year, she volunteered to participate.

PTA NEWS

The Tanana Parent and Teacher Assoc. was formed at the Tanana School on March 7, the program opened with a film "Good-by Mr. Germ." Boys and girls from Miss Amundson's room presented a play "The Lad and the North Wind."

The following officers were elected:
President - Ronald Nusunginya
Vice Pres - Elmer Gaede
Secretary - Josephine Roberts
Treasurer - Ruby Gaede

The new airport café, the first café in the village since the Gaedes had been there, and possibly the first eatery for decades, pushed additional energy into the village. Who would have imagined eating out in Tanana, meeting someone for coffee, or having something like a date? Ruby considered going there, yet she would have to ask Elmer. Her frugal and practical upbringing suppressed the inclination to pursue the subject. Why spend the money when she could make the items offered? It was tempting, though. If they offered root beer floats, her resistance would be shot. She had heard a whiff of conversation that the schoolteachers—Harriet and Herman—had indulged. She might have to inquire about their experience.

COFFEE SHOP OPENS

Pete and Joan Myberg opened up the Airport Coffee Shop Wednesday March 25th. The invite all folks to come out and try their foods.

SANDWICHES

Hot dogs, chili dogs, hamburgers, chili-burgers, cheeseburgers, bacon-lettuce-tomato sandwich, ham & cheese, grilled cheese, American cheese, salami bologna, liverwurst, egg salad, tuna salad.

<u>BREAKFAST</u>

```
  Ham & Eggs    Hot Cakes
Sausage & Eggs   Coffee
```

Seven variety of soups to choose from.
Pies, Danish pastry, Donuts
Pop, coffee, tea, milk and hot chocolate.
OPEN - 8:30 A.M. until 8 P.M.

Naomi's excitement was focused on her ninth birthday, on April 2. "And, Grandma Leppke is fifty years older. Almost exactly," she told everyone. "We are alike. Her birthday is April 1." Naomi was proud of that connection.

Ruby talked with her eldest about a party. Naomi did not mention balloons, nut cups, or streamers. Nothing was said of cutesy invitations or party favors. "I just want about six friends and a cake, with not too much icing." Even though Ruby was capable of putting on a party extraordinaire, she was relieved by her daughter's simple request.

The busy mother added birthday cake to her weekly baking. The cake wasn't as creative as in past years, such as when Naomi had begged for "one like a hen on Grandma Leppke's farm," or the mountain cake Ruby had made for her the year before, with miniature cars driving on a road to the top. The seven-minute frosting had been the perfect mix to cover up underlying cake crevasses, and the brilliant white sheen left no doubt that there was snow on the mountain. No, this year, Naomi wanted a confetti angel food cake with pale yellow frosting and white candles. "Not too sweet or sticky icing," she reminded her mother. That was easy.

Naomi's friends arrived in school clothes; they were not dressed-up girls. Thin-wale corduroy pants and shirts or sweaters prevailed. Naomi's short-sleeved blouse was striped in maroon, brown, and cream. Her hair was shorter than usual, and instead of braids, it was styled in two short pigtails that puffed out behind her ears.

The handful of girls included Marie, the sister of Naomi's grade-school crush, Chris Sommer, who was just as red-haired and freckle-faced as her brother,[84] and Sally Woods, Naomi's best friend.

After singing "Happy Birthday," but before eating cake, Mark, who had joined the party, pushed a gift toward his sister.

"Look! Look!" Naomi exclaimed when she unwrapped a jump rope with tiny bells attached to the red, wooden handles. For years to come, she would jump rope with gusto and dexterity: "high water," "low water," "eggbeaters," and more.

At this point, she practically lassoed her mother, who held her hand over her glasses in defense. "Why don't you put the jump rope on the table with your other gifts, and I will use your new camera to take a picture."

She did as instructed and opened another present. This one was just as dangerous in close proximity: a blue-striped girl-sized umbrella. She glanced at her mother and then carefully demonstrated its use, without flicking any edges into her guests' eyes.

Her parents had given her not only a Brownie camera, but also the doll she had circled in the Sears catalog. When she unwrapped the gift, she cooed, "Oh, just what I wanted." She snuggled the doll close and turned to her girlfriends, "This is Susie Lou Anna." Then she demonstrated how the doll had moveable legs and could sit beside the cake.

Those weren't the only offerings. Wrapping paper came off what appeared to be a book. Indeed it was. The Alaska photo book with cream-colored leather cover displayed a totem pole, igloo, and a snub-nosed passenger airliner, with the Alaska midnight sun setting behind it. It was in this book that Naomi placed a picture of her ninth birthday party.

Later, when Naomi skipped excitedly with her doll to school and showed it to Miss Amundson, the teacher's curt comment cut her short, "That is the ugliest doll I've ever seen." Her voice sounded loud in the empty and silent classroom. It was like a slap in the face. Naomi blinked hard, picked up the doll from her teacher's desk, and walked home. To her, the doll's golden-brown, short curls were like a halo, and the big blue eyes were almost real. "It's okay, Susie Lou Anna," she whispered, cradling the doll to her chest. "I love you."

Elmer offered Ruby a new opportunity. For her, it would be an opportunity to visit missionaries. For him, it would be an adventure to fly a great distance down the Yukon River. The tone of Ruby's letter to her parents was excited, even though it involved flying.

> "April 9 It was beautiful weather this month so we flew as a family to Russian Mission, downriver, about 400 miles, to visit with the Mennonite lay missionaries Stolfus and family and Eddie Hooley the school teacher. It was a 3 day trip. Russian Mission is an eskimo village of about 120 people. It isn't very far from the ocean."

Ruby and Elmer had met Mahlon and Hilda Stoltzfus when they had come down the Yukon River in a small outboard-motor boat with their three children. Previously, in 1949, Mahlon Stoltzfus and William Anders had flown their plane to Alaska to investigate mission opportunities for the Mennonite Church. Unlike the missionaries with Arctic Missions, who were supported by charitable people who believed in their cause, the Stoltzfus's were self-supporting and ran the village general store. Their service extended beyond the peoples' hearts and encompassed their physical needs as well.

Elmer's mother, Agnes, would have described the wayfarers as "PIT-i-ful people in a tin boat." Elmer had spoken of them as great trailblazers and an inspiration to everyone. He couldn't wait to see their endeavors. Once again, Ruby saw a need to encourage another missionary woman in a primitive and isolated Alaska village.

The village, approximately 450 air miles downriver from Tanana, was located where a fur trading post of the Russian-American Company had been established in 1842. Russian Orthodox missionaries built a log chapel shortly after that time. Following the sale of Alaska, from the Russians to the United States, in 1867, the village was called Russian Mission.

Instinctively, Ruby rolled up her sleeves for food preparation to take to the missionaries; among those things were butterscotch chip cookies and round raisin bread. She hated to use up the missionaries' meager food supply by her own family's eating, so she added a box of oatmeal and powdered milk for her family's breakfast. Elmer was a stickler on weight and balance in the plane, and she knew she couldn't take much.

Naomi sat in the kitchen, not helping but drawing in her hard covered army-green notebook. Ruby glanced at her latest picture. Nothing new. Another figure of a girl, with no skin, with blue and red veins and black outlined bones trailing everywhere. Would Naomi pursue medicine? Medical drawings? Ruby made no comment.

"How will we sit on the plane?" Naomi asked her mother without looking up. She knew where she and Ruth would be but didn't know if Mark would join them in the backseat, which would be plumped with army mummy sleeping bags, or be on their mother's lap in the front. In the back of her mind, she was also wondering which doll or stuffed animal she could take along. She settled on Tiny Tears because it was second to her smallest doll, which was Peter. Tiny Tears had more clothes, and her arms and legs moved, and, if she drank water from her bottle, she would wet her pants, which made her seem intriguingly real.

As it turned out, Mark was sandwiched between his mother and the airplane instrument panel, beside his daddy, and within full view of how flying took place. "I can help Daddy," he said with a grin. "We can fly the plane … let's go, Daddy!"

Anna had gotten her wish, and Mishal was her baby doll for the few days the Gaedes would be gone.

"We left Tanana at 8:30. There was some haze which looked like fog but when we approached it disappeared. Our first stop was Kaltag where we arrived at 10:30. XXXXNNNNGGGGLKUKLKLK Looks like Mark got a hold of the typewriter when I wasn't looking.

We saw some dog races, ate dinner, visited with missionary Nabingers, also visited with the school teachers, and Elmer saw a half dozen patients. We finally got off again at 3:30 PM and headed into some entirely new area for us. The weather was perfectly clear, calm, and about six above. We followed the Yukon river in general but made a few short cuts where the river curved off coarse Even though it was clear we didn't see Russian Mission until we were right about it since it was hidden behind a hill and kind of tucked into a canyon that opened down to the river.

The Stolfuses and half the eskimos in the village met us when we landed on the frozen river by the village."

Once the airplane engine shuddered to a halt and the propeller stopped rotating, Ruby unlatched the split door and hooked the top half beneath the wing. The lower half swung downward. There was Mahlon Stoltzfus. His balding head was covered with a cap, and his unzipped beige parka sported a red flannel shirt behind it. The man stooped under the wing and greeted them with a welcoming smile. Ruby turned Mark toward him, and Mr. Stoltzfus started to lift the preschooler to the ground. Mark stiffened his body and crooked his head backward to be sure his parents were following.

Ruby crawled out next, followed by Elmer. The two men shook hands and made small talk about the trip. Naomi and Ruth untangled themselves from their sleeping bags and backed out the airplane door on their own, each extending a leg and feeling for the metal step-plate before they reached the ground. Hilda Stoltzfus moved into the circle, hungry for conversation with someone who knew her culture and traditions. Her dark hair was pulled back neatly and covered with a silky print scarf. She had smiling eyes and a closed-mouth cautious smile. She and Ruby embraced gently.

Two of the Stoltzfus children stood nearby, Gareth, age eight, and Karl, age three. Since Russian Mission, and most villages in Alaska, did not have high schools, the two older girls, Gueen and Ruby, were attending a boarding school in Indiana. The boys wore black fur parkas with fluffy white fur ruffs. Little Karl's had a red felt patch with a white puppy sewn on either side of the front zipper. Just as Naomi and Ruth, he had moose-skin mittens attached to a yarn harness around his neck.

After a time, Vivian nudged her husband. "I'm sure the Gaedes would like to stretch their legs, get inside where it's warm, and have some supper too."

Elmer and Mahlon unloaded the plane, continued their best-buddies conversation, and caught up with the women and children, who had walked ahead.

Foot traffic had worn down single-track snow trails throughout the village, and the procession followed in a line to the Stoltzfus's rough-hewn two-story house, which backed into a steep hill. Snowbanks pushed up to the windowsills. A weathered picket fence, brown with age and no signs of paint, stood to one side, and thick logs chopped into eighteen-inch pieces were scattered hither and thither in front of the combination house-store. A flimsy-looking dogsled sat below the five or six steps up to the house.

> "The Stolfuses own the village store which is combined with their living quarters. They treated us royally and were so happy to visit with fellow Believer and Mennonites. We also visited with the Mennonite school teacher Eddie Hooley."

Eddie Hooley, a conservative Mennonite from Indiana, showed up to share supper with the "Mennonite Reunion." The lean, dark-haired man with straight hair parted on one side was in his late twenties or early thirties. He had a high forehead, light complexion, scant mustache, and thick beard, which was an asset for the Alaskan winters. His red parka showed signs of working outdoors, hauling wood, cleaning a wood stove, and other frontier activities.

Mahlon showed the Gaedes the small store. A long wooden counter stretched in front of ceiling-high shelves, arranged with colorful, large cans of spices, cooking and baking staples, bags of rice, and so forth. Or course, there were blue and white boxes of Sailor Boy Pilot Bread

Naomi and Ruth explored the surroundings with their eyes. They talked curiously and quietly between themselves about the tall shelves with canned items that could only be reached by a ladder; and the enormous pillow-like cloth sacks of flour and sugar. A large jar of multi-colored candy suckers on sticks particularly interested them. Regardless, they knew better than to ask.

> "Sunday forenoon we attended the Russian Orthodox Church. The service was conducted in the native language. We took some pictures."

Russian Orthodox church in Russian Mission.

The Russian Orthodox church was at one of the highest points of the village. The four-sided, weathered-gray, log multi-level structure with white-framed windows stood out against the snow like a black-and-white picture. Each of the three roof peaks held a white Russian Orthodox cross. Inside the narthex, icons filled the walls, including gold-haloed saints, filigree, and painted flowers. A white cross drew attention to the front wall, where there was a door leading to the altar table behind it.

Naomi and Ruth's eyes were wide and their mouths speechless. They had never seen the like. The churches they had been in were plain. Their grandparents' unpretentious, white Mennonite Brethren church on the Kansas prairie was filled with only a simple pulpit, hard wooden church pews, piano, and an attendance board. No pictures or ornaments. The chapel in Tanana was nothing more than a cold lean-to attached to the missionary's house. The girls sensed the sacredness of the place and saved their questions for later when they asked their parents the "whys" of the crosses with slanted foot-pieces, the odor of incense, the gold halos, and more.

> *"In the afternoon the Stolfuses held services in their store About 7 adults and 6 kids attended. He preached a very fine sermon. The rest of that clear warm afternoon we were outdoors seeing the village. We saw their huge fishtraps, pulled out of the river for the winter, and their steambath houses.[85] That evening we did a lot of good ole visiting and singing.*
>
> *Monday morning we were up by 7:00 and we all went to the school where the teacher served us fried mush."*

Fish trap at Russian Mission.

The school was a sturdy building with four-sided logs and a corrugated tin roof. A dark-green lean-to served as Eddie's living quarters, as well as a kind of arctic entry. A tall flagpole in front could be seen from most of the village.

"I wonder how loud that bell is," said Naomi to Ruth.

Ruth scrutinized the bell, mounted on a stocky four-legged log stand. "It's bigger than ours in Tanana."

A row of three fifty-five-gallon gas barrels, on a lower stand, added to the schoolyard, as well as an outhouse peaking from behind the school itself.

Fried cornmeal mush was a favorite of all three children. The edges could get tough when fried, and Ruth helped cut Mark's into small pieces. The oily smell of fried food blended with the sweetness of warmed syrup. The recently restarted, crackling fire in the barrel stove added to the warm and comfortable ambiance.

Schoolhouse and teacherage in Russian Mission

As much as both girls would have liked more, they turned their faces down and mumbled, "No, thank you," when asked about second helpings. Their mother had whispered to them earlier, "Don't eat too much. These people don't have much. I'll make you more mush when we get home."

UP IN THE AIR

"*The fellowship was all very wonderful and we were sorry to have to say farewell. By 9:00 AM we were again airborne and starting home. It was again clear and warm (18 degrees) so we flew about 100 miles and landed on the river by Holicochuck. Here we visited Mrs. And Mr. Parkens the Arctic Missions missionaries. The villagers were very friendly and insisted we visit every home. It was nearly 2:00 PM before we continued to Kaltag where we filled in gas. We then flew to Kokrines arriving at 5:00 PM, The river was very rough with snow drifts. We ate with the Scriptures and saw several patients and left by 7:00 PM.*

We were glad to arrive home by dusk after having an unusual beautiful, smooth, and safe trip. We had flown about 10 hours covering over 900 miles."

Ruby had no complaints about flying—to see the missionaries.

FRIED MUSH

```
3 C. water
1 C. cornmeal
1 ts. Salt
Boil water. Sprinkle in cornmeal while stirring
to prevent lumps. Add and mix in salt. Stir. Pour
into 9 x 5 loaf pan, cool to room temperature,
cover, refrigerate overnight. When ready to serve,
cut into thin slices, and fry in butter, or bacon
or sausage grease, until golden brown. Serve with
syrup.
```

CHAPTER 32

SPRING CARNIVAL AND SCHOOL FAIR

Tanana, 1959

SPRING CARNIVALS are annual events for villages in Alaska, and the mid-April competition and celebration signify a goodbye to winter and hello to the dramatic return to summer, which is marked by the Yukon River going out. The warm sunshine and longer daylight hours soften the snow, even if temperatures aren't that much above freezing.

In 1959, the Tanana Spring Carnival involved dog races for men, women, and children, along with snowshoe races for the age categories. These were held on the river. Neither Ruby nor Elmer joined in these races. All the same, they were intrigued by the excitement and the athleticism of the mushers, dogs, and other participants.

The river appeared clean and white, even while Front Street and the south-facing riverbank were black mud. The previous week at school, the children had been required to remove their shoes and boots in the hall and attend classes in stocking feet. Then, of all things, the Northern

Commercial store had advertised newly arrived 24- and 26-inch Murray bicycles. With no consideration of the road conditions or weather, riding bikes became the craze. The kids had no concern or caution. Wearing their winter parkas and mittens, they slipped and slid around the village.

Technically, April would be considered a month of spring; however, Alaskans speak of "breakup," when frozen rivers break up and when the frozen ground thaws and no longer holds puddles captive on the surface. The Gaede family and other villagers wore "breakup boots" to manage the grubbiness. Most of the tall, rubber boots were black; although in Mark's case, they were shiny red, that is, until he slipped in the mud on Front Street on the way to the river. Not only were his boots grimy, but the entire backside of his red parka. He scowled and looked at his mother to see if he would be scolded. She reached out her hand to pull him up and muttered a Plautdietsch expression of annoyance.

Tanana Spring Carnival, 1959

SPRING CARNIVAL AND SCHOOL FAIR

The Gaedes made their way down the riverbank, holding on to one another, and joined the other bystanders. Elmer had both his Kodak slide camera and his 8 mm movie camera strapped around his neck, and, with a broad smile and a few chuckles, he recorded the scene before him. Later, he would entertain guests with these pictures. Even later, he would hold spellbound his California family with movies and larger-than-life stories of Life Along the Yukon River.

Only racers and handlers got near the exuberant dogs, and only the Natives raced. It was clearly not a petting zoo for kids, but a serious competition.

The racers' faces showed beads of perspiration from exhaustion, and their coats were unzipped. Onlookers laughed and found amusing a male snowshoe contender who could not keep his footing, dogs that tangled in their harnesses and tripped the mushers, and the charm of youngsters trying out the sports in their own ways. All this was mixed with the yapping of dogs eager to race, the wild motion of them leaping in their harnesses at the starting line, and red tongues lolling out the sides of their dog-grinning faces at the return.

Ruby described the event in a letter.

> *"What a busy and variety of experiences we had this week. Starting Wed noon we had our village dog races and the traditional April Tanana Spring Carnival. The weather was warm, the snow on the river where they had the dog trails were soft and the dogs had a hard time. A native manages a hot dog stand to please the natives very much, Anna, Harriet and the Gronnings releaved the workers some too."*

Elmer caught Ruby on camera holding a hot dog in one hand, a cup of coffee in the other, and talking with a Native couple. No matter the disordered conditions around and beneath her, she herself was neat as a pin in her fur parka with hood tossed back, hair in place, and a lipstick smile. She was having a very good day.

Ruby did love hot dogs, yet, almost better was her taste testing of caribou. She explained in the same letter:

"Fri. nite the village had the caribou potlatch and they were so thankful for the caribou Elmer got for the potlatch. We had our first caribou roast and is it ever delicious, milder, softer, and finer grain than moose. Those who have had reindeer say it compares to that."

After the potlatch, the party spirit continued.

"The first night of the dog races the natives really whooped it up and Elmer was called out twice to sew up the after effects. The one native man was sent to jail in Fairbanks for 6 months. The other one gets a chance. The commissioner announced at the Community Hall that if there would be any drunks appearing at the hall he would lock up the place for a long time. That would hurt a lot as they love their many movies and dances they have there. Tonight there is another potlatch so we will see how things go."

Elmer's plane did not sit idle. The engine scarcely cooled off before he fired it up again. Not knowing where they would be the following year, there was an unspoken frenzy to fit in as much as possible at this time.

"Sunday morning we again took the three older children and took off

for Kokrines and spent the day with Scripters. It made our hearts sad that it was the last time together as they will be isolated soon because of the breakup of the river, and then in June they will be transferring and as yet do not know where for sure."

Ruby could relate to Maxine Scripter's uneasiness about an unknown future.

"Again we must be thankful that God does not permit us to see what the tomorrow brings as it is sufficient to live for one day. Wed. morn I started another of my bladder infections and Elmers leg was giving him a bad time. By Fri morn it was a battle as to who was the sickest and who got to stay I bed. Elmer tried to get up but had to come back to bed so I gave it a try and got the children off to school and by afternoon I told Elmer to scoot over and let me use the hot water bottle a while. It is Elmers sciatica nerve that give him all this trouble.

We have had zero and below, much too cold.

Elmer was able to go to work on crutches this morning. He also got his plane ready and he and Anna Bortel will leave tomorrow morning for Field Clinic at Anaktuvuk Pass, this place has a group of the only Eskimos in the Interior. They have no school so Anna wants to investigate that phase of the village."

This medical field trip would be to a group of Native people that, although in his healthcare region, he had never visited. The small band of

Eskimos migrated continually up and down Anaktuvuk Pass, above the Arctic Circle, and in the Brooks Range. Migrating for hunting or fishing was not unusual for the Native people. It was their lifestyle to move to fish camps in the summer and hunting grounds in the winter. Other tribes, however, had a place to return, a home base. At that time in Alaska history, the Anaktuvuk Eskimos were only then semi-settling in one area. Holding clinic was challenging.

"April 21, 1959

Elmer and Anna took off this morn, I felt uneasy about Elmer as he could not even put on his own shoes but I'm praying that he will make out O.K.

likkjj1/2/1/2/1/Mark has been helping again. Why is it so hard to get to a letter? Elmer got off to Anaktuvuk Pass with Anna, they had a few clouds and bumps on their way up. They thoroughly enjoyed their work there. Two public health nurses met them there, the all slept in one Quonset, Anna did the cooking.

This is really one of the most unusual villages in Alaska. The people live in caribou tents and they migrate considerably with the caribou herds. For summer they stay in one spot as there is no way for them to get around on foot, and there is no river to use a boat on. In winter they use their dog sleds. They live quite a ways from timber and therefore they get their timber in winter with dog teams so it lasts them through the summer.

The summers there are of course shorter than here. There are about 96 people in the village now. An old white man owns the very small store.

SPRING CARNIVAL AND SCHOOL FAIR

Elmer and Anna returned Thursday eve, only three days away. I did not expect them as bad weather was moving in and these CAA weather reports are very unreliable sometimes, it seems that all the fellas would have to do is step out of their doors and they would see it moving in but they just look out of the window in one direction and if that happens to be clear well the weather report then is clear for Tanana. Elmer did have a little trouble getting back that night, they had to fly around in some low fog and soup.

Elmer brought back red fox and wolverine furs, a mask made by the Eskimo men as a souveneer from the Pass. Plus good pictures."[86]

Elmer and Anna had returned two days before another first: the Spring Fair in the new Tanana school. For Ruby, it was one more chance to rub shoulders with the people in the village and to work alongside the teachers.

The *Northern Lights* advertised the Spring Carnival well in advance.

```
Start saving your pennies now for the spring
fair to be held in the school April 25, 1959.
NOTICE: Do your spring house cleaning
early! Save those white elephants for the
school fair. Save your books and comics,
bundle them up and donate to the school fair!
There will be a fish pond, hot dog stand, movies,
and many more stands.

NOTICE: The PTA would like donations of hand made
items to be sold at the school fair. Starting
making your items now!
```

The evening drew in everyone in the village.

Like a dog at the starting line, Naomi bounded with excitement to leave for the fair. Elmer was once again delivering a baby at the hospital, so it was up to Ruby to gather her children, herd them out the door, and, at the same time, remember everything she needed for the booth she was hosting.

When they arrived at school, Naomi either dragged Ruth behind her or raced around with Sally beside her. The fishing pond was oh so fun. It wasn't really a pond. It was a tall booth that "fishers" cast fishing lines over to see what would be reeled up on their lines: things such as a package of Juicy Fruit gum, a pair of socks, a little notebook, a set of metal jacks with a rubber ball, crayons, a bag of marbles, and so on.

Young and old tried the ring toss. Others sat before a man from the White Alice site who was "a very good Fortune Teller," or so reported the May *Northern Lights*. The men and boys lined up for the dart games, although an occasional spunky Native woman challenged them.

Just down the hall, and past the candy and popcorn booths, Walt Disney movies attracted all ages. Cake, cookies, and coffee were offered in another area. Naturally, the Gaede children found their way to the hot dog booth. Could those children ever get enough?

Ruby's booth was next to the White Elephant booth. She displayed homemade items for sale and was pleased with her efforts to raise money for the school:

> "At the school fair I had a souvenir stand, I sold $40 worth. The entire fair brought in $300 which is good for our little community. We have about $100 expenses. Since I am treasurer I have to record and take care of all this."

And, she did take care of business, even though she did not consider herself to be smart, felt embarrassed she had never finished high school, and she compared herself to her husband, who was a medical doctor. She had not taken the job to be honored or recognized. She just wanted to help out a good cause.

No, the bush doctor's wife was not in the limelight, nor in the local paper, as was her husband, who was the daring pilot, successful hunter, and Alaska physician who managed emergencies with minimum resources. Instead, she was quietly behind the scenes, leaving a legacy on the hearts and souls of countless people, keeping the home fires burning for her four children, and carefully adding and subtracting. The teachers and PTA were grateful she was a numbers gal.

Ruby had written her parents, "*We still have no news concerning this summer. I placed an order for ivory souvenirs for when we leave Alaska: ivory handled cake-server, meat fork, cake-breaker, salt and pepper shakers, and etched buttons.*"

If there was relocation, Ruby knew she would be responsible for packing, and she liked to plan ahead. If Elmer were transferred, where would it be? Would they still need the clothes and belongings they had accumulated in Tanana?

Naomi overheard her parents talking about the summer, not necessarily a relocation.

"I hope we can go to the farm this summer and see Grandma and Grandpa Leppke," she said, sitting at the kitchen table and working on one of the two jigsaw puzzles they had given her. One was of transportation, with an airplane overhead, a red Santa Fe locomotive with a yellow snout, a silver and blue Greyhound bus, and a chunky green delivery truck. None of these were a part of her world in Tanana. An Alaska transportation puzzle would have had a river barge, dogsled, and floatplane. Her heart loved both places, and the train evoked fond memories of her life in Kansas.

Her favorite puzzle, though, was the farm scene: a red rooster and yellow chicks, a pink pig eating an ear of corn with a smirk on its face, a white duck with red paddle-feet, a bright sunflower, a red barn, a galloping pony, and a striped tiger cat.

"Maybe there will be kitties under the porch at Grandma's."

Ruby didn't say a thing. She just kept stirring the pot of chicken noodle soup on the stove and tried to stop the thoughts spiraling downward in her head.

The next week, she wrote again, "*We still have no news concerning this summer, the children are learning to know what it means to wait upon the Lord.*"

And again, the following week, "*We know absolutely nothing concerning summer or next years plans. We trust the Lord will show us soon. Elmer did request that we might be here another year, should we get this request, we may not even get a vacation.*"

Would this be the Gaede's last Spring Carnival? Last potlatch? Would Public Health officials indeed make them transfer? No one seemed to know.

CHAPTER 33

ON THE MOVE

Tanana, 1959

BY THE FIRST OF MAY, the sun was climbing off the horizon around 5 a.m., and clinging to the sky until forced down, near 11:00 p.m. Unlike the sun, adults and children did not eagerly climb out of their beds at that early hour; however, like the sun, they grudgingly said "good night" to the late day. One Native woman told Ruby, "It's when we get turned upside down."

Things would become more bizarre. Unless people had eight to five jobs, there was no specific schedule. Natives tended to stay up and outdoors until they literally dropped, and then slept wherever they dropped until they felt rested, which was often the next day.

Although school was not yet over, the Gaede children were in summer mode. Their mother understood the evening phenomenon when the tardy sunset did not signal true and needed bedtime, and wide-eyed energy continued to course through their veins. Her dislike of tired, grumpy children at the breakfast table was her only incentive to call the children into the house on school nights.

Here in Alaska, Ruby watched the clock, not the sun, even though the sun had been her clock as a girl in Kansas. At this stage and place in her life, she would have found it easier to get cows into the barn to be milked, than children into bed, even with the bribe of bedtime snacks and daddy reading bedtime stories.

After sighing in exasperation from calling in the children for the nth time, she reminded herself that the end of school was drawing near. The *Northern Lights* school paper confirmed that with its final, May issue.

P.T.A. MEETING

```
The Tanana school P.T.A. met Friday evening, May
1, for its final meeting of this school year with
the president, Ronald Nusunginya presiding.

A report of our School Fair Committee was given
by its chairman, Fern Peters. The treasurer, Ruby
Gaede, gave the report of the Fair income.

It was voted to buy playground equipment with the
money.
```

Ruby Gaede *did* get her name in the paper after all. And, the school children would get swings and a slide for before and after school and recess. Until this time, they had devised other entertainment for recess, such as tag, marbles, jump rope, and hopscotch drawn with sticks on the dirt.

The *Northern Lights* clearly portrayed a picture of the kids' additional and preferred activities, most of which were outdoors:

```
Since school is almost out, we are asking some of
the school children what they are going to do this
summer:

Marie Sommer - "Play house outdoors."
```

```
Chris Sommer - "Work on "Weekly Readers."
Mickey Woods - "Go to fish camp."
Sally Woods - "Play on the beach."
Diane Miller - "Make mud pies."
Dennis Edwin - "Play marbles."
Loretta Byrd - "Go boat riding."
Freda Swenson - "Go swimming."
Judy Sommer - "Ride bike."
Ruth Gaede - "Walk in the mud."
Joyce Roberts - "Play in the mud."
```

Even with all the talk of mud, Ruby's housecleaning battle had left the ground and taken flight to the air.

"The water holes have dried up around the house so that housekeeping is a bit easier, but we live so close to the street and with quite a bit of traffic and it is dry enough to kick up a cloud of dust each time a truck goes by so I am keeping the windows on that side of the house closed."

Whereas the mother was utterly finished with mud splattered on the sidewalks, steps into the house, and play clothes, her girls insisted on making mud pies. It didn't do a lick of good that Ruby discouraged them otherwise. "Put your dolls in their stroller and take them to visit the secretary at the hospital," she suggested. They could have played paper dolls inside, like nice little girls, which they did enjoy—in the wintertime at 40 degrees below zero. Yet, with temperatures edging into the 60s, they were like chickens let out of confining coops. As soon as homework was done after school, and supper was finished in the evenings, or weekends welcomed their free time, they ran chattering out the door, hither and thither in all directions, making the most of what nature offered them.

Ruby compared them to "chickens with their heads cut off." Naomi had witnessed that on her grandparents' Leppke farm one summer, and it left an indelible impression on her young mind. "How can they still run without heads?" she had asked her mother in a whisper. Soberly, and disbelieving their crude death, Naomi had stood still until the chickens had fallen over dead. Ruby used that term matter-of-factly. It was just a part of farming and bringing food to the table; no different than pulling an ear of corn off a stalk, shucking it, and slicing off the kernels.

And, what did these rambunctious children do in the fresh air with no lawns or parks for a game of croquet, a sidewalk too narrow to chalk-draw a foursquare game with a ball, and no swimming pool or amusement park? As much as they loved to pedal their bikes as fast as their legs could go, they still made mud pies.

On a Friday night, the children were playing outside, behind the house, and Ruby felt no parental responsibility to steer them into the house for baths, snacks, and stories. Even though the sky was an uninspiring gray and the air chilly, the kitchen window was open slightly and let in the happy sounds of children playing. Music to a mother's ear. She surveyed the scene before her. All three had bowls, spoons, and sandy dirt.

"Ruth, what can we decorate these with?" asked Naomi. Her tightly buttoned cotton jacket showed smudged signs of outdoor play. It had definitely seen better days and would not make it as a hand-me-down to Ruth.

Ruth thought a moment, ran dirty fingers through her wavy hair, and looked around. "Pussy willows? Pine cones?"

She sprang up from where she had been kneeling and chased around in zigzags, scouting out the medical compound. Naomi headed in another direction. Mark, who had been sitting on the ground with his knees bent and a short-brimmed cap on his head, jumped to his feet and tossed the sloppy contents of his bowl into the air, shouting exuberantly in nonsense syllables. Some of the mess splattered his face, and he laughed even harder.

The noise was silly, yet "good" noise, and the satisfied mother turned her attention to Mishal, who was practicing climbing up and down the divan and pushing her nose against the front window. Whenever someone walked by, she laughed and patted an open hand on the window.

All laughter and chatter stopped at 7:00 p.m.

"The children were outdoors making mud pies and one was running for water from the spigot in front of the house and the other was returning with water, they met at the corner of the house full-speed ahead and knocked each other down. Ruth has just a small gash on the upper forehead but poor Naomi just cut up her lip and smashed it badly that Elmer took 5 stitches starting with one on the outside and the rest leading to the gum. She is really sick and has not eaten anything solid for two days now, the first day she managed to sip with a straw but when swelling set in she could not do that so I have been dripping egg-nog and chocolate milk into her mouth as she is lying down.

Tonight she was at the table and I had some mashed potatoes and she turned her face away in tears and would not try. I need to learn the Christian graces of a mother at a time like this, my heart aches for her and here is nothing I can do for her.

Ruth feels happy about her one stitch but feels a lack of attention that Naomi is getting."

Eventually, the swelling subsided, and Naomi took pleasure in mixtures Ruby put together in the new blender, especially those of moose roast, mashed potatoes, gravy, and a sprinkling of canned peas.

Ruth was fit to be tied with jealousy. When Naomi offered to share some of her custom-made supper, Ruth turned up her nose and stalked away.

"It's really good!" said Naomi. "Like when I put peas in the mashed potato and gravy lake I make."

Finally, Elmer removed the sutures, and all was well, except for a lump of scar tissue in Naomi's lip, which remained for decades later. That, however, was not an immediate consideration. Her parents had a more pressing concern.

> *"Naomi needs braces for her teeth badly. It was because of two of her front teeth were sticking forward that her lip was torn so badly. I will be glad when we can get proper dental care for both the girls."*

After that traumatic event, Ruby's letters increased with news of their relocation.

> *"Dear Loved Ones, News first! We have finally found out that we will be moving the first of Sept. Elmer asked for two weeks vacation to be spent here in Alaska which leaves us two weeks for the states which has to be used before Jan. The children are not nearly as disappointed as I thought they might be. We have no idea where we will go. At least I know I will pack."*

During the previous two years, Ruby's emotional and mental confidence had shifted from the uneasiness of surviving village life to thriving in Tanana and loving the people and life along the Yukon River. Surprisingly, she now met this announcement with equanimity. Only four years prior, she had been uprooted from her familiar Kansas life and transplanted over four thousand miles away, to a different climate and culture, to the wild, unknown of the Last Frontier. Then, two years later, she had pulled up stakes from the bustling city of Anchorage and had moved to the speck on the map of Tanana.

Perhaps her acceptance had to do with believing she had no choice. Perhaps because she was a submissive, Christian, Mennonite, stand-by-your-man woman. And, very likely, because she had grown up in a faith of trusting God for one's future. Whatever the reason behind her calm, there was some relief of knowing she would be packing—to go somewhere. Thus, she started playing with the puzzle pieces of obtaining packing materials and trying to cram in the pleasures of life in the village.

The future was uncertain. Campfires with meat roasting, greasy sparks spitting, and an umbrella of smoke in everyone's eyes were familiar and even comforting. Unmistakably the pages of her May letters seemed to repeat themselves with her fervor:

"Thursday nite we had our first wiener roast. Just our family. It was quite windy and we still wore long underwear but it was fun.

Friday night we had a hamburger fry with the women teachers, public health nurse and an inventory man from Anchorage.

The head nurse and I put on a picnic for the nurses.

Saturday we had a Chapel picnic for all those leaving, which included more than they thought as only Anna and Wally the X-ray tech know we are also leaving, not only the Gronnings and some hospital staff.

The other nite, I cooked chicken over a little fire on the beach, and invited Anna and Harriet to join us. Elmer was tied up at the hospital."

Among the details, she inserted, "Since I always have to bake all our buns every time, it always takes a little more time." As if she had "more time" with her already full baking schedule and dirty kids, who craved the outdoors.

Eating outdoors wasn't only an inclination of Ruby's. Village-wide, folks made the most of early summer, including a culminating school event.

<u>COMING EVENTS</u>

```
Seventh-Eighth Grade Banquet   May 7, 6 P.M.
Eighth Grade Graduation        May 12, 8 P.M.
School Picnic                  May 13, 10:30 A.M.
Grade Cards Issued             May 14, 9 A.M.
```

Ruby was not involved in any of these; however, Elmer spoke at the graduation on "The Practical Question." Since Ruby did not include a description of this twenty-five-minute speech, and neither did a *Northern Lights* issue, there is no clue as to what that question was.

Ruby had her own practical question: would she be able to reap a harvest from her garden before leaving? Regardless, between picnics and baking, she put in a garden. She was a country girl, and like the innate calling of a salmon swimming upstream to spawn, a bear hibernating, and geese migrating, springtime called her to hoe the ground, crumble the sandy loam between her fingers, inhale the smell of wet dirt, and plant seeds: carrots, leaf lettuce, broccoli, potatoes, and radishes. After the previous year's experience with unripened, green tomatoes in mid-August, when the frost dashed her hopes of a mature, red crop, and the Natives had looked at each other knowing the outcome, she did not plant tomatoes.

To give some of her plantings a jump-start, such as pansies, she nurtured them indoors, and when they were strong enough, she placed the seedlings in pots and moved them indoors and outdoors, depending on the temperatures. Oftentimes, at midday, they happily sat on the front steps, absorbing the warmth of the concrete, and turning their purple, yellow, and maroon faces to the sun. Ruby tended them carefully, and the cheerful sound of robins, which had returned for the brief summer, added to her satisfaction. The only birds she had heard all winter were "the old black crows," which, in actuality, were ravens and sacred to the Native people. Perhaps if she had known more about the intelligence of these annoying creatures, she would have been fascinated instead.

Elmer took his turn to scribble news to his parents.

"The ice went out at Fairbanks a couple days ago so we expect the Nenana ice to go this week and probably the ice here in about two weeks. The ice is getting fairly rotten so I'll get the plane off the river in the next couple of day."

And, in the nick of time, he did so, for shortly after Elmer heralded the impending event, Ruby followed on his heels with confirmation, and her two cents' worth, which really was not much for such an astonishing, thundering, and powerful act of nature.

"Thursday morning at 3:30 a.m. our ice went out and it was a thrill, Elmer had the nurse on duty blow the hospital fire whistle. The piercing sound awakened nearly everyone in the village so they could come out and take pictures. You of course realize that we have plenty day-lite by that time to take pictures."

A river pathway had already grown along the shoreline, and now, with the force of ice breaking loose upriver, the middle section buckled and moved forward, shoving enormous slabs of ice upright as it did so. The slabs would then lose balance and crash down on others ahead of them. It was a water and ice battle, and, as if there was a contest to beat the other chunks to the sea, a frenzied, ear-splitting marathon provoked by a mighty force behind it.

The water rose up the banks, along with fears of the village flooding. That year, Tanana was fortunate. The river and ice churned steadily forward, leaving a trail of smaller ice chunks bobbing, twisting, and crashing into one another. On successive days, trees pulled off riverbank edges and driftwood from sandbars joined the diminishing ice cakes that bobbed like ducklings after the main event had taken place. Once the river cleared from these smaller obstacles, the Natives would fire up their motorboats and chase the logs for fuel for their barrel stoves.

Breakup of the Yukon River was the final farewell to winter. At this same time, there were other farewells too.

> *"Harriet Amundson went to her home in Minnesota for the summer months. She hated to go as she has a broken home. She seemed to enjoy our home so much and considered herself a part of our family. Herman Romer was suppose to leave today and he is heavy-hearted and hated to leave. I had him and Anna over for his farewell breakfast and he says he is not really to leave so he will try again tomorrow. We feel like all 3 teachers belonged to our family."*

The schoolteachers' struggles to maintain lessons and learning in drafty, insulation-itching, dim-lit, Quonset huts with clogged oil lines had bonded the three of them. Throughout the entire year, Elmer and Ruby's ever-welcoming home and hospitality had warmed their hearts and physical beings, which served to connect the doctor's family with the teachers, as together they cared for one another and for the community.

ON THE MOVE

The Gaede family kept the air furrowed with their flying. If they were leaving Alaska, they had to squeeze in as much of the intriguing Frontier as they could.

> "Sat. morning we took off for Fairbanks at 8:00 and arrived at 9:30. It was a beautiful day and Mt. McKinley was just gorgeous in the distance. Mishal stayed home with Anna. We checked in at a hotel. $15 for one night and we were fortunate to have a room, as there was graduation at the University (of Alaska) and also the Base (Eielson Air Force) had an airshow. We shopped in the forenoon, mostly toys and groceries! We all had malts for lunch. In the afternoon, we watched the air show. It was really good and the sun was so hot we had a chance to absorb much needed sunshine.
>
> That evening we spent at the hotel. Mark played with his new floatplane in the tub, and the girls did the same with their small boats. It was so noisy since there are so many bars, there was screaming and talking and bottles clanging that I didn't get a nickels worth of sleep. Boy am I glad we live in simple Tanana.
>
> The weather was good Sunday and we went to S.S. and church. In the afternoon we went up the hill to the University grounds and Judy Orr a Freshman now Soph. showed us the campus. (We lived next door to her family when we were in Anchorage and Elmer hunted with her father.) We returned here at the hotel at 6:00 and cleaned up a bit and went to church.

Mark got such a kick out of the elevator, and called it the "alligator." He cried when we had to leave."

If Ruby's stomach wasn't upset by flying, it was with the bits of news Elmer kept receiving about their relocation.

"We were told that we could have a place at Cass Lake, Minn. And we were very happy, but a few days later they called and said nil to that, then gave Elmer the openings that were available so we chose Browning, Montana. Elmer will be M.O.C. (Medical Officer in Charge). There is much going on that is very trying, but we want the Lord to give us grace so that it will make us better children of His. They have been very rude and unfair with handling employees, and of course you well know that unless you drink and dance along with the big boss you just may not be popular and so always we must trust in the Lord rather than have confidence in men. The next months will be very trying for Elmer."

Elmer had his hands full with medical patients and the red tape and politics of the transfer. Ruby had her days full with packing, although her husband told her it was too early to start. With arms crossed tightly in front of her, she told Anna, "I cannot let this go and then try to throw everything together in two weeks." Naomi cried when her mother boxed up the basement playroom. Away went doll beds, Ruth's red and Naomi's white wooden chairs Elmer had made them, hard rubber farm animals, and the electric train. Ruth didn't show her emotions. She just got quiet and walked upstairs to her bedroom and closed the door. Most likely, she buried her face in her white stuffed cat, Puff.

Mark saw the tears streaming down Naomi's cheeks and her scarred lip quivering. He turned his face up to hers and tried to offer comfort, "I'll share my rocket ships with you. That will make you feel better." Ruby had written home, "*Mark has a craving for chocolate chips and calls them rocket-ships. Any time he has a tummy ache he thinks that rocket-ships will make it feel better.*" Naomi's sobs increased. "No. No." Perhaps if he had offered her butterscotch chips or cheese crackers, that might have distracted her, at least for the moment. Ruby took a corner of her apron and dried Naomi's tears.

If Ruby had let herself, she would have cried too. She wrote, "*I am so disappointed we did not get Minnesota, Elmer's request, too, so we could see some dear friends.*"

The hospital used coal in its mammoth furnace—coal that was brought in by barge each summer, in large burlap bags, and stacked behind the hospital. One day when Ruby and the three oldest children were wandering behind the hospital, Ruby showed them coal cinders, the remains of coal chunks after being burned for heat. As grimy as the porous lumps were, she actually asked the children to carry home what their hands could hold. She then showed them how to make a crystal garden—after they washed their hands, left black streaks in the bathroom sink, and gathered around the kitchen table, leaning on their elbows.

Somehow, among the letters, *Northern Lights*, *The Mukluk Telegraphs*, newspaper clippings, and other materials that were saved, the handwritten recipe for the Crystal Garden was discovered.

CRYSTAL GARDEN

Aluminum plate or dish. Roughly crushed cinder block or brick.

4 T. Water
4T. Bluing
4T. Salt
1T. Ammonia

Tin can and spoon to mix ingredients.

Place crushed chunks in plate or dish. Pour solution over pieces. Dabble on food coloring. Leave undisturbed. Cover with plastic wrap to slow down absorption - crystals will be larger and last longer.

CHAPTER 34

SUMMER FLIES BY

Tanana, 1959

"June 14 We now have sunrise at 12:55 am and sunset at 11:00 pm, the sun shines so bright against our bedroom window at 3:00 at night that I can hardly sleep. We are having a heat wave of 85 degrees during the day. Our small row of leaf lettuce is ready to eat."

The life-giving sun and rejuvenating temperatures beckoned Ruby outdoors. Sometimes, she took a break from weeding, arched her back in a stretch, and sat back on her heels, then like a prairie sunflower, turned her face to the everlasting sun, soaked in its warmth, and thought of the pleasant times at her Kansas home. Not of the backbreaking, face-sweating chores of plowing fields and harvesting wheat, but of rare picnics beneath tall cottonwoods, eating paprika-topped deviled eggs and juicy cantaloupe. Or, recollections of catching catfish with Elmer when they were first married, and standing knee-deep in a muddy Kansas creek, with her full skirt pulled up and hands plunged into the thick water. Those were good times. The mental getaway warmed her heart, and the sun toasted her face and arms.

Fishing in Kansas. Ruby with the man she loved: farmer-boy turned physician.

When Mark bumped into her, she opened her eyes with a start. With a proud smile, he presented his mother with a handful of feathery carrot tops. "Thank you," she said, looking at his sweet face. She didn't have the heart to tell him the carrots needed their fancy top hats to keep their bottoms growing under the soil.

Out of the corner of her eye, Ruby saw motion coming from the duplex. Naomi skipped toward her with her jump rope. Dust swirled around her ankles, and she sang with gusto,

> *"Cinderella, dressed in yellow*
> *Went upstairs to kiss a fellow*
> *Made a mistake*

And kissed a snake
How many doctors
Did it take?"

The girl's count was up to twenty-one when she stopped. Trying to catch her breath, she puffed, "Mommy, Mishal woke up from her nap ... She was crying ... but it's okay now ... Ruth is with her."

Ruby was confident Mishal *was* okay and imagined Ruth sweet-talking the child, dangling a stuffed animal over her head, or playing patty-cake.

"It being warmer the children play outdoors more and since we have no lawn they are always filthy which means more washing and cleaning. And, they are going barefoot now to. Right now, Naomi and Ruth are playing barefoot at the hospital playground in dress hats. To top it all maintenance dug another ditch close by and the children are like chickens when it comes to a freshly dug place, needing to add to the ruckus. Of course, they had to climb down inside to investigate. Boy, did that wet sand track into the house."

To try to distract them from the luring ditch, Ruby suggested, "Let's have a picnic down by the river. Ruth, run this note to Anna and see if she will join us."

"Mommy, will we have a fire?" asked Mark excitedly. "I will find the matches."

No matter where Ruby hid the matchbox, Mark was able to find it. He pushed a chair to the kitchen counter and climbed up with his sandy bare feet. Ruby stood with her arms akimbo and watched the three-and-a-half-year-old edge sideways along the countertop until he was by the refrigerator. He stretched short arms toward the cabinet door above it and nearly lost his balance.

"I can't reach them," he said. His eyes were wide with alarm.

"I know," replied his mother. She caught him in her arms and stepped on the chair to retrieve the matches. It was a stretch for her as well.

Without much thought, and out of habit, she packed the picnic box: plates, cups, a plastic bag of silverware, a quart jar of water, and whatever else was handy for a picnic. And, of course, the matchbox.

Ruth returned with a, "Yes, Mommy. Miss Bortel is coming."

Ruby handed her Mishal's lightweight cotton jacket, and the little-mother patiently wriggled Mishal's waving arms into the sleeves. "Come, Mishal. Let's go to the wagon," she coached her toddling sister.

The children took off gaily to the river shore, unaware that for their mother, this wiener roast was bittersweet and the last picnic with Anna.

"I spent as much time with Anna as I could as she left yesterday, she will spend 5 days at Barrow with Florence Feldkirchner, who was the head teacher here last year, and then some time in Valdez, where she taught before she came here, and then to her home in Ohio. I miss her already, she was my left arm here."

She wasn't the only one Ruby would miss. The Gronnings were being re-stationed.

"Monday evening Ken Hughes came from Anchorage to fly the Gronnings to Victory Bible Camp at Palmer. They put all their belongings in an old cabin behind their house until they know where they will be stationed next. I worked so hard to help them sort and pack."

During the coming weeks, Ruby would long for a familiar face to listen to her uneasiness. It would have been comforting to sit on the steps of the duplex's concrete porch with Margie or Anna, gaze over the restless and mesmerizing Yukon River, and just chat a bit. Sure, she talked about the practical aspects with Elmer. And, even though she recognized his tenseness and disgust at how Public Health was handling their reassignment from Tanana, she didn't feel an empathetic connection when she expressed her nagging worries.

After the children were tucked into bed, and she had slipped in beside her husband, she would stare up at the ceiling, still shadowy from the late sunset, and take a deep breath of courage to start a conversation. But, by the time her questions reached her lips, she would hear Elmer's chorus of snores begin. Then, she felt silly and even guilty. He had so much on his mind; his workload at the hospital was overwhelming. In addition to other surgeries, he was nearing fifty-five tonsillectomies. He wanted desperately to explore more of Alaska, and the red tape for the relocation was sticky and kept him ensnared.

It wasn't as though she didn't pray about her future, or she didn't believe God cared about her and her family; it just would have been nice to let her feelings trickle over to a listening, caring ear. Someone who could hear her heart, not just her mind. Someone who could vicariously share the weight of packing, preparing, and managing her children for the unknown and feel with her the sadness of leaving Tanana. She sighed often and then resolutely marched forward. Her letters to loved ones served in some ways as a therapeutic journal.

Elmer continued to play travel agent for Ruby, not per her request, but for his desire to share with her the places he had been on medical emergencies or field trips that he thought she might want to see. One of those places was Manley Hot Springs, approximately fifty miles upriver, as the crow would fly.

Two winters prior, he had gone to Manley Hot Springs on a fearfully cold February dusky day. He had received a call over the radio, "I think ol' Charlie is dying," the innkeeper at Manley Hot Springs had said urgently. "He needs you, Dr. Gaede." The bush doctor had followed through and risked his life to take off with his small plane, in the obscurity of a short winter day, when the dimensions of land and sky blended together, and the mind's eye could not be trusted. From start to finish, the series of events had been both a menacing and miracle story. Ruby had summarized the ordeal in one sentence, "*God's hand of mercy was the only way anyone made it.*"

At that medical emergency, Doc Gaede wasn't compelled to check out the hot springs. Now, in June of 1959, he was, and he thought Ruby and the children would enjoy the unusual wilderness phenomenon too. Besides, it was only a hop, skip, and a jump from Tanana and could easily fit into the weekend when he had time off work.

> *"This afternoon we took the 3 older children and flew to Manley Hot Springs a half hour flying from here. We saw the gardening they do there and took a bath in the water that comes out of the hot springs. One bubbly hot springs is 125 degrees and the other is 134 and that bath water was so hot even tho they had cold water running with it we just wilted in no time. The small pool is very crude and shabby but it is typical to bush Alaska."*

Ruby seemed to take pleasure in the excursion, as unusual as it was to lounge in a rough wood structure that was a combination greenhouse and spa. Steamy waterways were in sections of the floor, as well as streams of hot and cold water in chutes outside. By this time, the bush doctor's wife had developed an acceptance and appreciation of the efforts made, in the rawness of Alaska, to offer a concept of luxury.

> *"After the leisure bath we walked back to our plane and got our sandwiches and walk to where a float plane was docked and ate there. The mosquitos were of course terrible and we have to soak ourselves in repellent. We returned home by 6:00 pm. Wally, the lab technician who lives on the other side of our duplex babysat Mishal. She sleeps most of the afternoon."*

No matter how cold an Alaska winter gets, and even when the mercury has nowhere to go and settles to the bottom of a minus-60-degrees thermometer, mosquitos will not freeze away. Every summer, they eagerly reconstituted themselves. For sure, Ruby thought, if Pharaoh had first encountered mosquitos, he would have let the Israelites go. God and Moses would not have had to bring down more plagues.

Mishal seemed to be particularly plagued by the mosquitos.

> *"Mishal has very many mosquitos bits. Last night I check her room and found 4 the first time, she cried so I went back and found 3 more, cried again later and Elmer and I found 4 more after that. She is not outdoors much as they just chew on her to much, they swell on her and she scratches them till they bleed so I have long sleeved shirts on her to prevent that."*

Rev. Mel and Pat Jensen replaced Roy and Margie Gronning. Mel Jensen flew in for a preliminary look at the Arctic Missions' house and chapel. He was a tall man, a bit younger than Elmer, and built like a runner. His brown hair had long since disappeared toward the back of his head, and the top of his dome shone. His eyes smiled, and his congeniality made people feel at ease. The few days he was in Tanana, he stayed in the Gaede's basement.

After a quick assessment of the tiny mission house, Mel found a shovel and dug up the front yard. He had brought along seeds and planted a vegetable garden. Elmer and Ruby were impressed. Roy Gronning had been more relaxed about the upkeep of the physical aspects of the mission. Elmer described Mel as a "go-getter." Ruby expected the new pastor would inquire about white paint and tidy up the front yard picket fence as well.

As always, Ruby was a superb hostess and prepared full-course meals for their guest. The smell of piping-hot browned meat in a greasy skillet filled the air, and when Ruby placed a platter of crispy moose minute-steaks on the table, Elmer pointed out that it was from "Ruby's moose." Elmer looked at his wife proudly, and she, in return, smiled broadly. Mel set down his fork and knife and said in surprise, "Well, you'll have to tell me about that."

After Elmer and Ruby told the story together, each with a slightly different version, Mel asked Ruby if she would do it again. She thought for a moment. "Maybe, yes, maybe, if I didn't have to fly. Maybe, if I could drive with Elmer in a car, spot a moose, shoot it, and pack it out."

The men's conversation turned to other hunts. Ruby refilled the bowl of mashed potatoes, cut Mark's meat, and reflected on her first big game hunting experience. It really was quite an accomplishment and something not many women she knew had done. She felt good about herself. But now, with Elmer being transferred out of Alaska, would there even be another opportunity to shoot a moose? One thing was certain: she would miss eating moose meat.

After a few more exchanges with Mel, Elmer mentioned to Ruby, "Mel might be a good companion for a few more explorations."

It didn't end. Why wasn't her husband ever satisfied? His determination to squeeze in more long-distance flying trips before leaving Alaska kept her stomach churning. Ruby stopped drying her hands on her apron, looked her husband straight in the eye, and responded with emphasis, "Good!" Mel seemed practical, detailed, and steady. He would make a sound copilot. Perhaps he could prevent her husband from taking chances.

To her credit, Ruby did try to be a companion to her bush pilot husband. She gave flying her best effort. She tried to improve her attitude too. Subsequently, when Elmer flew Mel back to Nenana, Ruby accompanied them.

> "Saturday afternoon Elmer flew Rev. Jensen back to Nenana where he and his family were missionaries, until this new assignment. Mark and I went along, it was a cloudless day and beautiful but man was it bumpy and windy. It was a good thing I had dranamine for air sickness and oh I was glad to get my feet on the earth. I just do not have enough feathers to enjoy flying. We had up and down drafts of 500 ft in just a second, one up draft took us up to 5000 ft. it was 32 degrees up there. We had left Naomi, Ruth, and Mishal on their own and we got back at 5:00 and Wally had taken them to the hospital to eat as his guests."

Mark's tummy was not upset by the roller-coaster turbulence. "When I'm a big boy, I'll fly Daddy's airplane. By myself!" he declared.

Between adventures with Elmer, Ruby packed. The issue of packing was complicated enough, and much more when emotions were tangled into the process. It would have been easier if the emotions could have been boxed up and taped securely, along with dishes, toys, and towels.

> *"I am still packing, I shampooed our rug and rolled it up, I am still sorting clothes and then must write to Fairbanks cleaners and have them send me some spray or crystals which I can use for bear rugs as we want no moths in those things.*
>
> *June 21. We are past the longest day in the year and on our way to winter, it feels strange that we will not spend next winter in Alaska. The girls do not want to give up their parkas, mukluks, or mooseskin mittens. They want to wear them in Montana. I suppose as they see what the other children wear they will want to wear the same."*

The Jensens had been packing also, and two weeks after Elmer had flown Mel back to Nenana, the entire family arrived. Mrs. Jensen was delicately built, with thick, wavy brown hair surrounding her heart-shaped face. It didn't take long for Ruby to size her up, not in a judgmental way, but matter-of-factly and in an understanding way.

> *"The Jensens arrived safely, on the boat from Nenana. It was a strenuous trip for Mrs. Jensen as she is a typical woman and does not have a real need for adventure. She is a couple years younger than I. I sure do like her she is a real consecrated soul. Jensens did not have their stove as it is to come on the barge so I had them over quite a few times. Their children are Naoma 6 and Timmy 4."*

Nenana is on the road and train system, within a little over an hour's drive to Fairbanks. The Jensens had been used to procuring provisions more easily and quickly than they would in Tanana. In this small remote village, they would be dependent on air deliveries or by barge in the summer. Ruby reckoned Mel would most likely take in stride the isolation and inconveniences, more so than his wife, Pat.

"Elmer flew to Fairbanks and then to Fort Yukon. There is a new hospital nearly as large as we have here, also an old condemned hospital. The old hospital was part of missionary medical work that is being stopped now and P.H.S. will have to take over. There was an elderly Episcopal nurse still there, she helped Elmer with clinic.[87] He brought cottage cheese and bananas from town! What a treat to have something fresh! Mishal was so glad to see daddy back, she can repeat "I love you" so cute, and she said that to Elmer."

He wasn't home long. Walking briskly with his narrow necktie swinging, Elmer zipped around the hospital to check on patients and give the nurses instructions. Then, he dashed home for a quick change of clothes and jogged to the airstrip to refuel his airplane. Mel stood ready for action, and the men lifted off in front of their hand-waving wives and children. This time to fly to the windswept north coast of Alaska.

"The highlight of the week was Elmer and Rev. Jensen making a trip from here to Barrow, Point Hope, Kotzebue and returning Sat. night. The 3 day trip was reality mixed with nightmare. I will not go into detail as I want Elmer to write it up and then it will be very interesting for you to read. They had contrary weather the greater part of the trip. They certainly had Gods guidance in many decisions that had to be made in just a few seconds."

Yes, Elmer did write up the adventure story, which for decades later was interesting for everyone to read; whereas, Ruby continued with updates about preparations for leaving Tanana.

"I am not busy these days as you may think as I have plenty time to pack especially since I have another 4 weeks, but I use up a lot of energy with just concern. I feel so restless when Elmer travels. Also we must get definite dates set for my schedule as Elmer is flying the plane to Mont. I am concerned about him finding someone to fly down the Alcan highway with him. The children and I will come on our own with other transportation. I am complicating it a bit by considering taking the train from Fairbanks to Anchorage but if it is a day time trip it can be pretty. It takes so long and travels at a snails pace. A plane from Fairbanks to Anchorage is only 3 hours at the most and train is 10.

The packing of our goods is a real problem too as they do not want large crates because of weight even tho it came in large crates they had no equipment to handle it so I am concerned, if I pack in cardboard boxes that they will tear open with rough handling and also when they are on the barges from here to Fairbanks they could get rained on unless they are very carefully tarped. I fortunately have quite a few hard cardboard soap barrels, about 55 gallon size, and I will put much more than dishes in those.

We received word from a nurse that transferred from here to the Browning hospital that the doctors house in Mont. has three bedrooms. It is next to the nurses quarters and hospital. She said Browning was more isolated than Tanana. It has no airstrip, one train each day. The area is flat and treeless, the Blackfeet Indians are tough, there is a new high school and a new grade school, several churches."

Elmer continued to receive more specifics about his new job assignment, and Ruby faithfully kept his and her families informed about their plans.

"Elmer was told from Anchorage boss that we leave Tanana August 10. He must report the 16th in Browning. So now I am planning to fly with the children to Nenana instead of Fairbanks and take the train to Anchorage. Talkeetna is along the way and that is where the Scripters were reassigned and we will visit them for a few days. Then I will stay in Anchorage until I hear that Elmer has arrived in Montana. Then I will fly to Seattle and then take another train to Browning. Browning does not have an airstrip so Elmer will land at Cutbank and take the train to Browning too but he will of course arrive before I do."

Ruby wondered about a church in Browning. Would she be able to teach Sunday school to little Indian children? Would she and Elmer be invited to sing duets together? Perhaps he could play his accordion. Maybe there could be a music group they could join. She was hopeful. She wanted to trust God that Browning, Montana would be as satisfying as Tanana had been, and, perhaps without an airstrip in the small town, Elmer would keep his feet on the ground more often too.

RUBY'S BEST MOOSE ROAST

Brown roast on all sides in roasting pan with vegetable oil.

Sprinkle with salt and pepper.

Add water to pan, ¾-way up the roast.

Top roast with onion slices if available, either raw or sautéed.

Add 6 to 8 strips of uncooked bacon, if available.

Include carrots in chunks, if available.

Cover roasting pan.

Bake at 325 degrees for 3 to 4 hours, or until tender.

- Wild meat is dry. Adding bacon and water can help add fat, flavor, and moisture.
- Serve with mashed potatoes (instant or real) and gravy.
- Good with canned or frozen peas, if available.
- Leftover moose roast is tasty eaten cold with yellow mustard.

CHAPTER 35

FAREWELL TO TANANA

Tanana, 1959

"July 20, 1959. The days slip by so fast and I feel that I do not accomplish enough. Meal and bread baking sure do take up a lot of time."

Ruby stood in the kitchen. Her self-expectations as mother and wife were high. Did she really think keeping tabs on four children wasn't enough? Preventing Mark from disappearing over the riverbank to look for airplanes wasn't enough? Or that managing the uncertainty and nervousness of relocating wasn't an accomplishment in itself?

She took a deep breath, pulled back her shoulders, looked around, and tried to assess the most immediate need. There was no slack right now to wilt like a limp tea towel, draped over the back of a kitchen chair after drying dishes.

Mark wandered toward her and played with her apron ties.

"Mommy, when will we move?"

He asked this question often.

"In a few weeks. In August. Next month." His mother tried to explain but didn't know if he had a concept of days and weeks.

"I will go pack now," he said and scampered into his bedroom.

Ruby heard him toss items into a box and peeked around the door: he had collected a truck, some candy, a ball, and a miniature checkers game. He seemed cheerful enough, for which she was glad.

The wind-up kitchen timer buzzed. Without looking up from the kitchen table, where her head bent over a wide-lined paper tablet, Naomi called, "Mommy," as if the house was so large Ruby hadn't heard it herself. Ruby returned to check on cinnamon rolls in the oven.

The consummate baker had learned the doctor's house in Browning was partly furnished with some linens and some kitchenware. Yet, even in an era when many women baked yeast bread on a regular basis, she wondered if there would be baking tins and a rolling pin. On her packing list, she had crossed out, rewritten, and crossed out "rolling pin and cloth." Should she tuck them into her suitcase? Or, should she send them upriver in a packed box for the long expedition to Montana? What if they didn't arrive when she did? Unlike Tanana, Browning would have a fully stocked grocery store where she could purchase store-bought bread. She contemplated this possibility. At any rate, she felt the need to cling to her rolling pin and cloth. She could ponder this a few days longer.

Naomi fiddled with her pencil, pulled her elbows up on the table edge, and cupped her chin in her hands. "There's just so much to tell them," she sighed.

"July 27.

Dear Grandma and Grandpa,

We just packed most of our dolls.

We are going to have Ruth's birthday party tomorrow not on her birthday that is August 14 because we want to have it with her friends here. She wants pink candles. We are going on a picnic with some of our friends. Mommy and Daddy bought her a big big doll.

Mark sleeps in Ruths bed and Ruth sleeps in Mishals bedroom on the sofa.

XXXX Love Naomi"

No detail escaped the scribe's notice, and she felt it her duty to report the occurrences of her life, without embellishment or creativity—just the mundane facts.

"Mommy, be sure and put this in your next letter to Grandma and Grandpa Leppke," she said, folding the paper into three pleats. "May I invite Sally to make cookies now?"

The kitchen was already hot from making bread, and a clutter of baking bowls and tins were stacked beside the sink. Before Ruby could answer, Ruth wandered into the kitchen. "Can I help too?" She clutched her longhaired, white stuffed cat tightly. The last weeks, Puff was never far from the young girl's hands, and even at mealtimes, Puff snuggled beneath the table, on Ruth's lap. Ruby mused over the comparison. Whereas Ruth grasped the security of a stuffed animal, Ruby was reluctant to let go of the familiarity of her rolling pin.

Ruby nodded approval to Naomi's request. Why not, Ruby reckoned. Naomi would probably never see Sally, her best friend, again, and Elmer was doing his "what if I'm never in Alaska again" checklist, as well. The mother waved the girls out the door, and they skipped up Front Street to the other end of the village, occasionally jumping over mud puddles.

While the girls were gone and Mark continued his packing, Ruby tidied the kitchen and even sat down to type some lines to her parents: "*Elmer still does not have a companion. – and we have barely 3 more weeks until we leave. Our goods will go by barge to Fairbanks and the railroad to Seward then by boat to Seattle then on a truck van to Browning.*"

Her stomach knotted, thinking of her husband flying over the Alaska-Canada Highway, through Canada, to Browning, Montana. This was unknown territory for him as a pilot. Her head reminded her that he had flown for three years in the Last Frontier, and every time he had returned home safely. Her heart replayed the emotions of the death-defying details.

Should she worry? One thing she could do was pray and beg God for her husband's safety. Indeed, that was all she could do, for there would be no communication between the couple along the way. Not knowing, while traveling with four children, was a kind of blessing, for when she would write her 1959 Christmas letter, she would report to friends and family that "*… he had a safe trip with a real test near the Canadian, Montana border because of severe rain storms, they saw the cars beneath them stopped on the highway and needed to set down the plane for safety, but there was no place for them to land on the highway.*"

On August 1, 1959, Elmer scribbled in longhand, "*We've crated our goods of 4,600 lbs and we're waiting for the next barge to Fairbanks.*"

Heavily loaded freight-barge, riding just above the water-line.

On August 7, he wrote again, "Our house is stripped except for a few furnishings. We're practically living from tin-cans now. We have quite a few picnics. Today three of us families went blueberry picking. We only got a couple gallons. Last night, I took Rev. Jensen fishing for pike. Mt. McKinley was perfectly clear, shining in the evening sun.

> I'm getting the plane in good condition for the long run. I've worked out the flight plans nearly to completion so it'll be an enjoyable trip without much sweat.
>
> The Lord has answered our prayers for a plane passenger for me. He is a young married man we knew in Anchorage. I'll meet him in Nenana, the same time I see Ruby and family off on the train.
>
> The weather is finally clearing and now we have normal summer weather with daytime hi of 64 and nite low of about 40."

August 10, 1959. The day came to say farewell to Tanana. In June 1958, Elmer had written, "*We certainly enjoy life out here and we think this is quite a paradise.*" When Ruby had arrived in Tanana, she had wondered if she could be a good enough wife and mother in the small village. She had proven that to be more than true. The entire family had thrived. If anyone had his or her choice, they would have remained in that small Athabascan village along the mighty Yukon River, in the middle of Alaska.

That morning, the clear blue skies and calm air bolstered her spirits. Both the commercial plane she and the children would be flying in and Elmer's smaller plane would at least have a smooth first leg of their journey.

Ruby dressed carefully in a pale-lavender, below-the-knee summer coat over a dress. A coordinating scarf covered her head with only her dark, short bangs emerging above her glasses. Short-heeled, black leather sandals completed her outfit. Of course, she was wearing stocking hose.

Naomi, age nine, wrapped both arms around her lambskin teddy bear. Ruby had designed the bear for her first-born when her second-born had arrived to share the spotlight. The bear had a red knit tongue, black button eyes, and was filled with thin straw. Naomi appeared ready to sail in her white-trimmed nautical-blue dress with a broad collar.

Ruth's dark brown curls cascaded to her shoulders, and she modeled a lacy headband, as did Naomi. A navy summer coat covered the eight-year-old's full-skirted orange dress. She held a white box purse over one arm and gripped her Ruthie doll in the other. Just like Naomi, she wore black patent shoes with white anklets. Squinting into the sun, she rocked side to side nervously, her legs appearing more bowed than usual.

Mark and Mishal were the epitome of high-class adorability. Mark, age three-and-a-half, sported a gray suit, complete with a short-brimmed gray cap. His arms encircled a brown teddy bear, wrapped in a blanket. At eighteen-months, Mishal's black ringlets poked out of her lace-brimmed bonnet, which matched her pink coat. She bounced in Elmer's arms and chewed on her fingers. Bits of drool dripped on his green wool jacket. He didn't mind. He was happily holding *his* baby.

If a picture had been taken of the family, without showing the sandy gravel airstrip behind them and their dusty shoes, one would have thought this family was going to church or some cultural event. Ruby wouldn't have thought of leaving home or traveling in any other fashion, even if she would be pulling aside her skirt and balancing her semi-high heels to climb into a small airplane with four children.

Elmer was the odd person out in the scene. He did not wear a suit. A red cap contained most of his black, shiny curls, and his green wool jacket emitted a faint odor of picnic campfire smoke and bug dope, the latter used to ward off harassing mosquitos. He would not be visiting friends, flying commercially, or traveling on a train. He would be piloting his single-engine airplane, relying on months of bush pilot flying, and trusting God to take him over uncharted country, to reunite with his family on the other side of Canada. Apprehensive? He never let on.

Whenever Elmer flew his plane, it was his custom to pray before taking off. That final day, he gathered his family around him on the airstrip, and they bowed their heads, except for Mishal, who looked around, squinted her eyes, and giggled. "Our dear heavenly Father," he began, ending soon with, "… in Jesus' name, amen." Whispered "Amens" completed the goodbye ceremony.

For a moment, no one said a word, and the little family stood nestled together. Ruby raised her head and studied her husband's face. He was still as handsome as when she had first set eyes on him on the church youth group bus in Kansas. Still, her sweetheart. She blinked back tears.

"God be with you 'til we meet again," she said with a choked voice.

Her husband kissed her cheek.

"When will see we see you, Daddy?" asked Naomi anxiously, touching his jacket hem.

He cleared his throat. "In a short while." He handed Mishal to Ruby and bent down to hug his other three children.

"The pilot is ready. Let's get you loaded now," he urged gently.

From inside the chartered plane, Mark watched his daddy break into a run toward the red Family Cruiser with its single beige stripe and beige leading edges on the wings. Suddenly, the boy threw himself toward the window and shouted, "I want to go with daddy!" Ruth tried to soothe him. "We will see him in Nenana," she said. "He will meet us when we get on the train there." He had no concept of where or when that would be.

The plane's propellers rotated, and the engine shook to a start. Mark stretched his neck to keep his eyes on his father. Naomi and Ruth pressed their faces to the windows and watched the hospital compound, schoolyard, and log cabins with spirals of woodstove smoke disappear below them.

Farewell to Tanana.

The Gaede family at the Nenana train station, 1959.

Naomi at the Nenana train station, 2011.

CHAPTER 36

STARTING ANEW

Browning, Montana, 1959

RUBY'S CHRISTMAS LETTER that year was laid out chronologically. For August, she wrote:

> "The children and I flew to Nenana commercially, then took the R.R. to Anchorage laying over at Talkeetna for 3 days with the Scripters who had just moved there, Anchorage 5 days, Seattle 6 hours, thus visiting many dear friends whom we may never see again until that Great Meeting in the Air, when our Lord comes again."

As the train crossed the prairie and neared the small town of Browning, she noted the flat and treeless landscape. Windswept. No wide river or spindly spruce trees like she had experienced in Tanana. Barren. A picture painted in shades of browns.

Her foremothers, too, had relocated and arrived in Kansas by train. They had left the fertile farming fields in Southern Russia, crossed the ocean in the late 1880s, and found themselves at the end of the railroad line in the middle of Kansas with the promise of farmland. They found windswept hard sod.

She came from a long line of women who did what they had to do, without complaining, who knew their roles as wives and mothers. Who were durable. She, like her foremothers, sucked in her breath, whispered a prayer, and responded with perseverance.

At the same time, she was not superwoman or inhumanly stoic. She admitted honestly, *"We arrived in Browning tired and ready to collapse."*

How had she managed four active children, who had slept in different beds for eight nights, were off schedule, confined in airplanes and railroad trains, and had no idea where they would find home again? How many times had she listened to, "Are we there, yet?" and "When will we see Daddy?"

The train lurched to a stop at the Browning station, and she pulled her children together, waiting for the doors to open.

God had given her strength and also a surprise.

"Oh, oh!" she blurted out. "Daddy, Mom, Elmer!"

"We were greeted by 3 precious faces, Elmer and my mother and dad. What a surprise! Mother and dad had driven from Kansas and arrived the same day but a few hours earlier. Folks stayed nearly 3 weeks."

Ruby's tired shoulders, which had carried the responsibility of the children, complications of train and plane tickets, and connections could finally relax.

Mishal squealed in delight and waved her arms excitedly. Mark called, "Daddy! Daddy!" Naomi ran to her grandmother, got lost in her billowing skirt, and hugged her ample waist. Ruth stayed beside her mother.

STARTING ANEW

The reunited family crowded into the Leppke's two-tone, fin-tailed Dodge and drove up the hill to the doctor's house. The house had a sturdy stone exterior, and just the appearance offered a welcome of stability and security.

In her first letter to Elmer's parents, Ruby offered a brief written map of the new surroundings:

> *"Our present home is adjacent to the hospital, our section of the town is called the Agency, located on the north end of town and the schools are on the south edge of town and the girls have a ¾ mile hike to get to school.*

Naturally, the first room in the house Ruby explored was the kitchen. She opened drawers and stood on tiptoes to reach the tall cupboards. Were there mixing bowls? Baking tins? She needed to give the place a housewarming. She needed to turn a house into a home. It was time to get out the rolling pin.

The bush doctor's wife's last letter from Tanana concluded with, *"Please return this letter as I did not have time for an extra for my diary – future story book. Thanks."*

She did tell her story, not one she considered an adventure, but one of everyday life as a wife and mother in the Last Frontier. Simply stated. Bravely lived. Kindly remembered by those whose lives she had touched.

EPILOGUE

NAOMI IS THE FAMILY HISTORIAN. She relentlessly seeks to categorize, sort, organize, document, research, and display her family's heritage. At the same time, she values the relationships she and her parents had during their lifetime and carefully gives a voice to those teachers, missionaries, healthcare workers, and friends, many of whom did not have the ability or resources to stake claim to their contributions on paper or other media. And, although most were humble people and many were simply serving their God, it has been Naomi's pleasure to, pay them notice, even in a small way, and offer a glimpse of their lives to the reader.

Although Naomi's primary residence is in Colorado, she frequently visits the Gaede-80 homestead outside Soldotna, Alaska, where she stays in the family cabin, which she rebuilt after it burned in 2005. The Gaede siblings gather around her kitchen table and appreciatively savor rhubarb-cherry pies, round yeast bread, cinnamon rolls, and traditional Mennonite dishes.

It means a great deal to Naomi that, as an adult, she has been able to re-connect with two of her Tanana classmates: Sally Woods (Kookesh) and Chris Sommer.

Home for Ruth and Mark is the Gaede-80 homestead. They are seasoned homesteaders who find satisfaction being outdoors and in the woods, chopping firewood, cleaning up brush, picking berries, and doing what it takes to establish a home in the wilderness. They never tire of seeing a moose stroll, or frolic outside their windows, or on the Gaede-80 grass airstrip, even if they frown and mumble when that same moose strips off leaves and branches of a tree or bush they just planted.

Ruth carries gardening DNA from her mother. She continually putters with vegetable gardening, fragrant rose bushes, and indoor plants. Like her mother, she keeps the woodstove fire burning and enjoys a cozy home.

Music is in Ruth's genes too. Playing and arranging Christian music on the piano nourishes her soul and brings her satisfaction and comfort. As a young adult, she and Mark sat across the church stage from each other, on organ and piano benches, and accompanied the congregational singing.

Ruth married Roger Rupp, who is an airframe and powerplant aircraft mechanic. Elmer Gaede often relied on his son-in-law to repair his airplanes.

Mark can't remember when he wasn't in an airplane. He flew his father's planes before he was legal (age sixteen) to get a pilot's license. Just like his father, he is a bush pilot and currently flies a Piper J-3 Super Cub. He, too, is a hunter and shot his first moose and mountain goat at age nine. Following in his father's footsteps, Mark rebuilt the family house on the Gaede-80 homestead in 2018; in 2019, the chicken coop; and in 2020, the original hangar. He plans to plant a garden—just like his mother.

Mark married Patti Kvalvik, whose brother married Harold and Vera Johnson's daughter, Barbara (chapter 20.) In his adult years, Mark crossed paths with Chris Gronning.

Even with his fascination for fire, Mark did not become a firefighter. As Anna quipped, "Perhaps, he's destined to be a musician." This comment, made in jest, did come true.

EPILOGUE

Over time, Mark experimented with every possible instrument he could get his hands on. Though his experience with other instruments expanded his knowledge of sounds and techniques, in the end, it was the piano and keyboards that were his natural bent. He composed and arranged music, mostly by ear, which was a tremendous frustration to his piano teacher. At age twelve, he became the church organist. At this time, he continues to play on the church worship team, as well as write and record music. Although some of his compositions are originals, much of his focus is on old church hymns and turning these into more modern interpretations. His newest venture is creating videos using photos he has collected and adding soundtracks using his own musical arrangements. These can be found on YouTube and often on Naomi's Facebook page at Prescription for Adventure.

In January 1980, Mishal discovered that her birth mother, Dora Tooyak, was living in Denver, Colorado. Amazingly, at that same time, Mishal was also in Denver, living with Naomi. On October 19, 1980, at the age of twenty-two, Mishal met her birth mother. Ever since that time, Mishal has stayed in touch with her biological siblings and gracefully and gratefully integrated her two families.

Mishal attended the Colorado Institute of Art. Her artistic bent showed itself at age three when she copied graphics from a Cheerios box. She is adept with beadwork, various mediums of design and artwork, and sewing moose skin.

Mishal now lives in Fairbanks, Alaska, and is a Tribal Court facilitator for Tanana Chiefs Conference in Tribal Government Services. She often climbs into a bush plane to travel into Interior Alaska for work-related meetings. Being an advocate for Native people brings her abundant satisfaction.

The Gaede children deeply cherish their parents' history and homestead and their family's Alaska heritage.

the BUSH DOCTOR'S WIFE

To follow Ruby's life in Browning, Montana, and her continued relocations, read:
From Kansas Wheat Fields to Alaska Tundra: a Mennonite Family Finds Home.

To read about Elmer's adventures, fasten your seatbelt and read:
Alaska Bush Pilot Doctor.

Anna Bortel's passion for the Alaskan people's education and welfare fill two books:
'A' is for Alaska: Teacher to the Territory.
'A' is for Anaktuvuk: Teacher to the Nunamiut Eskimos.

All these people had a prescription for adventure, whether chosen or unchosen. What is *your* prescription for adventure?

You can find Naomi at
Facebook: Prescription for Adventure
www.prescripitionforadventure.com
blog.prescriptionforadventure.com

To order books
www.prescriptionforadventure.com
For speaking engagements
npenn@prescriptionforadventure.com
303-506-6181

RESOURCES AND FURTHER READING

Alaska Almanac. Portland, OR: Alaska Northwest Books, 2013.

A Century of Faith: Centennial Commemorative, Episcopal Dioceses of Alaska 1895 – 1995. Fairbanks, AK: Centennial Press, 1995.

Eagan, Timothy. *The Worst Hard Times*. Boston, MA: Houghton Mifflin, 2005.

Epp, Reuben. *The Story of Low German & Plautdietsch*. Hillsboro, KS: The Reader's Press, 1993.

Fejes Claire. *Villages: Athabaskan Indian Life Along the Yukon River*. New York: Random House, 1981.

Gaede-Penner, Naomi. *Honoring our Sacred Healing Place: Tanana, Alaska (Development, History, Community, & Cultural Significance of the*

Tanana Hospital Complex. Anchorage, AK: Alaska Area Native Health Service, 2008.

'A' is for Alaska: Teacher to the Territory. Mustang, OK: Tate Publishing, 2011.

'A' is for Anaktuvuk: Teacher to the Nunamiut Eskimos. Mustang, OK: Tate Publishing, 2016.

Alaska Bush Pilot Doctor. Mustang, OK: Tate Publishing, 2015.

From Kansas Wheat Fields to Alaska Tundra: a Mennonite Family Finds Home. Mustang, OK: Tate Publishing, 2015.

Goertzen, Peggy. *Miracle of Grace at Ebenfeld*. Hillsboro, KS: Ebenfeld Mennonite Brethren Church, 2001.

Huntington, Sidney, and Jim Rearden. *Shadow on the Yukon*. Portland, OR: Alaska Northwest Books, 1993.

Loewen, Royden, and Steven M. Nolt. *A Mennonite History Series: North America: Seeking Places of Peace*. Intercourse: Good Books, and Kitchner, ON Canada: Pandora Press, 2012.

Madison, Curt, and Yvonne Yarber, ed. *Josephine Roberts: Tanana*. Fairbanks, AK: Spirit Mountain Press, 1983.

Person, M.D., Jean. *From Dog Sleds to Float Planes: Alaskan Adventures in Medicine*. Eagle River, AK: Northbooks, 2007.

RESOURCES AND FURTHER READING

Stuck, Hudson. *Ten Thousand Miles with a Dog Sled.* Lincoln, NE and London: University of Nebraska Press, 1988.

Voth, Norma Jost. "*Mennonite Foods and Folkways from South Russia, vol I.*" Intercourse, PA: Good Books, 1980.

"*Mennonite Foods and Folkways from South Russia, vol 2.*" Intercourse, PA: Good Books, 1991.

On-line Writing Resources

Military deferment and service: https://www.law.cornell.edu/uscode/text/50/3806

http://freepages.rootsweb.com/~coleen/genealogy/alaskaorphanage.html

https://books.google.com/books?id=NLnCCQAAQBAJ&pg=PT265&lpg=PT265&dq=Russ+and+Freda+Arnold-+Alaska&source=bl&ots=fwMASwXwsL&sig=ACfU3U-2VGE-g1UIegXzZLzuC9MHAghKtSQ&hl=en&sa=X&ved=2a-hUKEwiB-O_1QKHR92DsYQ6AEwB3oECAQQA-Q#v=onepage&q=Russ%20and%20Freda%20Arnold%20Alaska&f=false

https://interactministries.org/get-to-know-us/history/ Interview with Russ Arnold, 2015: **https://vimeo.com/132160166.** 108 Campbell Dr. Ct., Palmer, AK 99645

RECORDS OF ALASKA NATIVES IN RELIGIOUS ARCHIVES.
Prepared By Larry Hibpshman, Archivist Alaska State Archives. April 30, 2014

The Mukluk Telegraph*, U.S. Public Health Service, Alaska Native Health Services, Area Office, Box 7 – 741, Anchorage, Alaska. Issues:
- July 1958
- August 1958
- September 1958
- November 1958
- February 1959
- April 1959
- May 1959

RESOURCES AND FURTHER READING

*Northern Lights**, Tanana, Alaska, Day School newspaper
   Charles Wheeler, editor:
   October 1957

   John Hawkins, editor:
   October 1958
   November 1958
   December 1958
   January 1959
   February 1959
   March 1959
   May 1959

Tanana Council News, January 17, 1959

* These publications can be found at www.prescriptionforadventure.com under Resources.

ACKNOWLEDGMENTS

WRITING THIS BOOK was like participating in Alaska's Great Race, the Iditarod. I couldn't have done it without people cheering me on at each checkpoint.

Thank you to the My Word Publishing Team. Polly Letofsky, you believed I had good stories and good stuff, and managed the details to get this book published. Delta Donohue, I couldn't have asked for a better editor. You were a stickler on punctuation, questioned every fact, and made the rough spots smooth. Victoria, I handed you over 500 pages with photos and footnotes, and you persevered in putting the parts together in an aesthetically pleasing and readable fashion.

Thank you, Sally Dolan and Diane Estlund, for getting me out the door by reading the first chapters; and Kathy Page for reading a section of the manuscript for "the feel of Ruby."

Freda Arnold, missionary who my parents visited along the Yukon River, added depth and detail to the few comments my mother had written and the one photo my father had taken. Our email exchange was like a window into my parents' missionary journeys." Thank you.

My heart was warmed through and through by conversations around the dinner table with my mother's brother, Wilbur Leppke, and nephew, Dean

Fast. They immersed me in specifics of my mother's childhood life in the early 1930s, answered questions about the farm and farmhouse, described what she carried in her lunch pail to school, explained traditions, and more.

Madelyn Fox, missionary in Interior Alaska, confirmed my childhood perceptions of village life in Tanana. I was constantly reminded of how much Alaska has not changed over sixty years. I appreciated you immensely.

Melissa Fogle, your willingness to read through the manuscript was a compliment and encouragement. You are a passionate reader of books on world culture, exploration, and resilient people. From all indications, Ruby's story passed the test of your "must-read books." Thank you.

Wayne Leman, I was honored to have you appraise my manuscript. Your skills as a linguistic, heritage of a Russian-Alutiiq family in Ninilchik, Alaska, love and respect for Native people, and fervor for recording family history were the perfect blend for evaluating and critiquing Ruby's Alaska stories. My gratitude runs deep.

My dear daughter, Nicole Penner Clark. This is the fifth Alaska book you've seen me through. You did not waver in your commitment to read every jot and title, countless long chapters, and redundant rewrites. Your suggestions for rearrangements of paragraphs and for dividing chapters added clarity to the stories. You kindly drew my attention to sections and phrases that were repeated or tangled due to cut-and-paste procedures. I could never have completed this book without your reinforcement of, "Mom. It really is a good story." I cherish you—and your input.

My siblings, Ruth, Mark, and Mishal added their memories and approved the descriptions and dialogues I created about them. These are their stories, too. We all had our perspectives, and the truth is broad.

READER'S GUIDE

1. Starting in 1930 and continuing until 1965, Dick, Jane, and Sally were the main characters in the classroom readers in the United States and other English-speaking countries. What demographic did these characters represent? How might indigenous children in Alaska have had difficulty identifying with them and finding meaning in the activities and settings portrayed? What are several changes you might suggest for a more suitable reading primer?

2. What strengths do you have from your upbringing that would have helped you adapt to life in Tanana?

3. Which amenities and conveniences would you have missed most if you had lived in Tanana? Explain.

4. If you had to order food for the year, what would you be sure you had enough of?

5. What are some of your family's food traditions?

6. Would the cold, dark winter have been difficult for you? Explain. What would you have done to keep your spirits up? Would you have been compelled, like Ruby and Anna, to venture outdoors, regardless of the season and weather?

7. Ruby loved a picnic and campfire. What are you passionate about doing outdoors?

8. Elmer and Ruby wore wool slacks and Army Surplus parkas for outdoor wear. How has below-zero clothing changed and improved since the 1950s? What difference has that made?

9. Mishal always wondered about her birth mother. Finding Dora, as well as her half-siblings, was immensely gratifying to her. Why do you think some adopted children are relentless about finding their birth parents, and others are not?

10. Ruby, with her lack of high school degree, felt inferior to her physician husband. What might you have told her?

11. How did Ruby's faith affect her choices, attitudes, and roles?

12. What was the main theme of the book?

13. What did you think of the writing style and composition of the book?

14. How did the book make you feel? What emotions did it evoke?

READER'S GUIDE

15. If it were possible, what questions would you ask Ruby about her life growing up in Kansas or her life in Alaska?

16. Were the characters clearly portrayed? How does Ruby's character develop from the first of the book to the end?

17. What chapter or scene did you resonate with the most? Why?

18. Would you recommend this book to a friend? If so, how would you summarize it?

19. Have you read any other books by this author? How would you compare them to this book?

20. How did you feel about the last chapter of the book? How might you have changed it?

21. How do you think the individual Gaede family members will transition to life in Browning, Montana?

22. If you could talk to the author, what questions would you ask her?

NOTES

1. Bush refers to the remote areas of Alaska, which are inaccessible by highways or railroads.
2. World War II pulled people from the farms, which were vital for food production. Young men were drafted. Women went to work in factories. Defense plants recruited workers and paid high salaries. This exodus from the farm left the United States in a critical food shortage. As a result, Congress enacted a draft deferment for farmers and farmworkers, along with specific requirements of livestock the farmer needed to have on his farm.
3. Government cheese was a commodity controlled by the government from World War II to the early 1980s. It was created to maintain the price of dairy when there was an artificial surplus of milk, which was then converted into cheese, butter, or powdered milk These hard, brick cheeses, and other food products, were used for welfare beneficiaries, the elderly receiving Social Security, and in schools.
4. In the 1950s, the term Hi-Fi High Fidelity came to replace the use of phonograph and record player.
5. Alaska achieved statehood on January 3, 1959.
6. On March 30, 1867, US Secretary of State, William H. Seward, agreed to purchase Alaska from Russia for $7 million. (The approximately 375 million acres is about one-fifth the size of the contiguous US.) The purchase was ridiculed by Congress and the press as "Seward's Folly" and "Seward's Icebox."
7. Cold War refers to the ongoing political tension between the United States and the Soviet Union, following WWII, approximately mid-1940s to 1990s.
8. The CAA—Civil Aeronautics Administration—was reorganized in 1958 and became the Federal Aviation Agency (FAA). In 1966, it became the Federal Aviation Administration.

9   1955 McDonald's menu: Hamburger – fifteen cents, fries – ten cents, coke (soft drink) – ten to fifteen cents.

10 White Alice was a nickname given to a telecommunications network built during the Cold War by the Bell System in the 1950s, along the western Alaska coastline and inland to consolidate and improve radio communication. "White" came from the aspect notion of the frozen North; "Alice" was an acronym for **A**laska **I**ntegrated **C**ommunications and **E**lectronics. Later a Distant Early Warning (DEW) radar system was added to detect incoming Soviet bombers.

11 To learn about the Gaede's life in Anchorage, read *From Kansas Wheat Fields to Alaska Tundra: a Mennonite Family Finds Home,* by Naomi Gaede Penner.

12 Prior to Anna's arrival, the Tanana Day School had operated under the dual system of both the BIA and the Territory. The BIA provided a teacher for the Native population, and the Territory provided a teacher for the non-Native students. The year Anna arrived, the school was staffed and maintained entirely by the BIA. Then, the following year, it became a Territorial School exclusively. Regardless of the entity in charge, the Native and non-Native children were taught together and not segregated.

13 *'A' is for Alaska: Teacher to the Territory* tells Anna Bortel's story of teaching in Valdez and Tanana, Alaska.

14 When there *were* schools in the villages, classes were taught first to eighth grade. Students were sent to Wrangell, in southeastern Alaska, for high school, where the climate and culture there were much different from Interior village life.

15 See Character Guide in the front of the book for character identification.

16 In July of 1876, seventy-five Mennonite Brethren (MB) families emigrated from South Russia to southeast of Hillsboro, Kansas. They called the area *Ebenfeld* which means "even field or flat ground." This name was used to denote a church, a community, and a school district. As early as 1890, the local German newspapers printed reports from Ebenfeld, giving it recognition as a valid settlement, even though it did not have a post office. Much of Ebenfeld's early history has been gleaned from Abraham B. Gaede's diary and church notes.

17 A cornet is similar to a trumpet but is shaped slightly differently, smaller, and has a warmer sound.

18 Low German and Low English have Saxon roots in the fifth century. Low English developed in Great Britain, with the European people who migrated there. Low German was the language of the remaining northern European people, including the Dutch and German people, as well as those in the Nordic countries around the North Sea. As a result of their common history, both languages have similar words and are linguistically connected, although there are many Low German dialects. Both languages were used before what we know today as English and German.

19 Sizeable populations of migrating Mennonites from the Netherlands carried their

NOTES

      mother tongue of Low German with them. When they fled religious persecution and migrated to Prussia (today's Poland) in the 1540s, the language helped them preserve a feeling of community and a sense of solidarity in their foreign surroundings. In Prussia/Poland, the people spoke a different dialect of Low German.

20 During this same time, Martin Luther translated the Bible from Hebrew and Greek into High German (1534). Johannes Guttenberg, who had invented the printing press in 1450, printed it in High German. As a result, the Mennonites and other religious groups that based their faith on the Bible learned High German (the standardized German of today), which was then used in the churches.

21 When the Mennonites, and other groups, accepted Catherine the Great's invitation to farm in Russia (the area that became Ukraine), the Mennonites were allowed to live in their own villages, conduct their own schools and businesses, and have their own churches. In all these affairs, they were allowed to continue the use of High German, rather than Russian or Ukrainian; at the same time, Low German was spoken at home. This perpetuated the use of both languages to the next generation.

22 The dialect specific to the Mennonites originating in the Netherlands became known as Plautdietsch, or "Flat German."

23 Litke means little song in German. The family name, correctly translated from German, was "Liedtke." However, in America, it was also spelled "Lietke," "Lidtke," "Liedkey," and "Litke." It is believed that bankers, and other local businesses with which the family conducted business, failed to translate the spelling properly from the German script. The immigrants were at their mercy for officially recording their names.

24 Isaac's father, Heinrich Leppke, had been poverty-stricken as well. As a young child, he worked hard on the farm and had little opportunity for schooling. He was illiterate. His signature on land transactions and loans recorded in the Marion County courthouse, Marion, Kansas, are indicated by an X, marked under the spellings of "Loeppke," "Leppky," and "Lepky." The original German script was "Löppke. Heinrich's certificate of church membership was spelled "Leppke," as is on his tombstone, and used by his descendants. Heinrich's son, Isaac, was determined to read. He went one week to an English school and learned enough to read the newspaper. Working for English-speaking neighbors increased his ability.

25 A soddy or sod house was common for settlers on the Great Plains. Wood was often scarce, and the thickly rooted grass was available and free. The sod was cut into rectangular chunks and stacked together. This living situation was not ideal, as it was vulnerable to rain, snakes, and tumbling down; however, for people trying desperately to eke out a living, it was often the only choice for shelter.

26 In 1988, the Arctic Missions' name was changed to InterAct Ministries.
27 To learn when and how Elmer Gaede became a pilot, read *Alaska Bush Pilot Doctor*.
28 To learn more about Rev. Inge Coleman, read *A Century of Faith: Centennial Commemorative, 1895–1995, Episcopal Diocese of Alaska*.
29 To make a barrel stove, Rural Alaskans take a fifty-five-gallon fuel drum, turn it on its side, set it on metal legs, cut a hole for a door in one end, and insert a stovepipe in the other. A flat piece of metal is attached to the top, which turns the heating source into a cooking source.
30 Old-time farm equipment had pour-in-place Babbitt bearings. The bearing material was heated to a molten state in a blacksmith forge or another source of high heat, then poured into a block mold, which was specific to the size and shape required for the piece of equipment.
31 Camp Innowok was a makeshift camp in the wilderness for Native kids. Ruby prepared meals for over fifty-five people in an improvised Visqueen cooking tent—and loved it, despite the hordes of mosquitos, and that on the first day, it rained twenty-four hours straight. At Solid Rock Bible Camp, outside Soldotna, she cooked indoors or up to sixty campers.
32 "Outside" is the term used by Alaskans for anywhere outside of Alaska, most often referring to the Lower 48 States.
33 In remote areas of Alaska, the government provided housing for the schoolteachers either within the school building or nearby.
34 Some documents state the population in the Tanana/Fort Gibbon area reached three thousand. In 2020, the population was around 245.
35 It was also the major source of employment until 1982, when it closed. (For more Tanana hospital history, see *Honoring our Sacred Healing Place: Tanana, Alaska, -- Development, History, Community, & Cultural Significance of the Tanana Hospital Complex*, edited by Naomi Gaede Penner, published by the Alaska Area Native Health Service, IHS, DHHS.
36 A potlatch is a Native gathering, typically in Athabascan and Tlingit cultures, that commemorates major life events, honors deceased village members, or is used to celebrate in general. Usually, this is done through song, dancing, storytelling, feasting, and gifting.
37 To read about Dr. Jean Persons, see *From Dog Sleds to Float Planes*.
38 Although Ruby and Elmer's fathers had grown up together, and their parents knew each other, Ruby had grown up in the Peabody area, whereas Elmer's family had settled in Hillsboro. The towns were not that far apart. However, the families did not attend the same church (social life) or schools, and "going to town," meant a different town.
39 The towns of Peabody and Hillsboro are approximately twenty-three miles apart.
40 Grandma Florentine Leppke died at age eighty-three. Grandpa Isaac Leppke died

NOTES

ten days later, at ninety-one. The doctor said he died of a broken heart.

41   Many Mennonites considered the game of pool to be sinful, very likely because it was played in a pool hall where drinking alcohol and smoking took place. Instead, they played the acceptable, in-home board game of Carrom, which is played with cue sticks or flicks of one's finger on a three-foot-square Carrom board with net pockets in the four corners of the board.

42   His letter does not clarify who this is. Apparently, his parents would have known by the woman's name. Perhaps it was the dairy farmer's wife who had collected his mail for the few days he was with his parents.

43   IIC status provided military deferment because of essential agricultural employment.

44   After living on rented farms for twenty-four years, they bought their first farm in 1943, two miles east of Hillsboro.

45   Decades later, missionaries, schoolteachers, and villagers in remote areas would order food from Amazon—with free shipping over a specific dollar amount and quicker delivery.

46   In 1937, Hormel developed the first canned meat product that did not require refrigeration. Spam, made from chopped pork shoulder, was a perfect meat source for the military and became a household "miracle meat" during World War II when beef was rationed. Its most popular uses were with eggs or in sandwiches. Ruby's favorite recipe was to cut thin slabs, dip them in egg batter, roll the pieces in crushed soda crackers, and fry. When daily fare most often consisted of moose, Spam was received as a welcome treat. In 2008, Spam's popularity would resurge.

47   Elmer purchased an airplane and took flying lessons the second year they lived in Anchorage, in the spring of 1956.

48   There would come a time when catalog ordering would be viewed as primitive, restrictive, and unfortunate. But, as is said, "nothing is new," and the popularity of buying from a catalog would gain popularity in the digital age of websites and ordering online. One thing would not change, the guesswork of sizes and the perception of actual colors.

49   The Natives called boats with outboard motors, "kicker boats."

50   The first recipe for s'mores was published in the Girl Scout Handbook (1927).

51   New International Version Bible (NIV), Proverbs 31:13–27.

52   When a family moves away from relatives and friends to a country with different cultural mores and an unfamiliar language, the members of such a household feel the bonds of allegiance to one another more than might be otherwise customary. This was the experience of Ruby's great-grandparents. They were the only Mennonite family on the S.S. Bolivia when they left South Russia in the summer of 1975. Their family of twelve arrived in Peabody, Kansas, on July 9 of that year. When the children grew up, they all settled within six miles of their "home place," and spending time with one another was their social life.

53 The barges, operated by Yutana Barge Lines, wintered in Nenana.
54 Breakup is the time of year when melting snow raises the level of the ice on Interior Alaska rivers, causing them to break apart and the ice to float downstream. This signals the return of river navigation. Barges run on the Yukon River between the first of June and the end of August.
55 When Elmer first arrived in Tanana, his welcome had been a knock on the door with a voice informing him, "Lee shot Floyd." To read about the murder, see *Prescription for Adventure: Bush Pilot Doctor*, chapter: "A Strange Village Welcome."
56 The commercial airplanes, and usually the charters, flew with wheel or wheel-ski combination landing gear. Elmer, and other bush pilots, typically put their planes on skis, which provided greater versatility for landing in general, emergency landing options, and for hunting. The airstrip in Tanana was kept clear for wheels. Sometimes Elmer landed on this strip, but more often, he tied down on the river, where the hospital maintenance man cleared an area with a CAT. (Alaskans refer to all bulldozers as "CATs" since Caterpillar was the brand of most heavy equipment in the early years.)
57 Changing from floats to wheels typically requires a hoist and is much more complicated than changing from wheels to skis, which really is like "changing a tire." All the same, the above comes directly from Ruby's letter.
58 Sputnik 1, launched by the Soviet Union on October 4, 1957, was the first human-made object to orbit the earth. Sputnik 1 weighed 183 pounds and orbited in 96.2 minutes. This achievement sent shockwaves through the American public, who had felt a sense of technological superiority; furthermore, they feared the Soviets could launch ballistic missiles armed with nuclear weapons at the United States. This sparked the space race between the Soviet Union and the United States.
59 *Unshackled* is the longest-running radio drama in history. It is broadcast around the world and translated into a number of languages.
60 The Lone Ranger debuted in 1933 and purportedly left the air in 1956. However, on into the early 1960s, the Gaedes discovered it on stations transmitting to Alaska.
61 Diamond Willow is not a particular kind of willow tree but is a description of a diamond-shaped canker knot formed in fungus-infected willow trees. Wood carvers and furniture makers prize the wood and whittle off the bark to expose the dark knots against the golden wood.
62 This is from the song "God Leads Us Along," by George A. Young.
63 Three years later, she would take ground school lessons; however, she would never solo and get her private pilot's license.

64 In contrast to 1958, in 2020, approximately 44 percent of the Tanana residents had achieved a high school degree, and 23 percent had attended college. Several had bachelor's and master's degrees.
65 The original name for margarine was oleomargarine, which was used as a less expensive substitute for butter. Whereas butter was made from churned milk, oleomargarine was made from animal fats. During the Depression and WWII, when there was a shortage of meat fats, the recipe was changed to use vegetable oils. It became known as oleo.
66 Exclamation of sympathy.
67 Grandma Elia was generous to the Gaedes. Ruby wrote, "I got the most beautiful fur mits from Mrs. Elia (lady that did my fur parka.) She used the legs of the fox fur and few scraps of my fur coat and moose skin for the palms. I just love them and will cherish them."
68 A "sourdough" is a person who has lived in Alaska for a very long time, as compared to a cheechako (chee-CHA-ko who is a newcomer or tenderfoot.
69 To hear Russ Arnold talk about his and Freda's ministry and life in Alaska, listen to https://vimeo.com/132160166.
70 Alaskans refer to Sailor Boy Pilot Bread crackers as "Pilot Bread."
71 A minimum of ten students is required by the State of Alaska to have a publically funded school. Some of the villages were, and are, so small that enrollment could not be met; therefore, most missionaries in remote areas of Alaska used homeschooling curriculum to educate their children.
72 Calvert Homeschool curriculum, established in 1896, is mission-based and is still used today.
73 In the spring of 2009, the river exceeded its banks, and without warning or hesitation, rushed into cabins as near the river as the Gaede's duplex.
74 Florence Feldkirchner worked for the Bureau of Indian Affairs and was being transferred to Barrow.
75 As of 2021, many people along the Yukon continue to get food for the year via summertime barges. It is also possible in many places to order food, with free shipping, from Amazon.
76 The whitefish, called such because of their white or silvery color, are sheefish found only in the arctic and subarctic North America and Asia. In Alaska, they are most abundant in the Kuskokwim and Yukon rivers and in the Selawik and Kobuk Kotzebue Sound. Their enormous size (up to sixty pounds and forty-two inches long), difficulty to catch because of their tremendous strength to fight, and delicious taste make them very desirable.
77 It is believed that tuberculosis was brought in by Russian and American whalers during the late-1700s to the mid-1800s. A medical survey in the 1930s estimated that over one-third of Native deaths in Alaska were attributable to tuberculosis.

78 Lazy Mountain Children's Home provided care for Alaskan children until the early 1960s.
79 http://freepages.rootsweb.com/~coleen/genealogy/alaskaorphanage.html
80 Pedal pushers were calf-length women's slacks popular in the 1950s.
81 Following this initial moose hunt, she did not volunteer to go hunting again in Tanana by airplane; however, several years later, when the family relocated to another part of Alaska, which was on the road system, she was more than willing to get up early or drive at dusk, with two guns between her husband and herself.
82 Men's: 1st – Jake Starr, 2nd – Peter Joseph, 3rd – Lester Erhart, 4th – Henry Kokrine. Women's: 1st – Clara Swenson, 2nd – Rebecca Swenson and Bertha Folger, 3rd – May Edwin, 4th – Gladys Erhart, 5th – Judy Woods.
83 First light was around 8:00 a.m. with daylight around 9:00 a.m., and sunset at around 6:00 p.m. with last light around 6:45 p.m. Increase in light per day around 6 minutes.
84 In 2009, Naomi flew to Tanana. She saw a red-haired young woman walking down Front Street. She called out, "Are you a Sommer's?" The woman was surprised and inquired how Naomi knew. Naomi replied, "How many Athabascans along this river have red hair?" They both laughed. Yes, it was one of Chris's younger sisters. In 2012, Naomi flew into Galena, Alaska, a large village downriver of about five hundred people. She learned that Chris Sommer was the village chief. They met in the school library. His red curls were gray, and his smile was welcoming and friendly.
85 Steambath houses were sweat lodges used by the Native people.
86 Elmer would write a chapter of the events in his book, Alaska Bush Pilot Doctor, and Anna would compose an entire book, 'A' is for Anaktuvuk: Teacher to the Nunamiut Eskimos.
87 St. Stephen's (Episcopal) mission hospital/ Hudson Stuck Memorial Hospital. After Dr. Grafton Burke retired, Public Health Services took over the property.

INDEX

A

Amundson, Harriet, 5, 320, 327, 334, 335, 370, 434
Anaktuvuk Pass, Alaska, 419, 420
Anders, William, 405
aprons, 24, 258, 259, 260, 316
Arctic Missions, 24, 258, 259, 260, 316
Arnold, Russ, Vivian, Darris, Sondra, Barry, Lynda, 5, 243, 246, 294, 296, 301, 303, 304, 305, 308, 473, 489

B

Birches (CAA station), 6, 241, 255, 256, 257, 258
Bortel, Anna, 3, 5, 36, 37, 38, 70, 202, 212, 233, 251, 253, 290, 320, 328, 329, 334, 364, 384, 394, 399, 419, 442, 470, 484
breakup, 3, 5, 36, 37, 38, 70, 202, 212, 233, 251, 253, 290, 320, 328, 329, 334, 364, 384, 394, 399, 419, 442, 470, 484
Bureau of Indian Affairs (BIA), 37, 38, 484
Burke, Dr. Grafton, 490
Byrd, Loretta, 427

C

Camp Funston, 53
Camp Innowok, 486

Carlson, Paul and Irene, 6, 173, 232
Christmas seals, 375
Civil Aeronautics Administration (CAA), 26
clotheslines, 286
Cold War, 17, 18, 483, 484
Conscientious Objectors, 54
crystal garden, 437

D

Distant Early Warning (DEW), 484
Doerksen, Dan and Wanda, 346

E

Ebenfeld, 52, 58, 100, 472, 484
Ediger, Agnes, 56, 57, 180
Ediger, John, 56
Edwin, Dennis, 427
Edwin, May, 490
Elia, "Grandma,", 6, 226, 312, 313, 489
Elia, Edward, 394
El Nathan Children's Home, 290, 291
Erhart, Gladys, 490
Erhart, Lester, 490
Estes, Clarence, 394

F

Federal Aviation Agency (FAA), 483
Feldkirchner, Florence, 5, 37, 38, 253, 442, 489
Folger, Bertha, 490
Fort Gibbon, 33, 87, 88, 486
Fort Riley, 53, 55

G

Gaede, Abraham, 61
Gaede, Agnes, 57, 67, 148, 303, 307, 312
Gaede, Alvin, 103
Gaede, Harold, 345
Gaede, Heinrich and Agata, 4, 51
Gaede, Henry, 4, 52, 53, 56, 307, 311

INDEX

Gaede, Lillian, 4, 62, 134
Gaede, Malinda, 104, 105
Gaede, Menno, 103
Grant, Chief Alfred, 219, 378, 399
Gronning, Rev. Roy, Margie, Chris, Bethany, 5, 69, 114, 115, 123, 126, 138, 162, 179, 196, 261, 265, 275, 279, 284, 285, 288, 302, 304, 319, 326, 338, 342, 361, 363, 373, 385, 399, 445, 446, 468

H

Hanson, Wally, 6, 380, 431, 445, 447
Harper Station, 86
Hayward, Gary, 394
Hooley, Eddie, 405, 409
Hughes, Rev. Ken and Vivian, 5, 288, 292, 384, 385, 442

I

Inge, Rev. Coleman and Anne, 5, 69, 377, 399, 486
Innowok Camp, 486
InterAct Ministries, 486
Isaac, Robert, 326

J

Jensen, Mel, Pat, Naoma, Timothy, 5, 445, 447, 448, 449, 457
Johnson, Harold, Vera, David, Barbara, 6, 468
Johnson, Louise, 290
Joseph, Peter, 490

K

Kaltag, Alaska, 247, 407, 413
Kokrine, Henry, 490
Kokrines, Alaska, 5, 241, 244, 247, 255, 293, 297, 301, 309, 314, 315, 413, 419
Koski, Jack, 245

L

Lane, Leonard, 6, 227, 229, 339
Lazy Mountain Children's Home, 5, 289, 290, 490
Leppke, Arnold and Mary (Ediger), 305
Leppke, Bertha, 4, 56, 58, 59, 60, 75, 101, 104, 114, 148, 176, 212, 235, 345, 490

Leppke, Florentine, 486
Leppke, Isaac, 4, 58, 61, 96, 486
Leppke, Lulu Mae, 4, 58, 59, 60, 73, 74, 78, 96

M

McQueen, Dr. Thomas, 333, 397
Mennonite, 1, 3, 5, 14, 29, 51, 53, 57, 58, 59, 78, 97, 99, 102, 103, 109, 122, 155, 192, 303, 339, 405, 409, 410, 431, 467, 470, 472, 473, 484, 487
Miller, Diane, 394, 427
Miller, Pete, 111, 338
Mission of Our Savior Church, 86
Mukluk Telegraph, 4, 223, 323, 474
Myberg, Pete and Joan, 402

N

Nason, Blanche, 290
Neufeld, Olga, 339
Nickovitch, Rod, 377
Northern Commercial Company (NCC), 26
Northern Lights school newspaper, 4, 38, 154, 191, 324, 327, 344, 360, 371, 377, 386, 394, 395, 421, 422, 426, 432, 437, 475
Nuchalawoyya, 85
Nusunginya, Mrs., 400
Nusunginya, Ronald, 402, 426
Nusunginya, Vernon, 394

O

Olsen, Mamie, 244
Orr, Jim and family, 6, 288

P

Person, M.D., Jean, 472
Peters, Fern, 426
Peters, Hardy, 377
Point Hope, AK, 6
potlatch, 183, 199, 418, 424, 486
Public Health Services, 4, 25, 109, 490

INDEX

R

Roberts, Josephine, 402, 472
Roberts, Joyce O., 427
Romer, Herman, 5, 328, 330, 371, 434
Ruby (village), 243, 244, 294
Russian Mission, Alaska, 5, 405, 406, 407, 408, 410, 411, 412

S

Schuking, Rose, 219
Scripter, Larry, Maxine, Bobby, Shirley, Nancy, 5, 246, 247, 254, 255, 257, 301, 304, 305, 308, 309, 313, 314, 315, 316, 384, 419
Smith, Marshall, 377, 395, 399
soddy, 61, 485
Sommer, Chris, 393, 399, 400, 404, 427, 467, 490
Sommer, Judy, 427
Sommer, Marie, 426
Sputnik, 190, 488
Starr, Jake, 490
St. James Episcopal Church, 5, 38, 69
Stoltzfus, Mahlon, Hilda, Gueen, Ruby, Gareth, Karl, 5, 405, 407, 408
Swenson, Clara, 490
Swenson, Frieda, 394

T

Tabor College, 21, 96, 103
Tanana Day School, 35, 36, 38, 40, 84, 253, 263, 271, 327, 484
Tanana School Christmas Program, 370
Tanana School Dedication, 399
Tanana School Graduation, 432
Tooyak, Beatrice, 237
Tooyak, Dora, 6, 214, 469
Town Council News, 387
Tryland, Tom, 203

W

Wheeler, Linda, 379
White, Alice, 27, 205, 327, 382, 422, 484
Woods, Judy, 490
Woods, Mickey, 427
Woods, Sally, 6, 399, 400, 404, 427, 467

www.ingramcontent.com/pod-product-compliance
Lightning Source LLC
Chambersburg PA
CBHW071643160426
43195CB00012B/1337